Bugenhagen's Jonah
Biblical Interpretation as Public Theology

Martin J. Lohrmann

Lutheran University Press
Minneapolis, Minnesota

LUTHERAN UNIVERSITY PRESS DISSERTATION SERIES

The Dissertation Series is designed to make available to libraries and individuals the scholarship and research of those pursuing advanced academic degrees. The final editing is that of the author and the publisher assumes no responsibility for errors of fact, interpretation, or attribution.

Bugenhagen's Jonah
Biblical Interpretation as Public Theology
By Martin J. Lohrmann

Copyright 2012 Martin J. Lohrmann. All rights reserved. Published by Lutheran University Press, an imprint of 1517 Media.

Library of Congress Cataloging-in-Publication Data

Lohrmann, Martin J.
 Bugenhagen's Jonah : biblical interpretation as public theology in the Reformation / by Martin J. Lohrmann.
   p. cm.
 Includes bibliographical references (p.   ) and index.
 ISBN 978-1-932688-71-9 (alk. paper) — ISBN 1-932688-71-4 (alk. paper)
 eISBN 978-1-942304-45-6
 1. Reformation—Germany. 2. Bugenhagen, Johann, 1485-1558. 3. Germany—Church history—16th century. 4. Luther, Martin, 1483-1546. 5. Bible. O.T. Jonah—Criticism, interpretation, etc. I. Title.
 BR305.3.L64 2012
 230'.41092—dc23
            2012001552

Table of Contents

Foreword 5

Chapter One: Johannes Bugenhagen as a Public Theologian 7
    Johannes Bugenhagen Pomeranus (1485-1558)
    Johannes Bugenhagen in Contemporary Academic Literature
    Bugenhagen's *Jonah* as Public Theology
    Outline of this Work

Chapter Two: Bugenhagen's *Jonah* in Historical Context 29
    Charles V and the Holy Roman Empire
    Two Lutheran Saxonies, Ernestine and Albertine
    Elector Moritz and the Augsburg Interim
    Lutheran Responses to the Augsburg Interim in Electoral Saxony
    Bugenhagen's Writings from 1547 to 1550
    Publishing *Jonah*

Chapter Three: Biblical Interpretation as Public Theology 68
    The Bible's Living Voice
    Jonah's Title Page: The Bible and Lutheran Theology
    Opening Arguments: *Praefacio, Argumentum, Loci*
    Biblical Interpretation as Public Theology
    On the Spirit and the Letter: Allegory and the Clear Word of God
    Quid sit, Quid effectus: Doctrines and Effects
    Jonah in Wittenberg

Chapter Four: Bugenhagen as Public Interpreter of Martin Luther ... 101
    Luther and Bugenhagen as Colleagues
    Bugenhagen's Funeral Sermon for Luther
    Luther as "Father"
    Luther's Lectures on Jonah, 1525/26
    Luther and Bugenhagen on the Office of Ministry (Jonah 1:2)
    Luther and Bugenhagen against the Louvain Theologians
    A Report of Luther's Reformation Breakthrough

Chapter Five: Repentance and Justification 134
    Otto Vogt's Essay on the "Jonascommentar"
    The Transition from Commentary to Tracts
    Contrition and Faith in Nineveh: The Tract on True Repentance
    Jonah's Sermon to Nineveh
    Justification by Faith Alone: The Tract on Human Traditions
    Ambrosiaster and Augustine on Faith Alone
    The Lutheran Epistle of James

Chapter Six: Justification in Action 176
    Faith and Tradition: The Tract against Montanism
    Case Studies: Clerical Marriage and Communion in Both Kinds
    Usus Christi in Worship and Everyday Life
    The Kingdom of God and the Bondage of the Will
    Conclusion to the Tracts on Jonah 3

Chapter Seven: Final Confessions 206
    Law and Gospel in Jonah 3
    The Ongoing Chastisement of the Saints: Bugenhagen and Jonah 4
    Bugenhagen's 1551 Assessment of His *Jonah*

Chapter Eight: Conclusions 224

Appendix One: Letter to Duke Albrecht of Prussia (May 1549) 229

Appendix Two: Dedication Letter to King Christian III of Denmark
    (October 1550) 235

Abbreviations 242

Bibliography 244

Endnotes 252

Foreword

This study is the fruit of many years of personal and professional interest in the Reformation era. The idea to focus my doctoral dissertation on one of Luther's colleagues first came when I heard a lecture by Dr. Martin Treu of Lutherstadt Wittenberg, who remarked that Luther was not a lone giant but worked for church reforms with many other people. I immediately wanted to learn more about this collegial side of the Lutheran Reformation.

Johannes Bugenhagen, a pastor and professor in Wittenberg during the Reformation, was a natural person to study. I thank my *Doktorvater* Timothy Wengert and my other faculty advisors – John Hoffmeyer, Jon Pahl, and J. Jiyakiran Sebastian – for their guidance in this project. As a dissertation, this research was accepted with distinction by the faculty of the Lutheran Theological Seminary at Philadelphia in the spring of 2010. As a published book, I hope it is useful and readable for scholars, pastors, students, and anyone interested in Reformation history.

Bugenhagen's 1550 Commentary on Jonah was not available electronically until I was nearly finished with the dissertation. In early 2007 I started studying a microfilm copy of the book loaned from Luther Seminary in Minneapolis. In the fall of 2008, I visited the Herzog August Bibliothek in Wolfenbüttel, Germany in order to see two original copies, among the few still in existence. I thank the Evangelische Kirche in Deutschland and the ELCA Wittenberg Center for offering the stipend which made my research in Germany possible. I also thank the staff at Krauth Memorial Library in Philadelphia for their great assistance, as well as the publisher, Leonard Flachman, for taking a chance on a new author. Many other people have provided great help and encouragement over the years, from the beginning of this project to its end: I am profoundly grateful.

Because the original text of the Jonah Commentary was relatively inaccessible, my dissertation included extensive Latin quotations in order to show my sources. Since then, Bugenhagen's *Ionas Propheta Expositus* has become available through Google Books (books.google.com). To save space here, I have removed most of the Latin text that had been footnoted in my dissertation. Those who would like to compare my translations with the original are invited to search the book online or to email: MartinLohrmann@hotmail.com. Bugenhagen's collected letters (*Dr. Johannes Bugenhagens Briefwechsel*) are also available online. The many biblical citations in this book are either translated directly from Latin or taken from the *New Revised Standard Version* (1989), depending on context.

I could not have done this research without the support of great friends and supportive family. Thanks to my cousin Cheryl Lohrmann for designing the cover. My deep love and thanks go to my parents, John and Linda Lohrmann, and to my entire family, especially to Carrie, Hilde, and our Jonah. This book is dedicated to you all.

Soli deo gloria.
Martin J. Lohrmann
Philadelphia, PA
Advent 2011

CHAPTER ONE

Johannes Bugenhagen as a Public Theologian

The decorative altarpiece in Wittenberg's City Church contains four panels painted by Lucas Cranach the Elder.[1] The central scene is Christ's Last Supper, which takes place at a round table. Seated there among the disciples, Martin Luther is shown turning to pass the cup beyond the immediate circle to an assisting worshiper dressed in sixteenth-century clothing. This shows that Christ's grace continues to be received in contemporary Christian communities through the sacramental meal. In the panel below that Last Supper scene, Luther is shown again. This time he is preaching to the Wittenberg congregation. The crucified Christ appears between Luther and the congregation, revealing the content of Luther's sermon. The panel to the left of the Last Supper shows Luther's colleague Philip Melanchthon baptizing an infant. Since Melanchthon was never ordained and is not known to have ever performed a baptism, this is a somewhat puzzling scene. Nevertheless, it reminds the observer that Melanchthon "baptized" the Evangelical Lutheran Church[2] as the author of its first theology book, the 1521 *Loci Communes*, and as chief composer of the Augsburg Confession and its Apology. These panels invite viewers to experience Christian faith through preaching, baptism and the Lord's Supper.

Yet there remains one more panel on the Cranach Altar. It depicts a third Wittenberg reformer and a third Lutheran sacrament. In the altar's right-hand panel, a white-haired Johannes Bugenhagen holds the keys that symbolize the power to retain or forgive sins (Matt. 16:18). One man, dressed well but looking back scornfully, walks away with his hands tied and his sins unforgiven. Another man, more plainly clad and kneeling with bowed head and folded hands, receives forgiveness through his confession and the absolution given by Bugenhagen, whose hand is on the forgiven man's forehead. Having served as head pastor at Wittenberg's City Church from 1523 almost until his death in 1558, this depiction of

Bugenhagen as Public Theologian • 7

Bugenhagen fits with the office of ministry that he held for so long in that place.

The Cranach Altar's image of Bugenhagen also provides a good image for understanding him as a theologian. His entire career was marked by a concern for the relationship between repentance, faith, and good works. In 1547, the same year that the altarpiece was dedicated, Bugenhagen began lecturing on the prophet Jonah at the University of Wittenberg.[3] In these lectures, he interpreted Jonah as a book that teaches how repentance and faith provide the foundation for Christian life. Cranach's painting captures the spirit of Bugenhagen's work as a professor, pastor, and church leader.

This Cranach Altar and Bugenhagen's Jonah Commentary are linked by history as well as theology. On the same Easter Sunday on which the Cranach Altar was likely dedicated (April 24, 1547), Wittenberg's ruling monarch, John Frederick of Saxony lost a key battle to Holy Roman Emperor Charles V at Mühlberg, about 50 miles up the Elbe River from Wittenberg. Emperor Charles had long been eager to end the religious controversies dividing his German subjects; with this victory would finally have his chance to bring the Protestants back to the Roman Catholic fold. His military victory led to the swift end of the Smalcaldic War and brought profound consequences to Germany. For one thing, Saxon power shifted to John Frederick's cousin, Duke Moritz. Charles' victory and Moritz' ascent made the future of German Protestantism appear to be quite tenuous. John Frederick had succeeded his uncle Frederick the Wise and his father John as a strong defender of the Lutheran Reformation. When Emperor Charles defeated John Frederick and Philip of Hesse, Lutherans had lost their two most powerful political supporters. Duke Moritz' sympathy with the Lutheran cause was still unknown. Adding to the uncertainty of the times, Martin Luther had died in February 1546, so that Lutherans were without key leaders in these new crises.

In his Jonah Commentary, composed in the years following the Smalcaldic War, Bugenhagen addressed the challenges of the time by calling his community back to the repentance and faith to be found in the short biblical book of Jonah. He connected the turmoil of his own time with the ancient story of Jonah by placing them all under faith in Christ's death and resurrection, writing: "All history is in the image of the passion and resurrection of Christ."[4] With the Easter experience as the foundation for all life, Bugenhagen offered his Jonah Commentary – or, as he called it, his *Jonah* – as an explanation of Lutheran teachings and as a public response to volatile current events.

Johannes Bugenhagen Pomeranus (1485-1558)

With few biographical resources available in English and only slightly more in German, Johannes Bugenhagen's life and work remain largely unknown, even among scholars of the period.[5] The following biographical sketch emphasizes Bugenhagen's activity as a reformer of church and society.

Johannes Bugenhagen was born on June 24, 1485 in the region of Pomerania, on the island of Wollin. There the Oder River empties into the Baltic Sea, at the present day border between Germany and Poland. Bugenhagen's homeland provided him with the Latin names "Pomeranus" (the Pomeranian) and "Dr. Pomer" that he would later carry as a reformer. Johannes' father Gerhard was on the local town council and may have served as mayor.[6] As a youth, Bugenhagen attended grammar school before studying at the University of Greifswald. There he became acquainted with northern European humanism. The influence of humanism shows in the first two entries of Bugenhagen's collected letters, which are an exchange between him and the Dutch humanist Johannes Murmellius.[7] At age nineteen, after only three years at the university, Bugenhagen left Greifswald to serve as rector of a Latin school in Treptow (modern day Trebiatow, Poland).[8] He taught there for over fifteen years. Bugenhagen also became acquainted with the abbot of the town's Premonstratensian (or Norbertine) monastery, a man named Johann Balduin who was interested in reforming the church. To this end, Balduin started a school to improve the monks' education and in 1517 invited Bugenhagen to lecture at that school as well.[9] Bugenhagen had been a priest in Treptow since his ordination in 1509, but it is not clear whether he ever took monastic vows.[10]

As a priest and scholar, Bugenhagen showed an interest in church reform before he heard about Martin Luther or the reforms emanating from Wittenberg. In a sermon given between 1517 and 1519, he preached for a return to biblical morality, mentioning the work of Erasmus of Rotterdam.[11] Of this time in his career, he later said that he had good intentions but did not yet know the gospel.[12] According to a later colleague named David Chyträus, Bugenhagen first learned about Luther's ideas in 1520 when he read *The Babylonian Captivity of the Church*.[13] After close and critical study, Bugenhagen found that he agreed with Luther. In a letter which no longer exists, he must have asked Luther about finding a *modus vivendi* (a way of life). In reply, Luther sent a copy of his newest book, *The Freedom of a Christian*, along with a short note: "You have written that I should prescribe a right way for you to live. A truly Christian person does not need moral precepts. For in faith the Spirit leads that person to everything that God desires and perfects brotherly love. So read this book. Not everyone believes the gospel. Faith is known through the heart."[14]

Within a year after receiving Luther's reply, Bugenhagen left Pomerania to enroll at the University of Wittenberg. He arrived in early 1521, just before Luther left for his trial before a young Emperor Charles at the Diet of Worms.[15] Bugenhagen took a room at Melanchthon's house and started to teach a private course on the Psalms, given mostly to his Pomeranian colleagues. His study grew popular enough that Melanchthon made it possible to open the lectures to the university, helping fill the teaching void created by Luther's absence.[16]

At the Diet of Worms, Emperor Charles declared Luther an outlaw. From April 1521 until March 1522, Luther stayed in hiding at Wartburg Castle. While he was there, reforms in Wittenberg continued. Changes such as the voluntary disbanding of the Augustinian monastery, the refusal of many priests to hold private masses, and the introduction of communion in both kinds (bread and wine) took place with Luther's approval.[17] At worship on Christmas Day, 1521, Luther's colleague Andreas Bodenstein von Karlstadt presided at Eucharist without wearing the traditional vestments and gave communion in both kinds to lay people who had not made private confession. This dramatic action and the next day's disclosure that Karlstadt, a priest, was engaged to be married met no resistance from Luther. It was not until religious images in the City Church were destroyed and Karlstadt started preparing a new church order that Luther voiced an objection. When Luther returned, he preached that reforms made without respect for other people's consciences and civic peace were useless.[18]

Because Bugenhagen did not yet hold a faculty or church position in Wittenberg, official documents do not record his involvement in the "Wittenberg Movement" of those months. In April or May of 1521, however, Melanchthon dedicated a Greek edition of Paul's Letter to the Romans to Bugenhagen.[19] Perhaps still addressing Bugenhagen's interest in a *modus vivendi*, Melanchthon wrote that Romans was not written for scholarly speculation or for creating new laws but was more like a catechism that teaches faith.[20] Melanchthon put this approach to Romans to work when he organized the *Loci Communes Theologici* by following its main points (*loci*); the "loci method" that Melanchthon used in organizing that book provided an interpretive model that Bugenhagen would also use throughout his career.

In September 1521, Bugenhagen sent out his first work as a Wittenberg reformer, an open letter to a friend in Pomerania, published under the title *Epistola de peccato in spiritum sanctum* (*The Sin against the Holy Spirit*).[21] While Frederick the Wise responded to the imperial edict of Worms by quietly ignoring it, the church in Pomerania had started enforcing the edict's demands to root out Lutheran teaching. Bugenhagen wrote this letter to encourage reforming colleagues back home. He explained that through justification by faith all sins would be forgiven except the unbelief that refused to turn to Christ for mercy.[22] Such a refusal was a failure to let the Holy Spirit work salvation.[23] With this letter about repentance and faith to his homeland, Bugenhagen entered the ranks of leading Wittenberg theologians.

Bugenhagen's status in Wittenberg also grew when he became pastor of St. Mary's Church (also called the City Church). The congregation's previous pastor, Simon Heins, had died in 1522. Originally, Luther's friend Nicholas von Amsdorf had been elected to fill the position, but disagreements between the reform-minded city council and the more conservative leaders of the All Saints Church (also called the Castle Church) led to Amsdorf's withdrawal from the nomination.[24] After Luther's fellow Augustinian monk Wenceslaus Linck also turned down the position, the city council and the congregation elected Bugenhagen to be their pastor, with Luther's support.[25] Bugenhagen's installation in October 1523 set an early example of congregation members taking part in the election of their pastor.

Bugenhagen set an additional precedent by being a married priest. He and his wife, Walpurga, had married on October 13, 1522. In a letter to Frederick the Wise's advisor George Spalatin, Luther asked if they might send a gift to support the honorable but impoverished priest and his bride.[26] Frederick responded to the politically questionable action of openly supporting married priests by sending food and money through Spalatin.[27] As a husband, Bugenhagen gave to Walpurga the "sovereignty of the keys as mistress of the house, and retained the authority of the sword for himself."[28] Almost thirty years later in the Jonah Commentary, Bugenhagen spoke similarly of his wife's authority. There, making an analogy between the priesthood of all the baptized and the office of ministry, he wrote, "The [priesthood of all the baptized] is also from God but is mediated by people or the church, which has from its spouse Christ the keys to bind and loose, as a wife in the house."[29] In Bugenhagen's analogy, pastors are leaders of equally worthy members of the church, just as a mother has a place of honor and authority among equally loved members of a household. This analogy does not simply bless the domestication of women's work; to the contrary, it shows that women used the same leadership and problem-solving skills needed in effective parish ministry or in business.[30] Walpurga accompanied her husband on many of his trips to organize church reforms in northern Germany and Denmark. Although little is known of her, Johannes often included greetings from Walpurga to the families of those with whom he corresponded, including the King of Denmark.

The couple enjoyed a good relationship with Martin and Katherine Luther. Bugenhagen performed the Luthers' private wedding on June 13, 1525 and presided over the public ceremony two weeks later.[31] In 1527, when an outbreak of the plague temporarily closed the university, Bugenhagen's family stayed with the Luthers. Historian Inge Mager noted that Luther and Bugenhagen's decision to stay together "is generally interpreted as a sign of pastoral responsibility for the Wittenberg congregation. However, the fact that both wives were pregnant and did not want to deliver far from home may also have been of equal importance."[32] Together with Martin and Katie Luther, Johannes and Walpurga set an early example of life in a Lutheran parsonage. In his 1525 tract on clerical marriage, Bugenhagen continued to write positively and publicly about marriage, quoting Proverbs 18:22: "He who finds a wife finds a good thing, and obtains favor from the Lord."[33]

This seemingly private category of "marital status" reveals Bugenhagen's public witness about how faith affects everyday life. Having served as pastor for Luther's wedding and himself been married over two years earlier, Bugenhagen knew that spiritual faith can positively impact physical matters like sexuality, child-rearing, and daily work. As much as any theological tract, Bugenhagen's personal life demonstrated his belief that faith in God provides the foundation for all aspects of life in God's good creation.

In the 1520s and '30s, Bugenhagen's skills as an organizer grew increasingly evident. In 1524, some members of the St. Nicholas congregation in Hamburg called Bugenhagen to be their pastor. His status as a married priest and Wittenberg's refusal to release him resulted in Hamburg rescinding that call.[34] Nevertheless, the book-length letter that he wrote to the church in Hamburg (first published in early 1526) shows that theology and practice were closely connected in Bugenhagen's thought. The letter's full title is *On Christian Faith and True Good Works, against False Faith and Fictitious Good Works; Furthermore, How One Should Establish Things through Good Preachers, So That Such Faith and Works Are Preached*.[35] Three themes that would later dominate the Jonah Commentary appear in this title: first, what Christian faith is; second, how faith keeps good works from becoming sources of self-righteousness; and third, how this relationship between faith and works can be fostered through public ministry and congregational life. Within five years of moving to Wittenberg, Bugenhagen had found a way to teach a *modus vivendi* shaped by faith alone.

In 1528, Bugenhagen was granted a leave of absence to travel to Braunschweig. There he gave local congregations their first governing constitution of the Reformation era when he wrote a church order (*Agenda* or *Kirchenordnung*) for the town. In it, Bugenhagen provided theological instruction, gave structures for organizing churches and schools, and instituted a common chest (*die Gemeine Kasten*) so that social relief could continue under a theology that no longer considered almsgiving to be a meritorious good work.[36] Although the idea for a common chest had been part of Luther and Karlstadt's earliest reforms, Bugenhagen's contribution to this new social initiative was critical. In the words of historian Carter Lindberg, "Bugenhagen's genius was to separate the fund for poor relief (*Armenkasten*) from the fund for schools, pastors' salaries, and the maintenance of the church (*Schatzkasten*)."[37] In this way, pastors could distance funds dedicated to their salaries from donations given to those in need. Evaluating the effectiveness of the common chest by studying receipts and accounting books, Tim Lorentzen has convincingly shown that "the doctrine of justification by faith alone did not automatically lead to empty chests."[38] Rather, Lutheran reforms led to quantifiably positive results in public welfare, education, and poor relief. Bugenhagen worked in Braunschweig for several months before going to Hamburg to complete similar tasks.

Bugenhagen's 1526 Letter to Hamburg and his church orders exemplify a central concern of the early Lutheran reformers: if good works of charity are no longer necessary or helpful for salvation, then how will social needs be met? Although Luther had already addressed the theological and social importance of good works in *The Freedom of a Christian*[39] and Melanchthon defined good works as the fruits of justification by faith in his 1521 *Loci Communes*,[40] critics continued to say that Lutherans had done away with charity and good works. Some Lutherans, especially Johann Agricola, did embrace their newfound freedom of faith in such a way as to deny the requirement to love one's neighbor.[41] The 1550s would see a second intra-Lutheran conflict about the role of good works in salvation. Bugenhagen, however, consistently asserted that justification by faith and service to the neighbor always go together. This position remained true from his earliest writings to the Jonah Commentary of 1550. While Luther and Melanchthon's works also show this commitment, the relationship between faith and works has a focus in Bugenhagen's writings that is impossible to overlook.

When Bugenhagen returned to Wittenberg in 1529, he took part in the official visitation of congregations in Saxony that oversaw church reform at the local level. He also participated in the meetings that produced the Torgau Articles, which served as the basis for articles 22 through 28 of the Augsburg Confession.[42] By the fall of 1530, Bugenhagen was on the road again, this time to

Lübeck in northern Germany. He stayed there for a year and a half, making another stop in Braunschweig. In 1534, he returned to Pomerania, where he visited congregations, advised church leaders, and wrote a church order for the entire territory.[43] In May 1536, Bugenhagen worked on and signed the Wittenberg Concord, which tried to settle disagreements among Protestants about the Lord's Supper.

A year later, Bugenhagen encouraged Luther to take a stronger position on the Lord's Supper in his Smalcald Articles than what they had set down in the Wittenberg Concord. In a private comment about Bugenhagen's role in those talks, Melanchthon said, "he is a hot-tempered man and an uncouth Pomeranian."[44] This complaint, however, appears to be the frustration of a close colleague and not a final judgment; in February 1537, both reformers signed the Smalcald Articles and Melanchthon's appendix to the Augsburg Confession, The Treatise on the Power and Primacy of the Pope. Melanchthon and Bugenhagen continued to live and work closely together in Wittenberg for another twenty years.

In addition to spreading church reforms in northern Germany, Bugenhagen and his family went to Denmark in 1537. There he crowned the new king and queen, ordained bishops, introduced a new church order, and reorganized the University of Copenhagen.[45] After that trip, Bugenhagen kept in close correspondence with Denmark's King Christian III, who remained a patron of Bugenhagen and other colleagues in Wittenberg. Two years after first arriving in Copenhagen, Bugenhagen returned to Wittenberg. In 1542 he made his last trip as a church organizer abroad to Schleswig-Holstein and the duchy of Braunschweig-Wolfenbüttel. After this, Bugenhagen stayed within Saxony. By this time he had written or edited church orders for Braunschweig, Hamburg, Lübeck, Pomerania, Denmark, Schleswig-Holstein, Braunschweig-Wolfenbüttel, and Hildesheim.

When Martin Luther died in February of 1546, Bugenhagen preached the funeral sermon at Wittenberg's Castle Church. His sermon expressed deep grief and love for the man he called "Father Luther." But as much as he voiced his great sorrow, Bugenhagen preached even more the same faith and hope that Luther had taught. While the sermon ranks among one of Bugenhagen's best-known works, Luther's death also stands as the moment when

Bugenhagen biographies begin to speak of declining "last years," even though Bugenhagen published regularly until 1552 and remained Wittenberg's head pastor through 1556.[46] Histories of the stormy years that followed Luther's death and the Smalcaldic War similarly overlook Bugenhagen's participation, even though he was still the leader of the church in Wittenberg. This book makes the case that Bugenhagen's work during that period offers rich historical and theological insights, especially as seen in his 1550 Jonah Commentary.

Johannes Bugenhagen in Contemporary Academic Literature

In the 1993 book *Beyond Charity: Reformation Initiatives for the Poor*, Carter Lindberg lamented that Bugenhagen's theological and exegetical work has been neglected in scholarship in favor of a focus on him as a church organizer. He wrote, "It is equally important to emphasize that Bugenhagen's contributions to poor-relief legislation and its enactment were embedded in the doctrine he learned from Luther. For Bugenhagen, Reformation doctrine and its institutionalization belong together as 'constitutive factors for the progress of the Reformation.'"[47] In an apparent coincidence, just as Lindberg's book appeared, German scholars had started researching Bugenhagen's theological writings from the 1520s for the precisely that reason. Three books were published in Germany on Bugenhagen's theological and exegetical work in 1993 and 1994. The following review of German scholarship on Bugenhagen as a biblical interpreter and theologian underscores Lindberg's observation that theology and practice always fit together in Bugenhagen's thought.

Recent attention to Bugenhagen's biblical commentaries began with Hans Hermann Holfelder's dissertation on Bugenhagen's influential Psalms Commentary (1524), published in 1974 as *Tentatio et Consolatio (Affliction and Consolation)*. Holfelder began by noting that with the 1908 *Bibliotheca Bugenhagiana*, a large catalogue of everything Bugenhagen published, editor Georg Geisenhof had intended to reopen Bugenhagen's life and work by showing that Bugenhagen had written much more than church orders.[48] In addition to the detailed bibliography, Geisenhof's work resulted in the printing of some newfound copies of Bugenhagen's sermons.[49] The *Bibliotheca Bugenhagiana* did not, however, produce the revival that Geisenhof sought. Though these hopes went unmet for decades, Holfelder's work marked the beginning of a new interest in Bugenhagen as an interpreter of the Bible.

Holfelder identified a core methodological challenge presented by Bugenhagen's work as an interpreter of the Bible: how should one study a biblical commentary as a work of theology? The modern division of labor between biblical scholars, systematic theologians, and church historians presents a significant obstacle to a coherent study of Reformation-era commentaries. While Holfelder hoped to integrate these fields, he focused most on Bugenhagen's interpretive methods rather than on theology or historical context. Holfelder chose to find the principles behind Bugenhagen's interpretation of the Psalms, but by narrowing the focus, he missed a more interesting historical and theological question: why was this long-forgotten Psalms Commentary so popular in its time? It went through five printings the first year it appeared.[50] What did it say to the readers who snatched it up? Despite overlooking questions like these, Holfelder's work remains important as the first to focus on Bugenhagen as a biblical interpreter.

In his second book on Bugenhagen, *Solus Christus* (*Christ Alone*), Holfelder tried to show a link between Bugenhagen's commentaries on Paul's epistles (1524/25) and the 1526 Letter to Hamburg.[51] He also tried to make connections between biblical interpretation, Lutheran theology, and practical reforms, which he had not undertaken in his study of the Psalms Commentary. To do this, he emphasized points at which Bugenhagen's theology expressed the paradoxical theses of Luther's *The Freedom of a Christian*: "A Christian is a perfectly free lord of all, subject to none. A Christian is a perfectly dutiful servant of all, subject to all."[52] Holfelder successfully showed that by the mid 1520s Bugenhagen already had a firm grasp of the Lutheran theology of the cross.[53] In Bugenhagen's thought "imitation of Christ as imitation in good works, in confession of Christ to the point of risking bodily death, and 'in works of mortification of the self' can only take its rightful place where it grows out of Christ's death and resurrection, which binds believers with Christ."[54] By focusing on Lutheran teachings about Christ's death and resurrection, Holfelder identified the heart of a theology that had been formed by the Bible, Luther's teaching, and practical experience in his parish.

But despite this fine expression of Bugenhagen's early theology, both of Holfelder's works reveal a clear problem in studying Bugenhagen: the need to find uniqueness, especially with respect to Luther and Melanchthon. This problem appeared in Holfelder's attempt to find points at which Bugenhagen might have diverged from his colleagues. The same need is also implied by contemporary descriptions of Bugenhagen as a great organizer, pastor, or practical theologian, as if Luther and Melanchthon did not think or work practically, pastorally or institutionally. These labels seem to come from the academic need to find originality in historical subjects. Such a view overlooks a more obvious and more likely hypothesis: that several reformers could work well together, even as they engaged different projects and expressed themselves in their own words. This book addresses the issue of originality by studying Bugenhagen's writings as occasions for him to express a shared faith in his own voice.

Two dissertations published in the early 1990s built upon Holfelder's research by focusing more closely on the historical context of Bugenhagen's early years as a reformer. Annaliese Bieber pushed Holfelder's search for intellectual origins by examining lectures on the Gospel of Matthew that Bugenhagen delivered from 1519 to 1521, before he left for Wittenberg.[55] Especially valuable for her insights on Bugenhagen's move to Wittenberg, Bieber noticed that by the end of the commentary, Bugenhagen had shifted from an Erasmian emphasis on moral reform to Lutheran themes of "law and gospel" and justification by faith alone. She also noticed a new emphasis on God's word converting people more radically than philosophy could, beginning with the conversion of the preacher himself.[56] By reading the context of Erasmian reform into this early work, Bieber highlighted a key moment in Bugenhagen's growing conviction that the Lutheran emphasis on faith active in love was more effective than the humanistic *philosophia Christiana*. In this, Bieber deepened Holfelder's search for the origins of Bugenhagen's theology.

Ralf Kötter's 1994 study took a different path to expand upon Holfelder's work.[57] Like Holfelder, Kötter studied the Letter to Hamburg as a bridge between Bugenhagen's first biblical commentaries and his later church orders. But Kötter added several compelling features to his study. First, he showed that the Letter to Hamburg expressed the same theological foundation as Bugenhagen's earlier works of biblical interpretation; it was consistent with those writings, not some kind of further development. Second, Kötter examined the letter's historical context to better understand Bugenhagen's reasons for writing it.[58] Kötter recognized that Bugenhagen was addressing fears of social chaos inspired by the Peasants War. At the same time, Bugenhagen also had to explain the increasingly hostile relationship between reformers and those who favored traditional Roman worship and structures.

Kötter challenged Holfelder's focus on how much influence Luther and Melanchthon had over Bugenhagen. Instead of looking for points of either divergence or imitation, he read the Letter to Hamburg through Luther's *The Freedom of a Christian* and Melanchthon's *Loci Communes* to see how Bugenhagen understood and expressed their ideas. While he sought to show continuity with Luther and Melanchthon, Kötter managed to present Bugenhagen as more than a mere imitator, with the result that he interpreted the Letter to Hamburg as itself a skillfully crafted work of the early Reformation. Still, his conclusions overemphasize small points of difference between Luther, Melanchthon and Bugenhagen in order to make claims for theological uniqueness. Rather than looking for differences, Kötter's own research implies another and more fitting conclusion: that Bugenhagen can be read and studied as an expert ambassador of Wittenberg's early theology, right alongside Luther and Melanchthon.

Also published in 1994, Volker Gummelt's *Lex et Evangelium* (*Law and Gospel*) studied Bugenhagen's Isaiah lectures, which had been delivered between 1522 and 1524. In this, Gummelt used a method similar to Holfelder's study of the Psalms Commentary, looking for central theological themes in Bugenhagen's early thought. Like Bieber and Kötter, Gummelt found that core Lutheran teachings stood more firmly in place in those early years than Holfelder had suggested, with law and gospel already providing the lens through which Bugenhagen interpreted the prophet. He showed how Bugenhagen read Isaiah as a preacher of the gospel; that is, the Old Testament prophets were not simply chronological predecessors of the gospel but living witnesses to God's eternal revelation in Christ.[59]

As Lindberg had surmised, these books better established Bugenhagen as a first-rate theologian who could teach the new Wittenberg theology in his own voice. In addition, they provide three major insights for this study. First, Bieber had noticed that a change in emphasis could occur within a series of lectures. That sets a valuable precedent for understanding the Jonah Commentary, which was composed between the years 1547 to 1550. Change over time is possible within such a lengthy commentary. Second, Kötter showed the value of interpreting the Letter to Hamburg through its historical context, paying attention to local debates within Hamburg and the larger setting of the Peasants War. Similarly, Bugenhagen published his *Jonah* of 1550 immediately after a major war and amid tensions with both Roman Catholics and other reformers. Just as Kötter found these themes by reading between the lines of the Letter to Hamburg, this study will read Bugenhagen's *Jonah* with an eye for outside influences that help interpret the commentary. Third, Gummelt's description of how Bugenhagen interpreted the prophet Isaiah is consistent with the way that he later interpreted Jonah as a preacher of law and gospel. We see that Bugenhagen had long been interpreting the Old Testament through the Lutheran teaching of justification by faith in Christ alone. By integrating these three insights, this study will show that Bugenhagen's *Jonah* is a profound and profoundly biblical confession of faith during a time of great uncertainty.

While not focusing purely on Bugenhagen's biblical commentaries, two other recent German works deserve attention. First, Yvonne Brunk's 2003 dissertation looked for the theological origins and practical effects of Bugenhagen's baptismal theology.[60] This theological focus allowed Brunk to examine works spanning Bugenhagen's career and across the genres of church orders, biblical commentaries, and pastoral writings. The concern for an integrated study culminated in the book's final chapter, in which Brunk studied the consequences of Bugenhagen's baptismal theology for congregational practice, especially as expressed in his church orders and in the 1551 tract "Von den ungeborn Kinder," which pastorally addresses miscarriages and stillbirths. Like other Bugenhagen researchers, Brunk dealt with the problem of Bugenhagen's uniqueness by focusing on his practical work. Nevertheless, she clearly showed that Bugenhagen grasped Lutheran theology like few others, especially in his ability to integrate faith and practice.

Brunk briefly included the Jonah Commentary as part of her study, observing from it that Bugenhagen's sacramental theology fit with his views of scripture and church organization. On his scriptural theology, she wrote in bold print, "For Bugenhagen, the scriptural principle is always a Christ principle, too."[61] This means that in Bugenhagen's thought, the Bible (like the sacraments and preaching) always points first and foremost to Christ and salvation through him. This is a great summary of Bugenhagen's biblical interpretation. Brunk also noticed that Bugenhagen's baptismal theology informed his critique of the Roman Catholic Church. In this way, she showed that his objections to Rome were grounded in theology, not mere polemics.[62] Finally, she cited the following poetic passage from the Jonah Commentary to describe Bugenhagen's rich view of baptism.[63]

> Faith is the chief promise of the first commandment, and even of the whole first table [of the law], which we receive in baptism when we are baptized into Christ and his death in the name of the Father, Son and Holy Spirit, and when we are incorporated into Christ and made one with him. Just as a bride is united [*copulatur*] with the bridegroom, so that two become one body and one flesh, so we are united [*copulamur*] by God the Father through the Holy Spirit to Christ, so that with Christ we might not be only one body but also one spirit, as Christ is God and human.[64]

This passage demonstrates the refinement of Bugenhagen's mature theology and his skill in expressing something as potentially ethereal as union with Christ. Brunk gave careful attention to the close relationship between the Bible and Bugenhagen's faith and practice. Her occasional discussions of the Jonah Commentary place that work solidly within the larger scope of Bugenhagen's thinking.

Where Brunk looked across all of Bugenhagen's writing to identify his baptismal theology, Tim Lorentzen examined Bugenhagen's church orders with the tools of social history. Lorentzen set himself the task of finding out how effective Bugenhagen's church orders really were. Did Bugenhagen's organizational skills make a difference in the real world? The 2008 book, *Johannes Bugenhagen als Reformator der öffentliche Fürsorge*, answered the question with a resounding "yes" by comparing theological writings like the Letter to Hamburg with the archival evidence found in accounting books, receipts, and other social artifacts.

Through this method, Lorentzen was able to move from discussion of Bugenhagen's theology to an evaluation of his effectiveness.

Lorentzen's book also introduced a new category for interpreting Bugenhagen as a public figure. In English, the title would read, "Johannes Bugenhagen as Reformer of the Public Welfare." This title moves Bugenhagen out of the relatively narrow confines of theology and into wider historical debates about public leadership and social action during the Reformation. This introduction of the "public welfare" element adds a great deal to appreciating Bugenhagen's contributions as a community leader. It honors the public and social nature of the reformers' work, even while insisting that their public activity was rooted in their theology.

Bugenhagen's *Jonah* as Public Theology

In that vein, this study examines the relationship between religious faith and daily life by focusing on a "public theology." Public theology is understood here to be a mode of discourse, a way of speaking about God. It is a "how" rather than a "where." It happens whenever individuals or communities enter into responsible religious conversation. The historian Martin Marty has used the phrase "mode of discourse" to remind us that we can speak in different ways in different settings without losing our integrity.[65] That is, if we hope to educate or inform people about our ideas, then our words should reflect our context. Speaking of a "mode of discourse" also helps avoid spatial metaphors like "public spheres" or "intersections" that often confuse rather than clarify. For instance, in his *Jonah*, Bugenhagen spoke publicly without physically leaving Wittenberg; he also could address students and parishioners in Wittenberg in a public mode, even in potentially "private" settings like lectures and sermons, by speaking to them as members of wider communities like the Christian Church, Electoral Saxony, and the Holy Roman Empire.

A public theology is also responsible to the public for what it says. While individuals and local communities may be fortunate enough to believe and worship as they please, a public theology insists that teachings and practices remain accountable to the wider community. Public theology also affirms that faith commitments have a role in shaping life in society. When describing public philosophy in the United States, Princeton professor Jeffrey Stout has written that democracy includes its own ethic "of holding one another responsible."⁶⁶ Democratic public discourse involves the freedom to speak, the ability to hold others accountable, and the duty to extend those freedoms to others. Turning to theology, Stout observed that public theologians have two main roles: interpreting religious faith within a community and clarifying that tradition publicly for those outside the tradition.⁶⁷ Although he did not use the term "mode of discourse," Stout recognized that public theology is a way of speaking and that the so-called public sphere "is not a place."⁶⁸ Rather, he said, "If you express theological commitments in a reflective and sustained way, while addressing fellow citizens as citizens, you are 'doing theology' publicly – and in that sense doing public theology."⁶⁹

As Wittenberg's head pastor and as an academic in his own right, Johannes Bugenhagen does not easily fit into contemporary categories like "systematic theologian," "biblical scholar" or "church organizer." This confusion of categories has appeared in the various approaches that contemporary researchers have used in studying Bugenhagen. Tim Lorentzen's recent study of Bugenhagen as "reformer of the public welfare" best connects Bugenhagen's public leadership to his work as a theologian. This study hopes to build on that insight. It asserts that Bugenhagen aimed to serve the public good through biblical interpretation and faithful actions. As the title to his Letter to Hamburg shows, Bugenhagen's interpretation of the Bible revolved around the interplay between Christian faith and "true good works," which for Bugenhagen always meant works of love for neighbors.

This approach accepts the risk of imposing the contemporary category of "public theology" into the history of the Reformation because it might prove helpful in integrating Bugenhagen's work as a teacher, pastor, and community leader. Stout's observation that the public sphere "is not a place" also helps us correct unhelpful understandings of Luther's "doctrine of the two kingdoms," which has often been used to divide personal faith from public accountability.⁷⁰ Interpreting Bugenhagen's *Jonah* as a work of public theology adds clarity to how the reformers understood the relationship between faith and daily life.

For Luther, identifying "two kingdoms" – one earthly and one heavenly – offered a way of addressing different contexts. It is a mode of discourse, not a division of the world into religious and secular interests. Because God rules both heaven and earth, the two kingdoms doctrine does not separate God from the world or church from state. Rather, Luther believed that a clearer understanding of the relationship between these two kingdoms might help human institutions work better: secular society could support the common good by fostering positive conditions for personal and communal faith; spiritual reform would in turn benefit society through more effective institutions and through good works of neighborly service. Luther taught that people could use this distinction between the heavenly and earthly kingdoms as a way to live out their personal and public roles as beneficially as possible.

Concern for the right relationship between earthly harmony and obedience to God resulted in Luther and his colleagues favorably invoking both Romans 13:1-7 and Acts 5:29. Romans 13:1 commands Christians to "be subject to the governing authorities," because such authority comes from God, punishes evil, and serves the greater good. At the same time, respecting authority does not mean excusing injustice through blind obedience. Himself excommunicated from the Roman Catholic Church for his teachings and declared an outlaw by the Holy Roman Empire in which he lived, Luther and his colleagues actively invoked Acts 5:29 as a conscience clause to support religious and civil disobedience: "We must obey God rather than any human authority."[71] The Augsburg Confession cited the same passage in its statement on obeying earthly governments.[72]

Instead of using the two kingdoms doctrine to describe even ideal "church and state" relationships, Luther more often spoke of three "estates" (or "walks of life") that God established to guide and nurture human life. These three estates are household, government and church. It is worth noting that "household" covered not just family life but all means of making a living.

> We know that there are three estates in this life: the household, the state, and the church. If all men want to neglect these and pursue their own interests and self-chosen ways, who will be a shepherd of souls? Who will baptize, absolve, and console those who are burdened with sins? Who will administer the government or protect the common fabric of human society? Who will educate the young or till the ground? Yet these duties [*officia*], which have been

commanded and approved by God, have been scorned and cast aside in the papacy, and the devil has foisted these monstrous acts of the monks upon men with horrible fury."[73]

Luther believed that God created human households, basic economic life, and political bodies in order to serve individuals and the common good. God created these "estates" with their respective "duties" to nurture and sustain life.

Like households and governments, Luther taught that God created the Christian Church to be a source for good in the world. Just as people work for the good of their families and just as good governments give order to community life and punish wrongdoing, so God created the church in order to teach the gospel, free souls from sin, and lead people into righteousness. The church on earth belongs to the created order. As such, it should not be confused with the kingdom of God, which remains mostly hidden until the final judgment.[74] Instead, the church on earth is a worldly institution created to lead people into divine knowledge and action.

These distinctions between "estates" provided an intellectual and biblical foundation for the Lutheran reformers' public work. They sought to walk between extreme positions that either collapsed human and heavenly rule into one or that totally separated spiritual faith from civil society. In debates with Rome, Lutherans stressed the hiddenness and humility of Christ's one church, which exists to serve the gospel and not worldly powers. However, in debates with more anti-institutional reform movements, they emphasized the goodness and necessity of the church on earth as the steward of Christ's good news in an otherwise corrupted world.

As a *public* theologian, Bugenhagen worked to foster the social and political conditions that might best reveal God's goodness to individuals and communities. As a public *theologian*, Bugenhagen knew that his role as a leader was to serve the Christian gospel rather than economic or political interests. By addressing such themes from a position of public accountability, Bugenhagen turned one of the shorter books of the Bible into a commentary of over 400 pages, as he taught his Lutheran theology and defended decisions that he and his colleagues had made. The Jonah Commentary carries additional significance as Bugenhagen's last major work. It stands as the fruit of nearly thirty years of experience as a pastor, teacher, and church reformer in Wittenberg and northern Europe.

Outline of this Work

For the most part, the following chapters are organized according to the commentary's own structure. To introduce readers to Bugenhagen's historical context, chapter two begins with a broad overview of Saxony's place in sixteenth-century Europe and gradually comes to focus on events surrounding Wittenberg from 1547 to 1552. This is the context of the dedication letter to King Christian III of Denmark which serves as the Jonah Commentary's introduction. Because Bugenhagen's efforts during this period have been mostly overlooked, this second chapter makes a significant contribution to historical research of the period.

After its introductory letter, the commentary then starts its study of Jonah. Therefore, chapter three examines Bugenhagen as an interpreter of the Bible. Attention to formal elements within the commentary like the title page, the division of chapters, and the preface acquaints readers with the book's physical layout and highlights key features of Lutheran biblical interpretation. This study of Bugenhagen's method of interpretation explains how it was possible for him to use a biblical commentary to address current events.

An examination of Bugenhagen as an interpreter of scripture also runs into the topic of Bugenhagen as a public interpreter of Martin Luther. Indeed, the religious controversies that dominated Lutheranism after Luther's death in 1546 frequently revolved around who could claim to have Luther on their side of social or doctrinal issues. This was true already in the years during Bugenhagen's composition of his *Jonah*, so that the commentary functions partly as a summary of Luther's teaching by a longtime colleague. Because of Luther's long shadow, chapter four discusses Bugenhagen's relationship to "Father Luther." Starting with a short summary of their early relationship, the chapter turns to Bugenhagen's funeral sermon for Luther to show how Bugenhagen valued Luther's legacy without turning it into a cult of personality.

A unique insight into Luther's life also arises here. While teaching justification by faith in the middle of his Jonah Commentary, Bugenhagen revisited Luther's original "breakthrough" and retold it from Luther's first-person point of view. This account adds new information to Luther's own descriptions of how he came to his evangelical faith. The account also points to the heart of Bugenhagen's own theology. On one hand, the commentary is vehemently anti-Roman because it was written during a time when Lutheranism faced serious political and military threats from Roman Catholic authorities. On the other hand, Bugenhagen told a story of Luther's breakthrough that is more indebted to the medieval Catholic tradition than usually understood. This chapter on Luther explains much of Bugenhagen's theology and allows a comparison between the two reformers' approaches to the book of Jonah.

Chapters five and six examine the four theological tracts that make up most of the commentary's 400 pages. They flesh out the earlier chapters, so that previous discussions of political context, biblical interpretation and Lutheran theology can be seen as fitting together in the body of Bugenhagen's book. The first tract sets the tone by interpreting Jonah 3 as an example of true Christian repentance, in contrast to human attempts to set things right. The second tract builds on that biblical interpretation to teach the Lutheran doctrine of justification by faith alone; in it, Bugenhagen's lifelong interest in the relationship between faith and works takes center stage.

Having examined the biblical and theological foundations of Lutheran teaching, the third and fourth tracts turn to worship and church life. As a writer of church orders and as a church leader, Bugenhagen was certainly not against formal liturgical practices or church discipline. Thus, his severe criticisms of many worship practices like the laying on of hands or making the sign of the cross focused on specific targets and not at the practices themselves. One target was the Roman Catholic Council of Trent, which had begun in 1545 and already decided against justification by faith alone. Closer to home, Bugenhagen took aim at Emperor Charles' religious settlement for his recently defeated German territories, which came to be called Augsburg Interim. That document sought to place Lutherans across Germany under Roman church authority again, by force if necessary. Taken together, these defiant tracts show Bugenhagen's mastery of Lutheran theology, Christian history and biblical interpretation, while also demonstrating the working relationships between faith, practice, and life in community.

This study nears its close with chapter seven, which follows Bugenhagen's final summary of Jonah 3 and his short but surprising interpretation of Jonah 4. If Bugenhagen made a unique historical contribution to the interpretation of Jonah, it comes in his six pages on Jonah 4, in which he read Jonah's anger with God in light of his main points about repentance and faith. His reading resulted in a sympathetic final judgment about the prophet Jonah, which differs from most other Christian interpretations, including Luther's. At the same time, this conclusion exemplifies Bugenhagen's conviction that faith always leads people back to God's grace and goodness. In light of the conflicts that theologians in Wittenberg faced between 1547 and 1549, his conclusion stands as Bugenhagen's final strong confession of faith and its importance for church order and the common good.

Through this "thick reading" of the 1550 Jonah Commentary, readers step into the lecture hall of the University of Wittenberg in the years immediately following Martin Luther's death and major political changes in Saxony. Readers come away from this commentary with a clear sense of how a first-generation reformer read the Bible and applied it to his world. In the Jonah Commentary, we see the great extent to which the Lutheran reformers believed their teaching about justification was a "biblical theology." As they saw it, the center of the Bible was God's free justification of the ungodly by grace through faith in Jesus Christ. As the central point of God's word, this teaching was also the center of history, so that Bugenhagen could assure his audience that "all history is in the image of the passion and resurrection of Christ." This faith then provided the foundation for Bugenhagen's work for social and church reforms.

The picture of Bugenhagen on the 1547 Cranach Altar shows the reformer with the keys of the kingdom to bind and loose sins. His Jonah Commentary, begun later that same year, no less presents faith in Christ as the divine key that delivers people from sin and opens up new possibilities for personal and public life under God.

CHAPTER TWO

Bugenhagen's *Jonah* in Historical Context

As a work of biblical interpretation, the 1550 Jonah Commentary can be studied for Bugenhagen's theological insights, especially as they engage what Jaroslav Pelikan described as the "catholic tradition" of the Christian Church. This chapter lays a foundation for that analysis by examining the commentary's historical context. Through this approach, we see that the *Jonah*'s biblical interpretation and doctrinal theology are rooted in its immediate context as a work of public theology. It shows the first-generation reformer Bugenhagen teaching that "pure doctrine" includes right action and social responsibility. To him, theology and biblical interpretation always address practical challenges for the sake of the common good.

Bugenhagen wrote this commentary in a setting full of conflict and uncertainty. Wittenberg had just endured the Smalcaldic War, in which Holy Roman Emperor Charles V battled Protestant rulers John Frederick of Saxony and Philip of Hesse. When Charles won, Wittenberg and the Saxon electorship (the privilege of helping elect the Holy Roman emperor) were taken from John Frederick in May 1547 and given to the leader of the rival Saxon house, Duke Moritz. The following spring, Charles and his advisers imposed a new religious policy on his Lutheran subjects. Himself a loyal Roman Catholic, Charles wanted this to serve as a temporary measure for bringing Lutherans back under papal authority for the sake of a united Christendom. Because this new religious law was composed at the 1548 imperial diet in Augsburg, it came to be called the Augsburg Interim. The transfer of political authority from John Frederick to Moritz and the imposition of the Augsburg Interim on German Lutherans presented serious challenges and became sources of division in the years to come. At the center of the controversy, reformers like Bugenhagen, Philip Melanchthon and Caspar Cruciger, Sr. chose to remain in Wittenberg and work within the new political and religious order.

Bugenhagen's *Jonah* offers a perspective on events after the Smalcaldic War that historians and theologians have largely forgotten. Although he was the general superintendent (head pastor or even archbishop) of Wittenberg's churches and a professor at the university, Bugenhagen is rarely mentioned in even the best recent studies of the period.[75] This chapter examines Bugenhagen's *Jonah* as a direct statement about life after the Smalcaldic War and under the Augsburg Interim. Further, the dominant theological interpretation of the time is that Melanchthon and his Wittenberg colleagues failed to lead Lutherans in this time of crisis and compromised their faith for political expediency. While such a view appears in studies that clearly prefer the view of Melanchthon's Lutheran opponents,[76] it is also present in the writing of more objective historians like Carter Lindberg and Robert Kolb.[77] This study, however, presents an alternative view: the stands taken by reformers in Wittenberg were valid and responsible Lutheran positions.[78]

This chapter begins with a sketch of Emperor Charles V's complicated relationship with his German subjects throughout his reign. This background is critical for understanding the situation facing Lutherans in Saxony after the Smalcaldic War. From that point, the chapter studies the policies of Duke Moritz of Saxony, whose power and influence increased after the war at the expense of his cousin John Frederick. The focus then narrows around Philip Melanchthon's efforts to address the Augsburg Interim. Finally, the chapter ends with Bugenhagen's own responses to the war and the Interim, beginning with writings from 1547 and concluding with the 1550 letter to King Christian III that opens the Jonah Commentary. The dedication letter, along with a similarly revealing letter written to Duke Albrecht of Prussia, has been translated and appears in this book's appendix.

Charles V and the Holy Roman Empire

By the 1540s, the Lutheran Reformation was not the story of a lone monk who took a conscientious stand against pope and emperor. Instead, in the years since Luther first stood trial before Charles V at the 1521 Diet of Worms, the Lutheran Reformation had found its definitive expression in the Augsburg Confession (1530) and spread beyond German lands to Scandinavia and Eastern Europe. But despite church reforms taking root across northern Europe, the people of Saxony still owed their highest political allegiance to Emperor Charles V.

From 1519 until his abdication in 1556, Charles V (1500-1558) worked tirelessly to protect his family's power.[79] The grandson of Ferdinand and Isabella, Charles was king of Spain and ruler over Spanish territories in the New World. Elected to be Holy Roman Emperor in 1519, Charles also led that confederation of German nations and free cities which spanned much of central Europe. And as heir to the Hapsburg dynasty, Charles ruled over lands including Austria, Hungary and Belgium. With so much territory under his command, Charles faced several obstacles to the smooth running of his truly global empire. The French, English and Turks all presented constant military threats. The popes during Charles' reign were also not reliable partners, often aligning themselves with France to keep Charles' power in check. They often ignored or delayed his calls for a church council that might settle the religious divisions in the empire. For their part, German princes and imperial cities balanced their financial and military support of Charles with grabs for more political or religious autonomy at home.[80]

Charles' antagonistic relationship with France shows the extent to which international politics directly and indirectly influenced the Lutheran Reformation. Bordered by Spanish, Hapsburg or imperial lands on every border, the French kings Francis I (1494-1547) and Henry II (1519-1559) sought to curb the power of Charles. During the 1520s, France and the Holy Roman Empire fought over land in northern Italy and southeastern France. This meant that Charles had to depend upon German support to fight his battles, even as religious changes were sweeping across Germany. In 1525 Charles took King Francis prisoner and held him captive for several months.[81] Before releasing Francis, he made the French king sign the Treaty of Madrid. Once in Paris, however, Francis renounced the treaty, saying that it had been made under duress and was therefore not binding.[82] Francis went to war against Charles again in the following years, allowing German rulers to support Charles politically and militarily even though they did not enforce his laws against the Lutherans, which had begun with the 1521 Edict of Worms.

These ongoing conflicts with France included the 1527 sack of Rome by troops loyal to the emperor. Wary of Charles' growing power, Pope Clement VII had chosen to ally himself with France. After Charles' army won a military victory in northern Italy, his soldiers continued south, conquering Rome and taking Pope Clement VII prisoner. But this was not a religiously motivated act of aggression against the pope. Instead, the 1527 sack of Rome took place with the support of many Italian allies and had more to do with the chaotic state of Charles' army and a complicated web of Italian and European politics than with the religious convictions of some German mercenaries.[83] In the 1527 sack of Rome, we see that political interests often shaped events far more than religious convictions.

King Francis not only started wars with Charles over the years; he also formed alliances with the Islamic Ottoman Empire in order to limit the Spanish, imperial, and Hapsburg interests that Charles personally represented.[84] In the sixteenth century, the Ottomans, led by Suleiman the Magnificent, were expanding their power across southeastern Europe and northern Africa. While many Catholics and Protestants in Europe saw religious justification for the wars against the Turks, the alliance between France and the Ottoman Empire gives good reason to see these wars as typical conflicts over land and power. A 1544 peace agreement between Charles and King Francis put an end to their quarrels until 1551, when Henry II (who succeeded his father Francis in 1547) crossed religious lines again and joined forces with German Protestants. Henry's military alliance with German princes helped bring the 1555 Peace of Augsburg, which first gave adherents of the Augsburg Confession legal standing in the Holy Roman Empire. In these conflicts, dynastic disputes often trumped a shared Roman Catholic heritage.

In addition to needing support for wars against France, Charles' rule over Germany was also influenced by the Ottoman Empire.[85] In 1529, the Turks had advanced into central Europe and set siege to Vienna. Charles arrived at the 1530 Diet of Augsburg with three main goals: to settle religious disputes, gather German support against the Turks, and address political reforms in Germany.[86] In the preface to the Augsburg Confession, Lutheran leaders similarly identified the main purposes of that imperial congress as being the need to respond to the Turkish military threat and to settle religious debates.[87] On June 25, 1530 German

Lutheran political leaders presented a statement of faith to the emperor. This was the Augsburg Confession.

The diet ended with Germans still supporting the emperor militarily. But because Charles rejected the Augsburg Confession, German monarchs and free cities formed the Smalcaldic League the next year. The league existed for the mutual defense of lands supporting the Augsburg Confession.[88] Elector John of Saxony and Philip of Hesse led the league. Elector John was succeeded by his son John Frederick in 1532. Throughout the 1530s, the occasion for self-defense did not arise because Charles needed German support abroad.

This changed in 1544, after Charles made a more lasting peace with France. On his eastern front, Charles' brother Ferdinand had also reached a settlement with the Ottoman Empire about Hapsburg lands in Austria and Hungary. Charles could now take action against the Protestants within his realm.[89] He planned to begin a war against Hesse and Electoral Saxony in a way that would not evoke the sympathy of other Protestants. In his favor, too, was the weakened state of the Smalcaldic League. Philip of Hesse's reputation had been damaged when his bigamous marriage became public in 1540.[90] Philip and John Frederick had also pushed the League beyond its original aims of self-defense when they invaded Braunschweig-Wolfenbüttel in 1542, giving Charles a legal basis for starting a war in Germany.[91] Charles explained his plan to divide and conquer in a letter to his sister of June 9, 1546: "I decided to begin by levying war on Hesse and Saxony as disturbers of the peace, and to open the campaign in the lands of the Duke of Brunswick [Braunschweig]. This pretext will not long conceal the true purpose of this war of religion, but it will serve to divide the Protestants from the beginning."[92] Rather than give cause for Protestants to come together, Charles took advantage of existing fault lines to start a war against individual members of the Smalcaldic League.

Two Lutheran Saxonies, Ernestine and Albertine

Charles succeeded in playing the two royal houses of Saxony against each other. In the 1480s Saxony had been divided so that it could be shared by the brothers Ernest and Albert of the Wettin dynasty.[93] The Ernestine branch received much of Thuringia and the land around Wittenberg, which brought with it the Saxon electorship (the right to elect the emperor). The Albertine branch ruled over a territory that included Dresden, Leipzig and that city's university. The lack of a university in Ernestine Saxony led Elector Frederick the Wise to found the University of Wittenberg in 1502.[94] Ernestine leaders Frederick, John, and John Frederick each protected Luther from the imperial edict of Worms and supported gradual church reforms.

Unlike his Ernestine cousins, Duke George of Albertine Saxony long opposed Wittenberg's brand of reformation. But when he died in 1539 without a surviving male heir, the duchy went to his brother Heinrich, who began to introduce Lutheranism that same year.[95] Heinrich's son Moritz then became ruler of Albertine Saxony in 1541. Early in his reign, Duke Moritz came into a conflict with Elector John Frederick. At the time, the diocese of Meissen was jointly protected by the two Saxon houses. Unilaterally occupying a nearby town to collect taxes from the local Roman Catholic bishop, John Frederick started introducing religious reforms there.[96] Defending Albertine interests, Duke Moritz prepared for battle against John Frederick; only the intervention of Moritz' father-in-law, Philip of Hesse, helped the two Saxon houses avoid military conflict.[97] Here is another example of political interests overriding shared religious convictions, this time on the Lutheran side.

At the June 1546 diet in Regensburg, Emperor Charles proposed to Moritz that he should remain neutral in the coming war.[98] In exchange, Charles would support Moritz' right to claim more land and suggested that he might transfer the electorship from Ernestine to Albertine Saxony.[99] Charles also agreed not to interfere with the religious life of the territory until the close of the Council of Trent.[100] In addition to potentially seeing his power increase, Moritz had to consider that Charles' brother, King Ferdinand of Austria, was his powerful neighbor to the south and east. For these reasons, Moritz agreed to Charles' proposal. Near the end of the diet of Regensburg, Charles published a declaration of war against John Frederick and Philip.

The Lutherans made the first move in the ensuing Smalcald War in the fall of 1546. While the emperor was in Bavaria with a small army, John Frederick and Philip thought to strike first and cut him off from troops still arriving from Italy and Austria.[101] They did not move swiftly enough. Charles soon raised a larger army and began taking the offensive. During the winter of 1546-47, Philip could not pay his army and he returned to Hesse.[102] Meanwhile, seeing John Frederick's weakened position, Moritz switched from neutrality to alliance with Charles and Ferdinand.[103] In early 1547, Moritz and Ferdinand attacked John Frederick's under-protected home territory. John Frederick fought back, with some early success. But thinking that Charles' army would not be able to cross the Elbe River, he did not prepare a strong enough defense. Charles' army crossed the Elbe at a ford and defeated John Frederick at the Battle of Mühlberg on Easter Sunday, April 24, 1547. Today a small monument at that spot commemorates the battle with a poem.

Was die Elbe niemals sah	What the Elbe never saw
Einst an dieser furt geschah	Once happened at this ford
Carl V hoch zu Roß	Charles V high on horse
Zog hindurch mit heer u.	Troß With ASrmy and wagons came across
24 4 1547[104]	April 24, 1547

John Frederick was taken prisoner and Philip of Hesse surrendered a short time later. Other Protestant rulers around Germany, such as Duke Ulrich of Württemberg, were also forced to submit to the emperor.

This victory seemed to find Charles at the height of his power. He was at peace with France, England, and the Turks, and had finally subdued the Protestants in Germany. Yet this victory would eventually sow the seeds for his more modest exit from the world stage. With Philip and John Frederick under arrest, Charles tried them and sentenced them both to the death penalty. Neither ruler was executed, but they were kept with Charles as his prisoners over the following years. Although Moritz had received land and the electorship for defeating his cousin, his new power remained limited by the fact that Charles had preserved Ernestine rights in Thuringia.[105] Charles' treatment of Moritz' father-in-law, Philip, also insulted the new elector. Along with other princes and leaders in Germany, Moritz came to see that Charles' new power weakened not only Hesse and Ernestine Saxony but all of the rulers within the empire.[106] When Charles asked Moritz to put the city of Magdeburg under siege for its continued insubordination in 1550, Moritz used the opportunity to maintain a ready army at the emperor's expense.[107]

Jonah in Historical Context • 35

Elector Moritz and the Augsburg Interim

After the Smalcaldic War, Charles went back on his word to Moritz that he would not make religious changes. As noted above, he had agreed to keep the religious status quo until the end of the Council of Trent. The council had officially opened in December 1545. By 1547, however, it was clear from Trent's decrees on justification and the sacraments that the council would not give Protestants a chance to make their case in front of the whole church. Especially distressing to Lutherans was the condemnation of justification by faith alone: "If anyone says that the sinner is justified by faith alone in Christ's righteousness... let him be anathema."[108] Furthermore, the relationship between Charles and Pope Paul was again strained, so that in March 1547 the council moved from Trent (within the Holy Roman Empire) to Bologna, which belonged to the Papal States.[109]

Taking church reform into his own hands, Charles commissioned a new religious settlement for the 1548 diet of Augsburg.[110] The Augsburg Interim, as it came to be known, was written by Charles' Spanish advisers, German Catholic theologians Julius Pflug and Michael Helding, and the Lutheran Johannes Agricola, who was then the court theologian for Elector Joachim II of Brandenburg.[111] Although Agricola had been a longtime colleague of the Wittenberg reformers, he got into serious disputes with Melanchthon beginning in the late 1520s and with Luther ten years later.[112] The document written by these theologians maintained the Protestant practices of clerical marriage and of giving both bread and wine to the laity in the sacrament of communion, at least until the Council of Trent made its decisions about them.[113] Other than these concessions, the Augsburg Interim would re-impose Roman Catholic practices and theology on Protestant lands. It was signed by the Archbishop of Mainz, Charles Sebastian, on July 31, 1548.[114]

Even before then, Protestant theologians had seen the document and immediately rejected it. Philip Melanchthon was the first to do so. At Moritz' request, theologians in Electoral Saxony were given a copy of the document for evaluation in March.[115] In April the theologians together published a "blanket rejection of the Interim's chief points."[116] This letter was signed by Wittenberg theologians Philip Melanchthon, Georg Major, and Caspar Cruciger, as well as by Georg von Anhalt and Johannes Pfeffinger, who were leading Lutheran theologians in Albertine Saxony from before the war.[117] By that summer, Melanchthon was referring to the Interim as the "Augsburg Sphinx" for its imprecise language and muddled ideas.[118]

The emperor started enforcing the Interim militarily in southern Germany and along the Rhine River.[119] As a result, many pastors either fled or went into hiding. Johannes Brenz went into hiding in Swabia, Martin Bucer fled Strasbourg for England, and Andreas Osiander left his longtime post in Nürnberg to take a professorship at the University of Königsberg in Prussia.[120] Luther's old friend Nicholas von Amsdorf, who had lost his position as the Lutheran bishop of Naumberg to Julius Pflug, moved to Magdeburg where he became a leading voice against the Interim. He was soon joined by Nicholas Gallus, the former superintendent in Regensburg, who taught for a while at University of Wittenberg before moving on to Magdeburg.[121] Georg von Anhalt, Lutheran bishop in Merseburg, was also eventually forced to step down, although he kept working there to advocate for reform under his Roman Catholic replacement, Michael Helding. Anhalt remained a close colleague of the Wittenberg theologians.[122]

Despite imperial pressure, Moritz had not yet conceded to the demand to introduce and enforce the Interim in Electoral Saxony. To Emperor Charles and King Ferdinand, Moritz insisted that his acceptance of the Interim would lead to kind of the popular uprisings that Charles wanted to avoid. As mentioned above, Moritz' leading Lutheran theologians had written against the Augsburg Interim from the beginning. Further, his political estates (Saxon nobility and city officials) also refused to endorse the Interim.[123] Instead, over the next year Lutheran theologians would meet with Moritz' political advisors to write new theological statements that might honor the emperor's wish for religious unity while upholding the Lutheran practices and beliefs that were prevalent in the land.[124] Beginning in the summer of 1548, the Lutheran theologians of Electoral Saxony met with court advisers and Roman Catholic leaders like Pflug and Helding.[125] Some of these meetings, such as the July 1548 gathering in Pegau, focused on points of doctrine. Other meetings discussed questions of worship and practice. Bugenhagen was present for the first meeting to discuss liturgical matters at Altcella in November 1548.[126] For the Lutherans, these meetings offered a chance to shape public policy and protect the evangelical faith in Electoral Saxony.[127] They also gave Moritz the opportunity to show Charles and Ferdinand that he was leading his reluctant citizens toward a viable solution.

Although Moritz' handling of the Interim gave rise to lasting theological disputes, his tactics were politically effective. Aware of his precarious situation, he had never fully agreed to accept the 1548 Interim. Instead, he shrewdly argued that endorsing the new religious decree would work against the emperor's ultimate hopes for stability and unity.[128] The meetings of 1548 and 1549 successfully convinced the emperor that Moritz was working to bring his Lutheran citizens into line.[129] He used that time to make new allies with other Protestant leaders. For although he had sided with Charles against other Lutheran lands in 1547, Moritz came to see that the emperor's victory meant less local control for German princes and a new subservience to the Holy Roman Emperor.[130] By 1550 Moritz was in talks with anti-imperial neighbors, including Hans of Küstrin, Albrecht of Prussia, and John Albrecht of Mecklenburg.[131]

As usual, the French were also eager to weaken Charles. The German alliance led by Moritz soon gained the support of King Henry II.[132] According to an apologia written at the time of the alliance with France, "the originator of the scheme was Maurice [Moritz] of Saxony."[133] Moritz had kept his army together at Charles' expense in order to ultimately use it against the emperor himself. Moritz "had long been in possession of Magdeburg, but for specious reasons he still continued to keep on foot the army which had been originally raised to reduce the city in Charles' name."[134] In the spring of 1552, Moritz and his allies – already gathered together in southern Germany for meetings – marched south, attacking the emperor's residence in Innsbruck and forcing him to retreat over the Alps.[135] Charles was on the defensive. Moritz then led the negotiations with King Ferdinand that brought about the 1552 Treaty of Passau. As Charles' biographer Karl Brandi put it, it was Moritz "who, standing forth at Passau, gave the final form to the Reformation settlement. He it was who laid down the preliminaries, which were to be permanently enshrined three years later in the Peace of Augsburg."[136] The 1555 Peace of Augsburg was the formal agreement that first gave legal standing to the faith of the Augsburg Confession within the Holy Roman Empire.[137]

To the theologians in Wittenberg, Moritz' reversal was a vindication. Their willingness to maintain civil peace while working for religious faithfulness had been helpful to Moritz as he planned to shape a different religious and political scene in Germany. In July of 1552, for instance, Bugenhagen expressed his satisfaction to King Christian of Denmark.

> Gracious king, as I was writing this letter, a hasty but certain message arrived that peace has been made in the empire – Christ be praised forever. As a sign that this is true, the soldiers in Dresden, here in Electoral Saxony, and in Magdeburg have been paid and released. But your majesty will without a doubt know well that the old elector [John Frederick] is free and that he had been following the emperor as an imperial prince up to now. Thank God, the prayer of the afflicted is not in vain. The world defiles Christ and those who are his, but God dignifies us. May God give us peace and a good government and keep us in his word. Amen.[138]

Bugenhagen's prayers for peace had been answered. Somewhat ambiguously, Bugenhagen also mentioned the release of John Frederick. As part of his negotiations, Moritz had requested the release of his father-in-law Philip of Hesse but not of his Saxon rival, John Frederick. Strangely enough, they learned that Charles had already released John Frederick, who had since then remained a part of Charles' entourage of his own volition.[139] Without saying too much about this turn of events, Bugenhagen thanked God for such a peaceful settlement and continued to pray for good government.

Lutheran Responses to the Augsburg Interim in Electoral Saxony

Although the Augsburg Interim was rendered void by the Treaty of Passau in 1552, theologians continued to argue about the controversies it had generated.[140] Especially for those who lost their homes and positions because of the war, the altered political landscape would continue to define their theological discourse. Magdeburg, where Moritz had staged his imperial siege, had become a central place for Lutherans fleeing or protesting the Augsburg Interim. The senior theologian in Magdeburg was Nicholas von Amsdorf, who had been among the first to bring evangelical reforms to the city in the 1520s. He was joined by Gallus and Matthias Flacius Illyricus, who left Wittenberg in order to write more freely against the Interim. Until his departure, Flacius had taught Hebrew at the University of Wittenberg. Other leaders in Magdeburg at the time were the superintendent Johannes Wigand and pastor Matthias Judex.

These theologians vehemently opposed Duke Moritz and the Augsburg Interim. They asserted that because of Moritz' alliance with the Roman Catholic emperor, the new elector's theologians in Saxony had themselves become servants of the papal Antichrist.[141] In contrast, Magdeburg's city government had refused to submit to the emperor or the Interim; publishers and authors also flouted the imperial ban on writings against the Interim.[142] Writings against the Interim soon expanded into personal attacks against Melanchthon, Bugenhagen and other theologians who had stayed in Electoral Saxony.[143] Of course, the Magdeburg theologians who despised Moritz and criticized their Wittenberg colleagues did not know that Moritz would soon become their liberator when the artificially prolonged siege of Magdeburg made possible the decisive military victory against Charles V in 1552.

The sudden change brought by the 1552 princes' revolt against Charles did not reconcile these Lutheran parties. A fault line had grown, which especially divided those in Moritz' Electoral Saxony from other Lutheran theologians across Germany. Leaders like Amsdorf, Gallus and Flacius criticized their former coworkers in Wittenberg for having betrayed both John Frederick and the memory of Martin Luther. It is true that controversies within relatively small movements can appear petty to people outside the group. In this case, however, the conflict started by the Augsburg Interim was about important differences over matters of faith and public life. Those in Magdeburg had resisted Moritz and Charles on principle and believed that they had been right to resist. Theologians in Wittenberg had accepted Duke Moritz as their new God-given sovereign after John Frederick formally surrendered in the so-called Wittenberg Capitulation of May 1547. They believed that they had been right, too, when they accepted their new prince and agreed to work with him for the good of the community.

The Wittenbergers had not switched loyalties lightly. On May 29, 1547 university faculty members wrote to the imprisoned John Frederick, asking whether or not they should stay in Wittenberg.[144] Bugenhagen asked if he might stay in Wittenberg due to his age (he was nearly 62 at the time), though he said he would obey John

Frederick's decision.¹⁴⁵ It does not appear as if these professors and pastors received a reply. Despite their acceptance of Moritz and the decision of many theologians to stay in Wittenberg, the initial relationship to Moritz was cool. After all, one of the few people identifiable at the Last Supper scene in Wittenberg's 1547 Cranach Altar is Duke Moritz. While Luther shares the communion cup, Moritz is receiving bread from Jesus in a way that equates him with Judas Iscariot.

Despite now living under this "Judas of Meissen," Bugenhagen and Melanchthon stayed in Wittenberg. After helping John Frederick's sons found a new university in Jena in 1547, Melanchthon and his colleagues met with Moritz to discuss their future in Wittenberg. At that meeting, Moritz told them that he wanted to keep the University of Wittenberg open and that he would protect evangelical faith in his lands.¹⁴⁶ The Wittenbergers responded favorably and requested new funding for academic and ecclesiastical work, which they received in early 1548.¹⁴⁷ Opponents would later describe this as the moment when Moritz successfully bribed Melanchthon and Bugenhagen to stay in Albertine Saxony, a rumor that renowned Melanchthon scholar Heinz Scheible has conclusively refuted.¹⁴⁸ Melanchthon's student and colleague Johannes Stigel later explained that Melanchthon thought he would have more freedom to write against the Council of Trent in Wittenberg than in a weaker state like Ernestine Saxony; also, for Melanchthon, Wittenberg was not enemy territory but "his mourning congregation."¹⁴⁹ Indeed, the university grew larger in the 1550s than it had ever been during Luther's lifetime, a fact only made possible by Moritz' support and Melanchthon's decision to remain.¹⁵⁰

As mentioned above, Moritz scheduled a series of meetings that included Lutheran theologians, Catholic bishops, and political advisers in order to delay the Interim's enforcement. Lutheran theologians had expressed their dissatisfaction with the Interim, yet continued to participate in these political debates out of a sense of public responsibility. This sense is visible in their work at the November 1548 meeting in Altcella. There they reworked the existing church order for Albertine Saxony, the 1539 *Heinrichsagenda*, which had been written by the reformer Justus Jonas and approved by Luther when Moritz' father Heinrich introduced church reforms to the territory.

Jonah in Historical Context • 41

At Altcella, the Lutherans tried to balance existing practices with the new requirements. For example, the Augsburg Interim demanded the reintroduction of the Corpus Christi festival into church life.[151] In response, the Lutherans allowed for observation of the Corpus Christi festival as required by the law, but "without the procession and the carrying around of the Sacrament and other misuses that go against Christ's order."[152] Since the holiday traditionally revolved around the procession and veneration of the Eucharistic host, this was a clear rejection of the festival and its theology. To obey the emperor, the festival could have a place on the calendar but become instead a chance to teach the Lutheran use of the Lord's Supper.

A similar strategy appeared in the religious document put forth at the Leipzig assembly (*Landtag*) of December 1548. This document patched together elements of statements made by Lutheran theologians at Pegau and Altcella; it was finally presented by Duke Moritz' core political advisers.[153] Because of its many authors, the Leipzig document has a complex compositional history. Nevertheless, even in such a convoluted text, several points followed the Lutheran theologians' suggestions very closely. One such point was mandatory fasting. The Augsburg Interim had re-instituted fasting and not eating meat on certain days.[154] In response, the Leipzig articles declared that the fasting re-imposed under the emperor was a strictly secular rule, maintained for the sake of civil peace and having no spiritual implications: it would be "observed as an external ordinance commanded by his Imperial Majesty."[155] By saying that practices like fasting have no intrinsic spiritual value when required by law, the Lutherans took the heart out of the imperial command to conform to Roman Catholic teaching. They made clear distinctions between religious truth and civil law. These comments did not go unnoticed by the Catholic bishops who attended the Leipzig *Landtag*. They saw that these suggestions would not achieve the emperor's goal of unity in faith and practice.[156]

Throughout their meetings, the Lutheran theologians of Electoral Saxony based their work on the doctrine of justification. This doctrine teaches that people are saved by God's grace alone through faith alone in Christ alone. From this position, the Lutheran theologians could claim freedom and flexibility with respect to secondary matters that do not concern salvation. These non-essential matters of faith and practice are called "adiaphora," a Greek term meaning something about which the Bible does not give a clear position. Earlier in the Reformation, adiaphora had included fasting, observing saints' days, and the use of images and music in worship. The usefulness of the category of adiaphora became apparent, for instance, when Martin Luther returned to Wittenberg from the Wartburg Castle in 1522 and preached that reforming various practices was less important than showing Christian love and compassion to others.[157] As early as the 1519 Lectures on Galatians, Luther used the word adiaphora interchangeably with the Latin *indifferentia* (undifferentiated).[158] In the 1531 Apology to the Augsburg Confession, Philip Melanchthon wrote that for the sake of good order and Christian love the evangelical church might reluctantly tolerate certain traditions and ceremonies that they otherwise felt did not serve the gospel.[159]

The doctrine of justification gave Lutherans great flexibility as their reforms spread to different lands. The Augsburg Confession declared, "It is enough for the true unity of the church to agree concerning the teaching of the gospel and the administration of the sacraments."[160] Also, concerning church rites, its article 15 stated that "those rites should be observed that can be observed without sin and that contribute to peace and good order in the church, for example, certain holy days, festivals, and the like. However, people are reminded not to burden consciences, as if such worship were necessary for salvation."[161] These articles expressed the Lutheran liturgical conviction that proclamation of God's word and sacraments comes first; everything else in worship submits to those means of grace. This freedom to accept, reject or simply tolerate various worship rites was the basis for the Albertine response to the emperor's Augsburg Interim. Rather than accept the Augsburg Interim as it was, Moritz' Lutheran theologians worked to devise a policy that would honor Charles' political authority yet conform to their central doctrine of justification by faith.

The legislative *Landtag* held in Leipzig in late December 1548 was the culmination of many smaller meetings that had taken place that year.[162] The *Landtag* brought the elector and his advisers together with representatives from the nobility and the cities. The Roman Catholic bishops Julius Pflug and Johannes von Maltitz were also present, eager to see the re-institution of traditional

Roman theology and worship; they were responsible for reporting on Moritz' activity to Emperor Charles and King Ferdinand. Moritz' goal was to stall acceptance of the Augsburg Interim without offending the emperor.[163] In addition to needing to placate imperial interests, Moritz also encountered pressure to accept the Interim from a Lutheran ally, Elector Joachim of Brandenburg. At the conference in Jüterbog that took place the week before the Leipzig *Landtag*, Joachim and his court theologian Johann Agricola wanted Moritz to approve the Augsburg Interim as it stood.

Because of Brandenburg's position, Melanchthon had not even been sure he wanted to attend the Jüterbog meeting.[164] The involvement of these Brandenburg theologians and officials who sanctioned the Augsburg Interim troubled Melanchthon. He wrote, "But what kind of grumbling will there be if we are seen there with [Agricola]? I do not condemn this arbitration, and yet out of respect I shrink back from his spurious activities because it is clear to see that the earlier abuses will be restated and confirmed."[165] Having spent the months since the introduction of the Augsburg Interim fighting the kind of surface unity sought by Agricola, Melanchthon worried about participating in a meeting where such positions might receive further validation. In the end, Melanchthon and Georg von Anhalt successfully defended Lutheran teachings about the sacrament of Holy Communion at Jüterbog. Brandenburg agreed to support the Altcella agreement rather than the Augsburg Interim itself.[166] Nevertheless, when Agricola returned to Brandenburg, he started saying that the Wittenbergers now accepted the Augsburg Interim and had written a new church order that both electors approved for their lands.[167] Berlin pastor Georg Buchholzer reported these words to Wittenberg, asking his colleagues if such things were true. Bugenhagen and Melanchthon denied it and further distanced themselves from Agricola.[168]

Although Agricola sought a policy that would give new imperial sanction to some aspects of Lutheran faith and worship, Bugenhagen and Melanchthon questioned why he would give up so much to achieve that. In their answer to Buchholzer and the Berlin pastors, they pondered the difference between the brutal realities facing Lutherans in southern Germany and the superficial unity sought by Agricola: "It is therefore a wonder why Agricola promises a golden age, when one so clearly sees the destruction of so many churches and the exile of pious and learned men with their entire families."¹⁶⁹ The Wittenberg theologians viewed the Augsburg Interim as a real religious and political crisis. For the sake of political order and civil peace, they were willing to engage in the political process that Lutherans in Magdeburg found so abhorrent. At the same time, their response to Agricola shows that they did not consider a superficial peace to be worth compromising their convictions.

Although willing to be flexible on some points, they would not concede on matters of practice where there was no agreement. Some points like fasting were fairly negotiable; others, like a return to the old communion liturgy, would not be accepted without a fight. "In such high matters of worship, one should not speak falsely about an intervention that would serve to confirm great errors that are openly against the first and other commandments, and that are against the doctrine of Christ's grace and justification."¹⁷⁰ The Lutheran theologians refused to concede unity where there was none, especially on the Mass and on the sacramental use of anointing. Instead they spoke of the need for ongoing discussions with Catholic bishops.

Again at Leipzig, however, Melanchthon's worries about simply being involved in negotiations proved well founded. In the week between Jüterbog and Leipzig, Moritz' advisers changed earlier documents without identifying their authorship.¹⁷¹ Because of this, Melanchthon and his colleagues' influence over the document presented at the Leipzig *Landtag* remains uncertain. In a dissertation on the so-called "Philippist" theologians (colleagues and students of Melanchthon), Luther Peterson wrote, "Scholars have usually attributed authorship of the [Leipzig] Interim to Melanchthon and his fellow theologians, but... a large share of the Interim, and even an important interpolation or two in Melanchthon and Cruciger's articles on justification and good works, stemmed from the pens and purposes of Moritz' legal advisors."¹⁷² Günther Wartenberg, researching the relationship between Moritz and the Lutheran theologians, also declared the Leipzig articles "a text by the advisers."¹⁷³

Melanchthon reminded the estates of this fact when he spoke at Leipzig. First, he said that because many other pastors had worked with him on the articles, they were not his alone to alter;

more important, he recognized that articles on ordination, confirmation, anointing, and the mass remained problematic.[174] When asked further what he thought about the statement on anointing, Melanchthon responded by saying, "this article is withdrawn and belongs to the conclusion, 'in other articles one should speak further with the bishops.'"[175] Here Melanchthon paraphrased the Leipzig articles' final paragraph (about the need for ongoing dialogue on certain points) to subvert the document by using its own language.[176] Rather than standing up for the articles, he let them be defeated.

Nothing definitive was decided at Leipzig. In Wartenberg's judgment, "Neither the secular estates nor the theologians ever approved the Leipzig Interim."[177] The articles were not approved by Moritz, the Saxon people, or the Catholic bishops. In coming months, Moritz would approve portions of the Leipzig articles for use in his original territory, but not in formerly Ernestine areas like Wittenberg. Even then, enforcement or pressure was minimal and the Catholic bishops remained unsupportive.[178] Rather than revealing the Lutheran theologians' willingness to compromise, the document put forth at the Leipzig *Landtag* was merely one more strategic moment in the ongoing tussles between Lutherans, the Catholic bishops, and politicians.

According to accounts from the time, Melanchthon and his colleagues considered the failure of the Leipzig articles to be a success. In a letter of January 6, 1549, Melanchthon wrote, "The events in Leipzig did not make changes in the church, because the controversy of the mass and the liturgy has been postponed for other deliberations."[179] The Lutheran theologians were pleased that they had delayed ratification of theologically questionable teachings and practices. They had survived another threat to their faith and could continue worshiping and teaching as they had, at least for a little while longer.

The Wittenberg theologians were not the only ones satisfied by the defeat of the religious statement put forth at the *Landtag*. While the Lutherans had been able to distance themselves from an awkward document, the political estates had themselves been the ones to vote the articles down. The Catholic bishops at the *Landtag*, Julius Pflug and Johannes von Maltitz, also rejected the articles as too Protestant and too different from the original

Augsburg Interim. This served Moritz greatly. In a letter to Emperor Charles, the bishops wrote favorably about Moritz, saying that he had tried to bring the Augsburg Interim to Saxony but the nobility and the cities rejected the religious settlement.[180] Through this statement from the Catholic bishops, Moritz continued to appear cooperative with the emperor without making any changes.

Nevertheless, rumors and reports of the Leipzig *Landtag* and the other meetings brought new confusion and uncertainty about what had taken place. In the months that followed, theologians in Electoral Saxony were forced to explain parts of the *Landtag* that they did not write and which had never been approved by them, the Elector, the estates, or the Catholic bishops. The ensuing controversies would largely be based upon half-truths about the Albertine theologians' role in shaping the document presented at the Leipzig assembly of December 1548. Melanchthon in particular came to be negatively identified with the statement that political advisers had submitted.

When the document presented at the Leipzig *Landtag* was finally printed, it was not by Duke Moritz or the Wittenbergers. Instead, Flacius and Gallus published it in Magdeburg as evidence against Melanchthon and the Albertine theologians.[181] With that printing, the title "the Leipzig Interim" was first bestowed on the document. This was misleading, since the document had happily been voted down by all sides at the *Landtag*. "Flacius pilloried Melanchthon as the one responsible for supporting the fatal conciliation of Christ and Belial: he accused Melanchthon of combining correct [doctrine] with Satanic teaching and leading people into error."[182] But to the Wittenbergers, participation in the political process was not a sign of unfaithfulness but a legitimate tool for giving input and helping make reforms. To the contrary, it might be argued that much good came from the work of the Albertine theologians. They participated in tense deliberations over several months which helped minimize violent confrontations and bought time for the eventual downfall of the Augsburg Interim. Had the theologians taken an immediate and unshakable position against the emperor and the new Saxon political situation, Moritz might have been in no position to lead a coalition against Charles.

Indeed, despite the serious critiques exchanged between Magdeburg and Wittenberg, it appears as if both parties contributed significantly to the preservation of Lutheran churches after the Smalcaldic War. Wittenberg's theologians and their colleagues quietly prevented any enforcement of religious changes in Electoral Saxony and avoided armed suppression of Lutheran worship and theology. Their participation in political discourse protected lives and defended the faith. At the same time, Magdeburg's stubborn resistance to the Augsburg Interim also served the Protestant cause by rallying anti-imperial sentiments and by giving Moritz the excuse to maintain the army that he later used against Emperor Charles. In retrospect, events between the 1548 Augsburg Interim and the 1552 Treaty of Augsburg led to great advantages for Lutherans in Germany at a time when their future had seemed the least certain.

Bugenhagen's Writings from 1547 to 1550

Bugenhagen's work sheds further light on this period and provides more sources for interpreting the activity of the Albertine theologians. In letters and in other public writings, he explained events in detail and defended the decisions that he and his colleagues made.

Understanding Bugenhagen's view also helps interpret his 1550 Commentary on Jonah. One of Bugenhagen's stated goals in publishing his *Jonah* was to show others what he had been doing and saying all along. In a July 1550 letter to King Christian, Bugenhagen wrote, "I would have much rather have sent Your Majesty my *Jonah the Prophet* right now, in which one can see what we did in our school by God's grace since the siege."[183] Because he had been lecturing on Jonah beginning in 1547, his work from that time could serve as a public record of his teaching during those controversial years. When the commentary was printed in October 1550, he expressed his hope that, along with the testimony of friends from Wittenberg traveling abroad, the commentary would explain his position. He wrote to Duke Albrecht of Prussia, "Whatever more Your Grace should want to know about us and the dangers we are still stuck in, truly calling out to God in public and at home without ceasing, all this Dr. George [Venetus] will certainly tell you. For this reason I am also sending your ducal grace my *Jonah*, which is fresh out of the great fish, that is, I just received it wet off the printing press. It will testify to your grace about me."[184] Bugenhagen's *Jonah* was published as a confession of his faith.

Already in the summer of 1547, Bugenhagen had written an account of Wittenberg's fall to the emperor during the Smalcaldic War. This documents stands as a public interpretation of the war, as seen in the work's full title, "How It Went for Us in the City of Wittenberg during the Recent War until We Were Liberated by God's Grace and until Our Esteemed School Was Reestablished by His Highness Duke Moritz, Lord of Saxony and Other Places; a Truthful History Described by Johannes Bugenhagen of Pomerania, Doctor and Pastor in Wittenberg."[185] Although this "truthful history" is more an impassioned first person account of events in Wittenberg than an unbiased and objective report of historical events, it described recent events in order to inform an interested public. Bugenhagen's account was evidently well received, as this short tract underwent three printings within the year.[186]

In this work, Bugenhagen asserted that the city did not capitulate to either Charles V or Duke Moritz out of cowardice, opportunism, or betrayal of John Frederick. Rather, John Frederick had advised the city to accept the terms of surrender that he signed.[187] What is more, Bugenhagen told some anecdotes about how graciously Charles V had treated the city. Upon learning that church services had been stopped at the Castle Church because of his presence in town, Charles insisted that services be held again as normal and not be stopped on his account.[188] Also, when he visited Luther's grave in the Castle Church, Charles left it undisturbed.[189] During the week of Pentecost, Bugenhagen described how he preached to the emperor's retinue from the Acts of the Apostles about the difference between the evangelical and papal teachings, asking those present to report accurately about the faith that they heard in Wittenberg.[190] He also described how Moritz restored full rights and privileges to his new citizens in Wittenberg.[191] Through such reports, Bugenhagen gave a public interpretation of events in Wittenberg that expressed the disappointment of losing the war and their beloved John Frederick, while also describing the unexpected relief of being treated humanely by the emperor.

While he was still leading the church in Wittenberg and teaching at the university, Bugenhagen took part in the meetings about the Augsburg Interim and explained Wittenberg's position to those outside of Saxony. As noted above, he was present at Altcella in November, 1548. He later wrote to Duke Albrecht of Prussia that it was around this time when, in a heated debate about wor-

Jonah in Historical Context • 49

ship, he said, "I offered this gray head of mine before I would accept the blasphemous priestly unctions, consecrations, benedictions, the canon of the mass, and so on."[192] In letters over the following months, Bugenhagen continued to write to rulers like Duke Albrecht, King Christian, and Count Franz of Lüneburg to explain events and defend the Wittenberg theologians from rumors that had started circulating against them.

Bugenhagen's *Briefwechsel* (collected letters) provides some important references to the Leipzig *Landtag*. In December 1548, Melanchthon and Georg von Anhalt traveled south from Jüterbog on their way to the Leipzig *Landtag*. They stopped in Wittenberg and told Bugenhagen about their meeting with Agricola and the Elector of Brandenburg. In a note that appears to have been made for his own records, he wrote,

> Pomeranus, with my own hand.
>
> Master Philip returned from Jüterbog yesterday and said to me, "I bring back entirely good news. Nothing new has been enacted other than that which we harmoniously proposed in Altcella. The Prince Elector of Brandenburg himself wanted to keep within our bounds and not undertake anything beyond what we will set forth in this assembly" (to which our people and our Philip are going today). Prince Georg von Anhalt said similar things to me yesterday at the table, just as our captain – a good man – publicly said. They all said this, and the princes and whoever else had gathered there were very glad about this harmony; for it is what we are now in fact writing to many people. And Prince Georg von Anhalt had added this word to Magister Agricola: he [Anhalt] would rather have let things break apart than weaken the pure teaching of our gospel by not mentioning that there are significant controversies, as if everything were extremely peaceful and harmonious.[193]

Bugenhagen's account is similar to a letter that Melanchthon wrote to Wittenberg professor Paul Eber on December 17. There Melanchthon described how glad he was to have defused Agricola's efforts at compromise, even though he was still worried that Agricola misinterpreted their work together.[194] After Jüterbog, the theologians of Electoral Saxony felt that they had successfully maintained good doctrine through their work at Altcella and their public objections to Agricola. Bugenhagen had been able to hear the latest news from Melanchthon and Georg von Anhalt immediately and in person.

After the Leipzig *Landtag*, Bugenhagen made a point of preaching against the articles that had been put forward there. Professor Georg Cracow, soon to be Bugenhagen's son-in-law, carried the message of Bugenhagen's preaching to Duke Albrecht of Prussia. Cracow reported that the Wittenberg theologians had not subjected the church to any old practices.[195] On the contrary, Cracow challenged the notion that the Wittenbergers had compromised the faith by saying that they had risen against impious ideas at Jüterbog.[196] Bugenhagen appended a small handwritten note to Cracow's report, assuring the Duke that this was indeed his position.

Such personal assurances of Bugenhagen's real position had become necessary, because many different reports were circulating around Germany. In a letter to King Christian of February 1549, Bugenhagen described one secretive accuser:

> Now a man without honor, whose name remains unknown, has printed three little books against us, in which he exhorts people to remain in the gospel. But he teaches nothing that is most important in these times. And the unnamed person goes on to say: "I want to remain in the gospel," and so on. "Who are you? What's your name?" "Don't ask. In the meantime, I want to gossip like this: I do not want to defect from the gospel, as the theologians in Wittenberg have done, etc." My king, we sit here amid many dangers, because we did not want to leave our church and this school. Until now, the devil could not kill us with his murder, because God kept us so graciously with his miraculous protection, thank God. So now the devil tries another way (John 8) and wants to shit on us with his lies, so that we might stink before Christians. But Christ says, "I do not seek my own glory; there is one who seeks it and judges it," etc. [John 8:50]. So we must comfort ourselves with this, because we need to know that Christ will not remain outside long.[197]

This interpretation of events to King Christian would remain consistent a year and a half later in the dedication letter that begins the Jonah Commentary. The Wittenberg theologians decided to deal with anonymous attacks by appealing to patience and by reminding the public that many students and theologians were still coming to the university to study the same Lutheran theology that had been taught there for decades. Nevertheless, rumors and complaints against the Wittenbergers gained traction and influenced colleagues across Germany. By early 1549 the Wittenberg theologians had received letters of disbelief or denunciation from pastors and political leaders in Berlin, Hamburg, Mansfeld, Prussia, and other places.[198]

As a sign of how widely opposition against Wittenberg had spread, Bugenhagen received a disappointing letter from Duke Albrecht of Prussia in April 1549.[199] A document supposedly written by Bugenhagen had come to Albrecht's attention, in which offensive views about adiaphora were expressed. Along with a short note asking how Bugenhagen could be saying such things, Albrecht passed this report on to Bugenhagen. Bugenhagen responded immediately. In his reply of May 25, 1549, Bugenhagen disavowed any responsibility for the document that had come to Albrecht.[200] Instead, he described events surrounding the Leipzig *Landtag* and gave his perspective on the challenges confronting the church in Electoral Saxony. His attempt to convince Duke Albrecht of his position, however, seems to have failed. Though Bugenhagen wrote several letters of defense and explanation to Albrecht over the following months and years, he eventually wanted to stop trying to defend himself; in a letter to King Christian, he wrote that the Prussian leader still refused to believe him.[201]

Although Bugenhagen's letter failed to win Albrecht over, it provides a valuable source for viewing the controversies from the Wittenbergers' perspective (translated here in Appendix One). Beginning with the request from Moritz that the theologians craft an alternative to the Augsburg Interim, Bugenhagen presented an accurate chronology of the theological meetings and gave summaries of those meetings' decisions. He told Albrecht that the document put forth in Leipzig was submitted in the name of the theologians, even though they had not written the final product. Further, he reminded the duke that the document had not been approved by the *Landtag* and resulted in no new changes, for which Bugenhagen had given thanks from his pulpit in Wittenberg.[202] Indeed, Bugenhagen's letter reinforces the idea that the Wittenbergers judged the defeat of the Leipzig articles to be a victory.

In addition to reports on the official actions of the *Landtag* and his own preaching, Bugenhagen referred Duke Albrecht to the testimony of Wittenberg residents who were abroad. As mentioned above, Georg Cracow had personally explained Bugenhagen's position to Duke Albrecht in February 1549. In the May letter to Albrecht, Bugenhagen commended Hans Lufft as another source for learning about the situation in Wittenberg. At the time, Lufft was in Prussia to secure publishing rights there.[203] Since the 1520s, Lufft had been one of Wittenberg's leading printers of reformation writings, including the 1534 German translation of the Bible and the first collection of Luther's works, which started in 1545.[204] He was also a respected town leader: in addition to serving on the city council, he began working as a judge beginning in 1545.[205] For this reason, Bugenhagen referred to him as "our judge Hans Lufft" when he wrote that Albrecht should ask Lufft what he had seen and heard in Wittenberg.[206]

Another person whom Bugenhagen recommended as a good reference to Albrecht was Georg Sabinus. Sabinus was a literature professor and the first rector of the University of Königsberg. He was also a favorite student of Melanchthon's, as well as his son-in-law.[207] According to Bugenhagen's letter, Sabinus was returning to Prussia from Wittenberg. Although he had wanted to wait until Lufft brought back the latest news, Bugenhagen's need to defend himself forced him to send this letter earlier. He wrote, "But because Dr. Sabinus, my dear lord and friend, is traveling back home to your majesty, I cannot help but write to your majesty. For I now have something certain and good to write, which Dr. Sabinus will also tell you, so that your majesty might believe me even more."[208] Along with Lufft, Sabinus would be able to testify personally about the Wittenberg theologians. Though the close relationships that Cracow, Lufft and Sabinus each had with Melanchthon and Bugenhagen might make them less than impartial witnesses, Bugenhagen was eager to let each of these men speak for themselves about what they had seen and heard in order to make his position known publicly and to defend his colleagues and himself from slander.

One Bible verse that Bugenhagen often used to describe Wittenberg's handling of the recent controversies came from Jesus' trial before the religious authorities. He wrote to Duke Albrecht, "The more we write, the more they find to complain about, so that I simply must say to such people: 'I have spoken nothing in secret, why do you strike me? Ask the ones who have heard' [John 18:20, 23]. This is what I asked Hans Lufft to do."[209] In addition to using John 18 to persuade Duke Albrecht of his innocence, this quotation gives another insight into the public nature of how Bugenhagen responded to the debates of the time. Through public writings, Bugenhagen hoped to present his views in an orderly, open, and theologically faithful way; he had said nothing in secret. He published his Jonah Commentary with the same intent.

Although he rarely answered critics with the same pointed criticisms that he received, there is one letter in which he named some Lutheran opponents. This letter to King Christian of Denmark from July 17, 1549 appears to have been sent to other recipients as well.[210] In it, he identified Flacius as the primary source of untrue accusations. Behind a cordial façade, Flacius had been writing "absurd pieces against the Wittenberg theologians."[211] Bugenhagen continued, "When he was still with us, he wrote secretly to other cities that we had turned the gospel entirely around. Now he pushes this idea with his utmost, wrecking our names with his hypocrisy. He writes to many that they should betray their lords and brothers, but – praise God – only to those who gladly hear bad things of us: '[beware of] danger from false brothers' [2 Cor. 11:26]."[212] While granting that Flacius' motives were likely based in the conviction of his conscience, Bugenhagen rejected the content of Flacius' writings about the Wittenbergers.

Bugenhagen also lamented that "the worthy Bishop Amsdorf" had joined the cause against them. He addressed four accusations that Amsdorf had made: first, they had reinstituted the Roman Catholic mass; second, they were commanding all parishioners to make weekly confession of all their sins; third, they had forbidden people to eat meat [on certain days]; fourth, like Judas Iscariot, they supposedly took money to betray the truth.[213] On matters of worship, Bugenhagen felt it enough simply to say that these things were patently false. On the fourth point, however, Bugenhagen gave King Christian a short history of Wittenberg's relationship with Moritz. After the Wittenberg Capitulation, Moritz had agreed to reopen the university according to its old constitution and privileges. According to Bugenhagen, Moritz funded this reopening and even paid for improvements.[214] "That certainly does not mean," he wrote, "that we took money to betray the truth. I did not betray my previous lord [John Frederick]. My gracious and imprisoned lord knows me well enough to know that I do not want to be a traitor to this lord [Moritz], either. We did not sin against them when, through God's gracious will, we stayed with our churches and schools, as they scream and write against us."[215] Acknowledging that money had been involved, Bugenhagen explained that this was not a betrayal but a practical case of providing financially for the university and churches.

Bugenhagen's response to a document on adiaphora written by pastors in Hamburg against the Wittenbergers stands as a further point of defense in that letter to King Christian. Bugenhagen explained that he and Melanchthon had answered the Hamburg pastors "with diligence and good consciences before God." But this reply had not satisfied Hamburg pastor and former Wittenberg student Joachim Westphal, who – in "the spirit of Flacius" – then set himself up as a judge over them. "Both of these judges," wrote Bugenhagen, "speak a verdict that they are right and we are wrong. We do not accept such inexperienced judges. Our thoughts and theirs are of today. Other people should judge: namely, the poor and afflicted church of Christ, which well understands such matters in these times."[216]

Here Bugenhagen shared his confidence in God and in the church. As much as Melanchthon and Bugenhagen tried to deal correctly the questions and challenges at hand, they would not presume to stand as their own final judges; at the same time, neither would they accept judgments from former colleagues who were not in their shoes. Instead, they would let Christ and Christ's oppressed and afflicted church be their judge. This is a stirring reminder that Christians can keep perspective in troubled times by remembering other believers across time and space who have known what it means to toil and to suffer for the faith. Citing Revelation 14:12, he wrote to King Christian: "This is the endurance [*patientia*] of the saints."[217]

The main body of the Jonah Commentary is largely silent about intra-Lutheran controversies. Indeed, when Bugenhagen began his lectures on Jonah in 1547, there were no such disputes to address. But by the time of the commentary's printing in October 1550, Bugenhagen's concerns had shifted from recovering after the Smalcaldic War to defending himself and his colleagues from other Lutherans.

The dedication letter that Bugenhagen addressed to King Christian III of Denmark thus reframes the entire work (translated here in Appendix Two). Without the dedication letter, Bugenhagen's *Jonah* could be read solely as a case for Lutheran teachings against the Roman church of his time. The main body of the commentary primarily teaches the doctrine of justification and its consequences. With the dedication letter, however, Bugenhagen's writings against Roman Catholic opponents also became ways to explain his position to other Lutheran colleagues and communities.

Dated October 1, 1550, this letter is similar in tone and content to the letters that Bugenhagen had written to Duke Albrecht and to King Christian in mid-1549, especially in defending the Wittenberg theologians from slanders abroad. It opens by dramatically applying New Testament words about the devil to his situation.

> Christ speaks, most favorable King, in John 8[:44] concerning the devil: "That one was a murderer from the beginning, and he does not stand in the truth because the truth is not in him. When he speaks as a liar, he speaks according to his own nature, for he is a liar and the father of lies," (that is, the fountain of lies) for he killed the human race from the beginning with his lies. One may see this today in the works of the devil, as he horribly works against us afflicted preachers and teachers of Christ's church.
>
> For when he desired, we surrendered our city on the advice, order, and persuasion of the most illustrious imprisoned Prince Elector (may God set him free by his grace). And the Imperial Majesty made us submit and obey peace with this promise: that he would not introduce anything against our religion which we have served to now according to the Augsburg Confession and from which we have not deviated by as much as a finger. The devil, seeing that he could not destroy us through murder (for Christ with his faithful angels preserved us), now clearly desires to defile and oppress us with his lies through adiaphoristic writers. They write many public works in all the world, that we theologians who are faithful servants of Christ (our many Christian churches which we have served so faithfully are witnesses for us and acknowledge our faithful ministry with thanksgiving) accepted money from our magistrates and

became traitors of Christ's gospel and that, despising all good order, we defect from faith to the doctrine of demons and worship of the Antichrist.[218]

As terrible as the lost Smalcaldic War had been and as hard as life under the Interim had become, Bugenhagen viewed the most devilish actions to be those of his fellow Lutherans. Neither imperial soldiers nor Catholic bishops had afflicted the Wittenbergers as badly as those whom Bugenhagen called the "adiaphoristic writers."

The use of this label "adiaphoristic writers" is striking. Having named his Lutheran critics in the letter of July 1549, Bugenhagen was likely referring to Flacius, Amsdorf, Westphal and others who wrote against the Albertine theologians. Yet the term "adiaphorists" had been coined by the Magdeburgers. It was normally used to defame the Wittenbergers and their allies.[219] Bugenhagen's use of the name shifted the derogatory title onto those who were making what he considered to be baseless and harmful accusations. It is conceivable that the "adiaphoristic writers" might refer to Melanchthon and other theologians in Electoral Saxony, but that is highly unlikely because of the high level of cooperation that Bugenhagen maintained with his colleagues in Wittenberg. Indeed, in the Jonah Commentary's dedication letter he continued to speak glowingly of the university's "blossoming" after the war, in contrast to those who derided it.[220]

Further evidence that he was referring to critics in Magdeburg appears when Bugenhagen cited Flacius and Amsdorf without naming them. Against the University of Wittenberg, Flacius had written, "As for myself, I do not doubt that, if only the theologians had been steadfast, the Wittenberg School would have been to-day much firmer than it is... The Interim sprang from the timidity of the Wittenberg theologians... Even a thousand Wittenberg schools ought certainly not to be valued so highly by pious men that, in order to preserve them unimpaired, they would rather suffer the world to be deprived of the light of the Gospel."[221] Bugenhagen quoted the line "a thousand Wittenberg schools," lamenting that such comments had caused Wittenberg to be seen as "a common pest to Christ's church."[222]

In another place, Bugenhagen referred to a supposed prophecy in which Martin Luther predicted unfaithfulness among his colleagues. According to Amsdorf, Luther had said, "After my death, none of these theologians will remain steadfast." Amsdorf had apparently learned of this statement from the recently deceased Wittenberg physician Augustin Schurff and included it in a 1549 tract against Bugenhagen.[223] Bugenhagen responded by insisting that Luther had never said such words and that his opponents were putting lies in Luther's mouth.[224] Searching Luther's works for this supposed prophecy using either the words of Amsdorf's German quotation or Bugenhagen's Latin, no direct match appears; neither of the two closest matches refers to Luther's colleagues in Wittenberg. In one Table Talk, Luther warned a group of lawyers not to interfere with theology after his death.[225] A more likely origin for Amsdorf's quotation is not from Schurff, but from a 1548 publication by Erasmus Alberus, a theologian who was also in Magdeburg. In his "Dialog vom Interim" ("Dialogue about the Interim") Alberus had repeated words he claimed to have heard from Luther, in which Luther predicted that Charles V might someday begin to persecute the gospel by appealing to self-interested princes, who would not remain faithful.[226] There is no indication in Alberus' work that the citation referred to any particular Wittenberg theologians.

But rather than turn the fight into one about personal memories of Luther, Bugenhagen appealed to the faith that he had continued to teach at the university. This theology, he asserted, was on clear display in his Jonah Commentary. Explaining his desire to publish this commentary for that reason, he wrote,

> Finally they shout, "Now you are all silent and do not want to console the church's afflictions." For this reason, most favorable king, I dedicate to your majesty and your name these my tracts, which contain useful and necessary material, especially for the Christian Church of this age, so that your majesty may read and judge. For God has given your Majesty an intellect, in order that it might know the great mystery of God in Christ and so that all might see that we have not been silent until now. For we have dealt publicly with this in our school from the beginning, since the city's surrender and the college's reopening.[227]

Bugenhagen hoped that King Christian and others would read this commentary thoughtfully and see for themselves that Wittenberg's teachers had not been silent or changed their faith.

Along with appeals to reason and usefulness, Bugenhagen submitted this work of biblical interpretation as a form of public testimony to his teaching and leadership.

On the charge that the Wittenbergers had created a new abomination in the so-called Leipzig Interim, Bugenhagen wrote that he owed no one an explanation. "Moreover, they will clamor, 'You must respond to the Leipzig Interim!' I do not need to respond, neither for it nor against it. For I am not personally aware of anyone's evil doctrine. Neither did our magistrate ever ask this of me; much less has he purchased it, whatever else is judged against us."[228] In this, Bugenhagen voiced again his consistent response to the Leipzig document: he and his colleagues had not been responsible for it, they had not been bribed to support it, it had not become official policy, and he was glad that it had been voted down.

Bugenhagen also pointed to the positive consequences of his teaching, especially in contrast to his opponents. He did not fail to remind King Christian that the vehement theological attacks on the Wittenbergers often included calls for political sedition.

> Then seeing their stubbornness and that sedition in this world against our magistrate is sought through such writings (to which we do not owe our response and strained cooperation and which are fatal to us at this time, as was spoken in Revelation 14:[12] "This is the endurance of the saints and those who have served the commandments and the faith of Jesus"), I say these things, reflecting on myself, that I am beginning to know something of silence and endurance, that which pious, erudite and prudent men among us have since tested.[229]

This conservative position against rebellion certainly sought the favor of King Christian and other rulers. At the same time, Bugenhagen wrote of a personal struggle and endurance that points to the deeply Christian sense of suffering on behalf of others and for the sake of peace. As a sign that his "endurance" had public interests at heart, Bugenhagen next called attention to the great harmony that existed in the community, especially at the university and among pastors.

> But I truly tell your Majesty that there is the highest harmony in our churches and schools and in all this land, not only in Christian doctrine, but also among persons and among

ministers. We rejoice and give thanks to God whenever we hear that others are in such harmony. But for others we pray to the Father in the name of Jesus Christ. And I remind all our brothers in this public writing that they apply themselves to observe this holy harmony through the Holy Spirit. "If by the Spirit you have put the body to death, you will live" [Rom. 8:13]. "But if you bite one another, see that you are not consumed by one another" [Gal. 5:15].[230]

With this, Bugenhagen pointed out the beneficial relationship between doctrine and action, between faith and good works. To Bugenhagen, a theology that taught sedition or division was an incomplete theology, because the fruits of faith are not division but patience, forgiveness, and reconciliation. Bugenhagen not only defended his theology with abstract ideas of peace but pointed to concrete examples of harmony in his community.

The dedication letter that introduces the Jonah Commentary has the clear rhetorical goal of convincing readers outside of Electoral Saxony that the Wittenberg theologians had dealt with recent events faithfully. Their opponents now included not only Emperor Charles V and Roman Catholic theologians, but other Lutherans who found fault with them and published their dissatisfaction abroad. Bugenhagen dismissed those objections as either lies or uncharitable interpretations of their decision to stay in Wittenberg under Duke Moritz.

Finally, Bugenhagen briefly connected the prophet Jonah with these events. Near the end of the dedication letter, Bugenhagen said that disputes among Lutherans were not about justification but were arguments about secondary matters. His *Jonah* would show that he had never stopped teaching justification by faith.

> For the Council of Trent already stands in blasphemy before Christ with these words: "If any one says that all sins are remitted to the one who believes with certainty that he has remission of sins, and that this is the faith which God requires of a sinner so that he may be justified, let that one be anathema."[231] For they say that this is not in Holy Scripture, in which this stands written against such pride, audacity, and especially false faith: "Who knows if God will turn and forgive?" [Jonah 3:9, Joel 2:14].[232] To which Paul responds, "Even if we apostles or an angel from heaven

should preach a gospel other than that which we have preached, and which you received from us, let that one be anathema" [Gal. 1:8, 9]. "No one is able to lay another foundation but that which has been laid, which is Jesus Christ" [1 Cor. 3:11].

And Peter, full of the Holy Spirit in Cornelius' house and in front of the Roman soldiers who were first among the far off gentiles to receive Christ's gospel from the apostles, stood against this blasphemy and for Christ's glory through the holy prophets. He said, "all the prophets testify about Christ that all who believe in him receive forgiveness of sins through his name" [Acts 10:43]. In this place, Peter – and the Spirit in any holy prophet of the law – negates this foul and blasphemous doubt, which the Papists teach against faith in Christ. Your Majesty will see in this my commentary, too: that the Holy Spirit did not and would not speak of this doubt, either in the Holy Scriptures or anywhere in Joel or Jonah. Therefore, stop fighting the acknowledged truth of the gospel.[233]

In Jonah 3:9, the people of Nineveh wondered whether or not God would forgive them. Throughout this commentary, Bugenhagen challenged any interpretation of that verse which encouraged people to doubt God's forgiveness. With this position, which included a clear condemnation of the Council of Trent's decrees on justification, Bugenhagen saw himself fighting for Lutheranism's central message. Using this commentary on Jonah to teach the doctrine of justification by faith, Bugenhagen demanded that readers stop opposing true expressions of the gospel like his.

Having been composed mostly before controversies broke out among Lutherans themselves, the main body of the Jonah Commentary does not directly address intra-Lutheran debates. Nevertheless, through this introduction Bugenhagen offered his lectures on Jonah as proof that he had always embraced and taught faith in Christ alone. He had opposed the early decrees of the Council of Trent. More to the point, he wanted to show that he had preached, defended and taught justification by faith, even while living under the Augsburg Interim. This dedication letter shows that the Jonah Commentary, which had begun as a work of biblical interpretation addressing the Smalcald War and the Council of Trent, was finally published as a defense of Wittenberg's handling of the Augsburg Interim.

This chapter's interpretation of the Wittenberger's work under the Augsburg Interim remains relatively novel in contemporary scholarship. Nevertheless, Bugenhagen scholar and biographer K.A.T. Vogt made the same points over 150 years ago. In his monumental work, Vogt concluded that Bugenhagen and the Wittenbergers had been telling the truth when they claimed innocence with respect to the charges going around Germany. Vogt wrote:

> At the Leipzig assembly (December 21, 1548), a document was eventually presented, the so-called Leipzig Interim, which was not edited by the theologians but by the Electoral councilors. This document held fast to the central evangelical doctrine of justification by faith but wanted to allow many things as adiaphora with respect to the ceremonies under the bishops' authority and other matters. To the estates themselves, this appeared offensive and threatening of the evangelical truth in the church. Melanchthon had perhaps shown himself a little too flexible in these negotiations; he was moved by the compassionate thought that it would be better to hold fast to the main point and not fight about such lesser matters, the adiaphora, than to expose the congregations to the danger of destruction and dissolution of church life, as had already started happening to those in southern Germany. Regardless, this Interim was not accepted, for which Bugenhagen publicly gave thanks in the church with the congregations of God. And he explained that the theologians had been wronged when people attached those offensive articles, against which they had argued, to them.[234]

Here Vogt noted the influence of Moritz' advisers on the so-called Leipzig Interim. Interestingly, even though Vogt mentioned the standard critique that Melanchthon was "too flexible" in those talks, he included a footnote which points to an authentic work by the Lutheran theologians at Leipzig, in which the they expressed their eagerness to find peace and unity, but never at the expense of true evangelical teaching. That footnoted document was written during the week of the Leipzig *Landtag*. In it, the theologians said they were ready to suffer the consequences of remaining true to their faith. They knew that, regardless of whatever suffering might arise, it would be their oppressors who were in the wrong. Willing to obey civil law and make some compromises for the sake of peace, they worried even more for their parishioners' spiritual lives. They were certainly ready to suffer harm for their convictions.

Therefore the teaching of right and true worship should nonetheless remain in our churches, namely, that all Christian virtues and works are commanded by God as worship, not these adiaphora like clothing or food, and that we should take care for the weak among us in the use of such things, so that we do not put these ones in danger because of them. And St. Peter says, "You should suffer with patience that which is necessary" [1 Pet. 2:19-20, 3:16-17]. If suffering now happens for small and unnecessary things, then the conscience becomes troubled. Therefore it is better to suffer in necessary, important, and well-grounded matters than to place oneself and the country and the people in misery on account of little things.

Should the Imperial Majesty be content with such adiaphora, then we would thank God; should his Imperial Majesty not be content, then we have this clear comfort, that we suffer for the other most important things that are publicly held in contempt of God's honor. For this purpose, the items which we have approved have mostly been customary in these lands, and several serve good order, such as consistency in festival, songs, etc.

But several others desire that one should consent to everything in order to prevent wars and destruction; this also cannot be, because one should not do evil so that good may come [Rom. 3:8]. Some say, "The Imperial Majesty will bring about such violence himself anyways and great sorrows will happen so that one should approve of this now." The answer to this is that we should not approve of wrong for this reason. And if we are not able to be responsible for this, so we ourselves cause such destruction, and that is truly something else to deal with.

The bishops on the Rhine now make the pastors in many lands quite desolate, so that in many places there are no pastors and servants of the church and the people are without public baptism, without the sacrament, without meetings in the churches, without sermons. Should now such punishments come over us (may God mercifully forbid it), it would be more bearable for our consciences. Because, no matter how cruel it might be, it would be the doing of other people. Therefore one should hold onto what is necessary; in other adiaphora one may have patience and the people should be instructed so that they do not put others in danger through impertinence or obstinance concerning adiaphora and then suffer from a bad conscience because of it. We will have enough to do on account of other greater matters.[235]

This statement demonstrates a willingness to suffer for Lutheran teaching and worship. It revolves around the consciences of the faithful, their spiritual health and their physical lives. There is also the recognition that martyrdom may result. Here Melanchthon and his colleagues addressed real instances of suffering, offering clear guidelines for working or not working with the emperor. These words, written during the Leipzig *Landtag*, stand as a public plea to keep the faith at great personal and political peril. The theologians who stayed in Wittenberg and in Moritz' lands had not compromised but had constructed faithful alternatives to the Augsburg Interim. By doing so, they ultimately helped prevent further armed conflict in Saxony and prepared the way for a greater peace.

Publishing *Jonah*

The study of Bugenhagen and his political context sheds light on the controversies that followed Luther's death in 1546. Wittenberg theologians mourned the capture of John Frederick but were willing to recognize Moritz as their new ruler. They were definitely not prepared to sacrifice their faith on the altar of political or theological accommodation. Neither Bugenhagen nor Melanchthon ever agreed to the compromise document that came to be known as the Leipzig Interim. Even in the face of fierce attacks from other Lutherans, they proved themselves willing to work patiently for the sake of Lutheran congregations.

Bugenhagen's official entry in the university records indicates that he started a series of lectures on the prophet Jonah when the school reopened in late October 1547.[236] He also reported on the school's reopening to King Christian III of Denmark in a letter from November 13: "On October 24 our school reopened and we began the public reading of lectures."[237] Similarly, he wrote full of hope to Duke Albrecht of Prussia later that month: "God's word – praise be to God – is strong with us and the land is beginning to get better again. The school is running marvelously again, the lecture hall is achingly full... If only it there might be a little quiet after this *Reichstag* [imperial diet], then even more would come to us."[238] "A little quiet," however, did not arrive for the professors in Wittenberg. The Jonah lectures continued to take place in controversial times.

Two years later, Bugenhagen wanted these lectures published so he could share his teaching with the wider world. On March 9, 1550, he wrote to King Christian about the forthcoming publication of his *Jonah*.

> They also unashamedly shout about us that we are now keeping silent. That is also not true: "Ask those who heard" [John 18:21]. We are not keeping silent, neither in the churches nor in the school nor in writing, as you also acknowledge for yourself. For they have shit themselves and have written evil works against the letter that I sent to your majesty – whose content addressed so many of these matters – because I sent it on to quite a few princes and great cities.
>
> The publication of all of Father Luther's books in large volumes, which is coming from here and which never appeared before, also shows that we are not keeping silent.[239] So is the German version of Master Philip's book *Loci Communes* in an improved printing and now in two sections.[240] The first has already been published; his *Epistle to the Romans* has also been reissued.[241] And I alone have five entire books, which I have read in our school.[242] Therefore they should each be considered to have been sent out, even if they have not yet been published.
>
> *They are not adiaphoristic nonsense, nor are they the lies and blasphemies of holy teachers of the gospel; rather, they are necessary writings about Holy Scripture, through which the Antichrist of 2 Thessalonians 2 is even more fully made known and revealed. And those who love the*

truth receive this and are even more fully confirmed, so that they can speak of sure faith; and even if an angel of heaven or another apostle should preach a different gospel, let them be anathema [Gal. 1:8]. This certainly means not keeping silent. Christ does this through our office.

I would have gladly seen my *Jonah* get printed half a year ago. It is a book written and presented publicly in our school against the false repentance or *Poenitentiam Papistorum* [papal repentance] which grasps the entire antichrist; it confirms true Christian repentance, which fully grasps Christ with his righteousness. In this book I have also written a sure history of how "human traditions under the name of the Holy Spirit and the Spiritualists" (whom the papists still call "Spirituals") carried on soon after the death of St. John the Evangelist. Additionally for this purpose there is a "history and confutation from holy scripture about Christian repentance, which Christ commended to us in the people of Nineveh."

But it could not appear. All presses were full of such books as I mentioned and I did not want to hinder them, nor should I have. But now a printer, to whom I gave the book, is reading it and is setting the type. He said that my *Jonah* should be printed around the day of Sts. Peter and Paul [June 29]. God grant grace for this and more.[243]

Along with Melanchthon's publications and the ongoing printing of Luther's works, the forthcoming *Jonah* would stand as a witness to Bugenhagen's theology and public teaching. Bugenhagen's invocation of writings by Luther and Melanchthon shows that he believed he could point to a kind of Lutheran canon to answer doctrinal questions. In fact, just before his death in 1560, Melanchthon also put this idea to use when he collected a *Corpus Doctrinae Philipicum* to summarize his theology and the teachings of the evangelical faith.[244] Bugenhagen's remarks about Luther and Melanchthon's works make it clear that he already considered such writings, along with his own forthcoming *Jonah*, to constitute full and satisfactory expressions of his doctrine.

This chapter has shown that the accusation that the Wittenberg theologians betrayed Lutheran theology is unjust. Instead, these theologians crafted responses to the Augsburg

Interim that were theologically faithful and politically viable. They offered a contrast to the more bellicose style of other Lutherans outside Electoral Saxony. This is not to say that the Albertine theologians preferred harmony to argumentation. On the contrary, this chapter has revealed many numerous instances of direct confrontation and a willingness to suffer for the faith. What emerged from Electoral Saxony was a responsible – and bold – public policy based on the doctrine of justification. As the following chapters will show, this public theology was not constructed hastily but was built on existing biblical and theological foundations that honored right action as part of right doctrine. As a work published amid civic and religious controversy, Bugenhagen's *Jonah* presents an extraordinary look into a theology built on justification by faith alone for the sake of congregations and communities who were facing tremendous threats to both their faith and their lives.

CHAPTER THREE

Biblical Interpretation as Public Theology

Bugenhagen published his Jonah Commentary in 1550 as a demonstration of his teaching and a defense of his activity under the Augsburg Interim. Although the following quotation was included in the previous chapter for what is says about the public debates of the time, it deserves mention again for its implications for biblical interpretation.

> Finally they shout, "Now you are all silent and do not want to console the church's afflictions." For this reason, most favorable king, I dedicate to your majesty and your name these my tracts, which contain useful and necessary material, especially for the Christian Church of this age, so that your majesty may read and judge. For God has given your Majesty an intellect, in order that it might know the great mystery of God in Christ and so that all might see that we have not been silent until now. For we have dealt publicly with this in our school from the beginning, since the city's surrender and the college's reopening.[245]

By saying "God has given your Majesty an intellect," he introduced this biblical commentary as a contribution to rational and beneficial public discourse. While affirming that scripture is the guide and authority for Christian life, Bugenhagen also expected his readers to use their minds to judge the validity of interpretations. This chapter puts us in the classroom with Dr. Pomeranus, in order to learn how he interpreted the Bible and applied its teachings.

We start by reconstructing the history of the *Jonah*'s composition, then move to a description of the book's structure and contents, beginning with the title page. Next, a study of commentary's preface helps introduce technical matters of biblical interpretation. The chapter ends by returning to the question of how Bugenhagen's work provides insights for understanding biblical interpretation in the sixteenth century and beyond. Because the history of biblical interpretation has recently become a field of its own, this examination will also prove valuable in broader conversations about Christian biblical interpretation.[246]

The Bible's Living Voice

First of all, why did Bugenhagen write a biblical commentary after the Smalcaldic War? The simplest answer is that it was part of his job. Bugenhagen had been lecturing on the Bible in Wittenberg (especially on books of the Old Testament) since he arrived there in 1521. So it should come as no surprise that when the university reopened in autumn 1547, Bugenhagen resumed his teaching duties by offering a new course on a biblical prophet. In the official record of the university, Bugenhagen explained why he had chosen Jonah:

> Today, at the third hour, I will begin to lecture on the prophet Jonah, in which we learn what it says in Psalm 51: "For behold, you love the truth, which is hidden, and you reveal your hidden wisdom to me." May Christ be among us in his Spirit.[247]

In scholarship today, it is common to study the Bible as a source for learning about ancient peoples, cultures, and worldviews. Even in Bugenhagen's time, it would have been possible to read Jonah as a source for theology, church history, or biblical anthropology. But Bugenhagen's entry describes his class as an inquiry into the Bible's living witness to believers across time. Specifically, he turned to Jonah as a source for learning about God's hidden wisdom and truth.

For Lutherans, the hidden wisdom of God is seen above all in what Martin Luther had called the theology of the cross. "A theologian of the cross teaches that punishments, crosses, and death are the most precious treasury of all and the most sacred relics which the Lord of this theology himself has consecrated and blessed, not alone by the touch of this most holy flesh but also by the embrace of his exceedingly holy and divine will, and he has left these relics here to be kissed, sought after, and embraced."[248] That is, a theology of the cross reveals God's power and goodness in the last places one would usually expect. By connecting Jonah and the "hidden wisdom of God," Bugenhagen showed that his study would not be confined to a disinterested or objective study of one book, but would call upon Jonah and the entire Bible to teach the wisdom of the cross. The final thesis of the commentary's preface reveals how centrally Bugenhagen viewed God's hidden wisdom as revealed in Jonah, as it declares: "All history is in the image of the passion and resurrection of Christ."[249]

While this statement may sound like a radical leap from the short book of Jonah itself, Bugenhagen was already here taking the interpretive step of following the New Testament. In Matthew 12, Jesus referred to the "sign of Jonah" to talk about his own death and resurrection. Jesus said, "An evil and adulterous generation asks for a sign, but no sign will be given to it except the sign of the prophet Jonah. For just as Jonah was three days and three nights in the belly of the sea monster, so for three days and three nights the Son of Man will be in the heart of the earth."[250] And in Luke 11, Jesus said that people should repent of their sins "just as Jonah became a sign to the people of Nineveh."[251]

From the beginning of his class, therefore, Bugenhagen read Jonah in conversation with the entire Bible. He also believed that Jonah had something to say to his contemporary context. For Bugenhagen, the Bible was a living voice given by God to teach faith in Christ. An analysis of *Jonah*'s structure shows how Bugenhagen would develop his biblical interpretation in order to let the ancient scriptures speak to people in his time. If the book had a modern table of contents, it would look like this:[252]

Title Page	$[A_i]$	1
Dedication Letter to King Christian III	$[A_{ii}]$	2
Preface to Jonah, with *Argumentum* and *Loci*	$[B_i]$	9
Jonah, Chapter 1[	$B_v]$	13
Jonah, Chapter 2	$[E_{vi}]$	38
Jonah, Chapter 3		
Tract on True Repentance	$[H_{ii}]$	58
True History of Human Traditions	$[L_{iii}]$	83
Montanus the Blasphemer	$[Q_v]$	125
From Tertullian[	$m_i]$	273
Summary of Jonah, Chapter 3	$[z_i]$	361
Jonah, Chapter 4	$[Bb_{viii}]$	384
Conclusion with Appendices	$[Cc_v]$	389
Pontificale Episcoporum (1510)	$[Cc_{vii}]$	391
Agenda Parochiarum (1512)	$[Ee_{viii}]$	408
Ritum Ecclesiasticorum (1516)	$[Ff_{vii}]$	415
Errata	$[Gg_{vii}]$	423

Of the book's 424 pages, eight pages are introduction, 77 are direct commentary on Jonah, and 303 belong to the tracts on Jonah 3. The appendices are 33 pages long. The few remaining pages either introduce the appendices or identify typographical errors (*errata*).

This table of contents shows the wide range of subjects covered in Bugenhagen's *Jonah*. In particular, Jonah 3 served as the launching pad for hundreds of pages about repentance, liturgical traditions, and church history. Bugenhagen's appendices also bring Roman Catholic church orders of the early sixteenth century into the conversation. How is this possible in a commentary about a single book of the Bible? It might seem as if Bugenhagen either abandoned his original goal of interpreting the prophet Jonah or unnaturally forced his discussion of contemporary events into his work of biblical interpretation. If either of those extreme alternatives were true, then Bugenhagen's work would appear either sloppy or strained. This chapter, however, offers a different thesis: that Bugenhagen's interpretation of Jonah allowed all these elements to fit together quite sensibly. Here biblical interpretation provided a firm foundation for both contextual theology and public leadership in a time of great uncertainty.

Jonah's Title Page: The Bible and Lutheran Theology

Bugenhagen's title page reads like an academic abstract, summarizing the entire book in just under 100 words. It is translated here:

> THE PROPHET JONAH EXPLAINED.
>
> In the third chapter there is a tract on true repentance, as Christ commended to us through the people of Nineveh, and a tract on false repentance, which comes through our works, as demonic doctrines brought forth after the apostles, and which excludes Christ.
>
> In the same, a sure history – carefully and judiciously collected by searching the Scriptures – about how after the passing of John the Evangelist from this life there began a defection from faith. These are demonic doctrines under the guise of the Word of God. They are seen through the prohibition of marriage and the cup, vows of celibacy, blessed ordinations and spiritualities (which have been called the perfection of the church and

which reign to this day and alone make people spiritual without the Holy Spirit through a new spirit and the Paraclete of the Montanists, etc).

Likewise, a chapter that purges away impious and blasphemous doubts.

By Dr. Johannes Bugenhagen Pomeranus
Printed in Wittenberg
by Veit Creutzer.
1550[253]

This title page aptly describes several of the book's main themes: repentance, true and false teachings, faith and doubt.

We notice first that the title – "The Prophet Jonah Explained" – stands above the rest of the text. Rather than being part biblical commentary and part theological tracts, Bugenhagen published the entire work as an interpretation of Jonah. Here the book's first two long tracts are clearly identified as direct commentary on the conversion of Nineveh in Jonah 3. He then also used the word *ibidem* ("in the same place") to describe the later tracts. If the "table of contents" calls attention to the potentially digressive tracts that make up so much of the commentary, then this title page affirms their place under "The Prophet Jonah Explained."

In terms of biblical interpretation, the title page connects the Old Testament prophet with the New Testament's words about Jonah. As mentioned above, the focus on repentance as a theme of Jonah was grounded in Christ's own use of that text. Further, in the Gospel of Matthew, Jesus spoke of the "sign of Jonah" as a sign of his own death and resurrection,[254] one of the few places in the New Testament that explicitly makes a typological reference to the Hebrew Scriptures.[255] This reference to Christ's words about Jonah lets readers know that Bugenhagen will interpret Jonah through the lens of Christ's death and resurrection.

Because of this connection, when the Lutheran "theology of the cross" enters this commentary, it does so on the basis of the Bible's own example; it is not an extra-biblical theological concept. In the same way, the connection between Nineveh's repentance and the Lutheran teaching of justification by faith is also grounded in an interpretation of the Bible that assumes continuity between the Old and New Testaments and contemporary life.

The opening page already offers three important points for understanding Bugenhagen's method of biblical interpretation. First, he practiced an inter-textual study of the Bible, in which Jonah belongs to the larger biblical message of faith and salvation. Second, Bugenhagen interpreted Jonah primarily through the death and resurrection of Jesus Christ. Far from reading Jonah as a book separated from Christian faith by time or theology, Bugenhagen believed that Jonah provided a true and abiding witness to God's free justification of the ungodly, an interpretation found in the New Testament itself. Third, because Jonah is about repentance and forgiveness, it is also about justification. Thus, Bugenhagen could legitimately expand his commentary to include his teachings about justification, especially to debate the Council of Trent and the Augsburg Interim. The introduction of theological themes grew out of the biblical texts. This title page shows how one little book of the Bible can speak to a range of other biblical passages and theological teachings.

Repentance (*poenitentia*) is a major theme in Jonah. The Latin *poenitentiam agite* can be translated as either "repent," "be penitent," or "do penance."[256] Thus, repenting refers simultaneously to a spiritual activity, an inner disposition, and specific worship practices. Like Luther and Melanchthon,[257] Bugenhagen sometimes spoke of repentance as a third sacrament: the sacrament of absolution or the sacrament of the keys. The stories of repentance found in Jonah and commended by Christ himself gave Bugenhagen a good basis in this commentary for examining how repentance fits within faith and worship. For these reasons, the long tracts in the middle of this commentary belong to the biblical teachings and worship that Bugenhagen discussed as he went through the book of Jonah.

The title page's final comment about "purging away impious and blasphemous doubts" is a sign of how Bugenhagen's concentration shifted over the course of the lectures. It refers to the ongoing debates between Lutherans and Catholics about "certainty of faith." As a corollary of justification by faith alone, Lutherans taught that confession and absolution deliver a total forgiveness of sins that one can know for certain through faith. Already in his "Explanations of the Ninety-Five Theses" (1518), Luther had written that

God promised certainty of forgiveness to troubled and penitent believers through the sacrament of absolution.[258] Certainty of faith formed part of Cardinal Cajetan's initial objections to Luther's theology when the two men debated in October 1518[259] and it became a point of condemnation in the papal bull that excommunicated Luther in 1520.[260] On the Lutheran side, the Augsburg Confession asserted that because God promises forgiveness through absolution, it should not be doubted as if it were a matter of human achievement or subject to human error.[261]

Although this debate about certainty of faith had existed for nearly three decades, the Lutheran teachings about justification and certainty of faith encountered their most forceful rejection in January 1547. At that time, the Council of Trent explicitly condemned anyone who taught those doctrines: "If anyone says that the sinner is justified by faith alone, meaning that nothing else is required to co-operate in order to obtain the grace of justification, and that it is not in any way necessary that he be prepared and disposed by the action of his own will, let him be anathema."[262] The council also condemned being certain of one's forgiveness.

> For as no pious person ought to doubt the mercy of God, the merit of Christ and the virtue and efficacy of the sacraments, so each one, when he considers himself and his own weakness and indisposition, may have fear and apprehension concerning his own grace, since no one can know with the certainty of faith, which cannot be subject to error, that he has obtained the grace of God.[263]

The line in this declaration that "no one can know" echoes Bible verses like Ecclesiastes 9:1, Joel 2:14 and Jonah 3:9, which were used against spiritual pride.[264] This doubt concerning one's full forgiveness is the reason for Bugenhagen's reference to Joel and Jonah near the end of his dedication letter: "Your Majesty will also see in my comments here that the Holy Spirit did not and could not speak of this doubt in the Holy Scriptures, neither in Joel nor in Jonah."[265] From the Roman Catholic point of view, despairing of grace was never theologically or pastorally desirable; nevertheless, in both late medieval theology and in the Council of Trent, certainty of faith was considered impious and arrogant.[266]

Trent's condemnation of the certainty of faith had been preceded by the "Thirty-Two Articles" written by the University of Louvain's theological faculty. These articles, which earned a special refutation from Luther shortly before he died, were submitted to Emperor Charles on December 8, 1544; the emperor sanctioned them as a guide for orthodox teaching on May 14, 1545.[267] Like the later canons of the Council of Trent, after condemning justification by faith alone,[268] the Louvain theologians attacked certainty of forgiveness.

> Faith by which one firmly believes and states with certainty that one's sins are forgiven for Christ's sake and one will obtain eternal life has no support in Scriptures, indeed is opposed to them, although in this life we must expect with firm and certain hope remission of sins through the sacrament of baptism and penance; in the age to come, however, eternal life.[269]

This single article is the focus of much of Bugenhagen's ire in the Jonah Commentary. As he mentioned in the dedication letter, Bugenhagen wrote to show that certainty of faith could indeed be supported by scripture. In fact, he would use Jonah 3:9, a text used by Roman theologians *against* certainty of faith, to prove it.

Although never explicitly stated because of a ban on published critiques, a rejection of the Augsburg Interim stood behind Bugenhagen's denunciation of "impious and blasphemous doubts." Like the Louvainian "Thirty-Two Articles" and the Council of Trent, the Augsburg Interim denied that one could be certain of forgiveness by believing the words of absolution. It stated, "Because of their own infirmity or indisposition people cannot believe without doubt that their sins are remitted."[270] Although Bugenhagen had started delivering his lectures before the Augsburg Interim existed, his *Jonah* was published more than two years after its introduction. The title page's final statement against "impious and blasphemous doubts" makes his opposition to the Augsburg Interim clear. Bugenhagen researcher Otto Vogt also came to this conclusion in his 1887 article on the Jonah Commentary, writing that its critique of Tridentine theology constituted a definite, if veiled, critique of the Augsburg Interim.[271] The title page thus presents clear indications of the biblical points at issue in the commentary and of the contemporary disputes he was addressing through it.

By looking at the title page, we have already discovered central aspects of Bugenhagen's interpretive and theological method. Nineveh's "true repentance" unites the commentary's various themes by tying repentance, justification and worship together. This is a decidedly pre-Enlightenment "biblical theology,"[272] which did not separate biblical interpretation from the Bible's contemporary relevance.[273] In this way, biblical interpretation, doctrinal theology, and contemporary debates were not separate fields of study but were cohesive and mutually-supportive endeavors in Bugenhagen's work.

Recognizing this connection between biblical interpretation and doctrinal theology in the sixteenth century sheds light on an early Protestant slogan, *sola Scriptura* (scripture alone). From page one, we know that Bugenhagen's *Jonah* will cover the Bible, apostolic traditions, church doctrine, liturgical practices, and controversies of the day. It appears to be anything but "scripture alone." But by understanding how biblical interpretation and theology fit together in early Lutheranism, *sola scriptura* takes on a different shape than it often takes today.[274] *Sola scriptura* did not mean the apparent need to either accept or reject a biblical worldview often at odds with scientific knowledge and daily experience.[275] Instead, Bugenhagen's tracts conform to *sola scriptura* just as much as his sections that directly comment on the Bible, because in them he sought to clarify topics first found in the scriptures.

In this attempt to understand theology and life in light of the Bible, the Protestant theologians were in continuity with the late medieval Catholic tradition.[276] All Christians of the late Middle Ages, including strong advocates of the papacy, desired to live first and foremost in conformity with the Bible. In their adherence to *sola scriptura*, the Protestant reformers differed from their Catholic contemporaries by arguing against the scriptural supports for a strong papacy rather than by merely separating scripture and tradition.[277] Indeed, Bugenhagen refused to pit scripture and tradition against each other. Instead, as seen in the title page's emphasis on defections of faith "brought forth after the apostles," Bugenhagen made his criticisms of Roman theology based on differences of interpretation rather than on a blanket rejection of "tradition."

To those familiar with the history of biblical interpretation, these characteristics appear typical for the period. But as discussed in chapter one, Bugenhagen's contribution to the history of biblical interpretation does not lie in the realm of theological or exegetical novelty. Instead, he stands out as an expert teacher and practitioner of early Lutheran biblical interpretation and theology. After all, Bugenhagen's *Jonah* functioned originally as a teaching text in the field of biblical interpretation. By interpreting Jonah and elaborating on its themes, Bugenhagen taught his audience to interpret the Bible, learn the biblical and historical sources of Lutheran theology, and apply biblical faith to contemporary life. If Bugenhagen is rightly remembered as one who put the faith into practice in his church orders, then the Jonah Commentary also highlights his great skill in connecting a biblical faith with daily life. Study of this commentary gives readers today the chance to sit in the classroom with Bugenhagen and learn what *sola scriptura* meant to the first generation of Lutheran reformers.

Opening Arguments: *Praefacio, Argumentum, Loci*

The title page shows the themes and methods that Bugenhagen wanted to highlight when his commentary was published in 1550. But to see how he initially conceived his lecture series in the fall of 1547, we turn to the *Preface to the Prophet Jonah*, which follows the dedication letter.[278] This was undoubtedly the place where Bugenhagen started his lectures in 1547. Previewing the Christological interpretation that accompanies this interpretation of Jonah from beginning to end, Bugenhagen opened the preface by quoting the New Testament:

> Christ commends the prophet Jonah to us when he makes him an example of his death and resurrection in Matt. 12[:40]: "This adulterous generation asks for a sign and no sign will be given it except the sign of the prophet Jonah. For just as Jonah was in the belly of the whale," etc. And he offers to us an example of the repentance and forgiveness of sins among the lost people of Nineveh, and he condemns the unbelieving and obstinate impenitence of the Jews, who repented neither at the preaching of Jonah nor at the preaching of the Messiah, God's Son.[279]

As discussed earlier, Jonah's greatest significance for Bugenhagen comes from Christ's references to Jonah. Jonah is a prototype of Christ, who died and rose again. He is also a preacher of repentance and faith. Further, according to 2 Kings 14:25-26, the prophet Jonah had been ignored in his time, just as Jesus would also be rejected.[280] Bugenhagen then connected the unbelief of Jeroboam's Israel with the unbelief of the Pharisees in Jesus' time, resulting in that sentence against the "unbelieving and obstinate impenitence of the Jews."[281]

Because anti-Jewish statements like these arose frequently in Reformation-era writings, it is important to discuss them here. Like Luther, Bugenhagen would speak about the triple threat of Jews, Turks, and the Pope to evangelical faith.[282] Although many of these attacks from the reformers look crude at best and inhumane at worst, such words in the sixteenth century did not constitute blind polemic or hatred but belonged to some attempt at persuasive logic and rhetoric, flawed as it was. Within Luther's logic of anti-Judaism, for instance, historian Steven Ozment has identified Luther's twin perceptions that Jews had undermined German-Christian economic stability and denied the theological teaching of justification by faith.[283] That is, Luther and Bugenhagen tried to base their condemnations on scripture and reason. Rather than dismissing their harshest words as baseless polemics or blind hatred, readers today will therefore do better to study and refute the faulty logic behind such arguments. This honors both the reformers' own commitment to rational discourse and the search for greater truth and justice in the present.

Bugenhagen's preface, written so that "we may love and understand the prophet Jonah,"[284] leads into an *argumentum* (opening argument), in which he summarized Jonah for its widest meaning.[285] This opening argument connects Jonah's mission to the idolatrous city of Nineveh with Lutheran efforts to reform the church in sixteenth century.[286] Yet, just where it looks as if Bugenhagen might claim exclusive truth for Lutheranism over Roman Catholic opponents, he returned to Jonah as being not only a prophet, but also a sinner.

> By fleeing, Jonah sinned most gravely against God, who sent him to the Gentiles. And later he was angry and murmured against God, that he had spared Nineveh. Paul had been a blasphemer and persecutor of God's church; Peter denied Christ; the apostles fought about primacy. Christ censured them, for in danger on the sea they did not invoke God and did not trust in God, to which Christ said, "Where now is your faith?" Therefore God protects his

chosen and beloved ones even in sin, so that they might not perish in eternity, even in the middle of the sea, in death and hell (as is often sung in the Psalms), even against the sentence of divine law, as you see in the people of Nineveh, etc.[287]

In the preface and then the *argumentum*, Bugenhagen made a series of interpretive decisions as he summarized Jonah. First, he again referred to the words of Christ, who spoke of Jonah as a sign of death and resurrection and of Nineveh as an example of repentance. He then connected Jesus' unrepentant and "adulterous generation" backwards to the Israelites of Jonah's day and forwards to the papacy of the sixteenth century. Finally, he applied not Jonah's virtues but Jonah's sin to his own community. In this, he taught that Christian life does not belong to any spiritual elite but to lost and dying sinners who call out to God. Most of all, Bugenhagen stressed what is a key element of Lutheran biblical interpretation: study of the text finally leads the contemporary reader to personal knowledge and experience of God's salvation. He wrote so that his audience might "love and understand" this strange prophet and see themselves his story.

The *argumentum* concludes with Bugenhagen's identification of nine theological points to be found in Jonah, which he called loci (points or touchstones). These loci introduce the main interpretive directions that the commentary will take. They also reveal the formal method of biblical commentary that Bugenhagen would use here. Melanchthon had developed this "loci method" of interpretation for his 1521 *Loci Communes Theologici*.[288] There he searched the Letter to the Romans to find the theological points (loci) that Paul had used to teach and persuade his readers. Melanchthon explained his method in that book's dedicatory letter.

> ...in this book the principal topics of Christian teaching are pointed out so that youth may arrive at a twofold understanding:
>
> 1. What one must chiefly look for in Scripture.
>
> 2. How corrupt are all the theological hallucinations of those who have offered us the subtleties of Aristotle instead of the teachings of Christ.
>
> But I am discussing everything sparingly and briefly

because the book is to function more as an index than a commentary. I am therefore merely stating a list of the topics to which a person roaming through Scripture should be directed. Further, I am setting forth in only a few words the elements on which the main points of Christian doctrine are based. I do this not to call students away from the Scriptures to obscure and complicated arguments but, rather, to summon them to the Scriptures if I can.[289]

Melanchthon's description of this loci method of biblical commentary as a kind of theological index is helpful for understanding Bugenhagen's *Jonah*. First, because Bugenhagen explicitly named loci that he found within Jonah, we know that he was intentionally using an established and formal method of biblical interpretation. Second, Bugenhagen's use of this method allowed the tracts to serve as elongated discussion of biblical themes rather than departures from them.[290] Finally, in the citation above, Melanchthon emphasized the usefulness of this method for teaching students how to read and understand the Bible, the exact context in which Bugenhagen also wrote his *Jonah*. As both a set of lectures and a publication, the book served as a pedagogical tool for teaching how to interpret and apply the Bible. Recognizing Bugenhagen's intentional use of this loci method corrects a notion raised by Bugenhagen researcher Otto Vogt that the Jonah Commentary suffered from a lack of intellectual organization, which, Vogt explained, "was not really Bugenhagen's thing."[291]

On the contrary, Bugenhagen's nine introductory loci suggest a focused and logically coherent theology rooted in the book of Jonah. They are as follows:

1   God calls and sends ministers of the gospel, even as we see that Jonah was sent to prophesy [Jonah 1:1].

2   And God calls even the gentiles, for God sends a prophet to the gentiles [Jonah 1:2]. Therefore the church has not consisted only of circumcised people, as we see in Rom. 3[:29]: "God is not only God of the Jews but also of the gentiles."

3   The saints have gone to ruin, like Jonah did, and have returned to God through their confessions; and they are subject to punishment: "Cast me in the sea and the sea will be peaceful for you" [Jonah 1:12].

4   The prayer of Jonah is the doctrine of justification. He says, "Those who do not flee to mercy chase vanities" [Jonah 2:8]. We are saved from true agony by God's mercy alone, which is Christ, and not on account of our righteousness.

5   The divine call does not err but is efficacious and converts people like the Ninevites: "For as the rain and the snow fall come down from heaven, [and do not return there until they have watered the earth, making it bring forth and sprout, giving seed to the sower and bread to the eater, so shall my word be that goes out from my mouth; it shall not return to me empty, but it shall accomplish that which I purpose, and succeed in the thing for which I sent it"] (Isaiah 55[:10-11]).

6   The conversion of the king and people of Nineveh [Jonah 3:5-10] condemns the perverse Jews, who did not repent from their corruption, avarice and idolatry after Jonah's preaching [Matt. 12:41].

7   The what and the how of repentance is clearly contrition and faith, as you see in the repentance of the people of Nineveh [Jonah 3:5-10].

8   A most learned disputation against Stoic fate: although God was sending destruction to Nineveh, God did not destroy it [Jonah 3:10]. Therefore, divine threats of violence are reversible, not necessary but changeable if people turn back to God: "unless you repent, you will all perish similarly, etc." (Luke 13[:3]), because the promise of grace is stronger; grace abounds among the elect as soon as the oath has been embraced. "As I live, I do not desire the death of sinners, etc." [Ezekiel 33:11].

9   All history is in the image of the passion and resurrection of Christ, for the reason that we said before [Matt. 12:40]. And even as Jonah grieved the shrub, so much more does God grieve human destruction, for God said, "You grieve over the shrub, which you did not labor over or make to grow, which was born in one night and perished in one night. And shall I not certainly spare Nineveh, that great city, in which there are more than 120,000 people who do not know their right hand from their left, and many cattle?" [Jonah 4:10-11].[292]

Each locus comes from within the book of Jonah. They are arranged in order from Jonah's call in chapter 1 to God's mysterious final question in chapter 4. Further, Bugenhagen often supplemented his points with verses from across the Bible that express similar ideas.

These themes, derived from the biblical text, are not grammatical or doctrinal; they are pastoral and personal: God sends ministers to preach an effective word; Jonah's prayer exemplifies justification by faith alone; the saints have "gone to ruin" and need forgiveness; God desires repentance, not destruction; Christ's passion and resurrection is at the heart of Nineveh's salvation and even all of history. Through these loci, Bugenhagen taught the main message of Lutheran biblical interpretation: God justifies the ungodly by grace through faith.

It is worth noting that the later tracts on repentance and human traditions are absent from this prefatory material. This suggests that Bugenhagen conceived of them later as ways to expand upon themes he was already covering in the lectures, especially the originally brief seventh locus on repentance. Even though the tracts seem to be later additions, the introductory loci gave them a solid exegetical, theological and methodological foundation. While correctly identifying the tracts as later insertions based on current events, Otto Vogt had overstated the apparent haphazardness with which Bugenhagen organized his lectures.[293] For as diverse as the later material becomes, it stays within the commentary's original themes: the ministry of the word, justification by faith, true repentance, and salvation through Christ alone.

Biblical Interpretation as Public Theology

In the middle of the commentary, Acts 10:43 became a key text that Bugenhagen used to connect his original loci with the later engagement with the Augsburg Interim. In that passage, Peter, speaking to gentile believers at the house of the Roman centurion Cornelius, concluded his testimony about Jesus Christ by saying, "All the prophets testify about him that everyone who believes in him receives forgiveness of sins through his name." This verse helped Bugenhagen connect the prophetic witness across the Bible with justification by faith alone. He emphasized the words *"all* the prophets" to call attention to Jonah's authority as a preacher of true faith and repentance.

This seems to have been a fairly spontaneous and unique interpretive move. In the Apology to the Augsburg Confession, Melanchthon cited Acts 10:43 three times to show that forgiveness of sins comes through faith in Christ; he did not explicitly use it to read Christian doctrine into the Old Testament prophets.[294] Luther also does not seem to have cited Acts 10:43 often in this way during his career. But confronting new challenges, Bugenhagen called upon this verse to demonstrate the thoroughly biblical foundations of justification by faith.

Acts 10:43 enters the commentary at the beginning of the tracts.[295] It is a sign that Bugenhagen was adapting the themes flowing from the opening *argumentum* into a broader defense of Lutheran teaching in light of the Council of Trent and the Augsburg Interim. After the first tract connects Nineveh's repentance with faith in Christ, the second evaluates true and false repentance in light of the doctrine of justification. That secondary move addressed a difficulty raised by Jonah 3 itself. Roman Catholics had used Jonah 3:10 to prove that Christians need to do penitential works for salvation: "When God saw what they did, how they turned from their evil ways, God changed his mind about the calamity that he had said he would bring upon them; and he did not do it." For instance, the 1530 Roman Confutation of the Augsburg Confession (the official response to the Augsburg Confession) cited this verse to oppose the Lutheran teaching that good works do not contribute to justification.[296]

Based on the introductory loci, it appears as if Bugenhagen did not originally intend for this to be a major point in his lectures. But as the lectures continued, Jonah 3 offered him the chance to address a text used against the Lutheran doctrine of justification. Additionally, he could also draw upon earlier work by Martin Luther and Philip Melanchthon, who had each commented on this verse.[297] This second tract therefore is also "commentary on Jonah," even as it expands into a defense of justification by faith alone and calls upon Christian writers from Augustine and Peter Lombard to Luther and Melanchthon.

After discussing Nineveh's repentance and the right relationship between repentance and justification by faith in the first two tracts, Bugenhagen proceeded to show how spiritual practices that obscured faith and worship entered the church over the centuries.

These last two tracts therefore mostly discuss worship practices and church history. While this might seem far afield, they follow logically from the previous two tracts, which had themselves been built on Jonah 3. The fact that they still belong to "The Prophet Jonah Explained" is visible in the title page, where Bugenhagen had named practices that the Lutheran reformers had long contested, including vows of celibacy, withholding the cup from the laity in Holy Communion, and ordination as a sacrament. Even more relevant for our discussion here, these were practices that Lutherans were contesting under the Interim. While the tracts themselves will be examined in later chapters, it is important to see that Bugenhagen's method of interpretation gave him a biblical foundation for publicly commenting on contemporary debates.

In using the genre of biblical interpretation as a way to approach church debates, Bugenhagen was following an established Lutheran practice. For one thing, the reformers had long identified the papal church with the New Testament Pharisees.[298] Bugenhagen could easily move from Nineveh's repentance to discussion of problematic practices in the sixteenth-century Roman Church. Thus, the practices that Bugenhagen identified on the title page as "defections" from biblical faith could fit neatly within a biblical commentary. This also gave him the practical ability to denounce practices prescribed by the Interim without ever directly naming the document itself, which would have risked legal reprisals.

Because of these close connections between biblical interpretation, theology, and liturgical practices, this study avoids using the term "polemics" even when describing the reformers' harshest language. It proves to be an unhelpful word for two reasons. First, there was no genre of "polemical theology" in the sixteenth century; that branch of theology was introduced during the Enlightenment era. Instead, the Jonah Commentary remained a work of biblical interpretation (and not a "polemical work") from beginning to end. Second, "polemics" does not have a well-documented history as a medieval Latin or German word. Instead, derived indirectly from Greek, the French word *polemique* appears to have been coined during the Thirty Years' War (1618-1648).[299] The German *Polemik* did not appear until it was borrowed from the French in the eighteenth century.[300] Even the older German word *Streitschrift* only started to appear after Bugenhagen's time, likely coined by the Lutheran theologian Cyriakus Spangenberg.[301] "Polemics," therefore, is not a label that Luther, Melanchthon or Bugenhagen would have used to describe their own writings. While sixteenth-century writers used rhetoric as scathing as any time before or since (including classical tools like satire, *argumentum ad hominem*, and *reductio ad absurdam*), the contemporary use of the word "polemic" is dismissive of an author's rhetorical or logical argument. Describing something as "polemic" becomes a way to dismiss what was at stake for participants in the social and religious debates of the Reformation.[302] As a "mode of discourse" it is patently unhelpful. In contrast, the logical arguments that Bugenhagen used to connect the Bible, Lutheran theology, sacramental practices, and contemporary controversies show that he hoped to build a persuasive case that might convince a reading public about his theology and its implications: "God has given your Majesty an intellect, in order that it might know the great mystery of God in Christ and so that all might see that we have not been silent until now."[303] Flawed or excessive as Bugenhagen's rhetoric may sometimes appear, it was still rhetoric, meant to persuade. To what extent it succeeded is for readers to decide.

The commentary's appendices add yet another element to this mix. Concluding his comments on Jonah by once more admiring Jonah's faith and witness, Bugenhagen wrote, "Glory be to Christ. AMEN. THE END."[304] After this, he briefly suggested that his students or readers make a correction to his 1546 commentary on Jeremiah, adding some insights from Caspar Cruciger and Martin Luther about the passage in question and leaving his audience with the first lines of Luther's hymn, "Lord, Keep Us Steadfast in Your Word."[305] The mention of Cruciger as recently deceased shows that Bugenhagen had been lecturing on Jonah for at least one year (Cruciger had died on November 16, 1548) and provides further evidence that he wrote at least some of the commentary well after the promulgation of the Augsburg Interim.

While Bugenhagen's final comments about Jeremiah 15 seem to mark an ending, the book continues for 33 more pages, with Bugenhagen's inclusion of three Roman Catholic church orders from the 1510s. Introducing these orders, he wrote,

> Because, however, regarding the history of traditions and spiritualities – just as began from the Montanists after the

passing of John the Evangelist from this life, etc. – two books that are not in everyone's hands have been cited (*Pontificale Episcoporum* and *Agenda Parochiarum*), some excerpts from these books have been added here. From them you see that in their blessings, consecrations, sanctifications, [signs of] the cross, sprinklings, and blasphemous prayers (Psalm 109[:7]: "May his prayer become sin"), they attribute to creatures those things which they presume make holy. They do not attribute this to Christ the son of God, the Lord of glory, who was made by the Father to be the victim for us. Instead they hate, blaspheme and persecute the gospel of God's great glory, our Savior Jesus Christ, which preaches such things in Christ alone.[306]

According to Bugenhagen, older Roman Catholic church orders were being cited against the Lutherans, even though few people had access to them. Bugenhagen wanted to publish these so that they could be better known and addressed more concretely. He published the first under the heading *Pontificale Venetiis excusum, anno Do: M.D.X.*; the second, *Benedictionale & Agenda Misnensis Ecclesiae, impressa Lipsig, Anno Domini, M.D.XII.*; and a third, *Ritum Ecclesiasticorum siue sacrarum Cerimoniarum SS. Romanae Ecclesiae, libri tres... sunt excusi primum Venetiis, anno Domini, M.D.XVI cum privilegio Papae Leonis decimi.*[307] The 1510 *Pontificale Venetiis excusum* was a papal order connected to Pope Julius II's wars against Venice. The *Agenda Misnensis Ecclesiae* of 1512 was a church order promulgated in Albertine Saxony under Johannes VI, the bishop of Meissen.[308]

Within these church orders, Bugenhagen often inserted parenthetical comments to show where he objected to a liturgical practice or to the theology supporting it. For instance, where the Meissen Agenda spoke of making the sign of the cross while blessing the baptismal font, Bugenhagen interjected, "Who consecrated the water for Christ in the Jordan?" He then identified St. Cyprian of Carthage as the source of this ritual and invoked Augustine against Cyprian on this point.[309] The portions of the *Ritum Ecclesiasticorum* that Bugenhagen included came in for his heaviest attack, as they talk about the sacrifice of the mass and papal authority. In each of the agendas, however, Bugenhagen returned to arguments that he had made in his writings on human traditions, suggesting that his parenthetical comments should be views as supplementing the teaching he had already given in the tracts on Jonah 3. The publication of these three church orders provides further evidence that Bugenhagen's *Jonah* used biblical commentary to address the controversies provoked by the Augsburg Interim, including the intra-Lutheran charges that Bugenhagen and others were re-introducing Roman Catholic worship practices.

On the Spirit and the Letter: Allegory and the Clear Word of God

Bugenhagen's opening comments on Jonah include a short discussion of allegory. This likely arose in order to address St. Jerome's interpretation of Jonah, which had influenced much of medieval interpretive tradition.[310] Jerome found two primary allegories at work in Jonah. First, based on Matthew 12, Jonah's life prefigured that of Jesus, so that everything that happened to Jonah has a parallel in Christ's life; second, because Jonah means "dove" in Hebrew, the book can serve as an allegory for the Holy Spirit coming to the faithful.[311] Jerome insisted especially on the first allegorical meaning, as it contrasted literal and spiritual interpretations.

> The world believes and the generation of Jews is condemned. Nineveh repents and unbelieving Israel perishes [Matt. 12:41]. They have the books, we have the Lord of the books. They possess the prophets, we understand the prophets. The letter kills them, we live by the spirit (2 Cor. 3[:6]). With them, Barabbas the thief is released (John 18[:40]); for us, Christ the Son of God is acquitted.[312]

Jerome explained the difference between "letter and spirit" as the difference between Jewish knowledge of the historical prophets and Christian belief in Christ as the eternal Word of God to whom the prophets refer. Jerome's commentary is thoroughly Christocentric, even to the extent that the historical Jonah disappears within an allegorical ("spiritual") retelling of Christ's life.

But Bugenhagen had a very different understanding of Jonah's central "spiritual" message than Jerome. In 2 Corinthians 3:6, Paul had written, "the letter kills, but the spirit gives life." St. Augustine explored this distinction in his *De Spiritu et Litera* (*On the Spirit and the Letter*), a work that was so influential for Lutheran theology that it became a required book in the University of Wittenberg's theology department.[313] Like Jerome, Bugenhagen recognized that Christ's use of Jonah as a type of his own death and resurrection gave biblical support for interpreting Jonah as a forerunner of Christ. And because Jonah is called the son of Amittai (which means "truth"), Bugenhagen was also willing to entertain allegorical interpretations of Jonah as "dove" and "son of truth." But where Jerome's allegorical interpretation equated Jonah with Jesus, Bugenhagen preferred a spiritual meaning about personal repentance and faith.

To introduce this reading, Bugenhagen explained what he meant by the distinction between "the letter and the spirit." For him, Jonah offered a "holy history" that taught God's encounter with humanity through law and gospel. As he challenged medieval methods of interpretation, he laid out his own interpretive rules for his students.

> You should take great care not to obscure the true holy history with inept and invented allegories, just as Origen did and, after him, none other than Jerome. Where they could not catch the right meaning in the word of Holy Scripture, even in the sacred histories themselves, they invented absurdities in the words and created foreign meanings through invented allegories, calling the literal word of scripture the killing word and allegory its true living spirit. In this way they so shamelessly distorted the word of Paul, "the letter kills but the spirit makes alive."
>
> Augustine refuted this error in *On the Spirit and the Letter* and correctly explained Paul's word. And yet, following their error, they imagined there to be a fourfold meaning or explanation of Holy Scripture, after which – as the Epicureans say – we could have no certainty from holy letters, and Holy Scripture should be like a wax nose, which can be turned now to the left, now to the right. This is insulting and contemptuous to the Word of God, in that through God's judgment and wrath we accepted human doctrines and mandates.
>
> But Holy Scripture has its own elegance and loveliness in speaking, for it has spoken often in figurative words, allegories, metaphors, and similes, which we clearly understand from other places from the clear word of God, the Law and the Gospel. And this knowledge of ours is the literal sense and grammatical exposition. It is not Spirit, as they say, nor is it uncertainty, rather we know the will of

God toward us with certainty from the word that God has revealed to us. The Holy Spirit speaks against the doctrines and rules of men in Psalm 5[:9]: "For there is no certainty in their mouth, etc." On allegory, see Luther's commentary on Galatians 4.[314]

Here is a remarkably clear summary of hundreds of years of Christian biblical interpretation. This quotation explains Bugenhagen's rejection of ancient allegory, the medieval *quadriga*[315] and his preference for a focus on "the clear Word of God, the Law and the Gospel."

In Bugenhagen's view, the proper distinction between letter and spirit is not the difference between literal and figurative speech. Instead, he employed an Augustinian distinction between human and divine teaching, in which *any* interpretation guided by a logic other than the gospel remains "the letter that kills."[316] Even though a firm grammatical or even theological meaning of any particular passage may be uncertain, the central message of God's salvation never is; the gospel – God's free justification of sinners through faith in Christ – is the "spirit that gives life." Conversely, even the most easily understandable text is not "spiritual" if it does not lead to life. Bugenhagen's definition of scripture's spiritual meaning as the proclamation of the gospel stood squarely in line with the earliest Lutheran tradition. For this reason, before continuing to direct exegesis of Jonah, he could simply footnote his thoughts on allegory by pointing to Luther's work on Galatians 4:24-31, saying, "On allegory, see Luther's commentary on Galatians 4.[317]

Luther's comments on Galatians 4 consider Paul's own use of allegory. There Luther asserted that "allegories do not provide solid proofs in theology; but, like pictures, they adorn and illustrate a subject. For if Paul had not proved the righteousness of faith against the righteousness of works by more substantial arguments, he would not have accomplished anything with this allegory."[318] Then, summarizing the value of Paul's allegorical interpretation of Hagar and Sarah in Galatians 4, Luther stated,

> Therefore this allegory teaches in a beautiful way that the church should not do anything but preach the Gospel correctly and purely and thus give birth to children. In this way we are all fathers and children to one another, for we are born of one another. I was born of others through the

Gospel, and now I am a father to still others, who will be fathers to still others; and so this giving birth will endure until the end of the world.[319] But I am speaking, not about Hagar's giving birth, who gives birth to slaves through the Law, but about free Sarah's, who gives birth to heirs without the Law, without works or their own efforts."[320]

For Luther, allegory's usefulness was based on first preaching the truly spiritual meaning of the Bible: the righteousness of faith given through Christ. Following Paul, Luther could use allegory, but only in service of preaching the more fundamental message of salvation. In Galatians 4 that meant proclaiming the difference between spiritual slavery and freedom.

Melanchthon had used allegory in a similar way. In the 1521 *Loci Communes*, he described of the Ark of the Covenant in terms of law and gospel: "There were two cherubim placed on the Ark, the law and the gospel; therefore it is impossible to teach correctly either gospel or law without gospel."[321] While a large spectrum of interpretations about these angels on the ark is no doubt possible, Melanchthon allegorized them into signs of God's word, revealed in the two modes of law and gospel. In a dissertation on Melanchthon's *Annotationes in Johannem*, Timothy Wengert noticed that Melanchthon overwhelmingly employed allegorical interpretation to highlight the encounter between God's word and humanity,[322] finding only two exceptions to this "*Logos*-centric" use of allegory: Jacob's ladder (John 1:51) and the bronze serpent (John 3:14-15).[323] Though Wengert did not mention this, Melanchthon probably did not allegorize those stories because Jesus had already applied them to himself; there was no reason for him to allegorize them further. This parallels Bugenhagen's treatment of Jonah. Bugenhagen interpreted Jesus' metaphorical words about the "sign of Jonah" literally. He did not feel the need to invent a new allegory in order to reach a "spiritual" interpretation. Instead, he commented (non-allegorically) on the literal (allegorical!) words of Jesus.

Bugenhagen's own allegory, therefore, presents Jonah as an example of how God saves through the preaching of God's word. Following Luther's guidelines, he gave a brief allegorical reading that emphasizes the right use of law and gospel.[324]

If anyone wants an interpretation of these names and this history, adding some allegories, one will want to do what truly belongs to sinful Christians and those still coming to their senses. But it is fine by me like this:

Jonah is a dove, that is, a Christian (as Christ said to us, "Be innocent as doves" [Mt. 10:16]). He is the son of Amittai, that is, a true preacher and confessor of the word of God, slain in sin by God's own justice, disobedient to God, and terrified by a bad conscience, fleeing from the face of God, as Adam and Eve did in Genesis 3, and as the children of Israel did on Mt. Sinai in Exodus 20, etc. And this poor sinner cannot flee the judgment of God, which is present and powerful everywhere.

Where did he flee? To the sea, that is, to the world and its concupiscence: "Do not love the world, nor the things which are of the world "(1 John 2[:15]). But first he went to Joppa, that is, this journey of perdition and death, which began beautifully, for sinners see beauty and satisfaction in fleeing from the face of God, just as Christ said in Matthew 7[:13]: "Wide is the gate and the road easy, that leads to perdition, and many take it."

Entering the true sea, one is cast down to ruin in it, according to Proverbs 18[:3]: "The sinner, when he has come to the depths, also despises." And this one is swallowed by the great fish, that is, the devil, who keeps him captive. Once there, he comes to his senses and believes in God's mercy, which is in Christ Jesus our Lord, and he calls upon the father, is liberated, gives thanks, and obeys God, etc.

Such is an example of how we may embrace the sacred histories, as examples of the wrath and mercy of God, just as Paul said in Romans 15[:4]: "Whatever has been written, was written for our learning, so that through patience and the consolation of Scripture we may have hope."[325]

This allegorical interpretation of Jonah is very different from Jerome's. Unlike Jerome, Bugenhagen did not care to equate Jonah as "dove" and "son of truth" with Christ. Instead, he turned to a different passage to apply Jonah to all faithful people: "be innocent as doves." Rather than prefiguring Christ, he equated Jonah as the "son of truth" to be a preacher of God's word, which was in fact his role as a prophet. Jonah's misadventures then exemplify a life within law and gospel, in which one comes face-to-face with one's own sin and is set free only by God's gracious liberation. Bugenhagen ended by asserting that such interpretations exist to console and nourish believers, quoting St. Paul's assurance that all scripture exists so that "we may have hope."

The difference between Jerome and Bugenhagen's use of allegory is not that the Lutherans were somehow more Christological or interested in letting "scripture interpret scripture." Indeed, one could say that Jerome's exegesis of Jonah is *more* Christocentric and uses *more* citations from the rest of the Bible to support its interpretation than Bugenhagen's did. The difference is one of means and ends. Where Jerome used allegorical interpretation to find spiritual insights into Christ's life, Bugenhagen's allegory focuses on the effect of law and gospel in the lives of believers. As a "son of truth" Jonah preached the good news of salvation. He confronted sin and error (including his own) in order to show that God alone frees people from sin, death and destruction. Thus, Bugenhagen's "allegorical" approach has the effect of inserting readers into this living "holy history" of the "clear word of God" which saves sinners.

Quid sit, Quid effectus: Doctrines and Their Effects

Because Bugenhagen saw dying and rising with Christ as the center of the Bible's meaning, his commentary shows no interest in the question of whether or not Jonah could have really lived inside the great fish for three days. Luther briefly noted this implausibility in his 1526 commentary, saying simply that the story would be regarded as a "lie and a fairy tale" if it were not in the Bible.[326] Bugenhagen did not make even this nod to human doubt. For him, the question of whether a person could live inside a fish was totally insignificant when compared to faith in the God who creates life out of death. Either God raises people from the dead or not. If God does that, then sustaining a person inside a fish might be unusual but not impossible for God. But if God does not raise people from death, then no proofs from marine biology make any difference. Therefore, Bugenhagen interpreted Jonah's time in the belly of the great fish as a chance to focus on the theology of the cross.

> Where human reason sees no liberation amid danger and despairs because of it, there God wonderfully and mercifully liberates through what is impossible. And so, where God hurls on us the castigations of a thousand dangers and death itself, from there God again reveals peace, power, and glory,

just as Hannah sings in 1 Sam. 2[:6-8]: "The Lord kills and makes alive, he brings down to hell and raises up. The Lord makes poor and makes rich, humbles and exalts. He raises the needy up from the dust, and exalts the poor from the dung heap, so that he might sit among princes and inherit a throne of glory," etc.

Similarly, the children of Israel saw this earlier at the Red Sea, with [the waters] like mountains to their right and left, [chased by] the scourges of Pharaoh and his army. Of course, no one could know of the glorious liberation. But Moses spoke to the agitated and yelling people: "Be silent! The Lord will fight for you and after this you will not see these enemies ever again" [Ex. 14:13-14].

Christ asked the Father that death might pass from him [Mt. 26:39] and "he was heard because of his reverence" [Heb. 5:7]. But how was he heard? With ridicule before the world, as they cried out under the cross, "If you are the son of God, come down now off the cross, etc." [Mt. 27:42]. He cast him to death and hell and then exalted him, setting him at his right hand, etc. "This was the Lord's doing, and it is marvelous in our eyes" [Ps. 118:23], a verse that spoke of the resurrection. It is right that Christ suffered and in this way entered into his glory.

Thus, Jonah pitifully expected to be swallowed, which is horrifying. For not only was he swallowed by the sea or even by the whale, spending three days and three nights there, but even through death and hell he was protected by God to life. He was stuck inside of death, neither able to die nor to know liberation.

This is what is sung in Psalm 4[:3]: "The Lord has made his holy ones wonderful; the Lord will hear me when I cry to him." And in Jeremiah's Lamentations 3[:37-42]: "Who can command and have it done, if the Lord has not ordained it? Is it not from the mouth of the Most High that good and bad come? Why do people grumble in this life? Everyone grumbles about their own sin. Let us search our paths and seek and return to the Lord. Let us lift up our hearts with our hands to heaven. We ourselves have sinned, etc." God has splendidly promised in Psalm 91[:14-15]: "Whoever loves me, I will deliver; who knows my name, I will protect. They who call to me, I will hear. I am with them in tribulation and I will raise them and glorify them. I will satisfy them with long days and show them my salvation."

These promises are ours today in this oppressed church. When we invoke the name of the Lord and are hopeful, God wonderfully liberates and glorifies his holy ones.[327]

In this passage, the plausibility of Jonah surviving for three days and three nights in the belly of the fish is equated with other miraculous deeds of the Bible, including Hannah's prayer that she might conceive and the Israelites' escape from Egypt across the Red Sea. Such miracles serve as signs of God's surprising power; they are not ends in themselves.

In commenting on Jonah's request to be thrown into the sea, Bugenhagen noted Jesus' prayer in Gethsemane: "if it is possible, let this cup pass from me; yet not what I want but what you want" (Matt. 26:39). In answer to his prayer, Jesus received ridicule, abandonment and death. And yet, this was not the work of a cruel or weak God, but the work of a God who confronted and conquered death through Christ. Similarly, Jonah had not known what would await him when he told the sailors to throw him overboard. In Bugenhagen's analysis, Jonah received the worst fate possible: "he was stuck inside of death, neither able to die nor able to know liberation." In this formulation, Bugenhagen anticipated the existential despair that Soren Kierkegaard described as "the sickness unto death" three centuries later:

> Thus to be sick *unto* death is to be unable to die, yet not as if there were hope of life; no, the hopelessness is that there is not even the ultimate hope, death. When death is the greatest danger, we hope for life; but when we learn to know the even greater danger, we hope for death. When the danger is so great that death becomes the hope, then despair is the hopelessness of not even being able to die.[328]

Bugenhagen's description of death and hell is not an abstract or distant death, but a very personal and real suffering that can only be relieved by God's grace.

While the "existentialist" label often applied to Kierkegaard does not exactly fit the worldview of the sixteenth-century reformers, a real sense of personal immediacy does characterize their view of life with God. In Lutheran theology, there is a consistent move from describing what a thing is (*quid sit*) to what it does (*quid effectus*).[329] This principle is at work, for instance, in Luther's paradoxical statement that "A Christian is a perfectly free lord of all, subject to none. A Christian is a perfectly dutiful servant of all, subject to all."[330] Far from simply declaring that someone is either free or bound, being a Christian leads to the effects of experiencing both deep freedom and service. In Luther's *Small Catechism*, the phrase "so that" repeatedly moves students from knowledge to action.[331] Luther understood faith to be an active power of God that brings concrete changes in the world, the church, and individual lives.

Melanchthon made early use of this *quid sit, quid effectus* dynamic in his 1521 *Loci Communes* when he wrote, "to know Christ means to know his benefits."[332] Because Christ's teaching changes lives, Christian knowledge is incomplete until people experience the benefits of reconciliation with God and neighbors. Melanchthon continued, "This, then, is Christian knowledge: to know what the law demands, where you may seek power for doing the law and grace to cover sin, how you may strengthen a quaking spirit against the devil, the flesh, and the world, and how you may console an afflicted conscience."[333] This emphasis on effects deeply informed early Lutheran preaching and ethics. As a theological method, it connects knowledge with results. This relationship between what a thing is (*quid sit*) and what it does (*quid effectus*) was constantly invoked in the works of Luther and Melanchthon.

Bugenhagen's interpretation of Jonah consistently makes this same move from knowledge to effect. Knowing the miraculous stories of people like Jonah, Hannah, or Moses is still only penultimate until people experience the freedom and truth that these narratives teach for themselves. As Bugenhagen concluded above, "Such is an example of how we may embrace the sacred histories, as examples of the wrath and mercy of God." The Bible presents truths to be embraced and experienced rather than known only in an abstract way.

The move from *quid sit* to *quid effectus* shows a Lutheran application of the Pauline distinction between the letter that kills and the spirit that gives life. It is a defining trait in early Lutheran biblical interpretation, on clear display in Bugenhagen's *Jonah*. Christians study and preach the Bible in order to share real experiences of liberation, comfort, and service. As seen in the examples that Bugenhagen presented – Hannah, Moses, Jonah, and Christ in Gethsemane – this message does not provide easy answers or simple vindication but confronts life's darkest moments, ultimately trusting that God alone creates life out of death. In this way, Bugenhagen's *Jonah* serves not only as a grammatical or interpretative aid for understanding a book of the Bible but as a direct model for how early Lutherans encountered and experienced the gospel both in the scriptures and in daily life.

Jonah in Wittenberg

This chapter began by asking, "Why did Bugenhagen lecture on Jonah?" The immediate answer was that it was his job as a professor on the theological faculty. After that, a study of Bugenhagen's interpretative methods showed how Jonah further provided Bugenhagen with a solid foundation for teaching Lutheran theology and addressing the Augsburg Interim. As this chapter reaches its conclusion, it is worth asking this question more pointedly: Why Jonah? What about this prophet spoke to Bugenhagen's context and made it compelling for his time? What did Jonah have to do with Wittenberg?

In Wittenberg today, there are few remnants of Elector Frederick the Wise's famous collection of relics. As the Reformation gained in influence, the relics were likely sold and their valuable metal cases and decorations taken for more secular usage.[334] One relic that remains in the Wittenberg City Museum, however, is one of three whale ribs that had formerly been displayed. It was claimed that they had come from the famous *Walfisch* that carried Jonah. Thus, at least during Bugenhagen's early years in Wittenberg, Jonah's story was physically on display in town. Less striking, but also significant, is that another longtime Wittenberg colleague was named Justus Jonas. Jonas connected his name with the story of Jonah and used a picture of Jonah as his personal crest.[335] In Bugenhagen's Wittenberg, then, Jonah was an easily accessible and visible witness to faith.

But Jonah did not merely represent an ancient story, sacred relic, or a clever personal reference. Most of all, Jonah and his troubles still resonated with people's lives. In the long citation above, after listing challenges faced by the prophets and the saints, Bugenhagen returned to his own time, saying, "These promises are ours today in this oppressed church. When we invoke the name of the Lord and are hopeful, God wonderfully liberates and glorifies his holy ones."[336] Bugenhagen clearly identified himself and his city's recent surrender with the despair faced by Jonah in the belly of the great fish. Even so, Bugenhagen did not make the parallel between Jonah and Wittenberg's trials in order to boast of their holiness. Instead he wanted to remind his audience that they would overcome only with God's help: "these promises are ours today." His choice of Jonah had immediate personal and communal significance as he interpreted the Bible to give strength to his students and church in a time of trouble and loss.

The passage cited above is one of a few instances when Bugenhagen explicitly inserted Wittenberg's recent history into his commentary. In another place, Bugenhagen named the lost war and the Council of Trent as twin opponents of Wittenberg's evangelical faith. There, commenting on Jonah 1:2 ("Get up and go to Nineveh"), he wrote:

> For this reason [unfaithfulness among the Lutherans], God started to threaten us through this war and through the Council of Trent, because he wanted to take the kingdom of God – that is, his word – away from us, which would cause us to perish for eternity. Therefore let us return to Christ and cry out to heaven with the people of Nineveh, repenting in the name of Jesus Christ that God might have mercy on us, etc. "Lord, keep us steadfast in your word." "Give us peace in our day, O Lord, for there is none other who can fight for us, etc." And as Christ admonished us [Matt. 6:33], "Seek first the kingdom of God and his righteousness, and all these things will be given to you."[337]

In this account, the Smalcaldic War and the Council of Trent were occasions for students and fellow Wittenbergers to repent of their sins and return to the word of God, without which they would certainly be lost. They were like the people of Nineveh, justly condemned to death because of their sins; and yet, the promised grace of the gospel remained theirs as well.

On this point, Bugenhagen identified himself as both a preacher and a penitent sinner. This matches the image of him as town confessor that greeted worshipers on the Cranach Altar in the City Church. As he had identified in his third his introductory locus ("the saints have all gone to ruin"), the book of Jonah reminds even the most faithful believers of their own ongoing need for confession. Jonah helped him teach that the people of Wittenberg should find comfort neither in self-pity nor self-righteousness but simply return to the Lord in confession and faith.

In the process of connecting Jonah with his own time, Bugenhagen cited two of Luther's hymns that asked for faith and perseverance during adversity: "Lord, Keep Us Steadfast in Your Word"[338] and "Give Us Peace in Our Day, O Lord."[339] By sprinkling Luther's hymns into his lecture, Bugenhagen taught his students to connect Luther's theology with prayer and daily life; Luther's legacy belonged both in the lecture hall and in the song of the church at worship.

Another mention of recent political events around Wittenberg appears in the commentary at Jonah 2:2, where Bugenhagen provided the simple heading *Clamaui* ("I called out"). Bugenhagen described it as a precious and unique treasure that when Christians cry out to God from darkness and the horrors of death, God has promised to listen.[340] To this theological assertion, he added his own thanksgiving and prayers for deliverance.

> I do not want to be ungrateful for the Father's mercy that the prayers of Christ's church liberated us in Wittenberg from this death in the year of our Lord 1547. And we hope that by invocations we are liberated hereafter from the coming war that we greatly fear as the highest danger. They intend this against us at the Council of Trent and Bologna: that through satanic cunning and violence they might sweep us away from the kingdom of heaven (that is, God's word and Christ's gospel), so that there might be no one upon the earth who invokes the Father in the name of Jesus Christ and who honors the Son just as the Father; rather that we, with our children and descendents, all be subjected again to the doctrines of demons.[341]

By the time Bugenhagen was commenting on Jonah 2, his language had grown increasingly confrontational: this passage vividly describes Roman Catholic plots (however real or imagined) against the Lutherans. Nevertheless, such comments still take place as part of the interpretation of Jonah because they come under the discussion of *"clamaui."* Here is *quid sit* and *quid effectus* in action: Jonah's "I called out" was not merely a historical statement by a long-dead prophet but the real cry of all faithful people across the generations who live amid uncertainty, fear and violence. By sharing his own prayers at this point, Bugenhagen modeled a way of reading scripture that connects the biblical story with daily life.

In terms of biblical interpretation, the passage above also makes an important point about Bugenhagen's understanding of the word of God. There he described the kingdom of heaven as itself being the word of God and gospel of Christ, highlighting the bond between the Bible and Christian communities where God's word is shared. Belonging to the kingdom of heaven means belonging to God's word. Although Bugenhagen could imagine God's word somehow being extinguished in Wittenberg, he believed that Christ would indeed arise for them.[342] He went on to pray, "O Lord Jesus Christ, do this so that when we have been liberated we can be the first to express thanks with Jonah [2:1]: 'I called out to the Lord in my anguish and he answered me.'"[343] Jonah's experiences of despair, imminent death and liberation might inspire similar faith in God's deliverance in the present. In its troubles, Wittenberg could still experience the kingdom of God by sharing in God's liberating and effective word.

This shift from desperation about the possible destruction of evangelical communities to a prayer of confidence in God's liberation shows how Bugenhagen's biblical interpretation worked. Though the Bible often speaks of hardship, afflictions, and despair, it ultimately teaches people to have faith, hope and love. Thus, for his *Jonah* to be a fully "biblical" commentary, Bugenhagen's work could not simply be a polemical tirade, an objective study of the Bible, or his complaint about troubles and sins. Rather, Bugenhagen ended even his most desperate statements with appeals to trust in God and God's enduring mercy.

Throughout this commentary, Bugenhagen interpreted Jonah primarily as a preacher of the eternal gospel that God justifies the ungodly through faith in Christ. Instead of presenting Jonah as a prototype of Christ as Jerome had, Bugenhagen presented a very human prophet whom God nevertheless used effectively to preach divine mercy. He summarized his own interpretation this way: "In the prophet Jonah, I will admonish Christ's church, of which the prophet Jonah was a member: he who sinned and fell away from God through unfaithfulness like Adam, but, coming to his senses and repenting, returned to God through faith."[344]

This commentary was written for a humbled land and a precariously positioned church, so that people might find in Jonah an example of what it means to turn back to God, receive new life, and proclaim God's liberation. It is a public call for repentance and, even more, for faith. As a work of biblical interpretation, this commentary clearly teaches themes like law and gospel, the spirit and the letter, justification by faith, and the *quid sit/quid effectus* dynamic, which moves readers from interpretation to action. Through biblical interpretation, Bugenhagen offered a strong response to the challenges facing Wittenberg in the years between the start of his lectures in October 1547 and the commentary's publication in October 1550.

CHAPTER FOUR

Bugenhagen as a Public Interpreter of Martin Luther

From the early writings that first inspired Bugenhagen to move to Wittenberg until his death in 1546, Martin Luther was a major influence in Bugenhagen's life and work. Bugenhagen's *Jonah* reflects this influence by presenting its author's view of what was most important about the faith that defined Wittenberg's worship, teaching, and public life. Studying Johannes Bugenhagen's relationship with Martin Luther adds insight into our understanding of the Jonah Commentary and sheds light on first generation views of the Lutheran reformation.

When Bugenhagen argued against the Council of Trent and the Augsburg Interim, he frequently turned to Luther's biblical interpretation, theology, and liturgical reforms. Also, Luther had published commentaries on Jonah in 1525 and 1526. We have seen already that Bugenhagen called upon Luther's explanation of allegory in the 1535 Galatians lectures and invoked two of Luther's hymns in his Jonah Commentary. By writing against the Louvain Theologians who had influenced the Augsburg Interim, Bugenhagen picked up another debate that Luther had begun in his last lectures on Genesis and in the 1545 tract "Against the Thirty-Two Articles of the Louvain Theologists." These nods to Luther peaked in Bugenhagen's third tract. There he defended the apostolic roots of the Lutheran doctrine of justification by recalling Luther's original "reformation breakthrough" and retelling that story from Luther's first-person point of view.

In this chapter, Bugenhagen's *Jonah* serves as a source for getting to know Bugenhagen as a public interpreter of his longtime friend and colleague, Martin Luther. Beginning with a short study of the two reformers' relationship, we see their shared conviction that the gospel leads to clear practical and pastoral effects. The sermon that Bugenhagen preached at Luther's funeral demonstrates this conviction and shows how he viewed Luther himself in light of the gospel message. Studying Luther through Bugenhagen also highlights areas of Luther's life often overlooked by historians and theologians, especially his pastoral concerns and his love of Christ's one church. As the historian Volker Leppin has stated, Reformation history will continue to offer profound insights into religious and social studies not by stressing Luther's uniqueness but rather by highlighting the catholicity and wider resonance of a movement that he, with many others, founded and nurtured.[345] Rather than viewing Luther as a lone giant of history, getting to know him through a colleague like Bugenhagen helps situate Luther in his immediate context and re-introduces him as a pastor, teacher, and public figure dealing concretely with real spiritual and practical problems. The chapter closes with the account of Luther's breakthrough that Bugenhagen included in his 1550 Jonah Commentary, a report that stands as a clear testimony to the origins and goals of evangelical faith.

Luther and Bugenhagen as Colleagues

Martin Luther and Johannes Bugenhagen worked together for over twenty years.[346] Already in September 1522, Luther expressed his desire that Bugenhagen remain nearby to help with church reforms, requesting to the Saxon court advisor Georg Spalatin that the Pomeranian receive a stipend for that purpose.

> Finally, in your work with the prince, might you see to it that Johannes Pomeranus receives one of those stipends that are now going to ruin amid sophistry. For after Philip, as a theology professor he is second in the city and the world (*in urbe et orbe*). And I have heard mentioned, indeed I know, that he is getting carried off to Erfurt.[347]

From the beginning, Luther valued Bugenhagen as a first-rate teacher and colleague. The following year, Luther was instrumental in Bugenhagen's appointment to pastorate at the City Church,[348] a position that Luther later described as "bishop of the church in Wittenberg."[349]

Their close working relationship is demonstrated in an exchange that took place on November 7, 1535, as Luther and Bugenhagen were on their way to meet papal legate Peter Paul Vergerio in preparation for the anticipated church council.

> [As they were gathering for breakfast] Luther joked, "Look! Here go the German pope and Cardinal Pomeranus, who are God's witnesses and instruments." In the course of their

conversation, the legate asked, "Do you ordain priests?" Luther answered, "Of course we do, because the pope won't consecrate and ordain for us!" Then he pointed to Bugenhagen and said, "And look, there sits a bishop, whom we have consecrated and ordained."[350]

While they could perhaps joke about what makes a person a pope, cardinal or bishop, this anecdote shows the view of ministry that Luther and Bugenhagen shared.[351] More important than hierarchical honors was the practical fact that the church needs ministers and bishops to preach the gospel and lead the people in worship and faith. In this exchange with a papal representative, they emphasized their freedom to ordain good pastors and appoint evangelical bishops if the pope refused to do it for them.

While Bugenhagen and Luther generally agreed about matters, one significant point of departure between the two arose when Luther heard that Bugenhagen had personally crowned the king and queen of Denmark shortly after arriving in Copenhagen in July 1537. According to a report from the time, "Luther became 'angry and displeased'" when he heard what Bugenhagen had done, accusing him of misunderstanding his office and its relationship to earthly power.[352] For his part, Bugenhagen appears to have been aware of the complexities and problems involved in his action. But he was willing to preside over the ceremony for the sake of civil peace and to advance reforms in a new territory.[353] Despite this disagreement, they usually held similar opinions and worked well together. Over the decades, Bugenhagen worked with Luther on church organization, doctrine, and the translation of the Bible into German.

Luther and Bugenhagen also seem to have shared a reputation for being gruff and easily provoked. Once, after calling the conscientious St. Augustine a mild-mannered "pious sinner," Luther said that St. Jerome, Justus Jonas, Bugenhagen and himself were more prone to angry outbursts.[354] Melanchthon also described Bugenhagen this way.[355] Melanchthon sometimes found that gruffer temperament in Luther and Bugenhagen "immoderate" in the Aristotelian sense.[356] But it never prevented those three reformers from working together over several productive decades.

Despite their rough edges, Luther and Bugenhagen shared a warm personal relationship. Bugenhagen was often at Luther's house during the conversations recorded in the *Table Talk*. When the plague struck Wittenberg in 1527, Bugenhagen's family moved into Luther's house, providing companionship and mutual support in difficult times. As often as Bugenhagen tended to agree with Luther, however, Bugenhagen found it necessary and possible to rebuke Luther and startle him out of his occasional melancholy. Luther once recalled,

> Right here at this table, when the rest of you were in Jena [in 1527], Pomeranus sometimes consoled me when I was sad by saying, "No doubt God is thinking: What more can I do with this man? I have given him so many excellent gifts, and yet he despairs of my grace." These words were a great comfort to me. As a voice from heaven they struck me in my heart, although I think Pomeranus did not realize at the time what he had said and that it was so well said.[357]

Whether he had spoken frankly or sarcastically, Bugenhagen's rebuke effectively startled Luther out of his melancholy. As Luther's pastor and confessor, he asserted at another time, "Dear Doctor, what I am telling you, you should accept not as my word but as God's word which He declares through me."[358] Luther explained this as an instance of being brought back to life through God's word coming from the pastor.[359] In these ways, Bugenhagen modeled the office of pastor as one who proclaims law and gospel to comfort consciences. In his ministry, he was able to extend that saving word to Luther himself.[360]

Bugenhagen's Funeral Sermon for Luther

Despite several bouts of serious illnesses and *Anfechtungen* (spiritual afflictions) over the decades, Luther lived into his sixties. He died in Eisleben where he had been born, on February 18, 1546. In Eisleben, Justus Jonas and the local court preacher Michael Coelius preached sermons before Luther's body was taken back to Wittenberg for its final rest.[361] There, Melanchthon delivered a classical eulogy in Latin and Bugenhagen preached the funeral sermon in Wittenberg's Castle Church.[362]

The biblical text on which Bugenhagen preached is 1 Thessalonians 4:13-14: "We do not want to hold back, dear brothers, concerning those who are asleep so that you may not be sorrowful as the others who have no hope." Commentators on this sermon have often noted its personable and apparently informal nature.³⁶³ Comparing Bugenhagen's sermon to Melanchthon's funeral oration, Susan Hedahl described Bugenhagen's message as personal and private, anecdotal and rambling, apocalyptic and eschatological, and "generally individualistic in nature."³⁶⁴ Comparing Bugenhagen's sermon to Melanchthon's Latin oration, it is not surprising that Hedahl found Bugenhagen's sermon to be both more personal and less formal. In this way, she correctly identified Melanchthon's elevated rhetoric and oratory; in another way, however, her comment missed a crucial difference in genre. Bugenhagen had also preached a formal message: while Melanchthon composed and delivered a classical funeral oration following the strict rules of Ciceronian rhetoric, Bugenhagen preached a Christian funeral sermon for a gathered assembly of mourners. Studying Bugenhagen's sermon as a formal composition reveals a much more coherent and intentional work than many interpreters have granted.

Bugenhagen's sermon is perhaps best known for its description of Luther as a biblical prophet and as the fulfillment of the fifteenth-century reformer Jan Huss' prophecy that a successor would come one hundred years later. Bugenhagen identified Luther as the angel from Revelation 14:6-7: "And I saw an angel flying through the midst of heaven. He had an eternal Gospel to proclaim to those who sit and dwell on earth, to all heathen and races and languages and nations. And he said with a loud voice: 'Fear God and give him honor, for the time of his judgment has come. Worship the one who has made heaven and earth, the seas and the springs of water.'"³⁶⁵ This connection between Luther and Revelation 14 was not original to Bugenhagen but had come as early as 1522; the comparison with Jan Huss had likewise been made early in Luther's reformation career.³⁶⁶ Still, it was high praise to name and validate Luther as a fulfillment of God's revelation in this funeral sermon. At other points in the sermon, Bugenhagen described Luther as "a dear man, a proper bishop and shepherd of souls" and "this holy apostle and prophet of Christ, our preacher and evangelist in the German territories."³⁶⁷ Such laudatory biblical language suggests Luther's exalted status as one almost belonging to another plane of existence.

But eulogizing Luther's life and even describing its apocalyptic significance was not the main point of the funeral sermon. Only the first third of the sermon speaks of Luther as a prophet or angelic messenger. In fact, immediately after connecting Luther to Huss' prophecy, Bugenhagen focused again on Luther's role as servant of the church and returned to his sermon text, "concerning those who are asleep." The sermon thus quickly moved from eulogy to proclamation of the gospel to the mourning congregation. Bugenhagen made this transition by describing Luther's thoughts on the death of Ambrosius Berndt (a professor at the university who had been related to Luther by marriage[368]) and by remembering Luther's own final years and days. Through these anecdotes, Bugenhagen was able to introduce Luther's reflections about death into Luther's own funeral sermon. Indeed, Bugenhagen explicitly said that he was telling these stories to comfort for those who mourn, the theme both of the Pauline text and of the anecdotes about Berndt.[369] He then gave a second reason for sharing these anecdotes: in conversations during Berndt's illness, Berndt had testified to Luther about the power of Christ's gospel.[370] Through these personal illustrations, Bugenhagen was able to let the dead speak to the living about Christian faith and salvation.

This second point especially fixed the listeners' attention on the gospel: Bugenhagen went on to tell how Luther himself relied upon this faith, returning to the Bible to reminding his hearers of the difference between those who die in faith as opposed to those who "have no hope." Thus, despite its initial lofty language of Luther as prophetic reformer and apostle of Christ, the sermon does not announce Luther's apotheosis based on an exemplary life. On the contrary, Bugenhagen's sermon describes Luther as being as much in need of repentance and good news as anyone. Luther's legacy was the recovery of a gospel that brought comfort to those who mourned and courage to those who faced troubled times, a message that Luther personally treasured and relied upon. No less than Melanchthon's orations, this sermon adhered closely to a formal literary style: namely, the public proclamation of law and gospel.

Even the identification of Luther with the angel of Revelation 14 says more of Luther's understanding of law and gospel than about any intrinsic personal greatness.

This angel who says, 'Fear God and give him the honor,' was Dr. Martin Luther. And what is written here, 'Fear God and give him the honor,' are the two parts of Dr. Martin Luther's doctrine, the Law and the Gospel, through which all of Scripture is unlocked and Christ, our righteousness and eternal life, is recognized.[371]

Because of this faith that Luther had helped unlock and bring to light, Wittenberg would not mourn as those who have no hope. And though Luther's appearance may have marked a key moment in history, Bugenhagen concluded that the biblical revelation of Revelation 14 "has happened before and still happens."[372] Luther's life, teaching, and preaching took place amid the interplay of God's activity with people, which is not static but keeps entering the world, sometimes as condemnation of sin (law) and sometimes as the announcement of forgiveness and salvation (gospel).

Like Luther, Bugenhagen had a strong sense of living in the end times.[373] But more important than vague talk of the end times, Bugenhagen clearly preached Christ's power to bring good news to those who mourn in the present. And if some might interpret Luther's death as divine punishment for sin, then Bugenhagen recommended that "we should improve our life, petition God our heavenly Father through Christ that we remain in the blessed, pure teaching concerning faith and be protected through Christ from the rabble and tyrants and against all portals of hell."[374] The sermon repeatedly pointed to law and gospel in order to bring comfort and good news to those who mourned. It thus enacted the evangelical preaching of the gospel that formed the basis of Luther's own work and ministry.

Luther as "Father"

For all the language of Luther as prophet and even angel, Bugenhagen opened and closed the funeral sermon by speaking of "our dear father, Dr. Martin."[375] Along with the professional title of doctor, "father" was the most common title that Bugenhagen and others gave to Luther. This was true not only in the funeral sermon but in writings before and after Luther's death. In a July 1527 letter to Bugenhagen about Luther's illness, Justus Jonas spoke of "our father Dr. Martin."[376] Bugenhagen's letters also often used the phrases "our father Dr. Martin" and "Father Luther" both when writing to Luther and when writing about him to others.[377]

What did Bugenhagen and others mean when they named Luther as father? An answer can be found in the way in which

Luther used the term with respect to his biological father, Hans Luther, and his spiritual father, Johann von Staupitz. In the dedication letter to the tract "On Monastic Vows" (1522), Luther wrote to his father Hans that only service to Christ overruled the commandment to obey parents. This service to Christ, Luther said, was not fulfilled through monastic vows; indeed, he said that he had sinned by disobeying his parents when he entered the monastery. But Luther found blessing in his time as a monk through the fact that his monastic service included a call to preach. "Therefore – so I am now absolutely persuaded – I could not have refused to obey you without endangering my conscience unless [Christ] had added the ministry of the Word to my monastic profession."[378] Only by meeting Christ through God's word had some good come of Luther's monastic vows: Christ had become Luther's true father. "Although [Christ] has made me the servant of all men, I am, nevertheless, subject to no one except to him alone. He is himself (as they say) my immediate bishop, abbot, prior, lord, father, and teacher; I know no other."[379] Luther believed that he had entered the monastery in violation of the commandment to honor mother and father. But God worked through this sinful decision to teach him true obedience through his ministry to God's word.

If Christ alone was Luther's "father," then why did Luther also continue to speak of his Augustinian superior, Johann von Staupitz, as father? Was this merely a formality or does it point to something more? From early in Luther's monastic life in Erfurt, Staupitz had overseen Luther's promotions in the Augustinian Order and encouraged his studies toward becoming a doctor of theology.[380] Even after a geographical and perhaps ideological distance had grown between them, Luther continued to call Staupitz his "reverend father in Christ."[381] Luther wrote in a letter of September 17, 1523, "Even if we have lost your favor and good will, it would not be right to forget you or to be ungrateful to you, through whom the light of the gospel first began to shine out of the darkness into our hearts."[382] Despite uncertainties about Staupitz' later relationship to the reformation in Wittenberg, Luther still cherished Staupitz as his father in the gospel. He repeated this in a Table Talk from 1532, saying, "Everything I have is from Dr. Staupitz."[383] What defined Staupitz as "father" was not simply that Staupitz had been Luther's monastic superior but that he taught him the gospel.

Staupitz' "fatherhood" was based in his teaching of Christ. The image Luther used about the "light of the gospel" likely alludes to Paul's summary of his preaching to the Corinthians (2 Cor. 4:6). Paul similarly described his preaching as a spiritual fatherhood: "For though you might have ten thousand guardians in Christ, you do not have many fathers. Indeed, in Christ Jesus I became your father through the gospel" (1 Cor. 4:15). In both of these instances, Paul hoped to reach wayward Christians in Corinth not through his earthly rank but as a loving witness to Christ's gospel. About obedience to such spiritual leaders, Luther's *Large Catechism* explicitly taught that one should honor spiritual leadership based on 1 Cor. 4:15.[384]

Staupitz fulfilled this role as a teacher of the gospel for Luther. Luther, in turn, filled it for others, including leaders like Bugenhagen, Melanchthon and Jonas. His "fatherhood" is therefore best interpreted as yet another way to describe him as a Christian teacher and preacher. The Lutheran meaning of "father" is about sharing the gospel. This should not be a surprise, as many traditions continue to use the title of "father" to refer to spiritual leadership and the priesthood. Still, in its evangelical use, "father" is a title connected specifically with teaching God's word of law and gospel. Even for Luther's closest friends and colleagues, this was an appropriate way to address the one who taught them the faith in a new and liberating way. In this way, Bugenhagen could also speak of Philip Melanchthon (who was more than ten years younger than him and who had never been ordained) as a father: a 1544 letter from Bugenhagen to Luther and Melanchthon opens with the titles "reverend fathers and teachers."[385] Thus, the phrase "Father Luther" did not come from the desire to create a new hierarchy or to serve vanity. Instead, it honored the gospel preaching and teaching that Luther, Bugenhagen and others hoped to model as church leaders.

Luther's Lectures on Jonah, 1525/26

By lecturing on Jonah, Bugenhagen was following a precedent set by Luther, who had also turned to Jonah amid political struggles. During the years surrounding the 1525 Peasants War, Luther lectured on the Minor Prophets, including Jonah.[386] In his preface to his published German Lectures on Jonah (1526), Luther explained why he was lecturing on this prophet.

> For some time, I have entered the lists and fought against these spirits and factions. Now that others have joined the fray, I have decided to take Scripture in hand again to feast our hearts, to strengthen, to comfort, and to arm them, lest fatigue and lassitude subdue us in our daily struggle. May God grant me grace that we, by His Word and the comfort of Scripture, may be refreshed and invigorated to fight with ever greater courage...
>
> I have therefore chosen to expound the holy prophet Jonah, for he is indeed well suited for this situation and represents an excellent, outstanding, and comforting example of faith and a mighty and wonderful sign of God's goodness to all the world... Furthermore, Jonah is also an object of comfort for all who administer the Word. It teaches them not to despair of the fruit of the Gospel, no matter how badly it appears to be devoid of fruit and profit.[387]

Luther turned to Jonah to hear God's promises and find strength amid weakness. Jonah exemplified the power of God's word to heal and refresh, to teach mercy and goodness, and to comfort preachers struggling in desperate times and circumstances.

All of these themes informed Bugenhagen's own interpretation nearly 25 years later without overshadowing it. For instance, after expertly summarizing Luther's work on Jonah early in the commentary, Bugenhagen went on to say that his own work would be different. On the first mention of Nineveh in Jonah 1:2, Bugenhagen wrote,

> Asshur founded Nineveh, as it says in Genesis 10[:11].[388] In fact, Nineveh means "splendid" or "beautiful." You see this in Paul, Romans 3[:29] that God is not only God of the Jews but also the gentiles, which you see in Father Luther's commentaries on Jonah. There you also read that God sends prophets before destruction, that the law of Moses does not pertain to gentiles, that Jonah's ministry was very great, that even the saints are sinners and sometimes sin gravely, presented to as examples of God's grace so that we do not lay claim to our own merit.
>
> Moreover, [you see] the cause of Jonah's disobedience, which includes the hatred of the Jews for the salvation of the gentiles, as you clearly see at the end of this Book of

Jonah. Also, [you see] the holy verdict that God is no respecter of persons [Acts 10:34], so that sinners are not judged and condemned by us but can be reformed by God's word. Moreover, [you see] that many people were punished at sea on account of the one man, Jonah, but that they were sinners too. There is also the locus from Romans 1[:18-32] that the invisible things about God are clearly seen from the creation, the history of which has remarkably shown the light of nature and to what an extent this light has been in vain. [Luther's writing also teaches] about the true and false god, true and false faith, Jonah's sin and Jonah's faith, as well as other subjects which you should not expect from me, for I will not discuss them. But when you read the most blessed treatment of them in his commentaries, you will rejoice.[389]

Bugenhagen's admiration for Luther's earlier work would not result in imitation. Instead, he summarized topics that he would intentionally not cover. While a comparison between these points and Bugenhagen's loci shows them to be similar, Bugenhagen's *Jonah* and Luther's Lectures on Jonah differ greatly overall. The primary difference arises not in theology but in method. Where Luther mostly employed a verse-by-verse style of commentary to interpret Jonah, Bugenhagen's loci method allowed him to go deeper into themes he encountered in the text. His extended discussion of repentance in the tracts on Jonah 3 especially resulted in very different conclusions about the end of Jonah's story than Luther had reached. In fact, Bugenhagen's sustained focus on repentance led to an interpretation of Jonah 4 that was different from statements he himself had made at the commentary's outset.[390]

The loci method also allowed Bugenhagen to refer to the recently deceased Luther in his commentary to help him advance his argument. While that may seem natural enough, it is technically strange that Luther should enter into a work of biblical interpretation as a character. For instance, when discussing how God sends prophets in times of crisis, he included Luther in his list. Just as God sent Lot to Sodom, Jonah to Nineveh, Jeremiah to Jerusalem, John the Baptist to Judea, and the apostles to the ends of the earth,

> in the same way even now at the end of the age, God, our Lord Jesus Christ, sent Father Luther and holy prophets or

preachers, when it was revealed again through the Holy Spirit from the Holy Scriptures of the Gospel, to pope and papacy, as it had been said of our age in Revelation 14[:6]: "I saw an angel flying through the midst of heaven, who had an eternal Gospel," etc. so that God's elect may be liberated by the knowledge of our Lord Jesus Christ.[391]

Despite its elevated language and similarity to what Bugenhagen had preached in his funeral sermon for Luther,[392] this is no simple hagiography. Luther's importance stemmed from his role as a preacher of God's gospel. What the Spirit called Luther to do was a task shared by prophets, apostles and pastors, who continue to be sent by God to preach the gospel. As discussed in the previous chapter, for Bugenhagen the Bible is a living voice for a living church; its story includes the horizon of contemporary events.

Bugenhagen's choice of Jonah in 1547 was itself another way to follow Luther's example. Luther had lectured on Jonah amid the chaos of the Peasants War. He discovered that Jonah "rhymes almost exactly" with the Lutheran situation of the time, because Jonah preached the word of God to an unbelieving generation and showed that forgiveness comes through faith.[393] Luther also felt compelled to return to biblical commentary after the fighting and factions of the Peasants' War: according to him, the devil "has sowed his tares everywhere," both among the spiritual "enthusiasts" and the "mad bishops and princes."[394] This required a return to the word of God. Luther's condemnation of abuses by political and religious authorities led to censorship of some portions of his Jonah Commentary in Augsburg and to the arrest of a publisher in Leipzig.[395] Over twenty years later, Bugenhagen similarly turned to Jonah to show how Jonah's preaching of repentance and faith to Nineveh once again paralleled recent experiences in Saxony.

In the preface to the Latin lectures, Luther described the main points that he wanted to examine in the Book of Jonah. First, Jonah's call (*officium*) was to serve as preacher to the gentiles.[396] Second, the conversion of the evil city of Nineveh reveals the power of the word of God to change the world through preaching.[397] Third, Jonah served as a model of Luther's conviction that the believer is *simul iustus et peccator* (simultaneously justified and sinner), because in Jonah one clearly sees sin among one of God's holy prophets.[398] If even the prophets sinned, then one cannot find or create a pure and unblemished church in this life, because sin always affects human reason and institutions. This point was relevant to Luther's disputes against both "spiritualists" and the papacy, who, however differently, claimed more inherent holiness for the church on earth than Luther thought humanly possible or biblically warranted. Fourth, moving from Jonah's sin to his liberation, Luther emphasized the forgiveness of sins and justification by faith alone: neither the people of Nineveh nor the prophet earned their own salvation.[399]

With his nine opening loci, Bugenhagen expanded upon Luther's four points, adding his own nuances and concerns to the text, especially the emphasis on repentance. But Bugenhagen's final two points have no exact parallel in Luther's work. These themes had invoked Jonah as an example against stoic fate (locus 8) and as a sign of Christ's passion and resurrection (locus 9). Certainly, he and Luther held these ideas in common. Bugenhagen's identification of them, however, highlights his specific concern for faithful action and his willingness to think of the angry Jonah of chapter 4 as still able to receive God's forgiveness and liberation. Though it would be possible to interpret the refutation of "stoic fate" as a statement against John Calvin's teaching about predestination or divine election,[400] Bugenhagen seems to contrast the resignation of stoicism with liberating effects of contrition and faith. This addition shows Bugenhagen's encouragement for the people of Saxony to keep practicing their faith and not fall into moral or political resignation.

The second additional point, about Jonah's story belonging to Christ's passion and resurrection, also reflects the position of the later Luther. In a Table Talk probably from the late 1530s, Luther wished that he had written better about Jonah than he had.

> But this history of the prophet Jonah is so great that it's nearly unbelievable. It even looks deceptive and nonsensical, like one of [Aesop's] fables. If it were not in the Bible, I would laugh at it like at a lie. For if a person wants, simply consider how Jonah could have spent even three hours in the great belly of a fish, let alone three days, without becoming part of the fish's nature, flesh and blood? He should have died a hundred times under the earth, in the

sea, in the fish, etc. But isn't that exactly what it means to live in the midst of death? Compared to this, the miracle at the Red Sea looks like nothing.

There is also something foolish about him. For after he had been released and saved, he started ranting and raving and making himself quite useless about a small thing like the little shrub [4:9]. This is a great mystery. I am ashamed of my exposition of this prophet, that I touched the main topics and purpose of the miracle so weakly.[401]

Although Luther lamented that he had not written well enough in his commentary on Jonah, the first paragraph cited above shares much in common with his published lectures of 1525/26. There he compared Jonah's survival inside a big fish to a fable. He also described that miracle in terms of the Latin hymn that he adapted into German as "Mitten wir im Leben sind" ("In the Midst of Life").[402] For these reasons, his regrets were probably not about how he had interpreted the first three chapters of Jonah.

The lament expressed in the final paragraph must have been over his exposition of Jonah 4, in which the prophet sat outside of Nineveh, angry enough to die. Luther regretted that he had discussed this last part of Jonah "so weakly." Indeed, Luther paid little attention to this chapter in his published lectures.[403] In the Latin version, he offered there a short version of Jerome's allegorical interpretation.[404] In the 1526 German publication, Luther presented this chapter as an example of Jonah as both saint and sinner,[405] before presenting three allegories of the entire book, in which he only mentioned Jonah 4 as a foreshadowing of the Pharisees' rejection of Jesus Christ.[406] In neither edition, however, did he express anything laudable about Jonah in his comments on that chapter.

Bugenhagen's lectures on Jonah continue a line of thinking that Luther had only hinted at. Rather than leaving Jonah angry at God and ready to die in chapter 4, Bugenhagen interpreted the book's final chapter as another example of life under the cross of Christ. The final locus of Bugenhagen's preface does not consign Jonah to the lost but includes him among the fallen and redeemed.

> All history is in the image of the passion and resurrection of Christ, for the reason that we said before [Matt. 12:40]. And even as Jonah grieved the shrub, so much more does God grieve human destruction, for God said, "You grieve

over the shrub, which you did not labor over or make to grow, which was born in one night and perished in one day. And shall I not spare Nineveh, that great city, in which there are more than 120,000 people who do not know their right hand from their left, and many animals?" [Jonah 4:10-11].[407]

In this interpretation, Jonah's anger about the shrub points to God's compassion for the doomed people of Nineveh and, by extension, to God's compassion for Jonah himself. More clearly than Luther had, Bugenhagen followed the inner logic of Jonah 4 to identify a point about God's forgiveness that Christian interpreters have often missed. If an angry prophet could have enough compassion to grieve a shrub, how much more does God grieve all human suffering, including the ranting of an angry prophet? This point will be further explored in chapter 7. For now, it is enough to note that the differences between Luther and Bugenhagen's commentaries on Jonah say more about Bugenhagen as an able interpreter of the Bible and Lutheran theology than show major theological differences between the two reformers.

Luther and Bugenhagen on the Office of Ministry (Jonah 1:2)

Luther and Bugenhagen both interpreted Jonah as a living voice speaking to their time. In their respective quests to find biblical insights during times of political disorder, they found Jonah to be an example of one who experienced and preached law and gospel. Comparing their approach to Jonah as a minister of God's word shows how well Bugenhagen understood Luther's teaching and still felt free to express it in his own words.

The two reformers believed in the power of God's word to perform what it says. They each commented in this way on Jonah 1:2, in which God told the prophet to "Go at once to Nineveh, that great city, and cry out against it." Luther interpreted God's call to preach as a last gracious warning given to an otherwise doomed world. The world would be judged on the basis of its response to God's word given through the prophets. From Luther's perspective in the volatile 1520s, the world's response was not encouraging.

> For whenever God's wrath is about to be kindled, He usually first sends His Word to save a few. Thus He sent Noah before the deluge came (Gen. 6); He sent Lot before He destroyed Sodom (Gen. 19); and Abraham, Isaac, and Jacob before He despoiled Canaan; Joseph and Moses before He

afflicted Egypt. And thus He here also sent Jonah and Hosea before He did away with Israel, and Jonah before He determined to overturn Nineveh. And thus God also sent Christ, His Son, into the world before the appearance of the final wrath at the Last Judgment. After Christ's death not only Jerusalem but also Rome and the whole Roman orbit and empire were shattered.

At present we are also enjoying this same mercy, and the bright light of God's Word is shining on us, which is unmistakable evidence of impending disaster. God wants to save a number of us before disaster strikes and destroys us if we do not improve. But sad to say, we are surely behaving badly, and the punishment has already set in to a large extent.[408]

As a precursor to God's wrath, God sends messengers of the word to serve as means of grace so that some might be converted to God. According to Luther, this was the pattern of the Bible and of human history itself. Human disobedience across time also showed that faith in God's word and God's power to save was not something that people heed well; it is often despised and rejected. Published as it was in 1526, "the punishment" that Luther identified as already having begun included the bloody rebellions and social upheaval of the Peasants War.

As mentioned above, Bugenhagen added "Father Luther" and all faithful preachers to this list of divine messengers. Having summarized Luther's arguments about Jonah's call to preach, Bugenhagen could have moved on to another verse. But since he was working under the locus that "God calls and sends ministers of the gospel, as we see Jonah sent to prophesy,"[409] Bugenhagen expanded his discussion to comment on the office of ministry.

> Observe that there is a twofold call in God's church. One is directly from God and not from people (Gal. 1[:1]). This is the calling of the apostles and prophets like Adam, Noah, and Abraham, who were not called by people or by the church but were placed through the Holy Spirit and they established the church through the word of God, [to stand] even against the gates of hell [Matt. 16:18]…
>
> The other calling is also from God but is mediated by people or the church, which has from the bridegroom Christ

the keys to loose and to bind, like a wife in the home. It can commend and transmit the public ministry of the church through people who have been properly examined to be bishops and preachers, just as Paul prescribed to Timothy and Titus. This call or election is publicly confirmed by elders in the church with public prayer and the imposition of hands, and – as it written – they also commend the ordinand to the church that he will serve.

1. The call or election shows that the person ordained as a public servant of Christ in the church has been examined.

2. The imposition of hands signifies that they present him to God for public ministry, so that in the future he should serve God in the gospel of the son, and not they themselves (Rom. 1[:1-6]), just as the priests of the law were prepared by the imposition of hands in the law.

3. The one praying asks God through those present that Christ give the ordinand the Holy Spirit for this ministry, so that it might bear much fruit to the glory of God and the salvation of many...

... Christ instituted and gave his church true ministers, first immediately, then through humans – apostles and the church – so that they might preach the gospel and administer the sacraments of Christ and forgive sinners all their sins in Jesus' name, saying "Go into all the world and proclaim the good news to the whole creation. The one who is believes and is baptized will be saved; but the one who does not believe will be condemned" [Mark 16:15-16]. "Receive the Holy Spirit. If you forgive the sins of any, they are forgiven them; if you retain the sins of any, they are retained" [John 20:22-23]. "'So that you may know that the son of man has authority on earth to forgive sins'... And they glorified God, who had given such authority to human beings" [Matt. 9:6-8].

This is enough on vocation. [410]

As general superintendent of the churches in and around Wittenberg, Bugenhagen had been responsible for ordaining countless candidates for ministry over the years. While it might appear as if Bugenhagen let the episcopal side of his work interfere with the professorial side through this tangent on church organization, his conclusion (*hactenus de vocatione*: "this is enough on vocation") reminds the audience that this discussion of Christian ministry took place as part of his first locus on Jonah: God calls and sends servants of the word.

This longer treatment of vocation shows a significant difference between Luther and Bugenhagen's lectures on Jonah without implying that Bugenhagen was showing "extra-Lutheran" originality. This was not a digression or accidental segue into a new theme. Instead, Bugenhagen applied the locus on ministry as seen in Jonah to a practice of the church. In this way, he was using the Bible to teach the biblical origins and ongoing relevance of contemporary practices. This methodological difference between the commentaries of Luther and Bugenhagen provides a good example of the loci method's value for addressing both the scriptural text and its application to daily life.

Because these comments on Jonah 1 come early in the lectures, they were likely prepared and delivered before the Wittenberg theologians learned of the Augsburg Interim. For this reason, Bugenhagen talked here about the traditional "laying on of hands" at ordination without a sense that it was controversial. The Augsburg Interim, however, would soon require the laying on of hands by an ordaining bishop as a guarantee of unbroken apostolic succession.[411] Later in the commentary, therefore, Bugenhagen revisited this point, making sure to identify it as a free act and an external sign, not as a guarantee of God's approval or a necessary condition for valid ministry. Many pages (and probably many months) later, Bugenhagen wrote in the tracts,

> All Christians receive the Holy Spirit in Christian baptism without the laying on of hands because there we are reborn through water and the Holy Spirit, as Christ says. We are baptized according to the institution and words of Christ, but it is Christ who baptizes with the Holy Spirit, as John the Baptist says. This Spirit is renewed in us and is forever renewed in us through the preaching of Christ's gospel, that the Son of God who was made the victim for us, Christ alone, is our righteousness and salvation before God and not our works done according to God's law, let alone the works, religiosity and superstitious worship of human traditions…

"Anyone who does not have the Spirit of Christ does not belong to him" (Rom. 8[:9]). Therefore to identify the laying on of hands with the illumination of the living spirit, as Tertullian dares to say,[412] is blasphemy and impiety...

These prayers of the apostles [Philip and Peter, in Acts 8 and 10] were not in vain without the laying on of hands, I say, because the prayer of faith has the promise of God attached to it with a sure certainty. For [Christ] says, "Truly, truly, I tell you, anything you ask the father, praying in my name, it will be done for you" [John 14:13]. But the laying on of hands does not have such a promise from God, no matter what Tertullian and the Montanists attach to it with the illumination of the living spirit."[413]

In this passage from the Jonah Commentary's last tract, Bugenhagen qualified his initial comments about ordination. Confronted with the Augsburg Interim's requirement that the laying on of hands be the way "by which those who are consecrated to the offices of the church receive the grace by which they become fit, suitable, and capable," Bugenhagen nuanced his earlier stated position to emphasize faith, baptism, preaching and prayer.

This shows how Luther's teaching informed but did not limit Bugenhagen's comments on Jonah; it also shows how Bugenhagen's commentary adapted over time to address the challenges of the Augsburg Interim. By emphasizing the "prayer of faith" as the efficacious liturgical action in ordination, Bugenhagen could take the *ex opere operato* element out of the rite. His position mirrored the response of the Wittenberg theologians to the Augsburg Interim from their first critiques[414] to the later document written in Altcella.[415] In these documents, the Lutherans did not reject the laying on of hands (a practice they had freely retained) but emphasized instead the role of faith and God's Spirit. Bugenhagen's loci method allowed him to teach Lutheran theology and ecclesiology within a work of biblical interpretation.

Luther and Bugenhagen against the Louvain Theologians

Just as Bugenhagen expanded upon Luther's teaching about ministry and would improve upon Jonah 4 in a manner consistent with Luther's later reflections, so he also picked up Luther's last refutations of papal supremacy. Luther and Bugenhagen identified the papacy with "spiritualistic" Christian movements both past and present, especially the ancient heretical movement known as Montanism. The Montanists had been a sect among early Christians that claimed direct revelation from the Holy Spirit.[416] Already in the 1520s Luther equated the Montanists with any group claiming a revelation of the Spirit that went beyond the Bible. He did this, for instance, in his lectures on 1 John, in which he accused Protestant and Catholic opponents of appealing to revelation beyond the Bible.[417] In a section of the Smalcald Articles added in 1538, Luther explicitly accused the papacy of "enthusiasm" or "spiritualism" because of the many rules or practices that had little or no scriptural basis.[418] Bugenhagen's frequent use of "Montanism" in the Jonah Commentary already had a firm place as a standard Lutheran epithet for denouncing practices not found in the Bible.

One of Bugenhagen's "Montanist" targets was the theology faculty of the University of Louvain, who had written against the Lutheran doctrine of justification in 1545. Because the Council of Trent and the Augsburg Interim used similar language to the Louvain Theologians' "Thirty-Two Articles," his condemnation of them also served as a critique of both Trent and the Interim. By deriding the Louvain theologians and referring to Montanism, Bugenhagen could veil his critiques of the Interim, which banned the publication of dissenting opinions. This was a real threat, as Melanchthon had nearly been declared *persona non grata* in Electoral Saxony twice in 1548 for his early statements against the Interim.[419] But while it was illegal to write against the Augsburg Interim, there was no such law against condemning Montanists or the theological faculty of the University of Louvain.

Bugenhagen's references to the Louvain Theologians also show how well he knew Luther's teaching and methods. Bugenhagen's *Jonah* mirrors much of Luther's outline in "Against the Thirty-Two Articles of the Louvain Theologians," published in the fall of 1545. Luther's first nine articles against Louvain are helpful guides in interpreting the direction that Bugenhagen's *Jonah* took against the Augsburg Interim. Luther had written:

> 1. Whatever is taught in the church of God without the Word is a godless lie.
>
> 2. If it is declared an article of faith, it is a godless heresy.

3. Whoever believes it is an idolater and worships the devil instead of God.

4. St. Paul's declaration that the doctrines of men reject the truth stands [Titus 1:14].

5. That there are seven sacraments the heretical and idolatrous men assert without the [authority of the] Word.

6. Baptism, a sacrament for the remission of sins and eternal salvation, is to be administered to adults as well as to children.

7. In spite of this, the doctrine of the synagogue of those at Louvain regarding baptism must be condemned as heretical.

8. We condemn as heretical the spirit of the Anabaptists which condemns true baptism on account of the faults and unworthiness of men.

9. For thus one may also condemn government (yes, also the ministry of the Word) on account of sin or the unworthiness of the person. But that is seditious.[420]

Luther moved from the word of God to human teachings, corruption of the sacraments, and political chaos. His strong condemnation of the Louvain theologians' doctrine of baptism came not from their own words (which are innocuous enough)[421] but from the rejection of justification by faith alone, which he believed implicitly undermined the unconditional promise of salvation given in baptism.[422] Luther's view of sedition also appears in these opening articles, where he wrote that poor political – and even ecclesiastical – leadership is not an excuse for rebellion. As in the Augsburg Confession's pairing of Romans 13:1 with Acts 5:29, such obedience must not come at the expense of faith or serve to justify tyranny. Charles V had approved the "Thirty-Two Articles" as official imperial policy on March 14, 1545. Therefore, Luther did not attack Charles or the law, but chided "false flatterers" in order to make a strong but indirect critique of imperial policy. He also reminded the emperor that rulers are not be in the business of writing doctrinal statements. Among Luther's last articles appear the following:

72. How shamefully and to eternal ruin they disgrace the most glorious name of Emperor Charles, the prince of so

many people, and his time, when they pretend that he confirmed their so sacrilegious and satanic monstrosities.

73. It is not the business of kings and princes to confirm even the true doctrine, but to be subject to it and to serve it, as it is said in Psalm 2[:10], "Now therefore, O Kings, be wise; be warned, O rulers of the earth."[423]

Luther showed pragmatic (if not terribly subtle) discretion in minimizing the emperor's role in approving the "Thirty-Two Articles." Nevertheless, when juxtaposing his article 9 and article 73, one meets a political theology similar to what Melanchthon and Bugenhagen attempted to do under the Augsburg Interim. First, they rejected sedition, as Bugenhagen did in his dedication letter to King Christian. Second, they did not allow deference to authority to justify passivity or tyranny. Instead, like Luther indirectly criticizing an imperial declaration while prodding Charles to remember his real obligations as ruler, the Wittenberg theologians forged a path between sedition and capitulation. They aimed for a principled resistance, which they considered to be consistent with Luther and the Bible. Where political authorities overstepped their bounds, theologians had the right and duty to object.

As scholar Gerhard Lohfink showed in his article "Kommentar als Gattung (Commentary as Genre)," the insertion of contemporary events and theological issues into Christian biblical interpretation has been in practice at least since Hyppolitus of Rome's Daniel Commentary around the year 200.[424] By referring to the Montanist heresy and the Louvain theologians to condemn the theology of the Augsburg Interim, Bugenhagen was following a long tradition. In the lectures on Jonah, Luther had spoken of the need to return to the Bible to counteract the "raving" of princes, papacy, and peasants. Luther also condemned the Louvain Theologians in his late lectures on Genesis, beginning with Genesis 48:21. Since Luther started lecturing on Genesis 45 in January 1545,[425] it is likely that he started to condemn the Louvain Theologians in his lectures as soon as the "Thirty-Two Articles" came to his attention that spring. His first mention of "the asses in Louvain" appeared in comments on Genesis 48, where he cited Jacob's deathbed promise to Joseph to affirm certainty of faith.

> This is solid and firm consolation. In it alone the godly can find rest. Therefore the devil perpetually assails it. Thus

recently the asses in Louvain had the audacity to defend
purgatory by publishing articles under the seal of Emperor
Charles by which they betray their stupidity and madness
and openly declare that God has increased their blindness a
hundredfold, since they try to extinguish the light of that
promise which God, in His wonderful goodness and mercy,
has again kindled in our churches.[426]

Inserting contemporary controversy into biblical commentary was not new or unusual. Luther himself had recently employed this element of biblical commentary. Bugenhagen's mention of Montanism, Louvain Theologians, and current controversies within his Jonah Commentary therefore was in line with Luther's biblical commentaries and his political strategy.

A Report of Luther's Reformation Breakthrough

Having examined the personal and working relationship shared between Luther and Bugenhagen, this chapter now investigates a report of Luther's original Reformation breakthrough that Bugenhagen included in his *Jonah*. This account adds unique details to Luther's own descriptions from the 1545 preface to the Latin Works and the Table Talk.[427] The imprecision of those sources has led to scholarly disputes about the moment and nature of Luther's so-called "breakthrough." Attempts to date the breakthrough have ranged from 1512 to 1518.[428] Bugenhagen's account appears to support an earlier dating, while also suggesting that Luther's breakthrough included a process of gradual certainty about his insights into the gospel throughout the 1510s.[429] Because Bugenhagen himself does not seem interested in identifying a single moment at which this breakthrough took place, the word "development" better describes the increasing clarity with which Luther came to his conviction that God justifies the ungodly through faith in Christ. This analysis uses the words "breakthrough" and "development" interchangeably.

Bugenhagen's account of Luther's breakthrough appears in the third tract, entitled "Montanus the Blasphemer." In this section of the Jonah Commentary, Bugenhagen accused the church in Rome of the ancient heresy of Montanism, consistent with Luther's previous usage. To contrast Rome's claims of spiritual revelation through the papacy, Bugenhagen reported that Luther's theology had always been grounded in scripture. At the same time, Bugenhagen showed that Luther's insights about justification were supported by time-tested church writers like Jerome, Augustine and Peter Lombard. Thus, according to Bugenhagen, Luther's breakthrough came from both his engagement with scripture and the witness of respected church writers. It therefore provided a contrast from the "Montanist" spiritualism that the reformers rejected. After all, had the reformers' faith been invented by Luther, they would themselves have been guilty of Montanism.

Within the commentary, the report allowed Bugenhagen to teach the Lutheran doctrine of justification by faith alone over against his contemporary opponents. It might have also shored up Bugenhagen's credentials as an insider within the Lutheran reformation. Finally, Bugenhagen's positive invocation of early and medieval church writers uniquely emphasizes Luther as a reformer within Christ's one church.

> Father Luther often told me in the presence of many others: "I used to be amazed at Paul's argument for the justification of the ungodly [Rom. 4:5] and to rejoice in Scripture when I read the exceptional consolation of the Holy Spirit and God's promises of grace in Christ, but I did not understand it because I was a most righteous monk, being confident in my works and merits, in monastic vows, and my rules and observances; I ran after papal indulgences; and the mass was for me the highest righteousness and holiness and a sacrifice for the sins of the living and the dead in the pope's purgatory. I invoked the saints, whose merits and intercessions I could acquire with fervent fasting and sacrifice. For I made them my mediators, to placate the wrath of God for the forgiveness of my sins. Now I know this to be true idolatry against the first commandment; but at that time through such things we imagined ourselves to be true worshipers of the true God while we condemned as heretics those who even murmured anything to the contrary.
>
> "And therefore this phrase, 'the righteousness of God,' in the Epistle to the Romans [1:17, *et al.*], which Paul wrote to us as a highest consolation against our righteousness (which we always seek in ourselves and which we cannot find unless we Pharisees are blinded) was poison to me, and I abhorred it and reluctantly sang from the Psalms: 'In

your righteousness, deliver me, O Lord' [Ps. 31:1, 71:2]. For I understood, as did all those who were under the pope, that what was called the righteousness of God was nothing other than certain judgment and the wrath of God against my sins, that is, the righteousness of the law.

"I did not know that through the preaching and the Holy Scripture of Christ's church there was a twofold judgment of God, one of the law and another of the gospel, and likewise a twofold righteousness of God, one of the law and another of the gospel. In the world the judgment and righteousness of the law is known, but it is not performed; but – as the prophets announced – David's son, our Lord Jesus Christ, would bring about the judgment and righteousness of God through the gospel when he was upon the earth, as in Jeremiah 23[:5]: 'He will make judgment and righteousness on the earth, etc.' This I did not know, just as to this day all the papists are ignorant, because they hate the gospel of the righteousness of God, which is Christ in us through faith.

"And I impatiently put up with what Jerome rendered in the Psalm [24:5]: 'he receives blessing from the Lord and righteousness from the God of his salvation,' as it says in the Latin. The Greek has '*Eleemosynam*: 'and mercy from the God of his salvation.' I did not know that these [mercy and righteousness] were the same and that therefore Jerome's translation was correct. But then I read in Augustine: 'the righteousness of God, that is through faith in Christ, which God imputes to us unworthy people and so justifies the ungodly freely through grace,' as it says in Book IV of *De Trinitate*, which is also quoted in the *Sentences* of the Master [Lombard], Book III, distinction 35: 'It is said that the righteousness of God is not only that by which he [God] is righteous, but also that which he gives humans when he justifies the ungodly.'

"And I found in Paul, Romans 3 etc., that Augustine also had gotten this from Paul's words. Thus the door was first opened to me and I entered into all Holy Scriptures and the gospel of Christ, by understanding this phrase alone: the righteousness of God. For my righteousness perished by knowing the righteousness of God in Christ Jesus our

Lord, of which Peter spoke in Acts 10[:43]: 'To this all the prophets bear witness, that all who believe in him receive forgiveness of sins through his name.'"

In this and similar ways, Father Luther often spoke to us.[430]

Bugenhagen began and ended this account with the assurance that it was received from Luther's mouth in the presence of others. His report certainly shares a similar style with Luther's own reminiscences, especially descriptions of how the scriptural phrase *iustitia Dei* (the righteousness of God) troubled him until it became a gate to a new and heavenly understanding. The peculiar way of speaking in the first person singular as Luther's *ipsissima verba* and the fact that Bugenhagen follows Luther's narrative style may indicate that this account came from reliable notes on conversations with Luther or from Bugenhagen's personal reminiscences. Despite these stylistic similarities, significant historical factors still need to be considered.

One might criticize this account as a historical source because it appears over thirty years after the time it describes, raising questions about the reliability of such a distant memory. A first response to such an observation comes in recognizing the public nature of Bugenhagen's *Jonah* and the controversies with other Lutherans that had arisen during the years he was writing it. At the time, Nicholas von Amsdorf was among those leveling charges of unfaithfulness against the Wittenberg theologians. Unlike Bugenhagen and Melanchthon, Amsdorf had been at the University of Wittenberg since its founding in 1502; he became a professor of theology in 1511 and was among Luther's first supporters. It was therefore in Bugenhagen's best interest to present Luther's breakthrough as accurately as possible. Although this is an "argument from silence," Amsdorf and others did not criticize Bugenhagen on this point in their writings against Bugenhagen and the Wittenbergers after 1550.

Second, there is the question of whether Luther's own memory of his earliest insights was reliable. If not, then even a precise transcription would not guarantee historical accuracy. Volker Leppin, for instance, has argued that Luther's recollections about struggling with *iustitia Dei* were shaped by later controversies with Rome over that subject; that problem might not have been present from the first moments, as Luther would later describe it.[431] Indeed, the first Table Talk to mention the "breakthrough" and its relationship to *iustitia dei* is dated 1533.[432] Leppin posed this question in order to attend more closely to the earliest sources. His greatest evidence for Luther's emphasis on *iustitia Dei* coming at later time is the absence of that phrase in a May 30, 1518 letter to Staupitz. In that letter, Luther described Staupitz' teaching about *poenitentia* (not *iustitia dei*) to be the key for his new understanding of the gospel.[433] Leppin argues that because this letter is closer to the time it describes, it is therefore more trustworthy; its failure to mention *iustitia Dei* indicates that this was not a major concept in Luther's early thought. Given his general skepticism about a historical breakthrough moment, Leppin's study of *poenitentia* in the 1518 letter advances his preference for a gradual development in Luther, dismantling what he considers to be a later idealized story.

A first way to address this challenge to the priority of *iustitia Dei* comes by recognizing that Luther's letter to Staupitz served as the introduction to the "Explanations of the Ninety-Five Theses." In such a context, the emphasis on *poenitentia* is not surprising and indeed to be expected. Rhetorically, Luther's public description of his personal journey would provide a sympathetic point of entry for readers, who could then connect Luther's theological and pastoral insights with the disputed practice of indulgences. The letter also reveals how Luther viewed the indulgence controversy as one small part of a larger theological problem. By no means did Luther suggest that he had never considered problematic points of doctrine or worship until Tetzel started preaching too close to Wittenberg. On the contrary, this letter and the following explanation of the 95 Theses reveal that Luther had already mastered the theological vocabulary he would use in the controversies to come. If anything, the focus on *poenitentia* in the 1518 letter to Staupitz shows how carefully Luther chose his words to reach his audience and to teach them the best way to interpret the otherwise relatively narrow issue of indulgences.

This first observation about rhetorical context is supplemented by another point which notes the long-standing interrelation between key Reformation concepts like *iustitia Dei*, *poenitentia*, and *fides*. Rather than imagining a series of theological challenges that Luther hurdled in succession, textual evidence suggests that these concepts belonged together; Luther's view of God's righteousness both shaped and was shaped by his experience with the penitential system. This argument for a fairly well-developed theology in the early Luther is made possible by attending to the specifics of Bugenhagen's account, especially the quotations from Augustine and Peter Lombard.

Bugenhagen's citations of Augustine and Lombard contain some errors. Yet these may actually support the claim that this presentation was received orally from Luther and not invented or dramatically altered by Bugenhagen. Had Bugenhagen wanted, he surely could have taken exact quotations from the books he cited. Instead, slight inaccuracies remain. For example, *De Trinitate* Book IV refers to Romans 4:5 ("God, who justifies the ungodly") as Bugenhagen mentioned. However, the sentence that matches the line cited in Lombard comes from *De Trinitate* Book XIV: " ...just as it is said about God's righteousness: it is not only that by which God is himself righteous but also that which God gives to a person when he justifies the ungodly."[434] The common theme is that God's righteousness justifies sinners. But even in the more direct citation, Bugenhagen (or Luther himself) embellished the text with evangelical phrases such as "through faith in Christ," "God imputes to us," and "freely through grace" that are not in Lombard or Augustine.

Not only do these inconsistencies potentially support Bugenhagen's reception of this account, but they also point to the heart of Luther's early theology. Both passages from Augustine explain the centrality of God's righteousness in justifying sinners. Though this similarity makes the difference between the *De Trinitate* quotations (Books IV and XIV) appear negligible, the two quotes are different enough to stand as two sources for Luther's theological development. *De Trinitate* Book IV reads, "For the soul is resuscitated through repentance, and in this mortal body the renewal of life is begun by faith that believes in him who justifies the ungodly."[435] This short passage contains three words that became central to Luther's theology: *poenitentia, fides,* and *iustificatio* (repentance, faith, and justification). In this citation, Augustine connected God's justification of sinners, the faith of the believer, and the renewal of a person's soul through repentance. Within this framework, it is unlikely that Luther's focus on *poenitentia* in the letter to Staupitz came at the exclusion of other theological concepts. Rather, it suggests that Luther chose *poenitentia* in that 1518 letter as the best way to introduce new readers to his wider thought, in which key gospel concepts already hung closely together.

Finally, in terms of personal history, the two books that Bugenhagen cited were books that Luther had encountered as early as 1509. Luther read Augustine's *De Trinitate* and Lombard's *Sentences* as he prepared for his doctor of theology degree. The ninth volume of the Weimar Edition of Luther's Works contains the notes (*Randbemerkungen*) that Luther made in the margins of those books. They include a comment that Luther made on the title page of his monastery's copy of Augustine's works: "Saint Augustine died in the year of our Lord 433. It is now 1509. He died 1076 years ago."[436] To be sure, finding a "Lutheran" Luther in these *Randbemerkungen* and other early sources has proven impossible for scholars. For this study, however, the critical historical question is whether *iustitia Dei* could have been present in Luther's earliest thought, rather than being imposed later by a more established Luther or Lutheranism. Based on the texts cited by Bugenhagen, this is definitely possible.

Though Luther and Bugenhagen's reports came decades later, there is evidence that *iustitia Dei* was on Luther's mind as he studied for his doctorate. Commenting on Augustine's treatment of John 5:26 in *De Trinitate*, Luther noted, "For [Christ] himself is our life, our righteousness, and our resurrection through faith in his incarnation."[437] Here Luther connected Christian righteousness with faith in the risen Christ. While this quote by no means presumes a fully developed evangelical theology in Luther, it reveals that "the youngest Luther" (as the historian Heiko Oberman put it)[438] was thinking about justification by faith early in his academic career. These gradually developing insights could then grow into firm beliefs, from which no amount of pressure or controversy would shake Luther in the following years.

By pointing to Luther's early readings in Augustine and Lombard, Bugenhagen's account presents a new source in Luther research, in which Luther may have been coming to his gospel breakthroughs about *iustitia Dei* and justification by faith already as a doctoral student and a young teacher. It suggests that Luther, uncertain about the meaning of *iustitia Dei* as encountered in books like Romans and the Psalms, studied the Bible and the tradition with that specific problem in mind. Looking for resolution, Luther discovered that God's righteousness is the righteousness with which God justifies the ungodly, an external righteousness received only by faith in Christ. He made this discovery not through his own reasoning but by noticing it in authoritative texts of his day, namely, in the works of Augustine and Peter Lombard. In short, Bugenhagen's account presents a Luther steeped in the traditions of Western Christendom.

This is not to say that Augustine was more important than Paul in Luther's early thought. Rather, these questions seem to have struck Luther through his daily monastic life, as Bugenhagen reported him saying, "I reluctantly sang from the Psalms: 'In your righteousness, deliver me, O Lord' [Ps. 31:1, 71:2]." In this way, Luther's theological struggles had a liturgical and devotional base. From this small piece of information, we meet a Luther who took his personal prayer life seriously and nurtured it through his theological studies.

A survey of Luther's first lectures on the Psalms (1513-15) and Romans (1515-16) supports Bugenhagen's claim that Luther's insight about the twofold righteousness of God was at the heart of Luther's theology early in his career, while leaving room for ongoing refinement in his thought. Psalm 71:2, for instance, was one of the verses that Bugenhagen cited in this account. In his first lectures on that verse, Luther wrote, "whoever does not hope in God who justifies the ungodly cannot be delivered in God's righteousness or be rescued."[439] Although he was using techniques gleaned from medieval methods of biblical interpretation and borrowing language from Augustine's *De Spiritu et Litera* to do so, Luther proceeded to distinguish between law and gospel in that place.[440] He did that in order to contrast human righteousness with God's righteousness, which is seen in the cross and which alone brings salvation through faith.[441] Built on Augustine, his interpretation is not far from the established tradition. But the interest in justification and the citation of Romans 4:5 in Luther's early exposition of Psalm 71 is remarkable and supports Bugenhagen's account.

By the 1515/16 Lectures on Romans, Luther was citing Augustine's passage about God's twofold righteousness regularly, although he usually cited *De Spiritu et Litera* rather than *De Trinitate*. For instance, commenting on Romans 1:17, he wrote,

> In human teachings the righteousness of man is revealed and taught, that is, who is and becomes righteous before himself and before other people and how this takes place.

Only in the Gospel is the righteousness of God revealed (that is, who is and becomes righteous before God and how this takes place) by faith alone, by which the Word of God is believed, as it is written in the last chapter of Mark (16:16): "He who believes and is baptized will be saved; but he who does not believe will be condemned." For the righteousness of God is the cause of salvation. And here again, by the righteousness of God we must not understand the righteousness by which He is righteous in Himself but the righteousness by which we are made righteous by God. This happens through faith in the Gospel.[442]

Several elements of Bugenhagen's account are present here, including a quotation from Augustine, the distinction between divine and human righteousness, the unique revelation of the gospel, and the reception of God's righteousness through faith alone. Again, without insisting on a fully developed theology in the "youngest Luther" or assuming a single moment of heavenly inspiration, one finds striking similarities between Bugenhagen's account and Luther's earliest writings, lending support to an earlier dating of Luther's gospel breakthrough than is often granted. Important for this study, the account clearly demonstrates Bugenhagen's exemplary understanding of Luther's teaching.

A final piece of evidence for Bugenhagen as a reliable witness is found in a 1542 Table Talk, in which Luther and Bugenhagen each shared their earliest insights about the gospel. It puts them in the same room at the same time, talking about their respective breakthroughs, which supports Bugenhagen's claim that Luther had told him this "in the presence of many others." One version of this report shows that students were asking about Luther's first insights about the gospel, as it begins with the heading: "Which locus first moved the Doctor?"[443]

[Luther:] "I was in error under the papacy for a long time, not knowing how badly I was stuck. I sniffed at something but did not know what it was until I came to the line in Romans 1[:17]: 'The one who is righteous lives by faith.' That helped me; I saw which righteousness Paul was talking about, because earlier in the verse also stood *iustitia*, righteousness.

"When I rhymed the abstract and the concrete together – righteousness and being made righteous – and became certain of this, I learned to distinguish between the righteousness of the law and the righteousness of the gospel. Nothing was lacking for me before, except that I had made no distinction between law and gospel, thinking it was all the same and saying that there was no difference between Christ and Moses except for time and perfection. But when I found the right distinction – namely, that the law was one thing and the gospel another – then I broke through."

Then Dr. Pomeranus said, "I also started to come to a different opinion when I read about the love of God, which is meant passively. That is, it means the love with which we are loved by God. Before this, I understood love to be active, so that we love God." Dr. Luther said, "Yes, it is clear about love, that often in the Scriptures it means that love with which God loves us. But in Hebrew the genitive cases having to do with love are difficult." Pomeranus said, "But of course they are clarified later by other passages."[444]

Once again, "Lutheran" themes like law and gospel, righteousness, and faith are all found together in a single account of the breakthrough, making it difficult to speculate whether one concept alone came first. However, because Romans 1:16-17 itself contains the words "gospel," "salvation," "faith," and "righteousness," this abundance of theological vocabulary could be as much due to Paul's original juxtaposition of these concepts as to Luther or Bugenhagen's selective memories.

As a final word of caution, the most suspicious part of Bugenhagen's account comes in the closing reference to Acts 10:43. This particular passage is much more characteristic of Bugenhagen's *Jonah* than Luther's reminiscences. Luther did not mention Acts 10:43 in any of the Table Talks about his earliest insights, nor did he refer to it in his 1545 Preface to the Latin Writings. It is, on the contrary, ubiquitous in the second half of Bugenhagen's Jonah Commentary as a text that connects Jonah's preaching in Nineveh with the forgiveness that comes through faith in Christ. As a transitional point in the text, however, this verse might have helped Bugenhagen reconnect his account of Luther's breakthrough with the larger argument about faith and repentance.

Bugenhagen's account of Luther's breakthrough has resulted here in a search of other sources like Luther's early lectures and writings, the Table Talk, and the works of Augustine and Lombard. Taken together, they show the thorough grasp Bugenhagen had of Luther's theology, its key themes, and his ability to teach these themes to others. By invoking Luther, Bugenhagen not only bolstered his own credentials among his audience but also taught them the biblical and historical roots of Lutheran theology. This report also shows the continuity of Lutheran thinking with late medieval Catholicism. Here we meet a Luther steeped in monastic prayer and the classical writings of the Latin Church, who combined attention to the Bible and the Christian tradition with personal experience of the gospel. Bugenhagen's account shows Luther engaging the Bible and emerging with an understanding of the Christian faith that was grounded in the tradition, yet ground-breaking for his day and beyond.

This chapter has examined elements of Luther's life and work that Bugenhagen valued most. Luther's early writings had inspired Bugenhagen to leave a secure and prominent position in order to move to Wittenberg and enroll in the university. Within a few years, Bugenhagen's life was further changed when he got married, was elected pastor of the City Church, and became a leader in Wittenberg's reformation movement. Bugenhagen's funeral sermon for Luther emphasized him as a sinner in need of grace rather than as a divine figure. That sermon was no rambling or romantic panegyric but a clear articulation of the gospel that Luther spent his life teaching. It applied Christian comfort and hope to the grief and uncertainty of the community. He and his colleagues would remember Luther as a father in the faith and they would mourn his death even as they continued to preach the same life-giving gospel.

This chapter's focus on Jonah's call to preach has also shown how easily Bugenhagen referred to Luther's earlier writings, while remaining free to expand upon them or take the argument in a different direction. In this, Bugenhagen revealed his self-confidence as a theologian and church leader who could present his own ideas of what was most beneficial for his audience rather than simply parrot Luther's words. In the same vein, Bugenhagen's account of Luther's gospel breakthrough in Luther's own words also reveal how well Bugenhagen knew and could articulate key Lutheran teachings. In Bugenhagen, we find an excellent public interpreter not just of Lutheran theology but of Martin Luther himself.

CHAPTER FIVE

Repentance and Justification

The majority of Bugenhagen's commentary on Jonah 3 consists of four long theological tracts. Based in the story of Nineveh's repentance, they teach justification by faith and its implications for Christian doctrine and worship. While the tracts are rich sources for learning how Bugenhagen connected biblical interpretation with daily life, they also present the greatest obstacle for understanding the Jonah Commentary. Why are they here? What do they have to do with Jonah? These next two chapters will show that the tracts on Jonah 3 are neither digressions nor overzealous "polemics" but are central to the commentary's overall message.

The first tract contrasts the repentance of Nineveh in Jonah 3 with worship practices that the Lutherans had worked to reform. It juxtaposes two verses – Jonah 3:5 ("The people of Nineveh believed God") and 3:10 ("God saw their works") – to shore up biblical support for the Lutheran teaching of justification. After this, the second tract takes this biblical argument to an examination of justification by faith alone across Christian history. It also includes a comparison of St. Paul's letters and the Epistle of James, which Bugenhagen interpreted through Paul, Jerome, Melanchthon and others. When the Jonah Commentary was published in 1550, these first two tracts would have especially defended Bugenhagen's teaching to Lutheran critics.

With the third tract, Bugenhagen began an interpretation of church history that sets the apostolic faith of the New Testament against various heretical movements of early Christianity, especially Montanism. As far afield as this section may seem to wander from Jonah 3, it is directly grounded in the work of the previous tracts: from the Ninevites' repentance and their free justification by faith alone, Bugenhagen turned to the application of that doctrine in the worship life of the early church. The fourth tract is the commentary's single longest section. It elaborates on previous themes by using the examples of Tertullian, Cyprian, and others to show that even the most highly esteemed writers of the early Latin Church were fallible and could lead the church into error. Taken together, these tracts on Jonah 3 reveal Bugenhagen's deep engagement with the history of biblical interpretation, church history and Christian worship. They stand as his last major statement about faith and practice, while offering a valuable historical summary of first generation Lutheran theology.

Otto Vogt's Essay on the "Jonascommentar"

In his 1887 study, which was the only detailed examination of the commentary until this one, Bugenhagen researcher Otto Vogt catalogued many of the *Jonah*'s themes and outlined its content and its logic. Vogt was also able to physically locate the church history books that Bugenhagen used in preparing these tracts. For instance, he found books that contained marginal notations from Bugenhagen's hand and he identified a 1539 edition of Tertullian's works prepared by the humanist scholar Beatus Rhenanus as the source for major portions of Bugenhagen's knowledge.[445] In this, Vogt established that Bugenhagen had built his historical and liturgical arguments on firm and academically responsible historical foundations.

This study remains indebted to these insights from Vogt's work, while trying to present a more holistic view of the tracts. Vogt, for example, took it for granted that the commentary addressed the controversies of 1548 and 1549, but rarely provided evidence for that claim. He believed that the emphasis on certainty of faith revealed Bugenhagen's protests against the Council of Trent and the Augsburg Interim. He deduced that because the theologians' meeting at Pegau (July 1548) had not definitively addressed this topic, it must have been a live topic at the time of Bugenhagen's lectures on Jonah.[446] Vogt also noted that Bugenhagen's emphasis on the proper liturgical use of anointing with oil constituted his response to another point left unresolved after the Altcella meeting of November 1548.[447] Based on the historical and compositional analysis of the commentary given in chapters two and three of this work, Vogt's assessment appears to be correct.

Further evidence for Vogt's correct chronology arises in his observations about the "Johannine Comma," a disputed passage from 1 John 5:7-8.[448] While Bugenhagen's discussion of that passage fits thematically with the sacramental theology discussed in the third tract, it also provides outside help in dating the commentary's composition and points to another outside influence on the Jonah lectures. In a 1985 article on Luther and Bugenhagen's views of the Johannine Comma, Franz Posset noted that a new edition of the New Testament, which included the disputed lines, was being printed in Wittenberg in 1549.[449] Because Bugenhagen had been in Wittenberg during the plague of 1527 when Luther lectured on 1 John and because those lectures had yet not been published, Posset reasoned that Bugenhagen had unique firsthand knowledge about Luther's rejection of the passage and therefore protested its inclusion while he was lecturing on Jonah.[450] Although Posset did not provide the month in which this new edition appeared, the episode supports Vogt's contention that Bugenhagen was composing the commentary and delivering his lectures into 1549.[451]

Bugenhagen's rejection of the Johannine Comma in his *Jonah* is one reason that the work as a whole may have fallen into obscurity. According to Vogt, in 1734 a Lutheran Orthodox theologian named Jäncke wrote that Bugenhagen's emphatic position against the Johannine Comma likely made the book unpopular in its own time, because many Lutherans had come to accept the passage as genuine.[452] While Vogt believed that Bugenhagen's relationship to Melanchthon was the more general reason for the commentary's relative neglect,[453] Jäncke's insight points to a broader theme important for this study: Lutherans were already fighting over the best interpretation of Martin Luther. While it was common knowledge that Luther's 1522 translation of the New Testament followed Erasmus' original decision to leave the disputed verse out, later Lutherans thought that Luther had re-inserted it later in his life.[454] For his part, Melanchthon cited the verse favorably in his 1535 *Loci Communes* and was followed by influential theologians like Flacius and Martin Chemnitz.[455]

Despite later Lutheranism's acceptance of 1 John 5:6-8 as authentic, Posset sided with Bugenhagen. His article rejected the notion that Luther ever included the Johannine Comma; Richard Muller, a historian of biblical interpretation, has agreed. In his study of this verse, Muller identified Johann Agricola, not Luther, as the source of the Johannine Comma's reappearance in Lutheran Bibles.[456] On this topic, Bugenhagen's *Jonah* presents today's readers with a lost aspect of Luther's teaching.

Because Vogt's essay focused on Bugenhagen's condemnation of Roman Catholic theology, he sometimes described Bugenhagen's *Jonah* as too polemical. In one place he called it a "handbook of polemics against the Catholic Church."[457] However, Vogt concluded the article with a broader and more generous assessment.

> It also shows how Bugenhagen engaged the controversial pamphlet wars of his day, namely, those among the Evangelicals themselves. In a manner consistent with his fundamental style, he presented a sober and positively constructive work, while also not avoiding controversy by introducing some cozy and undisturbed pastoral still life. The work is always directed to distinct main points; above all, it reveals the firm foundation of Evangelical conviction for listeners in the lecture hall and in the church. He did this by remaining bound to the doctrines regarded as inviolable by Protestants of the time. For his part, he showed an honest zeal for nurturing the still-weak understanding of the gradual historical development of God's revelation from the Old Testament into the New Testament and beyond. He made his tireless work and penetrating examination for the sake of preserving the church's teaching office and giving it a solid scholarly basis. In this, he followed where Melanchthon, and before him Erasmus, had led the way![458]

In German, this is one enthusiastic sentence, in which Vogt described the great interplay between biblical interpretation, Lutheran doctrine, engagement with controversy, and love of Christ's church that arises in this commentary. More than simply a "handbook of polemics," the tracts in the Jonah Commentary functioned in the classroom and in print as a primer on theology, history, and the relationship between faith and action. Although this study cannot guarantee Vogt's final level of excitement, Bugenhagen's tracts on Jonah 3 certainly offer unique insights into the religious life of the mid-sixteenth century.

The Transition from Commentary to Tracts

Despite the shift from textual commentary to theological tracts, the first tract on Jonah 3 follows the comments on Jonah 2 fairly smoothly. One reason for this natural transition is that Bugenhagen was already using the loci method, so that he could add extended commentary on theological themes that arose in the text. An earlier example of this in Jonah 1 was the discussion of vocation, which Bugenhagen included in his exegesis of Jonah's initial call to preach. In Jonah 2, Bugenhagen continued this approach, presenting Jonah's prayer from the belly of the great fish as a song of thanksgiving for God's liberation and as an exercise in confession and forgiveness, law and gospel. This method had also given Bugenhagen the freedom to connect the Smalcaldic War with the prophet's experience of just punishment for sin and gracious liberation.[459] He put these words into Jonah's mouth as the main point of the prayer of Jonah 2: "Chiefly, I will acknowledge this grace and your benefits: that you have restored me from death and I will live to give thanks all my life."[460] The sinful prophet was redeemed from death by God's mercy alone. Jonah served as a sign of Christ's death and resurrection and as a comfort for all troubled believers, including those in Wittenberg.

While the commentary had already made several clear statements against the papacy in its opening pages, Bugenhagen made his first mention of the Louvain Theologians' ninth article against certainty of faith when he commented on Jonah 2:8: "Those who worship vain idols forsake their true loyalty." A section heading appears in the margins at that point, entitled: "Exposition of the first commandment."[461] Lutherans had long taught that faith alone fulfills the first commandment,[462] so that the ensuing discussion of the first commandment introduced a contrast between Lutheran faith and Louvainian doubt. From this point onward, Bugenhagen commented on Jonah 2 mostly to refute his theological adversaries.

> They believe and trust in empty things, in their own works of satisfaction for sins and merits for eternal life, which are vanities of vanities [Eccl. 1:2] and idolatrous worship, which they vigorously perform and devise for salvation. But to Christ, to whom alone this honor has been given (for there is no other name given to humans by which we can be saved [Acts 4:12]), they do not bestow the least honor, and they even forbid – as you see clearly in article nine of the Louvain theologians – that Christ be honored by believing that we have forgiveness of sins and eternal life on account of Christ. Of them, Christ speaks from the prophet Isaiah [29:13], "they worship me in vain, teaching human doctrines and commands" (Matt. 15[:9]). It is against the first

commandment, "You shall have no other God" [Ex. 20:3].[463]

With this passage, Bugenhagen began the argument that dominates the tracts on Jonah 3, in which justification by faith triumphs over the doubts about salvation and reliance upon human works encouraged by the Louvain theologians and the Council of Trent.

This "article nine" became Bugenhagen's shorthand criticism of the Augsburg Interim, which likely appeared around the time he was commenting on this verse. Promulgated in May 1548, the Interim contains a passage nearly identical to the statement of the Louvain theologians: "Because of their own infirmity or indisposition people cannot believe without doubt that their sins are remitted."[464] And, for the first time in the commentary, the surrounding pages show Bugenhagen calling for a strong confession of faith and clear rejection of papal errors.

> Therefore in this psalm [Jonah 2] or this thanksgiving, Jonah later remembered the good deeds of God the liberator. He also recognizes that this thanksgiving and confession of faith extends to us, so that we condemn error, human doctrines and commands, contrived worship, and the false religion of hypocritical liars [1 Tim. 4:2]. They even teach the lie about the righteousness of their works. And they have trampled on the conscience, always doubting and never believing or being certain of their salvation. In their anguish, they cannot call upon God by faith, because they have defected from faith to demonic lies, though in this they all have the appearance of saints (1 Tim. 4[:1]).
>
> This is against those know-it-alls today, who say that the gospel should indeed be preached, but without condemning abuses and papistic errors, and instead tolerating them in order to serve the peace, for according to them it says in Hosea 4[:4], "Let no one scold, let no one protest." And Micah 2[:6-7], "They say one should not speak of such fallings, for such falls will not touch us; we will not be confounded; is this the way the house of Jacob should be consoled? Do you think the Spirit of God cut off? Are these his doings?" etc. But Micah [2:10-11] adds, "they will be devastated because of their grievous uncleanness. If a

Repentance and Justification • 139

preacher should be an empty spirit and tell lies, saying 'I will preach of drinking and gluttony,' such a prophet would be fit this people." Micah speaks truly against this in chapter 3[:7-9], "The seers shall be confused, and the diviners put to shame; they shall all cover their lips, for there will be no word of God. But I am full of strength and the Spirit of the Lord, with justice and might, that I dare to announce to Jacob his transgressions and to Israel his sin. Hear this, you rulers of the house of Jacob and princes of the house of Israel, who despise justice and pervert that which is right," etc. And St. Paul in Galatians 1[:10], "Do I now preach to humans and am I captive to human favor or to God? If I was pleasing people, then I would not be serving Christ."

Together with these authors, Jonah here condemns a defection from God's word. He says, "Whoever trusts in empty things makes void the grace that God promises from eternity through the gospel of Jesus Christ for all people." God revealed this soon after the Fall through the word: "The seed of the woman shall crush the serpent's head" [Gen. 3:15]. Such people relinquish the grace and favor of God, accepting instead empty things and vanity of vanities. With these they will never have a good conscience before God but be afraid and insecure under God's wrath for eternity. [465]

This extended call for a confession of faith and condemnation of error came quickly on the heels of the commentary's first mention of the Louvain theologians. Also, the critique against "know-it-alls" (*sapientuli*) who thought it best not to confront the papacy suggests that Bugenhagen had specific people in mind who were using Bible verses to justify a wrong-headed appeasement (probably Johann Agricola). Bugenhagen rejected this option, referring to more verses from Micah to counter others apparently cited favorably by his opponents. His references to Micah 3 and Galatians 1 show his desire to take a stand based upon biblical promises.

The transitions surrounding the tracts on Jonah 3 help address questions of chronology. First, the verse-by-verse commentary of Jonah 1 and 2 concluded with Bugenhagen referring his audience one last time to Luther's lectures on Jonah for topics that he would not address. "For other things that pertain to this song [Jonah 2], read the comments by Father Luther."[466] Having recently introduced themes like certainty of salvation, confession of faith, and right worship of God that were not precisely in his introductory loci, Bugenhagen proceeded to develop Jonah 3 with new purpose. Just as the end of Jonah 2 helps introduce the tracts, their conclusion reveals that Bugenhagen had undertaken these themes as a way to address new controversies on the basis of Jonah 3.

Hundreds of pages later, the tracts conclude with a more traditional verse-by-verse commentary, which Bugenhagen entitled a *repetitio*. The *repetitio* begins:

> We spoke at the beginning of chapter three about true repentance, which Christ commended to us through the people of Nineveh, preferring the Ninevites' repentance to those unrepentant and hypocritical Pharisees and Jews, who do not acknowledge his righteousness before God. We have also refuted the false repentance of our works, works of satisfaction for sin, and merits for eternal life, through which the gospel of the Son of God has been obscured.[467]

In the *repetitio*, Bugenhagen stated that his summary of Jonah 3 should still be understood in light of the tracts' previous arguments.

Chronologically, Bugenhagen probably composed the tracts as his next step in his lectures once he came to the end of Jonah 2. He could have conceivably written the tracts after making relatively brief comments on Jonah 3 and 4, adding the transitional sections later, but there is little evidence of that. In either case, it is clear that the tracts arose out of the need to address the Augsburg Interim, which probably came to Bugenhagen's attention around the time he was finishing his commentary on Jonah 2. As a whole, the tracts on Jonah 3 demonstrate Bugenhagen's freedom and skill as a biblical interpreter to let his Jonah lectures serve as the occasion for teaching Lutheran theology and worship in the face of serious challenges.

Faith and Good Works: The Tract on True Repentance

Bugenhagen first refuted the Louvain theologians' teaching against certainty of faith at the end of his comments on Jonah 2. In the first tract on Jonah 3, he advanced this argument by focusing on Jonah's preaching and Nineveh's repentance. As a way to identify and refute false repentance, the tract's heading mentioned the early Christian heretic Montanus. This was the first mention of Montanism within the commentary's main body.

> A tract on true repentance from the sacred writings, against the false and hypocritical repentance of the papacy, which is from the human traditions that St. Paul calls the doctrines of demons and the hypocrisy of liars, etc. [1 Tim. 4:1-2], and which began after the apostles by Montanus and the Montanists under the name of the Paraclete and institution of the new spirit, whom today they call "spirituals" who have followed after this.[468]

Here Bugenhagen introduced Montanus and his teaching about the new spirit, a theme that would come to dominate Bugenhagen's ensuing interpretation of church history. He also tied Montanus directly with the papacy and spiritualism of his own day, grounding this critique in the "doctrines of demons" predicted in 1 Timothy 4. This interpretation of Montanism and the papacy then served as the basis of how the Bible and Christian history would inform his debates with contemporary opponents.

The opening page of this tract also includes the first citation of Acts 10:43. This passage served as the foundation for Bugenhagen's interpretation of Jonah as a preacher of Christian faith rather than a preacher of works or doubt.

> In this chapter the earnest repentance of the Ninevites is described. Fearing God's judgment, which is all that Jonah preached without any immediate promises, they believed in God and converted from their evil ways, pursuing God's mercy and the forgiveness of sins. In this same way and based upon the sacred writings, we teach that repentance in Christ's church is contrition for sin and faith in Christ, with a new, obedient life through the Holy Spirit, who is given to us in Christ Jesus, all of which you see here in the people of Nineveh.
>
> The papists teach another repentance – without faith in Christ, without the Spirit, without God's promises – based entirely on contrition, auricular confession, and satisfaction. That is, they teach that it is entirely our works, without Christ, just as the Louvain theologians teach in article nine. Such a faith is condemned in the Scriptures, which says that whoever firmly believes their sins are forgiven has eternal life on account of Christ. Woe to you impudent liars and blasphemers who are against the Lord and against his

Christ! Full of the Holy Spirit in the house of Cornelius, Peter condemns you, saying in Acts 10[:43], "All the prophets testify about him that everyone who believes in him receives forgiveness of sins through his name." You ask how the Ninevites could believe in God and truly repent when they had not heard promises of grace from Jonah? I will speak of this later.[469]

This is Bugenhagen's manifesto for the tracts: he insists that the preaching and repentance of Jonah 3 exemplifies Christian faith and practice. Through Acts 10:43, Bugenhagen would present the prophet Jonah as a preacher of grace: "*all* the prophets testify" to this forgiveness through faith in Christ. With this text, Bugenhagen then applied his discussion of Jonah to his theological and liturgical analysis of repentance (*poenitentia*) in worship and Christian living.

First, Bugenhagen wanted to show that Nineveh's salvation was based on faith. To do this, he reminded his audience that Jonah 3:5 comes before Jonah 3:10. After hearing Jonah preach, Jonah 3:5 reports that "the people of Nineveh believed God." Preaching led to faith. At the end of the chapter, Jonah 3:10 then says, "When God saw what they did, how they turned from their evil ways, God changed his mind about the calamity that he had said he would bring upon them; and he did not do it." Faith came before Nineveh's fasting and before God's recognition of their works. Although the text says that God decided not to destroy Nineveh after seeing their works, Bugenhagen was quick to point out that faith came first and was the origin of the good works of repentance that followed.

Luther had made this same observation in his 1525 lectures on Jonah.[470] It is therefore natural that Bugenhagen picked up on it. Strangely, though, this focus is absent from Bugenhagen's opening loci. There the doctrine of justification appeared in Jonah's prayer from the belly of the great fish, more in accord with Jesus' identification with the sign of Jonah in Matthew 12. However, the Augsburg Interim's threat against justification by faith alone likely inspired Bugenhagen's to turn to Jonah 3:5 with a new intensity. In the *repetitio* of Jonah 3 that follows the tracts, Bugenhagen once again stressed the importance of these verses by printing the words in capital letters: "And the people of Nineveh believed in God."[471]

Following Bugenhagen's typical method of interpretation, we find here three main supports for faith alone. The first is Jonah 3:5, in which Jonah preached and Nineveh believed God, placing their hope in God's mercy alone. Second, because Christ commended Nineveh's repentance in Matthew 12:41, their repentance exemplifies a Christian life of faith that includes sorrow for sin. Third, Peter's speech in Acts 10 affirmed Jonah as a preacher of Christian forgiveness, for according to Peter "all the prophets" – Jonah included – preached forgiveness of sins through faith in Christ. Confronted with powerful political and theological opponents, Bugenhagen asserted that Jonah's preaching and Nineveh's repentance provided biblical evidence for what the Lutherans were teaching. Whatever twists, turns, and apparent digressions Bugenhagen's tracts may take, these three biblical passages (Jonah 3:5, Matthew 12:41, and Acts 10:43) provide the bedrock for everything that follows.

To move his theological convictions into the realm of worship and personal piety, Bugenhagen also cited the parable of the Pharisee and the tax collector from Luke 18:9-14. This passage had appeared earlier in the commentary as a way to contrast spiritual pride with godly humility,[472] but it eventually grew into a refrain by which to compare true and false repentance. Due to its importance, Luke 18:9-14 is cited here in its entirety.

> [Jesus] also told this parable to some who trusted in themselves that they were righteous and regarded others with contempt: "Two men went up to the temple to pray, one a Pharisee and the other a tax collector. The Pharisee, standing by himself, was praying thus, 'God, I thank you that I am not like other people: thieves, rogues, adulterers, or even like this tax collector. I fast twice a week; I give a tenth of all my income.' But the tax collector, standing far off, would not even look up to heaven, but was beating his breast and saying, 'God, be merciful to me, a sinner!' I tell you, this man went down to his home justified rather than the other; for all who exalt themselves will be humbled, but all who humble themselves will be exalted."

Many of the themes of Bugenhagen's *Jonah* appear in this parable, including fasting, good works, and justification. It therefore came to serve as shorthand for all of Bugenhagen's critiques.

For instance, when speaking against "the sophists" of his own time, Bugenhagen equated a proud or self-satisfied repentance with the Pharisee of Luke 18.

> Christ already condemns this idolatry in the Pharisees, who trusted entirely in themselves for righteousness (which is unbelief, impiety, and idolatry against the first table of the law) and who reject others (which is against love of neighbor and the second table of the law, so how can they be justified?). They dared to speak of this faith in their works and merits before God, "I thank you that I am not like other people – the unjust, adulterers, thieves – and also not like this tax collector. And I give you a tenth of all that I have, that is, I fulfill the law exactly. For this, I am in a state of perfection and do works of supererogation," just as the monks say today, "I perform everything in the law and more than is commanded to me. For I fast twice on the Sabbath." But this is a work that is not owed but comes from human traditions, in the guise of religion, as false worship of God for all who trust in it, from the doctrines of demons and not from the Word of God. But Christ clearly pronounces the sentence of condemnation there against them, "I say to you, this tax collector went to his home justified before this Pharisee."[473]

For Bugenhagen, this parable showed how the apparent fulfillment of the law can actually violate the commandments to love God alone and to love neighbors. Whenever good works are not based on faith in God's mercy, they earn God's condemnation as signs of pride. Equating the Pharisees of the New Testament with practices prevalent in his day, Bugenhagen applied the parable to the difference between monastic good works and the Lutheran teaching of God's free justification of the ungodly.

Bugenhagen also showed his devotion to the Augsburg Confession from the beginning of this tract. First, he repeated his seventh locus: there are two parts to repentance, namely, contrition and faith. This is the definition given in the 1528 *Instructions for the Visitors of Parish Pastors in Electoral Saxony*[474] and in the Augsburg Confession, article 12.[475] Second, he talked about good works as part of the "new obedient life through the Spirit." This was consistent with the Augsburg Confession's article 6, which says that "faith is bound to yield good fruits and that it ought to do good works commanded by God on account of God's will and not so that we may trust in these works to merit justification before God."[476] Third, when people perform the good works that come from faith, Bugenhagen followed the Augsburg Confession's use of Luke 17:10 to remind believers that their response should be: "We are worthless slaves; we have only done what we ought to have done."[477] Here is evidence of Bugenhagen's assertion to King Christian of Denmark that he had not deviated "by one finger" from the Augsburg Confession or from Luther's teachings.

Although the relationship between faith and good works would become the basis for another intra-Lutheran controversy in the early 1550s, there was no hint of confusion or controversy in the *Jonah*'s teaching on the subject. In fact, Bugenhagen's entire career was marked by the clear and consistent explanation of how good works fit in a life of faith. We recall the full title of the 1526 letter to Hamburg: *On Christian Faith and True Good Works, against False Faith and Fictitious Good Works; Furthermore, How One Should Establish Things through Good Preachers, So That Such Faith and Works Are Preached.*[478] The right distinction between faith and good works was not only the center of the tracts on Jonah 3 but had long been one of Bugenhagen's points of emphasis as a teacher and pastor.

In fact, the Letter to Hamburg itself uses Jonah 3 and Luke 18 to discuss repentance and good works. Discussing the kind of spiritual fasting and sorrow that manifests itself by wearing sackcloth and ashes, Bugenhagen had written,

> This example [of mourning for sin] is called a death and a hell in the Scriptures, as we see in Psalm 6[:5] and in many other places. In such a death or hell the godless despair, but the faithful will be helped out. But while they are in such a state, they perform certain works that in other settings would be empty or worthless, even foolish, but which God reckons as good for faith's sake, as when the tax collector or public sinner beats his breast [Luke 18:13]. The same is true when the Ninevites put on sackcloth (that is, meager clothing) in which they wore their sorrow [Jonah 3:5-8]. So they sat in ashes, not just the people but the horses, cows, sheep and other domesticated animals too, and they would not let anyone eat or drink. They had to wrap

themselves in the sackcloth and cry out from their hunger with loud voices to the Lord.

That is definitely a ridiculous mockery, but for the sake of faith – that they believed the prophet Jonah's sermon – God saw their foolish works as good, which he would not have seen in the godless no matter how more exquisite they might have been (as we have proven sufficiently already from the Scriptures). But concerning their works it is written in Jonah 3[:5], "Then the people of Nineveh believed in God, and let it be announced that there should be a fast (that is, no one should eat anything, as the text says) and put on sackcloth, both great and small." When our hypocrites do such external works, they think that it counts just as much. But there is none of the seriousness with them as there was with the Ninevites.[479]

Without faith, wearing pitiful clothing, sitting in ashes, and forcing animals to fast are ridiculous things to do. But because they were done with contrite hearts, God saw the good works of repentance in Nineveh as external signs of inner faith.

In the Jonah Commentary, too, Bugenhagen reminded his audience that God knows people's inner hearts and does not need external works to know whether a person is contrite and faithful. "God saw true repentance and sincere conversion in the hearts of the Ninevites and he heard their cries and invocations of faith: 'For the people of Nineveh believed in God.' As Jeremiah 5[:3] says, 'O Lord, do your eyes not look for truth?' and Acts 15[:9], 'He has made no distinction between them and us, cleansing their hearts by faith.'"[480] This is identical to Luther's comments in the 1525 Latin lectures on Jonah that God, who knows human hearts, saw the Ninevites' works as external signs of an internal faith.[481] It is a sign of his strong theology that Bugenhagen could make relevant points in the late 1540s that resonated with his earlier writings.

Bugenhagen had also mentioned Jonah 3 in his 1535 church order for Pomerania. In that order's article on fasting, he first praised fasting as a good practice before warning that it easily leads to hypocrisy and self-righteousness. For this reason, his order forbade pastors from commanding fasts as they had done before. But Bugenhagen continued,

Nevertheless, in special situations it is very good to admonish the people to fast, so that we call on God with universal and special need, as the people of Nineveh did; for then we do it for the sake of prayer, so that our prayer is a prayer of faith and might not be hindered by a heart weighed down by gluttony and drunkenness [Luke 21:34].[482]

Made holy by faith, Nineveh's fasting was a sign of their repentance and conversion to God. It also encouraged the sober watchfulness that Jesus spoke of in the New Testament. With this discussion of faith, fasting and good works, this first tract on Jonah 3 picks up themes that were consistent with Luther's reading of Jonah, the teachings of the Augsburg Confession, and Bugenhagen's earlier works.

The positive use of fasting also entered the Jonah Commentary in this first tract. This time, rather than speaking of the recent war and the surrender of Wittenberg as he had before, Bugenhagen spoke of other ongoing troubles, to which fasting and public repentance remained appropriate responses. "Therefore, today we who are also in distress and public calamity may call all the people together to repentance, so that with fasting and sorrow they may be humbled before God, crying aloud and asking for pardon and liberation. This is our custom, that is, we are in the habit of making lamentation, just as Joel called the people (Joel 2[:15-32])."[483] Though he had not identified the "public calamity" specifically, the reference to a dramatic passage like Joel 2 (which includes the verse, "Why should it be said among the peoples, 'Where is their God?'") demonstrates a heartfelt and pressing need to address ongoing struggles in Wittenberg. At the same time, Bugenhagen noted that Joel did *not* say that fasts make satisfaction for sin in themselves; instead, those who turn to the Lord with fasting, prayer, and repentance remember that they are saved by God's mercy alone.[484]

Jonah's Sermon to Nineveh

The people of Nineveh believed in God and were delivered from destruction. But how did they come to know and believe in a merciful God? On this point, Bugenhagen differed from both Jerome and Luther. With his allegorical method, Jerome had answered this question by equating Jonah's emergence from the fish with Christ's resurrection from the dead: in this way, the resurrected Christ had personally preached to Nineveh.[485] Having heard a sermon from Christ himself, Nineveh learned the gospel and repented. Luther, avoiding Jerome's allegories, nevertheless agreed that the sermon given in Nineveh had consisted of more than only the few words that Jonah 3:4 reports: "Forty days and Nineveh shall be destroyed!" Luther explained, "When [Jonah] preached, he used his own passages to prove that God's wrath was coming against the people of Nineveh. He explained to them that God had sent him, and he set forth and declared to them their sin and the cause of God's wrath, etc."[486] Luther believed that what the Bible mentions was only a summary of Jonah's larger sermon.[487] Also, both Jerome and Luther insisted that Nineveh was a "great city of God," based on the Hebrew and supporting scriptural passages.[488] Jerome cited John 1:3 as proof that God had built Nineveh through Christ ("all things were created through him"),[489] while Luther pointed to Genesis 10:11 and the Latin Vulgate, which said that Nineveh was founded by Noah's descendent Asshur.[490] As a "city of God," Nineveh was able to receive God's message in faith.

Though he agreed that Nineveh was a great city of God, Bugenhagen understood Jonah's sermon and its effect quite differently. He followed another line of interpretation about Nineveh that Luther had used in his lectures on Genesis. A descendant of Noah, Nimrod, had founded the ancient kingdom of Babel (Gen. 10:10). Luther supposed that Babel then become idolatrous, at which time Nimrod's cousin Asshur left Babylon to establish Nineveh. In his lectures on Genesis, Luther explained, "Nineveh is called a city of God because it had the true religion and was preserved by God on account of the good man Asshur, who, being intolerant of idolatry, abandoned ancient Babylon and migrated toward the northern regions, toward the Japhethites, and there gathered a little church."[491] From this line of reasoning, Luther went on to praise the Ninevites' faith.

> The Assyrian kingdom is given great praise in the Scriptures, not only on account of its civil administration but on account of its religion and because it believed the preaching of the one man Jonah, who had been sent to them. It had not only a king and monarch but also other classes, namely, princes, priests, etc. If they had been like our princes, cardinals, and bishops, they not only would have kept Jonah out but would

even have killed him. And the godly descendants of Shem, even though they had deteriorated, nevertheless received the Word and returned to the former way; and the Lord received them in mercy.[492]

With Luther's Genesis lectures likely in the background, Bugenhagen firmly stated that Nineveh had been founded by Noah's faithful descendants. Therefore, the people of Nineveh could believe Jonah's preaching on the basis of the original gospel promise that God gave to Adam and Eve: "the woman's offspring shall crush the serpent's head" (Gen. 3:15). Bugenhagen summarized Nineveh's astonishing response to Jonah's sermon by supposing that "the Ninevites had the gospel from Adam, Noah, and the patriarchs."[493]

Unlike Luther, though, Bugenhagen believed that Jonah had preached nothing but those few words of wrath.[494] Instead, when the Ninevites heard Jonah's words of judgment, they recalled the gospel that they had known since the time of their founding. "Now terrified, therefore, about God's judgment and condemnation to death through Jonah's preaching, they grabbed hold of the earnest preaching of their father [Asshur] about God's mercy. They believed in God, hoping that, already condemned by God's wrath, they might still pursue God's mercy."[495] Relying upon the promises of grace given to Adam and Noah, Bugenhagen then imagined that the people of Nineveh began to preach for themselves.

> Thereafter, as much as they greatly and rightly feared God's wrath, they did not then despair. Rather, through faith they grasped God's mercy, the promise of the woman's offspring from God, Abraham's seed, that is, Christ the Son of God, who alone was made to be the Father's sacrifice for us and who liberates us from the righteous condemnation of the law. It says, "They believed in God." They did not get this from Jonah's preaching, but all the way from the time of the patriarchs, from Adam and before the flood, as we said before.
>
> And you see this: the people of Nineveh who believed began preaching a much more gracious sermon to other Ninevites than the one Jonah had preached. For it was the preaching of repentance and the forgiveness of sins. They cried out and pleaded that God turn from the fury of his wrath, which Satan had brought upon them. Praying by

faith and hope that they would receive mercy, they preached the cooperation of fasting and putting to death of the old Adam, as Jesus says, "This kind [of demon] cannot be cast out except through fasting and prayer [Mark 9:29]."[496]

Several elements of Bugenhagen's theology are present here. First, preaching God's wrath through the law can bring healing to a troubled people when it leads to sorrow for sin (contrition) and a return to faith. Even so, the law never works by itself: the Ninevites themselves combined Jonah's wrathful message with the gracious promise to deliver people that God had first given Adam and Eve. Bugenhagen saw the twofold nature of God's word as law and gospel working together to bring salvation. The effects of faith, repentance and deliverance were signs that Nineveh had truly experienced godly preaching.

Nineveh received God's mercy through faith alone. Despite condemnation and guilt, the people did not despair but trusted themselves entirely to God's mercy. This effect of law and gospel is similar to Bugenhagen's insistence in Jonah 2 that people should not wallow in despair but learn to trust God even more during times of adversity. Finally, as he had done in the Pomeranian church order, Bugenhagen provided for a positive use of fasting and good works. Careful not to suggest that good works merit forgiveness of sins, he commended fasting and prayer as tools for fighting the devil, based on Jesus' words in Mark 9:29. This treatment of Jonah's preaching advanced Bugenhagen's broader arguments about the power of God's word to bring salvation, the role of faith in receiving justification and forgiveness, and the right understanding of good works.

After continuing to comment on the differences between true and false repentance, Bugenhagen himself summarized four points about Jonah 3, based on specific verses.

> First, "And the people of Nineveh believed in God" [3:5]. They did not trust in their own works.
>
> Second, "And all shall turn from their evil ways and from the violence that is in their hands" [3:8]. They eagerly grabbed hold of true repentance, not trusting in those works which are signs of repentance, sorrow, fear, and grief, and are not repentance themselves.
>
> Third, "Who knows?" [3:9] Horrified by the terrible works they had done, they doubted God's mercy, just as

our papists say about works of iniquity on top of everything else. They not only doubt, but they even teach doubt! That is very far from the Ninevites wanting to trust in their works, which had been idolatrous and merited condemnation rather than justification.

Fourth, the Ninevites who believed preached to others: "Who knows? No one among you knows God's mercy amid this wrath and terror. Therefore, against the law's terror and the preaching of the holy prophet Jonah, we preach this gospel to you so that God might be converted, repent, and turn away from the fury of his wrath and we might not perish so that you may even believe in God as we believe in God." Thus, Nineveh was saved by faith among those who could do nothing through their works except doubt and despair.[497]

This is as close as Bugenhagen ever came to verse-by-verse commentary on Jonah 3. And yet, the first tract's discussion of true and false repentance has clearly served as an interpretation of that chapter. The four points retell in brief all that Bugenhagen had discussed up to that point. Further, the doubt expressed in Jonah 3:9 ("who knows?") was a doubt in their own abilities and merits rather than uncertainty about God's power to save. In the later *repetitio* of Jonah 3 that follows the tracts, Bugenhagen spent even more time explaining that point.[498] Here, however, Bugenhagen was satisfied to differentiate between the Ninevites' uncertainty and the uncertainty taught by the Augsburg Interim.

The first tract ends with a series of Bible verses that describe true repentance as humility before God. These examples include Christ's prayer in the garden of Gethsemane (Matt. 26:36-46), the parable of the Pharisee and the tax collector (Luke 18:9-14), King David's confession to Nathan (2 Sam. 11:13), the prophet Joel's pleading with his people (Joel 2), the call to trust God amid suffering (Lamentations 3), and God's promises to restore a ruined Jerusalem (Zechariah 8-9).[499] Bugenhagen's biblical references climaxed with a quotation of Isaiah 58:6, a passage in which the Lord denies any attempt to win favor through fasting: "But this is the fast that I choose: to untie those whom you have unjustly bound, to undo the thongs of the yoke, to let the oppressed go free, and to break every yoke."[500] Summarizing his first tract, Bugenhagen gave these Bible verses as examples of how humility brings true faith, forgiveness, deliverance, and love for others.

Justification by Faith Alone: The Tract on Human Traditions

The Jonah Commentary's second tract is entitled, "A true and certain history of human traditions against justification by faith, from the time of the apostles to us, which we recite here against false repentance."[501] The title thus bridges the discussion of repentance that preceded it and the history of religious traditions that will follow. The section opens with an impassioned case for justification by faith alone. "*Sola in Christum fide iustificamur coram Deo*" (we are justified before God by faith in Christ alone).[502] Even the word order in Latin points to a faith alone that has Christ at its center (*sola in Christum fide*). As these opening lines indicate, this tract defends the Lutheran teaching of justification by faith alone.

After briefly presenting the typical Lutheran teaching of justification, it addresses objections by commenting on the Epistle of James. In a passage frequently invoked against the Lutherans, that New Testament letter states, "You see that a person is justified by works and not by faith alone" (2:24). To present a Lutheran reading of that verse, Bugenhagen first called upon Ambrose and Augustine as right interpreters of faith and good works, asserting that their interpretations of Paul correct unhelpful interpretations of James. After citing these early Church writers, the tract leads readers through some of Melanchthon and Luther's writings, too. Finally, Bugenhagen began to move to his "true and certain history of human traditions" by showing how justification by works had clouded the church's proclamation of Christ from the earliest moments of its history, often through its worship life.

Of all the parts of the *Jonah*, this tract is the most theological. Far from being the disorganized diatribe that Otto Vogt's article suggested, this tract follows the formal rhetorical conventions of a *confutatio* (confutation), which "requires a person to break down the opponents' arguments."[503] On the heels of the previous positive statement about Nineveh's saving faith and consequent good works of repentance, Bugenhagen here anticipated criticisms of justification by faith alone by providing evidence from the Bible and the Christian tradition, tackling biblical verses that opponents had used to teach justification by love or good works.

As seen in following citation, Bugenhagen started this second tract by quoting St. Paul and preparing the way for a detailed defense of justification by faith alone. He also turned objections about the possible overuse of the Lutheran slogan *sola fide* into a sophisticated theological discussion of Christ's work as savior.

"We know that a person is not justified by works of the law" (much less by other works) "except through faith in Jesus Christ. And so we believe in Jesus Christ, so that we might be justified by faith in Christ and not by works of the law, because no one will be justified by works of the law of all flesh" [Gal 2:16].

The enemies of Christ, who have persecuted the gospel, ask where this *sola* was written, when we proclaim that we are justified by faith alone, which the whole world knows and which we understand and openly teach. By faith alone in Christ we are justified before God. They see this repeated often in Paul, "not by works of the law but by faith" [Gal. 2:16] and in Romans 3[:27-29], yet still these inept people do not see it: faith alone.

We do not simply say "faith, faith, faith, believe, believe, believe" as our adversaries say, thereby making false accusations against the genuine gospel of Christ. But we say with the entire Scripture: believe in Christ, [have] faith in Christ the Son of God, who in our flesh was made the sacrifice for our sins by the Father so that we might become the righteousness of God through him, etc. Just as Peter, full of the Holy Spirit in Cornelius' house, preached in Acts 10[:43]: "All the prophets testify about Christ that everyone who believes in him receives forgiveness of sins through his name."

Therefore, when we speak of faith alone, we speak of Christ alone, because Christ alone is our righteousness and eternal life before God, not works of the law, that is, good works, which God commanded to us in his law and which showed the Son of God to be obedient to God the Father. But they take this honor away from Christ, although the Father presents Christ to us in the gospel, him whom we cannot receive as ours except through faith alone. For only this way of receiving has been commanded in God's gospel. For you cannot receive or grasp this gift from the Father with your hands or feet or works or afflictions, much less through the capes or rules of monks or other human religious practices and traditions, or any other way whatsoever. But we grasp this entirely by faith alone, and it is our Lord Jesus Christ, the Son of God.

For Christ alone is grasped by us through faith alone and is for us the righteousness of God before God. "The righteousness of God is through faith in Jesus Christ in all and upon all who believe in him, etc." (Rom. 3[:22]). And in 1 Corinthians 1[:30-31]: "[Christ] became for us wisdom from God, as well as righteousness, sanctification, and redemption, so that [as it is written], 'Let the one who boasts, boast in the Lord.'" "There is no other name given to people by which we can be saved," (Acts 4[:12]). And Jeremiah 23[:6]: "And this will be the name that they shall call him" (that is, the name that shall be known and preached in the world, just as the Angel said to Mary, "the child to be born of you will be called the Son of God" [Luke 1:35]): "THE LORD IS OUR RIGHTEOUSNESS."

The "Lord Jehovah" is the name of Christ's nature, because he is true God. "Our righteousness" is the name of Christ's office in the church, for because of him we are righteous before God and are children of God. The first name – "eternal king at the right hand of the Father's glory" – is confessed by the papists together with us. But the second – "eternal priest" – they negate to such an extent that we are persecuted because of it. This is the hatred of Cain against Abel until the end of the world.[504]

This is an expert theological defense of "faith alone" by using biblical passages and theological reasoning. It anticipates objections and refutes them with other relevant verses. It even made it possible for Bugenhagen to characterize the difference between sixteenth-century Catholics and Lutherans as being about Christ's office as "our righteousness." Though the parties shared the same theology of Christ's divinity and humanity and used the same scriptures and ancient authorities, Lutherans had come to apply *solus Christus* in a unique way.

At the same time, Bugenhagen recognized that the Lutheran message could turn into a reductive and banal mantra: "faith, faith, faith; believe, believe, believe." He responded by pointing to faith not as a set of ideas but as actual trust in Jesus Christ. And he did not simply separate a merciful Christ from a wrathful Father.

Instead, his explanation of Jeremiah 23:6 identifies Jesus Christ with "the Lord Jehovah" in a way that only Trinitarian theology can: it sees God Almighty in the crucified Christ. While Luther had explained Jeremiah 23 in this same way in his Preface to the Old Testament,[505] Bugenhagen highlighted the effect of this Christological teaching. The passion with which he wrote stems from his belief that theology impacts real life: the content of theological doctrine (*quid sit*) always stands in relation to its real life results (*quid effectus*). The office, or activity, of the crucified Lord Christ is to change the world through faith.

Continuing to explain his Trinitarian theology, Bugenhagen attributed all preaching of this message to God the Holy Spirit. This appears in the passage above, for instance, when he emphasized the Holy Spirit's role in Peter's sermon to Cornelius. He knew that faith does not come from human striving or by simply repeating, "faith, faith faith, believe, believe, believe" as if it were a magic spell. Instead, faith is a work of the Holy Spirit: "It is not an easy thing to believe in Christ, but it is the Holy Spirit itself in us."[506] Later in the tract, Bugenhagen also used the phrase *per solum Spiritum sanctum* (through the Holy Spirit alone) to describe the Holy Spirit as the only source of a faith that is properly directed toward God.[507] Thus, the presence of the Holy Spirit among Christians cannot be a cause for boasting or self-righteousness but is another proof of God's grace, given freely and without respect to merit.

With its emphasis on works, the New Testament's Epistle of James presents one of the most direct challenges to justification by faith alone. James had also been invoked to support the sacrament of anointing (also called extreme unction) that Lutherans rejected. Therefore, Bugenhagen continued his discussion of justification by commenting on this letter. He asked, "Who then is this James, from whose epistle today's papists produce various meanings against the writings, teachings, and councils of the holy apostles, who were all assembled at that council of Jerusalem?"[508] Following the tradition that this St. James had been present at the Council of Jerusalem described in Acts 15, Bugenhagen wondered how James' epistle could contradict that first church council, where Peter declared that God had cleansed the gentiles through faith and that they too would be saved by grace. Similarly, Bugenhagen noted that James' teaching about Abraham's justification through works contradicts clear statements in Genesis 15:6, Romans 4:2-5, Galatians 3:6-9, and Hebrews 11:8-19.

Next, Bugenhagen cited Jerome and Eusebius of Caesaria to question the letter's status as an apostolic work. "Jerome wrote in the *Catalogue of Church Writings* that the esteemed Epistle of James was certainly planted by someone who wrote under his name;" the fourth-century Christian historian Eusebius also concluded that James was probably not authentic, even though many churches used it.[509] Bugenhagen's citation of Jerome and Eusebius followed Luther in reminding readers about questionable aspects of James, as the reformers argued against its emphasis on justification by works and its role as a proof text for the sacrament of anointing.[510]

But Bugenhagen did not simply deal with James by rejecting it. Instead, he re-interpreted it on the basis of justification by faith, as taught in other parts of the Bible. Like Luther and Melanchthon, Bugenhagen also found much good in this letter, despite its uncertain origins and apparent conflict with Pauline theology. For instance, Luther had written in a preface to James, "Though this epistle of St. James was rejected by the ancients, I praise it and consider it a good book, because it sets up no doctrines of men but vigorously promulgates the law of God."[511] Luther's lectures on Jonah also cited the Epistle of James favorably, especially the lines "mercy triumphs over judgment" (2:13) and "Elijah was a man with feelings like us" (5:17).[512] While Luther had used historical-critical tools to deny the letter's apostolicity, he did not deny edifying elements of the letter, even if he could not quite bring himself to call it "gospel." The Augsburg Confession likewise quoted James approvingly where it clarified the difference between faith as objective knowledge "which even the devils have" (James 2:19) and faith as trust in God's promises of forgiveness.[513]

Philip Melanchthon even found a positive use for James in Lutheran theology, in a roundabout way. In the Apology to the Augsburg Confession, Melanchthon called upon James to explain the Lutheran teaching of faith and good works. Comparing James with Romans 2, he wrote, "Therefore just as these words ('the doers of the law will be justified' [Romans 2:13]) are not against us, so we maintain the same thing with regard to James's words that 'a person is not justified by faith alone, but also by works' [James

2:24], because people who have faith and good works are certainly pronounced righteous."⁵¹⁴ Melanchthon reasoned that the Epistle of James assumes justification by faith. Just as Paul talked about good works in Romans in order to teach justification by faith alone, so James could be read as affirming the Lutheran position.

Like Luther, Bugenhagen doubted that James was written by the James of Acts 15, even as he defended its value as word of God. Like Melanchthon, he attempted to re-interpret the letter in light of other passages that teach justification by faith alone. In the following citation, he explained how James could be read within the larger scope of the Bible's teaching, which for the Lutheran reformers always meant justification by faith in Christ.

> You must know that on account of this letter we Christians cannot negate the entirety of the Holy Scriptures, which testify to Christ, that Christ alone is our righteousness before God, just as Peter said: "All the prophets bear witness," etc. [Acts 10:43] and as Christ's gospel was preached from Adam even to us, of the promised seed [Gen. 3:15]. And we speak with confidence that "even if an angel from heaven should preach another gospel, let that one be anathema" [Gal. 1:8]. "If Abraham was justified by works" (which could not mean ceremonial laws, because there were none at that time) "he has glory, but not with God. For what does the scripture truly say? 'Abraham believed God and it was imputed to him as righteousness,'" etc. [Rom. 4:2-3].
>
> We cannot negate Christ the eternal priest, that is, the propitiator and mediator, who sits at the right hand of the Father and intercedes for us. This honor, mediation and reconciliation, is given to the son of God, so that – just as we cannot give honor by our works – we cannot deny it even if a thousand such Epistles of James were produced against the Holy Scriptures of the prophets and apostles of truth, who say that Abraham was justified by faith, not works, according to obedience to God's commandments and to placate God. These are the two works of Abraham and all who believe, namely, first to believe and then to obey. Of this Christ speaks: "If you are children of Abraham, then do the works of Abraham" (John 8[:39]), that is, believe and obey; and "this is the work of God, that you believe in him who sent me" (John 6[:29]).

In this way, it is shown to humans that to obey is truly to believe, just as God said to Abraham after the sacrifice of his son: "Now I know that you fear God, because you have not withheld your only born son for my sake, that is, for the sake of my command, and you obeyed me. The offering is a sign showing your faith to all the world, so that you will be the father of many peoples, who will be children of Abraham, not by flesh but by faith, believing as Abraham believed" (Gen. 22[:12, 17, 18]).

[God said,] "I know," that is, "I cause to be known," just as Augustine rightly interpreted, "The tree is known by its fruit," just as James himself says clearly in his letter, "by people's works is hidden faith shown" [James 2:18b]. And we are accustomed to seize onto these words and rightly to interpret justification in James through the Holy Scriptures, as even the teachers of the church interpreted these words according to Scripture, not against Scripture, up to those places where he cited the Scripture concerning Abraham and Rahab [James 2:21-25]. There, all the teachers have deserted that fellow James for some kind of holy religion favoring the Scripture of the Holy Spirit.[515]

Rather than simply dismiss James, Bugenhagen interpreted it by means of other passages and thereby turned it into a word of encouragement for Christians. He did this first by contrasting James with Paul's teaching about Abraham's justifying faith in God. The two seemingly opposite views between Paul and James, however, began to come into harmony with Bugenhagen's observation that to believe is the same thing as to obey: faith and works rightly belong together. At the same time, he avoided the conclusion that good works are preconditions for justification by citing Augustine in order to remind readers that God already knows the human heart without seeing works. Expanding on God's comments about seeing Abraham's faith in Genesis 22, Augustine had explained that God's "seeing" affirms an already inner reality. By the end of ugenhagen's passage, then, James has confirmed the Augustinian idea that good works are the inevitable fruits of faith rather than conditions for salvation. He concluded that the Lutherans rightly subjected James's statements about works to scripture's wider understanding of justification in order to qualify James's interpretation of Abraham and Rahab, which earlier church writers had also rejected.

To build up James as a useful text, Bugenhagen walked his audience through other Lutheran works. First, he pointed readers to a publication by the humanist reformer Andreas Althamer on James.[516] He then developed Melanchthon's idea that the "analogy of faith" of Romans 12:6 gave reason to interpret one book through the witness of another, from which he showed that James not only assumed justification by faith but also taught the certainty of forgiveness opposed by Bugenhagen's Roman Catholic opponents.

> Already in early days we spoke and wrote a satisfactory interpretation of these words from Holy Scripture, which is neither disagreeable to the grounds of faith or against the honor of the mediator Jesus Christ. Althamer wrote on this Epistle in a learned and Christian manner. And with Christian effort, our Philip – knowing that prophecy ought to be [interpreted according to] the analogy of faith (Rom. 12) – satisfactorily tried to interpret these words about justification in James faithfully and according to God's word. Our discussions for and against this epistle [of James] are extant, from which a satisfactory interpretation of these words can be elicited.
>
> But what do we achieve among the papists? We have stirred up a hornet's nest. For from this epistle they simply negate what all Holy Scripture clearly claims: that Christ alone is our righteousness before God and not our works. They say (in the Louvain theologians' ninth article): "Faith by which one firmly believes and states with certainty [that one's sins are forgiven for Christ's sake and one will obtain eternal life has no support in Scriptures, indeed is opposed to them]." Yet they cannot deny Christ to Christians who have known the truth of the gospel, for even now Christ is destroying the Antichrist and will put an end to him by the brightness of his coming, as Paul said (2 Thess. 2[:8]).[517]

Beginning the passage by defending the Lutheran interpretation of James, Bugenhagen appealed to decades of theological work on this question, especially by Althamer, Melanchthon and the Lutheran reformers in general. Although he despaired of the effectiveness of reasoning with opponents, he remained convinced that the weight of biblical theology was on justification by faith alone rather than in human works of merit and uncertainty about forgiveness.

As in many places in the Jonah Commentary and other writings, the citation above identified the papacy with the biblical Antichrist. This accusation was not made lightly or indiscriminately. 2 Thessalonians 2 says that the "man of sin" will sit "in the temple of God." From this, the Lutheran reformers believed that the greatest temptations and adversaries would arise within the church itself. As the undisputed center of Western Christendom and as an institution perennially in need of reform, the papacy had long been an easy target of critique. More concretely, Lutherans in Germany were under direct military threat from the Roman Catholic emperor, his allies, and the pope. Still, it was not simply earthly power or even religious vice that earned the papacy the label of Antichrist from the Lutheran reformers. Instead, throughout the Jonah Commentary, Bugenhagen identified the Antichrist with the papacy specifically because of its resistance to the forgiveness of sins through faith. Because the Lutherans considered this doctrine to be the central insight of the Bible, the Christian tradition, and the living faith of the church, the Roman hierarchy's outright rejection of this teaching was the most significant basis for language about Antichrist.[518] The fact that the popes did indeed wield formidable power and used coercion throughout the era of the Reformation added real-life urgency to this theological debate.

From this theological objection against the papacy, Bugenhagen added a criticism against the hierarchy's right to institute new sacraments. On this issue, the Epistle of James again came into play. James 5:14 is one of two New Testament supports for the sacrament of extreme unction or anointing; the other is Mark 6:5. The Lutheran reformers did not count this as one of the sacraments because they believed it did not have Christ's command or promise in the gospels. This lack of biblical institution meant that its claim to provide divine grace for salvation was not trustworthy and could lead people into false confidence or unnecessary worry based on the ritual.

According to Bugenhagen, the Roman hierarchy not only used James to count extreme unction as a sacrament of the church but also to justify the institution of new rituals. Putting words into his opponents' mouths, he wrote,

> If James could institute the new sacrament of extreme unction, which was not instituted by Christ, then we bishops

are able to make and bless anointings that Christ did not institute. And [we are able] to teach or say that we can give the Holy Spirit and that we can bless other created things through the oil that we have blessed. We can even institute other things. We can establish new sacraments that Christ did not institute as new canons – that is, laws – and impose them on people to vex and injure the consciences that Christ has set free with his blood, etc.[519]

Here Bugenhagen confronted the hierarchy's view of its own authority. He challenged the logic which said that if James the Apostle had started a new sacrament, and if James' successors could rightfully follow his lead, then his spiritual heirs should have the same right to introduce or approve new practices.

While this may not entirely reflect the papal position, it was very close to the teaching of the Augsburg Interim, which stated, "it is also clear from the same Jerusalem Council that the church has the power of making canons for the benefit of the church, for all its power is for the edification of the church and not for its destruction."[520] Although the Interim invoked the Jerusalem Council of Acts 15 rather than the Epistle of James for this statement, we see the object of Bugenhagen's critique. For him, the Interim's "new canons" were euphemisms for the imposition of rituals that had usurped the more basic apostolic faith.[521]

Also evident in this excerpt from the Augsburg Interim is a difference on the doctrine of sin. The Augsburg Interim asserted that the institutional church serves only to build up Christian faith and not tear it down. Bugenhagen, however, insisted from the outset of his commentary that Jonah and other prophets and saints were also sinners: "The saints have gone to ruin" (locus 3). The institutional church and its leaders are able to hurt faith as well as help it. The warnings about the Antichrist further encouraged him to watch out for danger arising within the church. This danger was not limited to the papacy, but – as seen in the *Jonah*'s dedication letter – could come from any quarter, including other Lutherans. Bugenhagen disagreed that everything the church does is edifying; instead there is great capacity for sin in Christians and their institutions.

As a counterargument to the clerical prerogative to institute new canons, Bugenhagen turned again to the doctrine of ministry.

"They [the bishops] do not know this mandate of Christ: preach the gospel [Mark 16:15], and teach the people to obey everything that I have commanded you [Matt. 28:20]."[522] Above all, the apostles' first task had been to teach and preach Jesus' message, not to institute new spiritual rules or practices. Bugenhagen's decision to turn the debate over papal primacy into a discussion of ministry is similar to Luther's explanation of the office of bishop in the Smalcald Articles[523] and Melanchthon's position in the Treatise on the Power and Primacy of the Pope: "Christ gave to his apostles only spiritual authority, that is, the command to preach the gospel, to proclaim the forgiveness of sins, to administer the sacraments, and to excommunicate the ungodly without the use of physical force."[524] Having been present at the 1537 gatherings in Smalcald that had discussed and approved both of those documents, Bugenhagen was following a well traveled path.

After rejecting the right to institute new practices, Bugenhagen addressed the practice of anointing with oil even more directly. Luther had already written against extreme unction in *The Babylonian Captivity of the Church* with two main points. First, sacraments are instituted by Christ alone and not by apostles; second, the contemporary use of anointing did not resemble the practice as it had developed in the early church.[525] The influence of Luther's first critique is visible in the *Jonah* when Bugenhagen described the office of ministry as preaching and teaching, not instituting new sacraments or law. Luther's second objection also appeared in this tract, but in a more complicated way. In Luther's view, the anointing taught in James was for the physical healing of sick people: "Are any among you sick? They should call for the elders of the church and have them pray over them, anointing them with oil in the name of the Lord. The prayer of faith will save the sick and the Lord will raise them up; and anyone who has committed sins will be forgiven" (James 5:14-15). Luther believed that James' anointing referred to either the use of ancient medicine or to a unique rite for miracles in the early church.[526] Luther also noted that the promised physical healing and forgiveness are not attached to the anointing but to the prayer in Jesus' name. In contrast to these words about physical healing, the sacrament of extreme unction had come to be administered almost exclusively before death, so that Luther wryly observed that unction did the opposite of what it promised: confirming people in death rather than restoring them to life.[527]

Bugenhagen expanded Luther's critique by arguing that the real Christian sacrament of anointing is baptism.[528] For him, the Bible's language about holy anointing describes the coming of the Holy Spirit in baptism and not some other sacrament. He supported this assertion with a list of Bible verses about being anointed by the Holy Spirit, including Jesus' own claim to have been anointed by the Spirit of God in Luke 4:18.[529] At the end of the list of biblical passages, Bugenhagen appealed to Eusebius of Caesarea and told his audience, "Read the *Ecclesiastical History* by Eusebius concerning the anointing of Christ – book one, chapter one – and you will rejoice."[530] What did Eusebius write that made Bugenhagen rejoice? Introducing his Christian history with a description of Jesus Christ, Eusebius affirmed Christ's divinity and asserted that Christ's anointing was never one of human oil but one from the Spirit of God and the "divine oil of gladness."[531] As he had done in his discussion of James' authenticity, Bugenhagen invoked Eusebius as an early church authority who agreed that the anointing in James did not have its origins with Jesus.

Speaking of this anointing of the Spirit, Bugenhagen cited 1 John 2. In his citation of that passage, Bugenhagen interrupted the biblical text to provide his own parenthetical comments.

> 1 John 2[:20, 26-27]: "You have this anointing from him who is holy" (it does not say, by our apostles' false and deceptive oil of sanctification) "and you know all things. I do not write to you as if you are ignorant of the truth but because you do know it and you know that no lie is of the truth. I have written these things to you about those who would deceive you. For the anointing you received remains in you. And you do not have a need for anyone to teach you, rather the anointing itself teaches you about everything that is of the truth and is not a lie" (that is, the anointing is the Holy Spirit in Christians, who leads them into all truth through the word of God and the gospel of Christ, as Christ said [John 16:13]. All others are not of the truth but are lies from the teaching of demons) "and just as the anointing has taught you, abide in him, etc."[532]

In these asides, Bugenhagen called attention to the difference between the anointing of the Holy Spirit through Christ and the sacrament of extreme unction. In Bugenhagen's reading, John described the spiritual anointing given at baptism; other anointings or promises of the Spirit were "not of the truth" and led people away from the gospel of Christ. The naming of "our apostles' false and deceptive oil" was, of course, his critique against the misuse of anointing by the papacy and its potential reintroduction via the Augsburg Interim.

A further combination of biblical interpretation and contemporary controversy entered the tract when Bugenhagen, still arguing against this sacrament, recalled another proof-text sometimes used to support unction. This text had long been cited as Daniel 9:24, but was either a very strained reading of the text or an inauthentic interpolation.

> Many years before our time in the great and small schools, among learned and unlearned, there was this saying, as if from some prophet. It was repeated endlessly and widely known: "When the Saint of saints will come, he will stop your anointing." This was thrown at me in my youth in preaching and written in books of sermons and other books. I heard and learned this from unlearned teachers of youths; all knew about this along with me, who thirty years ago also paid attention to the writings of the papists.
>
> We inquired which of the prophets had said this against the Jews, as this saying was widely interpreted, but no one could show the place, because these words were not written in any prophet, or in the Hebrew text, or in any translation, or even in a Greek edition. But some said it was in Daniel, although nothing like this is written in Daniel 9[:24], "eternal righteousness will be brought up and vision and prophecy will be confirmed." These other words, however, are not read anywhere in Holy Scripture.
>
> But now in this age, through the preaching of Father Luther, this widely known prophecy began to be fulfilled. "When the saint of saints will come, he will stop your anointing" began also to be understood as that which began with the papists and their fathers, who said this as if it were from Daniel – I do not know from what oracle – as with Caiaphas' prophecy in John 11[:50], in which they being ignorant foretold the truth among themselves... The prophecy says to them, "your anointing – that is, human

anointing, a human tradition, and a human invention – is not God's anointing."533

Among other things, this passage provides one of the few instances in which Bugenhagen reflected on his life before the Reformation. Remembering an obscure prophecy that he had been taught as a student or a young teacher at least thirty years prior, Bugenhagen presented himself as an earnest and inquisitive student of the Bible and the tradition.

This citation, "when the saint of saints comes, he will stop your anointing" appears in medieval anti-Jewish writings by pseudo-Augustine and the scholastic theologian Duns Scotus.534 Luther also used this saying against the Jews in his 1538 tract "Against the Sabbatarians," although he identified it as extra-biblical rather than coming from Daniel 9.535 The context for both Scotus and Luther's citation of this text was, as Bugenhagen noted, the refutation of Judaism: the Jews supposedly lost their blessing with the coming of Christ, the saint of saints. Bugenhagen, however, turned it upon the papacy, asserting that they had spoken it against themselves in the same way that Caiaphas had prophesied correctly, albeit ignorantly, about Christ's saving death.536 For Bugenhagen, Father Luther's clarity of teaching about the gospel and the sacraments marked the end of the sacrament of anointing, a use of this apocryphal verse against Rome beyond what Luther had taught about it.

Ambrosiaster and Augustine on Faith Alone

Returning to justification, Bugenhagen turned again to early church writers to help defend *sola fide*, justification by faith alone. To this end, Bugenhagen frequently cited a Romans commentary which he attributed to St. Ambrose but whose author is now commonly called Ambrosiaster, a name first coined by Erasmus of Rotterdam.537 The other Latin writer most frequently invoked in this section is Augustine, bishop of Hippo in North Africa, who had written against Manichean, Donatist, and Pelagian opponents. As Bugenhagen's account of Luther's gospel breakthrough showed in the last chapter, Augustine deeply influenced Lutheran theology and the course of the Reformation. Bugenhagen's use of Ambrosiaster and Augustine here also mirrors the Augsburg Confession. The Confession's article 6 cites Ambrosiaster to support the teaching that good works come from faith and are not conditions for justification; article 20 refers to Augustine's *On the Spirit and the Letter* to support faith alone.[538] Through a detailed study of *sola fide* in these two early church writers, Bugenhagen's tract would continue to teach the Lutheran view of justification over and against contemporary objections.

Bugenhagen's first support for *sola fide* came from Ambrosiaster's interpretation of Romans. Here he followed Luther. In his translation of the New Testament, Luther had added the word "alone" to Romans 3:28: "For we hold that a person is justified by faith alone apart from works prescribed by the law."[539] In "On Translating, An Open Letter" (1530), Luther defended this "alone" by appealing both to the text's internal logic and the precedent of Ambrosiaster. "Moreover I am not the only one, or even the first, to say that faith alone justifies. Ambrose said it before me, and Augustine and many others."[540] Bugenhagen held fast to this explanation from Ambrosiaster about justification by faith alone.

> In the commentary on the Epistle to the Romans in which he explained justification by faith in a tract from Paul's words, how often does St. Ambrose speak of faith alone? Today's papists having been fighting terribly against what he said there. Where Paul says in Romans 3[:24], "they are justified by grace freely as a gift," Ambrose adds, "they are justified freely, not because of any works nor on account of merits, but by faith alone they are justified as a gift of God." The papists and their holy teachers should listen to this exposition of St. Ambrose.[541]

Bugenhagen's citation exactly matches Ambrosiaster's comments on Romans 3:24.[542] Further, the rhetorical question about how often Ambrosiaster talks about faith alone is legitimate: that commentary's treatment of Romans 4:5-6 mentions *sola fide* four times and explicitly emphasizes justification by faith alone and not by works.[543]

After citing Ambrosiaster to advance the Lutheran doctrine of justification as interpreted from Romans 3 and 4, Bugenhagen then enlisted Augustine to discuss the role of love (*caritas*) in justification, especially in light of Romans 5:5: "God's love has been poured into us through the Holy Spirit that has been given to us." Like the statement about justification by works in James, the role of love in justification was a challenging point for the Lutherans. The Roman

Confutation of the Augsburg Confession, for instance, had stated that Lutherans mistakenly kept love out of their doctrine of justification. "It is not enough to say we are justified only by faith because justification pertains to faith and love."[544] Along with other New Testament passages, the Roman Confutation cited 1 Corinthians 13:2: "If I have all faith so as to remove mountains, but do not have love, I am nothing."[545] Having started by defending justification by faith rather than works, Bugenhagen now examined the relationship between faith and love.

Here Bugenhagen drew greatly from Augustine to teach a theme that was at the heart of his own deepest personal convictions. For in addition to having spurred Luther's early theology, Augustine had also apparently been central for Bugenhagen's own "conversion" to Lutheran teachings. Melanchthon's 1558 funeral oration for Bugenhagen, for instance, mentioned that Bugenhagen's early engagement with Augustine had coincided with his first encounter with Luther's writings.[546] Also, the statutes of the University of Wittenberg required regular classes on Augustine's *On the Spirit and the Letter*, so that Bugenhagen had personally lectured on that work as recently as 1545.[547] Bugenhagen had a clear command of Augustine's works and decades of experience reasoning with Augustine on the themes of faith and love.

Bugenhagen taught that love and goods works are fruits of justification and not reasons for justification; faith comes before either love or good works. He then gave his audience an example of how to use Augustine against Augustine in case opponents said that Augustine taught justification by works, even works of love.

> Therefore, when they throw words from Augustine to you against justification by faith and against the honor owed to the only Mediator, respond, "the words I hear are not, in fact, Augustine's meaning. Augustine expressed his meaning and intention in clear words when he said, '"Now, having duly considered [and weighed all these circumstances and testimonies, we conclude that a man is not justified by the precepts of a holy life, but by faith in Jesus Christ]."'
>
> If they say, "Augustine thinks that the law of faith is love," then respond, "Augustine does not mean our love, that is, that our works of the law are merits for justification, because he clearly says this: 'We are not justified due to our

merits, but freely by grace.' If they will not allow this to you, then deny Augustine, lest you deny Christ as our righteousness; and listen to the Holy Spirit speaking in Peter, 'All prophets testify to Christ,' etc. [Acts. 10:43]; and in Paul, Colossians 2[:10], 'In Christ you have come into fullness,' etc.; and from Christ [Matt. 15:9], 'in vain do they worship me, teaching human doctrines and laws,' and see what follows in Isaiah [29:13] which Christ is quoting from; then add this, 'even if an angel from heaven should teach another gospel, let that one be anathema'" [Gal. 1:8].[548]

The two citations that Bugenhagen provided from Augustine exactly match the final sentence of *On the Spirit and the Letter*, chapter 13.[549] Bugenhagen thus gave his students Augustinian answers to questions about the relationship between faith and good works of love. At the same time, it is important to note that this imagined conversation ends not with Augustine but, to avoid denying Christ, with for four citations from the New Testament. As much as Augustine could be used to support the Lutheran position, Bugenhagen ultimately preferred turning to the Bible rather than relying upon even the greatest early church writers.

To emphasize that even Augustine should be read in light of the Bible, Bugenhagen cited Augustine's *De baptismo, contra Donatistas* (*On Baptism, Against the Donatists*).[550] The Donatists had been an early Christian group that demanded people be re-baptized if they had renounced or hidden their faith during times of Roman persecution. Augustine refuted the Donatists' claim to have the beloved bishop Cyprian on their side. He wrote that no council was above the Bible, including those over which Cyprian had presided. Instead, Augustine argued that Cyprian himself said that all local councils remain subject to scripture and brotherly admonition for the sake of "holy humility, catholic peace, and Christian love."[551] In this instance, Augustine had used Cyprian against Cyprian to insist on the priority of the Bible and the well-being of Christian communities in times of controversy. Bugenhagen's use of this passage, then, turned Augustine's words about Cyprian into an example of how to use Augustine against Augustine! To Bugenhagen, Augustine would never approve of uses of his work that contradicted justification by faith alone.

He then referred to Augustine's *De fide et operibus* (*On Faith and Works*). From chapter 7 of that work, he quoted, "faith comes first, so that whatever pertains to a good life is subjected to it. For a good life cannot follow in a person unless faith precedes it."[552] In chapter 14, Augustine answered the hypothetical assertion "that saving faith does not suffice without works" with the words of Paul: "a person is justified by faith without works of the law."[553] To clarify the point that Paul did not thereby condemn good works, Bugenhagen cited Augustine's explanation that "they follow justification and do not precede justification."[554] Not only did Augustine's *De fide et operibus* support the Lutheran doctrine of justification in general, but its discussion of the relationship between faith and good works fit exactly with Bugenhagen's point in this tract.

Bugenhagen's discussion of *De fide et operibus* ends by calling attention to two biblical passages. The first of these was the "foundation" metaphor used by Paul to show that justification comes from Christ alone: "For no one can lay any foundation other than the one that has been laid; that foundation is Jesus Christ" (1 Cor. 3:11). Bugenhagen then summarized Augustine's argument, invoking the Lord's Prayer as well: "At the foundation, Christ alone is our righteousness and our good works are the fruit of Christ's righteousness, for which we pray, 'Your will be done in heaven and on earth.'"[555] Once again, Bugenhagen turned Augustine's already well-suited text into an explicit affirmation of justification by faith alone. The great value he continued to place on good works performed out of love and faith shows that this was not an abstract matter for Bugenhagen but something grounded in serious concern for Christian communities and the common good.

The second biblical reference that Bugenhagen picked up from Augustine was the story of the Canaanite woman who approached Jesus and asked him to heal her daughter (Matt. 15:21-28). Augustine had wondered how this woman was saved through faith alone in a way that would not invite lawlessness or impiety.[556] He concluded that she had repented of past sins and amended her life when she said, "even the dogs eat the crumbs that fall from their masters' table." By trusting in Jesus rather than in herself, the Canaanite woman had humbly reached out to Christ for healing and received it. Augustine then observed that precisely this connection between faith and repentance was the proper way to interpret James' statement that "faith without works is dead." By using this particular quotation in his commentary on Jonah 3, Bugenhagen demonstrated an astonishing ability to carry on a discussion between New Testament texts, early church writers, and his own theological setting. In the end, Bugenhagen's use of Augustine resulted in having Augustine himself solve problems raised by the Epistle of James by means of a passage from the Gospel of Matthew.

The Lutheran Epistle of James

To this point in this second tract, Bugenhagen had taught justification by faith alone, refuted justification by works and the sacrament of anointing as interpreted through James, and turned to Ambrosiaster and Augustine for support of *sola fide*, even with respect to love and good works. He then brought this theological argument to its peak by turning to Melanchthon and Luther's treatment of James. After his final citation of Augustine, he wrote, "Philip Melanchthon has frequently and sufficiently interpreted the words of James in the *Loci Communes* and other places."[557] The paragraph that follows then cites Melanchthon's Apology to the Augsburg Confession and its discussion of James.

This use of the Apology began with the assertion that James can be valuable as long as justification by works is not assumed.[558] Next, Bugenhagen reasserted Melanchthon's insistence upon "forensic justification," in which God justifies people by simply declaring it and without respect to internal or external merit. Supposing that James implies this declaration of justification, James might then be found to agree with Paul that "the doers of the law will be justified" (Rom. 2:13). Melanchthon could consider such an interpretation to be harmonious with Lutheran teaching: "As we have said, the good works of the saints are righteous and please God because of faith. James preaches only the [works] that faith produces, as he shows when he says of Abraham, 'Faith was active along with his works' (2:22)."[559] With this, the Apology asserts a theology of good works that is always subordinate to but never separate from justification by faith alone. Melanchthon's basis for reading forensic justification into James had been based on a previous passage in that letter:

> James said a little earlier that regeneration takes place through the gospel. For he says, "In fulfillment of his own purpose he gave us birth by the word of truth, so that we

would become a kind of first fruits of his creatures" [1:18]. When he says that we are reborn by the gospel, he teaches that we are reborn and justified by faith. For the promise concerning Christ is grasped only by faith when we set the promise against the terrors of sin and death. James does not, therefore, hold that we are reborn through our works.[560]

With this, the Lutherans claimed James for themselves. Bugenhagen's borrowing from the Apology effectively summarized his own position. It also supported his main thesis in the Jonah Commentary: the Bible and the apostolic tradition teach justification by faith alone so that repentance, good works, and love can follow, as seen in the conversion of the evil city of Nineveh. To make his point, Bugenhagen did not only pick from Lutheran-friendly parts of the Bible like Romans 3-4; he also confronted passages that appear to refute justification by faith alone, including Jonah 3:10, James 2:24, and 1 Corinthians 13:2. In this way, he presented a strong *confutatio* of the Augsburg Interim and taught his audience how to articulate the foundations of Lutheran teaching themselves.

Bugenhagen concluded this section by noting that the Epistle of James begins by talking about prayers of faith. Luther had also approvingly cited this part of James in his Large Catechism: "But ask in faith, never wavering, for the one who wavers is like a wave of the sea, driven and dragged by the wind. Therefore, do not suppose that such a person – of two minds and fluctuating in every way – receives anything from the Lord" (James 1:6-8).[561] With this reminder that James begins with prayer and faith, Bugenhagen reaffirmed the Apology's conviction that James' Epistle, rightly understood, was grounded in gospel faith. Finally, this passage was used to counter the Augsburg Interim's teaching that one cannot have certainty of forgiveness through faith. On the contrary, both James and Luther taught that confidence in prayer was a holy gift and not something to be doubted. In this way, Bugenhagen asserted that the Epistle of James can indeed be interpreted as teaching the gospel.

Bugenhagen's last word to his audience about James referred them back to Luther's preface on that letter: "You see Father Luther's judgment on the Epistle of James in the German translation of the New Testament."[562] This is something of a vague conclusion, because he did not note which of Luther's comments on James he had in mind. Luther's general opinion about James was ambivalent, because Luther did not consider it to be an authentic apostolic letter and its teaching about justification was easily misleading.[563] On this latter point, Luther guessed that James "wanted to guard against those who relied on faith without works, but was unequal to the task."[564] Luther's well-known description of James as "an epistle of straw" was likely an illusion to 1 Corinthians 3:12, which lists building materials like stone, wood, and straw in contrast to Christ, who is the solid foundation on which to build faith.[565] That is, James is weak material with which to build faith. Presumably referring to Melanchthon's writings, Luther also said that he would not begrudge efforts to build a case for faith from James and personally found much that was edifying in this letter.[566] For these reasons, Bugenhagen's nod to Luther is a final recommendation to use caution when interpreting it. This shows again how well Bugenhagen taught both the Bible's content and a Lutheran method for reading scripture.

    The remainder of this second tract sets the stage for the discussions still to come, in which Bugenhagen identified points at which the Christian tradition had failed to observe Christ as the only source of righteousness before God.[567] He started with the Ebionites, an early sect that baptized and taught Christ's resurrection but did not believe that Christ was divine. In this way they negated *sola fide* and the doctrine of the Trinity.[568] Bugenhagen then applied this same critique to the moral rigor of Jews and Muslims. His main argument against Ebionites, Jews and Muslims was not based on Trinitarian doctrines but on the benefits of receiving grace through the crucified Christ. Bugenhagen extended this critique to his immediate opponents, the theologians behind the Council of Trent and the Augsburg Interim. "For all sects that deny Christ alone to be our righteousness before God, like our papists, imagine their works, worship, and monstrous religiosity to be justification and salvation."[569] This emphasis on receiving Christ's righteousness was the basis for repeated critiques against heretical groups within early Christianity, as well as against Jews, Muslims and the papacy.[570]

    It is worth noting that Bugenhagen added a short reflection here upon Mohammed and the Qur'an. He admired the Qur'an's portrayal of Christ as being conceived by the Holy Spirit and born of the Virgin Mary, as well as its description of Jesus as a great prophet and miracle worker who rose from the dead. He then addressed the accusation that worshiping Christ is idolatrous. First, he said that knowledge of God's transcendence is not the same thing as knowing God's mercy revealed in Christ. This is identical to his objections against the Augsburg Interim: as infinitely transcendent as God is, Christ's death and resurrection most clearly reveal God's true greatness. His final judgment about Islam was typical for the period: he believed that it combined the Arian rejection of Christ's full divinity with a Pelagian emphasis on justification by works.[571]

While not a great model for ecumenical or interfaith dialogue today, Bugenhagen's discussion of Islam reveals two important points. First, he showed that he was willing to engage Islam seriously and not merely dismiss it. Though he judged (more likely prejudged) Islam to be a Christian heresy, he knew its sacred text and admired elements of its faith and practice. Second, he articulated a positive understanding of his own faith; he did not simply define his position by denouncing the other. His objection to Islamic teachings was based on his pastoral concern for the practical effects of religious teachings on individuals and communities. Despite its shortcomings, Bugenhagen's discussion is constructive at least on these two points of honoring another tradition and arguing on the basis of positive proposals for human well-being.

In these first two tracts, Bugenhagen made his case for justification from the Bible and the Christian tradition. He repeatedly turned to his conviction that "Christ alone is our righteousness before God" to make exegetical, doctrinal and liturgical points. If salvation, love, and good works come through faith alone, then he defined the first and last heresy as this: "Christ is not the righteousness of God for us, rather our works and our endurance are our righteousness. Therefore, we are not justified by faith in the promised seed, but we make satisfaction to God for our sins through our works and we merit eternal life and a special crown in heaven."[572] For Bugenhagen, any view that minimized Christ's work in salvation was a sin against the first commandment, limiting God and God's salvation given freely through Jesus Christ. As both a *confutatio* and a positive statement for justification by faith alone, Bugenhagen's first two tracts reveal a theology rooted in scripture and tradition for the sake of experiencing God's grace. They skillfully call upon a wide range of sources with skill and teach their insights in a clear way to students and readers.

CHAPTER SIX

Justification in Action

The third and fourth tracts make up more than half of the book's total pages. While they take many turns through Christian history and theology, they advance Bugenhagen's teaching on justification by applying it to worship and daily life. Building on previous arguments, Bugenhagen reminded his audience that lofty religious ideals in worship, spirituality, and morality easily become their own idols. From this perspective, Bugenhagen made his case that the papacy of his day was more like the spiritualism of the Montanists than the preaching of the apostles. Noting the emphasis on faith taught by Peter, Paul, and John, Bugenhagen traced an apostolic theology of justification by faith that continued from the Apostle John to the bishops Polycarp and Irenaeus. In contrast to this orthodox genealogy, Bugenhagen claimed that the second-century heretic Montanus was the spiritual father of laws and traditions that had obscured the gospel in Western Christendom over the centuries.

Fitting his role as "reformer of the public welfare," Bugenhagen emphasized the practical consequences of justification for worship and daily life. He studied things like celibacy, monastic vows, communion in both kinds, fasting, and consecrations for how well those practices expressed the repentance seen in Nineveh or whether they encouraged people to trust in themselves. Not coincidentally, each of the liturgical issues that Bugenhagen addressed from history gave him the chance to argue against the Augsburg Interim without having to name it.

Faith and Tradition: The Tract against Montanism

Through his use of Christian history, Bugenhagen showed his familiarity with Luther and Melanchthon's writings even as he forged his own path. In 1539, preparing for the coming Council of Trent, Luther and Melanchthon each wrote books about faith and tradition. Luther's *On the Councils and the Church* refuted the notion that the Christian tradition (including its church councils) was infallible. According to Luther, the sole task of councils is to preserve the faith of Jesus Christ over time, making clarifications and condemning error if necessary, but otherwise not imposing new burdens or rules on Christians.[573] Similarly, Melanchthon's *On the Church and the Authority of God's Word* taught how the early church writers could be read most beneficially.[574] After a short survey of the early ecumenical councils, Melanchthon discussed what was laudable and what should be avoided in early writers, including Origen, Tertullian, Cyprian, Basil, Jerome, Augustine, and Pope Gregory I. Melanchthon affirmed the unity and holiness of the church across time, while differentiating local customs and institutions from universal faith. He wrote, "Let us, therefore, hear the church when she teaches and admonishes, but not believe merely because of the authority of the church. For the church does not originate articles of faith; she only teaches and admonishes. But we must believe because of the Word of God when, to be sure, admonished by the church, we understand that a particular opinion has been handed down in the Word of God truly and without sophistry."[575] Bugenhagen's work in the third tract calls upon both Luther and Melanchthon, commending Melanchthon's work by name and by providing an account of Luther's gospel breakthrough that centered on Luther's engagement with the Bible and Christian tradition (as studied in chapter 4).[576] While Bugenhagen's liturgical focus took a different path than Luther and Melanchthon's 1539 writings, his study of worship and daily practices started with the same belief that the doctrine of justification grounds all aspects of Christian life.

While covering wide swaths of Christian history, this third tract was also directed to Bugenhagen's specific time and place. The emphasis on Montanism allowed him to connect an ancient heretical movement (which had been condemned for going beyond the Bible in its teaching) with live doctrinal debates and political pressures. The tract's title stated this connection very plainly.

> Montanus the Blasphemer, as if from the word of God and under the name of the Spirit of the Paraclete, created specious institutions and perfections of the church after [the time of] the apostles, [and is] father of the traditions that oppress the gospel and church of Christ until even now.[577]

According to Bugenhagen, the papacy was guilty of Montanism. In the early church, Montanus had been a priest who claimed that the age of the Holy Spirit had arrived and been revealed to him, his fellow prophets Maximilla and Priscilla, and their followers. They followed a strict lifestyle and believed that their prophecies were ongoing revelation from God.[578] To other Christians, their requiring something beyond the apostles' teaching meant that they had added a mediator besides Christ and deviated from the shared faith of the church.

But before blindly accusing his opponents of such a heresy, Bugenhagen positively defined the gospel. He took his definition of the gospel here from the end of the Gospel of John. Because John was the disciple who supposedly lived the longest, Bugenhagen could consider this passage to be a kind of last word from the apostles to later communities of faith. Citing John 20:31, Bugenhagen peppered it with his own parenthetical comments.

> He says, "But these things have been written (as you see from the beginning until now), so that you might believe that Jesus (who is truly human) is the Christ (that is, the Messiah of God promised to us in the law and the prophets), the Son of God (that is, true God). And that through believing (John adds this part about the use of Christ or justification by faith against any other righteousness for all time) you might have life in his name."[579]

Bugenhagen pointed to this verse's Christological content and its concern for right application of the faith. The parenthetical comment in the second sentence mentions the *usus Christi* (use of Christ), which brings real-life results. As noted in chapter 3, the reformers consistently connected what a thing is (*quid sit*) with what it does (*quid effectus*), so that the gospel consists of both a certain knowledge and the effect of that knowledge. Here Bugenhagen identified this connection between right knowledge and right application as being the point of the biblical text itself: "that through believing you might have life."

The error of the Montanists had not been their doctrine of Christ or desire for better lives. Instead, the Montanists erred by believing that there was a holiness and spiritual perfection beyond what the New Testament taught. This is the point at which Bugenhagen connected Montanism with both the papacy and other "enthusiasts" of the sixteenth century.

> Why do you papists condemn your father Montanus and call him a heretic? He taught nothing against the articles of faith, except that he was the first to do what you do. For he is father and author of your holiness and all your spirituality and spiritualism. For all spirits who defect from faith by a name other than the Holy Spirit gaze upon his dreams and his lies, just as in our own time the Anabaptists and other fanatical spirits did. Whenever one criticizes or condemns them from Holy Scripture and the words of Christ's gospel, they respond, "Not everything has been written; the Spirit in us teaches all, the letter profits nothing."[580]

Just as Montanus had added new ideas about spiritual perfection to orthodox articles of faith, so Rome had added new spiritual requirements to the apostolic faith over the centuries. The practices that Bugenhagen criticized were hardly wrong in themselves. But once an institution insisted upon them, they could obscure or replace the gospel message. As seen in the quotation above, mistaken views about these practices often come through confusion regarding the letter and the spirit and the substitution of new laws for Christian faith.

It is instructive that a supposedly "polemical" book like Bugenhagen's *Jonah* identifies intolerance as a symptom of false spirituality. Here we find that Bugenhagen equated spiritual pride with the Pharisee of Luke 18, the Montanist error, and the papacy's intolerance of Lutheran preaching. Speaking of "our papists," he wrote,

> they do not believe in Christ, that they might be made righteous before God, children of God, and heirs of eternal life on account of Christ alone who was crucified for us; rather they believe in their own observances for their justification and merit of eternal life. And they judge others who do not recognize their observances not to be the church of Christ, just as it was written of the Pharisee in Luke 18[:9]: "they trusted in themselves that they were righteous and regarded others with contempt."[581]

Even though the Montanists and the papacy had orthodox teachings, their pride in higher spirituality had become idolatrous. Such pride also damages Christian community and love of the neighbor, because it regards others with contempt. In this case, the intolerance that Bugenhagen lamented was Rome's refusal to grant that Lutheran teachings were authentic interpretations of scripture and tradition. This intolerance was manifested in both theological decrees and the very real threat of military force.

As an alternative, Bugenhagen taught that tolerance based on a shared faith in the gospel demonstrates the presence of the Holy Spirit better than the appearance of outward unity. After citing Eusebius on the pride of early heretics and after condemning bishops in his own time, Bugenhagen paraphrased 1 Corinthians 13:1-3 and John 13:35 to speak of love as the inevitable fruit of faith.

> If I speak with the tongues of mortals and angels, and if I have prophetic powers and so on, but do not have love, then I am nothing, that is, I am not a child of God but an unfaithful and condemned person. And even if I have all faith, that is, such a great faith that I dare to do heroic miracles in Christ's name and move mountains, yet do not ever show love but instead follow ambition, lust, avarice, superstition and false teaching in my assigned Christian office, then it is a certain sign that I am nothing before God, that I do not believe, do not have faith in Christ my righteousness, just as Christ said: "By this everyone will know that you are my disciples – that is, truly Christians – if you have love for one another."[582]

Love is the great sign of a life of faith. Bugenhagen therefore found it ironic that Roman Catholic opponents arguing for justification by love (*caritas*) rather than faith could show such little love to the Lutherans. "How then can insane people, who do not have love, force their love upon us? For they cannot have it unless they believe in Christ."[583] Though it is possible here to wonder if Bugenhagen was himself guilty of not loving his opponents, in his own context he was in the place of relative powerlessness with respect to the pope and the emperor. Though the question of how tolerance was practiced within Lutheran Saxony would require another book, we do know that the Lutheran doctrine of adiaphora was one strategy employed for living with differences within the territory itself.

The appearance of love as a theological point brought Bugenhagen back to his argument in the previous tract: good works of love do not justify sinners but are signs of justification. Again citing Augustine's *De fide et operibus*, he reminded his audience that justification by faith provides the right foundation for worship and for good works of love shown to one's neighbors.

Love does not justify but is a fruit of justification. As Augustine says in the book *On Faith and Works*, good works or works of the law (that is, love of God according to the first table and love of neighbor in the second table) follow righteousness and do not precede being made righteous, as we have said here and in other places before. That is, the good works that God commanded, which are love of God and love to the neighbor, do not justify and are not the good tree. Rather they come from righteousness, that is, they are fruits of the good tree which has been made good and righteous, so that it is possible to bear loving fruit of righteousness [Matt. 12:33].

These works are not righteous in themselves, but are solely God's righteousness, mercy, grace, eternal love towards us, kindness, blessing, honor or good pleasure (which are all the same in God toward us) to those who are in Christ Jesus our Lord (Rom. 8). For this is not in us (Rom. 7), except when it is given to us through the Holy Spirit by hearing the gospel [Rom. 10:17] when we believe in Christ. Just as it says in Romans 5[:5, 8]: "God's love (with which God loves us from eternity before the foundation of the world in Christ) has been poured into our hearts by the Holy Spirit that has been given to us." That is, now we also know in our hearts that God loves us in Christ, because while we were still ignorant of our sin and under God's wrath, what clearly follows is that God commends his love to us, etc. [Rom. 5].

But the Pharisees are dreaming to themselves about I don't know what kind of love when they trust in themselves that they are righteous and regard others with contempt (Luke 18). They declare that today's monks are in a state of perfection, which therefore perfectly fulfills the law so that they can do works of supererogation: "I fast," he says, "twice on the Sabbath," that is, "I not only perform the law but even go over and above what God has commanded," which they call works of supererogation...

And it would be about our Pharisees when Paul speaks of the righteousness of the Jews and the repentance of the gentiles, that is, of the conversion to Christ (Rom. 9[:30-32]): "What then shall we say? That the gentiles, who did not strive for righteousness (like the tax collector), have received righteousness, yet this is the righteousness that comes from faith. On the other hand, Israel, which did strive for the righteousness of the law (like the Pharisee) did not succeed in the law's righteousness. Why? Because it was not from faith but entirely based on works of the law. For they stumbled over the stumbling block" [Psalm 118:22].[584]

Although he did not refer to Jonah 3 here, Bugenhagen's argument is identical to his earlier interpretation of Nineveh's repentance: faith in God's mercy comes before works of repentance or love. By trusting God, people begin to fulfill the commandments for the first time, honoring God above all else. They then perform the good works that grow out of faith in God. As Paul and Augustine taught, these works of love are pleasing to God as fruits of righteousness. By contrast, justification by works has more to do with the self than with God. Despite the best intentions, therefore, an emphasis on good works can then become the "stumbling block" that causes people to trust in something other than God.

Bugenhagen's bold accusations against self-righteousness again beg the question of whether he and his Lutheran colleagues merely replaced one source of spiritual arrogance with another, this time, an arrogance based on the doctrine of justification. There are two arguments against that accusation. As mentioned above, Bugenhagen lived under Charles V's superior military force and the clear condemnations of the Council of Trent. Writing from a position of relative weakness, Bugenhagen could advocate for a political and theological tolerance that would have been impossible for him to reciprocate, at least on that lofty level.

More important, Bugenhagen did not imagine that justification by faith alone or even Christian love was something to boast about. Instead it was a perpetual call to humility and service, because justification continually inspires repentance, forgiveness of sins, and a new obedience. Forgetting one's need for repentance obscures the gospel. This self-reflection was a part of Bugenhagen's own ministry and teaching.

For this reason, it necessarily follows that many teachers have not been able to teach and explain this article of faith correctly: "I believe in the forgiveness of sins," that is, the article of justification in which Christ alone, who was crucified for us, is our righteousness before God and not our works. That is, God forgives us our sins and imputes to us his righteousness on account of Christ, whom we receive by faith.[585]

In the Apostles' Creed, believers regularly confess their faith in the forgiveness of sins. But far from being a routine and simple affirmation, Bugenhagen pointed out that recognizing the continual need for forgiveness is one of the hardest things to believe. Bugenhagen's appeals to love and justification by faith were not signs of supposed spiritual superiority but were personal and communal calls to return to God in humility and trust.

This is the immediate context in which Bugenhagen gave his account of Luther's breakthrough.[586] It is also one reason why Bugenhagen did not portray Luther's gospel insight as either novel or meritorious. Instead, Bugenhagen presented it as being entirely grounded in the Bible, prayer, and respected church writers. Had Bugenhagen presented Luther' insight as an amazing new invention, he would have fallen into the very Montanist heresy of claiming new spiritual revelation or perfection that he was deriding. And had Luther's actions inspired new holiness or perfection, this would have also imitated the spiritual hypocrisy that justification by faith alone claimed to reject. Rather, Bugenhagen's account has Luther teaching that "we Pharisees need to be blinded" to see that justification is about God's mercy, not human striving.

In the same way, Bugenhagen evaluated the contributions of previous generations in light of their teaching about God's righteousness. This was especially true of the work that had served as the primary theological textbook of the Middle Ages, Peter Lombard's *Four Books of Sentences*. In this monumental twelfth-century work, Lombard collected quotations from the Bible and church writers on various topics of theology. Bugenhagen wrote that Lombard's teaching about the Trinity and Christology were good, but he was weak on application.

> In the Master's *Sentences* the articles of our faith on the divine Trinity and the two natures in one Christ are rightly and most blessedly defended. But as has been said, when it comes to the righteousness of God through faith in Christ (that is, the use of Christ, who became incarnate and glorified for us, who sits at the right hand of the Father,

and who intercedes for us) there everything gets confused, the good sayings with the mistaken ones, about human love, works and merits. There Christ alone is not our righteousness, mediator, reconciler, salvation or savior before the Father; or rather, they do not recognize this, though it is clear that there Christ is nothing. Neither do they teach the sacraments correctly but obscure Christ for us, along with the light of his gospel through human doctrines and traditions.[587]

Rather than setting forth wrong teachings, Bugenhagen complained that Lombard presented a number of sometimes contradictory or unhelpful sources, which then confused rather than clarified church teachings.

In this, Bugenhagen shared Luther and Melanchthon's conviction that church writers should be evaluated on their adherence to the doctrine of justification, which they viewed as the center of scripture. Luther had also praised Lombard's greatness while lamenting the conflicting citations and irrelevant subjects that sometimes clouded the *Sentences*: "Peter Lombard was a very diligent man with a superior mind. He wrote many excellent things. He would really have been a great doctor of the church if he had given himself wholly and truly to the Holy Scriptures, but he confuses the Scriptures with many useless questions."[588] In one way, what Lombard had done was to compile and catalogue the riches of Christian theology in a new and vibrant way. According to the reformers, however, the downside of his compilation method was new confusion about how best to evaluate and apply all that information.

Unlike Lombard's method of piling sources upon sources to teach the faith of the Bible, Bugenhagen believed that Augustine had taught a more nuanced *sola scriptura* principle. He further noted that Augustine's principle was present in canon law itself.

> For [Augustine] wrote most blessedly to St. Jerome something that they even have in their papal decrees, distinction 9. He says, "I have learned to yield this respect and honor only to the canonical books of Scripture: of these alone do I most firmly believe that the authors were completely free from error. And if in these writings I am perplexed by anything which appears to me opposed to

truth, I do not hesitate to suppose that either the manuscript is faulty, or the translator has not caught the meaning of what was said, or I myself have failed to understand it. As to all other writings, in reading them, however great the superiority of the authors to myself in sanctity and learning, I do not accept their teaching as true on the mere ground of the opinion being held by them; but only because they have succeeded in convincing my judgment of its truth either by means of these canonical writings themselves, or by arguments addressed to my reason."[589]

In this passage, Augustine placed himself under the authority of the Bible alone. Where it was a mystery to him, he let it remain a mystery and sought clarification through further study. His submission to scripture did not keep him from turning to other writers, but simply placed them under the Bible as well. Also, the reliance on *sola scriptura* did not do away with logic or even the technical work of examining ancient manuscripts. Instead, Augustine continued to value human reason and clarity of thought as part of what it means to interpret the Bible well.

This Augustinian position on scripture and reason is very near to the stand that Luther took at the 1521 Diet of Worms: "Unless I am convinced by the testimony of the Scriptures or by clear reason (for I do not trust either in the pope or in councils alone, since it is well known that they have often erred and contradicted themselves), I am bound by the Scriptures I have quoted and my conscience is captive to the Word of God."[590] While scripture, tradition and reason are not necessarily in opposition to each other, the reformers had received from Augustine their clearest guide for understanding the relationship between the Bible and how to apply it for the well-being of Christians and communities.

Case Studies: Clerical Marriage and Communion in Both Kinds

The *Jonah*'s move from theology to specific worship practices elaborates on earlier arguments. In particular, Bugenhagen focused on clerical marriage and the sacrament of Holy Communion to show how theology affects practice. Since the early 1520s, married priests and giving wine to the laity at communion had been two of the most visible signs of the Reformation. These were also two of the points still being disputed under the Augsburg Interim, which provisionally allowed for these practices until the Council of Trent would make its decisions about them; as expected, Trent eventually rejected the Lutheran views. Bugenhagen's arguments for clerical marriage and communion became ways for him to connect biblical interpretation with important and very public church practices.

Again, the emphasis on Montanism directly served Bugenhagen's argument. These disputed practices in the sixteenth century were very similar to the ancient charges leveled against the Montanists. In his history of Christianity, Eusebius wrote that Montanus "taught the dissolution of marriages," instituted laws about fasting, and collected money in the church to attract and pay his supporters.[591] To these classical charges against the Montanist sect, Bugenhagen added, "he [Montanus] taught that only in celibacy is there chastity and the spiritual life (and not in marriage), even as the papists blasphemously say today."[592] Identifying the prohibition of marriage and forced fasting with New Testament warnings about false teachers, Bugenhagen then cited 1 Timothy 4: "Paul preached about these two things, *exempli gratia*, when he spoke of traditions and deceptive doctrines, 'They forbid marriage and demand abstinence from foods.'"[593] Once again, Bugenhagen wove together the Bible, church history, and current events to present theological, historical and logical rationale for Lutheran practices, especially as taught and experienced in Wittenberg.

Bugenhagen then presented ways in which the church's teaching about celibacy and virginity had turned from good suggestions into burdensome commands. For instance, Bugenhagen identified vows of celibacy as a sin against the second commandment, because with them one's righteousness presumes to come through a human vow of chastity rather than by calling upon God's name.[594] He also claimed that clerical celibacy violated not only God's law but natural and civil laws as well: "For God created, instituted, ordained, and blessed marriage, as we affirm."[595]

In this context, Bugenhagen praised St. Ulrich of Augsburg, a tenth-century bishop who opposed a new papal mandate for universal clerical celibacy.[596] Ulrich had supposedly written a letter against mandatory clerical celibacy to Pope Nicholas I. This apocryphal letter was known in Wittenberg and had been published there in 1520.[597] Luther mentioned it in his 1521 reply to Jerome Emser and in the lectures on Genesis given late in his life.[598] In Bugenhagen's estimation, Ulrich "wrote against Pope Nicholas, condemning him from sacred letters most learnedly that he was tragically wrong to oppose the marriage of priests, which had been granted by God."[599] Building on Ulrich's scriptural defense of clerical marriage, Bugenhagen pointed out that many otherwise laudable Christians had been seduced by opinions about spirituality and personal holiness; he pointed especially to Pope Gregory VII, who had made the abolition of priestly marriage a key part of his eleventh-century reforms.

Forging an even more direct link between Montanism and the papacy, Bugenhagen turned his eye to Tertullian and Cyprian. Tertullian (ca. 160–220), the first Latin writer to comment at length about the Trinity, had joined the Montanists later in his life. He also pointed out that Cyprian of Carthage (d. 258), a heroic bishop and martyr, had added rituals to the liturgy and introduced strict penitential canons for Christians who had denied their faith during Roman persecutions. Bugenhagen wrote, "Thus Tertullian erred, being seduced by the Montanist spiritualism. After him, the holy martyr Cyprian erred when he accepted false consecrations and anointings from the majority (which promised the Holy Spirit or the Holy Spirit's grace to people, which is like the Montanists)."[600]

With respect to these early leaders, especially the great Cyprian, Bugenhagen's point was not to tear them down but to show that error and sin remained among the church's greatest leaders. "God sent an effective error, even through among his elect… according to Christ's word: 'For false messiahs and false prophets will appear and produce great signs and omens, to lead astray, if possible, even the elect'" [Matt. 24:24].[601] This "effective error" from God was the humbling of otherwise commendable leaders, which shows "that the saints have gone to ruin" (Bugenhagen's fourth locus) in order to inspire all Christians to lives of repentance.

Based on sources including Eusebius, Augustine, Lombard, and Gratian's *Decretals* (an influential collection of canon law), Bugenhagen identified Cyprian with practices like rebaptism, the institution of penitential canons, increased standards for clerical holiness, and new ritual consecrations. He then linked those ceremonies and the emphasis on spiritual holiness with the papacy. His objection was not to deride the ceremonies or rules themselves but to attack the notion that these rituals forgive sins or create holiness. He then considered the simple words of the Lord's Prayer: "Will it then not be enough when we pray in the name of the Son, 'Forgive us our sins?' Is it not then enough that we believe in the forgiveness of sin on account of Christ alone? Then has God's righteousness, which is through faith in Christ, been abolished? How are we the ones who are crazy?"[602] The problems that Bugenhagen raised about consecrations and anointings always returned to this question of forgiveness of sins through Christ alone. In this case, he contrasted a complicated holiness code with one little phrase from the Lord's Prayer, which he believed gave a more reliable basis for confession and absolution.

Bugenhagen held the same view of the sacraments: they exist in their simplicity to nurture faith and restore sinners to God and to the community. Bugenhagen named three sacraments: baptism, the Lord's Supper, and the sacrament of absolution.[603] Reflecting upon Augustine's famous definition of a sacrament as a sign of a sacred reality,[604] Bugenhagen wrote that even this can be a misleading statement because Christ himself never talked about signs. "Christ does not call it a sacrament or sign, but he calls it a true baptism into his church, his true body and blood at his meal, true repentance and forgiveness of sins or absolution from sins. However, I do not deny that they are signs presented outwardly by the minister, but I desire the truth itself, which is Christ's word of institution, to be preserved in the church even in the names used."[605] Because of the Lutheran emphasis on what a thing does (*quid effectus*), Bugenhagen was less interested in definitions or symbols than in the real reception of grace that Christ promised in and through the sacraments.

Confronting those who wanted to add more to Christ's word and sacraments, Bugenhagen introduced his argument against the so-called Johannine Comma (first mentioned here in chapter 5). "Adding more" was indeed his main argument against this passage. While critics of the insertion as early as Jerome said this passage was added to refute the Arian heresy, Bugenhagen suggested that it had likely been added by the Arians themselves to detract from the fullness of God's revelation in Christ. In the authentic passage, the "three that testify" to God's life given through Christ are the Spirit, water and blood (1 John 5:6-12). Bugenhagen interpreted these testimonies to be God's Word – given and preached through the Holy Spirit – and the sacraments of baptism and the Lord's Supper.

In Bugenhagen's eyes, the parallelism of the added phrase subordinates the Son and the Spirit in an Arian fashion. "There are three that testify in heaven, the Father, the Word, and the Holy Spirit, and these three are one. And there are three that testify on earth: Spirit, water and blood, and these three are one." Following the Comma's internal logic, Bugenhagen reasoned that if the Father, Word and Spirit are one in the same way that the Spirit, water and blood are one, then the Word and Spirit are less than the Father because the water and blood are less than the Spirit from whom they derive their power. Such logic, Bugenhagen argued, is against the broader meaning of John's gospel and epistle, which stress the fullness of God's salvation through Jesus Christ and the promised Holy Spirit.[606] Bugenhagen praised Erasmus of Rotterdam for identifying this passage as highly spurious; he implored printers and those who worked with them to keep it out of new editions of the New Testament.[607]

While apparently having little to do with Montanism or church order, Bugenhagen's discussion of the Johannine Comma serves as an important point of transition in the tract. To this point, he had made a predominately theological argument about church practices based on the doctrine of justification. He was writing against those who would add human works to salvation. At this pivotal place, the "Spirit, water and blood" of 1 John 5 introduce a study of the church's ministry of Word and sacrament according to Christ's institution.[608] In the pages that follow, the tract makes a sustained examination of the relationship between faith and practice, insisting that worship and Christian living work together under the doctrine of justification. A rich source for liturgical studies, ecclesiology, and Christian history, Bugenhagen's *Jonah* presents a Lutheran view of worship with the same depth as Luther's *Babylonian Captivity of the Church*. Although this study cannot follow all of Bugenhagen's trails, several are worth highlighting, sometimes as much for their colorful rhetoric as for their theological content.

On purgatory, for instance, Bugenhagen noted that the passage in 1 Corinthians 3 containing the phrase "cleansing fire" also included the images of watering, planting, building, and precious stones. He dryly remarked that of all these images, only the word "fire" had been taken literally.[609] Addressing the "indelible character" received through ordination or monastic vows, Bugenhagen sharply said that only mark received is the mark of the beast (Rev. 14[:9]).[610] With harsh objections like these, it is clear that Bugenhagen was as capable of using words to sting as anyone in his day. At the same time, these comments were not baseless diatribes but remained rooted in scripture, experience, and the threats of the Augsburg Interim, although perhaps wanting in charity.

Because the prohibition of marriage was one of the hallmarks of Montanism (and a debated point under the Augsburg Interim), Bugenhagen's defense of clerical marriage become a major theme of these last two tracts. Believing that dedicated virginity is certainly one good way to honor God, Bugenhagen also recognized that it was not the only way, nor might it even be the best way. In any case, virginity never merited salvation or eternal life for its own sake.[611] Commenting on the virgins of Revelation 14:1-5, Bugenhagen wrote that this "was not a physical virginity, which even the Turks have;" instead, the virginal followers are Christians who know and follow Christ.[612] Physical virginity, while a God-pleasing spiritual gift given to some, never guarantees salvation beyond that offered to all people through faith.

While Bugenhagen was by no means free of the "hierarchy of gender" that assumed male dominance,[613] he gave positive examples of women who showed their Christian faith without vows of celibacy or monastic regulations. His primary example was the prophet Anna from Luke 2:36-38, a widow who spent all her time fasting and praying in the temple and who immediately told others about the infant Jesus. Like Simeon, Zachariah, Elizabeth, and John the Baptist, the prophet Anna was not in the temple to fulfill monastic vows; she was there "because she was a prophet, that is, a woman full of the Holy Spirit."[614] He went on to say that faithful men and women across time have served God equally well and without being defined by either marital status or gender.

> Therefore, God's holy people, full of the Holy Spirit, whether men or women, have always detested and condemned the demonic teachings that started from the serpent in Paradise (that is, human traditions, doctrines and mandates through the hypocrisy of liars [1 Tim. 4:1-2]). And they have served God according to God's word reverently and chastely, freely and spontaneously through their vocation, whether in marriage or outside of marriage, through faith in the Son of God through the Holy Spirit.[615]

Bugenhagen expressed the Lutheran teaching that the highest Christian calling is to live a life rooted in God's word and shared in service to others. Although this emphasis on gender equality in spiritual matters did not challenge the fact of social inequality between the genders in everyday practice, it removed marital status and gender as conditions for spiritual worth.

Still rooted in a male-dominated worldview, this belief in spiritual equality did bring some practical social results. For instance, the reformers' emphasized education and literacy for girls.[616] They also supported care for the elderly, the poor, and widows through the institution of the common chest, as discussed in chapter 1. In fact, the Jonah Commentary's lone mention of the "common chest" arises in a passage affirming the spiritual and social status of widows. First, he showed that the apostles and early church valued the spiritual and social lives of women who were not virgins by the care they gave widows. Second, he pointed out that this same apostolic social impulse was visible in Germany through the common chest, which supported schools, preachers, widows and orphans.[617]

Speaking of "today's elders and preachers of the gospel" who had married, Bugenhagen described several beneficial results of this practice, especially the end of a double life among the clergy.[618] Instead of struggling with an unnecessary burden or hypocritically vowing celibacy and then keeping a mistress, married pastors could enjoy open, honorable, and legal relationships. Bugenhagen said that such pastors marry out of love for both the divine and natural goodness of marriage. They have children, whom they raise "in the fear of the Lord, to the glory of Christ, and for the benefit of the public and the church." These ministers serve the church "no less than before," and "give thanks to God that he led them into this kind of life."[619] This is a ringing endorsement of marriage. It presents family life as a blessing for individuals and for communities, who are blessed and served through the gift of children. Leaving pastors free to remain single, Bugenhagen nevertheless commended clerical marriage as a practice that could be entered into with thanksgiving and joy.[620]

Having himself been married since 1522 and having published works on clerical marriage since 1525, Bugenhagen's advocacy for marriage is a major part of his life's work. He believed strongly that the partnership found in marriage was a great personal and social good. Although it does not confer the forgiveness of sins like baptism, communion, and absolution, God created it and gave it as a blessing for human life. Through marriage God affirms the good creation of men and women, of sexuality as part of God's plan, and of children as the fruit of such unions.

With such a positive view of marriage, Bugenhagen was not able to end this tract without making one more statement against the papacy and other contemporary theological opponents. Citing Matthew 19:6 ("what God has joined together, let no one separate"), Bugenhagen asserted that this verse was not only written against those who separate individual spouses but also against those who keep men and women from marriage in general.[621] "They are not the creators of virginity or celibacy, as many fatheads falsely take pride in, but of much wickedness and filth. This is certainly not from the spirit of Christ, as their father Montanus imagined, but was invented by the spirit of the Antichrist, which Paul calls the doctrines of demons" [1 Tim. 4:1-5].[622] Bugenhagen's positive views of marriage and his personal experiences stand behind this condemnation. Clerical marriage was not simply a theological issue. It was a matter of flesh-and-blood reality that teaches God's love and care for real people and not some ideal spiritual community. Bugenhagen's own love for his wife and family certainly confirmed his theological position and added an existential passion to his debate against papal teachings.

Having refuted the practice of mandatory priestly celibacy for a final time in his career, Bugenhagen returned to his opening identification of the papacy with the ancient Montanists. As at the tract's beginning, this point was not made haphazardly but with concrete goals. According to Eusebius, the Montanists instituted new spiritual laws, especially rules prohibiting marriage. The New Testament letter of 1 Timothy also connected false teachers with rules against marriage and with the institution of new religious regulations. From these sources, Bugenhagen went through Christian history with an eye on the gradual rise of monastic celibacy and the prohibition of clerical marriage. These became touchstones for identifying points where the church had departed from the apostles' earliest teaching on justification in favor of other opinions about purity and righteousness. Speaking directly to his situation under the Augsburg Interim and summarizing major themes in his life's work, Bugenhagen's third tract shows him to have a firm grasp on the history of Christian communal life and the application of God's free justification to the life of believers and communities.

Usus Christi in Worship and Everyday Life: The Tract on Tertullian

The Jonah Commentary's final tract carries the short title, *Ex Tertulliano*.[623] In Bugenhagen's view, many of the traditions and spiritual practices that were causing problems in the sixteenth century came "from Tertullian." The North African theologian Tertullian had been attracted by the spiritual discipline of the Montanists and their emphasis on the perfection of the Holy Spirit.[624] As a sometimes orthodox and sometimes Montanist writer, Bugenhagen identified him as the bridge connecting Montanist spiritualism with Latin Christendom. The shift here from Montanus to Tertullian represents Bugenhagen's final view of how extra-biblical and heretical practices entered the church of his time. In this final tract, Bugenhagen studied some of Tertullian's works to show how easily worship can be co-opted to serve personal or collective pride and lead people away from faith.

At the opening of the tract, Bugenhagen reminded his audience that Tertullian (like Montanus) had taught the central doctrines of Christian faith correctly, including the Trinity, the two natures of Christ, and the resurrection of the body. But Tertullian had also "confirmed and advanced Montanist traditions and spiritualism… which obscured the righteousness and use of Christ."[625] Bugenhagen went on to show that Tertullian's primary error was an improper "use of Christ" (*usus Christi*) that stressed human righteousness through rituals and holiness at the expense of salvation through Christ's work.

The topics that Bugenhagen chose to address show the influence of sixteenth-century events on his historical study. In his refutation of Tertullian, he examined the liturgical practices of anointing, making the sign of the cross, and the imposition of hands. These related directly to the Augsburg Interim's view of the sacraments and Holy Communion. Anointing is the primary sign of the sacrament of extreme unction; the imposition of hands is central to confession, ordination, and confirmation; and the sign of the cross is a liturgical action belonging especially to the Mass. Although Tertullian taught correctly about baptism and the Lord's Supper, Bugenhagen believed that the things he added, including "external anointing, the sign of the cross, and the imposition of hands," had not come from the Bible or the apostolic tradition.[626]

Instead, he showed how Tertullian turned practices like these into new conditions for the forgiveness of sins and holiness. He lamented, "O God, how many Christians have suffered evil consciences because of these blasphemies?"[627] Bugenhagen then connected this mistaken emphasis on ritual purity with the threats of his own time. "Our papists are no different even in the present day. If Montanus was the worst heretic, then our papists are the worst heretics. For today they hate, condemn and persecute faith in Christ and debase justification by faith, while they have nothing other than Montanist traditions and spirituality."[628] After a broad critique like this, Bugenhagen provided concrete examples of how those practices negatively impacted Christian communities. Again, he did not simply tear down the rituals, signs, and works that he found objectionable but acknowledged that these traditional practices have had positive and beneficial uses when not overshadowing God's free gifts of grace.

For instance, he considered the laying on of hands to be very valuable. He himself was portrayed on the Cranach Altar as laying hands on the head of a penitent sinner! Nevertheless, he applied his critical principle to the sacrament of absolution. God's forgiveness is received by faith, not the laying on of hands. The laying on of hands is, however, a reliable outward sign of what God has done. Regarding ordination, Bugenhagen had already mentioned that the laying on of hands was something he practiced when he ordained new pastors.[629] He noted that many passages support the laying on of hands, including Jacob's blessing of Joseph's sons (Gen. 48:14), Moses' blessing of Joshua (Deut. 34:9), and several places in the Acts of the Apostles. However, once it was being mandated by the Augsburg Interim, Bugenhagen emphasized that the laying on of hands is never itself the effective sacramental action. In ordination, the laying on of hands is an external sign that a particular person has been called to preach and use the sacraments in a community; the office of preaching does not depend on this ritual, as seen in the ministries of Matthias and Timothy (Acts 1:26 and 16:1-5), which do not mention this sign.[630]

Similarly, the laying on of hands when anointing the sick is commendable but not necessarily efficacious. James 5:15 says that the "prayer of the faith" heals people, not the application of oil. Bugenhagen observed that if laying hands on the sick were a necessary part of making the prayers efficacious, it would cast doubts on the benefits of praying for absent friends, travelers, prisoners, and enemies.[631]

Bugenhagen believed that the papacy, by minimizing the inner role of faith and requiring the outer signs, had turned things like anointing and laying on hands into obstacles for believing and receiving God's grace. To prove this, Bugenhagen continued to recall the Louvain Theologians' ninth article, the Council of Trent's canons on justification, and (implicitly) the Augsburg Interim's article against confidence in the forgiveness of sins: "Because of their own infirmity or indisposition people cannot believe without doubt that their sins are remitted."[632] This denial means that people must depend on external signs like anointing and the laying on of hands, which do not have Christ's direct promise attached to the them. Without the confidence that God really has forgiven sin and given new life, Christians are left to trust in the fulfillment of external rituals. Practices like anointing, the laying on of hands, and making the sign of the cross can certainly serve faith, as long as they not become substitutes for faith.

Bugenhagen put forth a similar argument to deny the sacrament of extreme unction. As shown in the discussion of James in chapter 5, he rejected it primarily because it does not have a clear biblical basis. In this fourth tract, Bugenhagen identified Montanus, Tertullian and Cyprian as the originators of the blessings and consecrations with oil practiced in the church.[633] He then noted that Jesus' commission to his disciples to go preach the kingdom of God, heal the sick and cast out demons did not depend on their anointing (Matt. 10:10-15, Mark 6:7-13, Luke 9:1-6); rather, he supposed that the anointing mentioned in Mark alone was a local medical practice and not spiritual anointing.[634] Pushing a *reductio ad absurdum* argument, he recalled the story of the unnamed woman who anointed Jesus for his burial (Mark 14:3-9) and asked why it should not have inspired a law about making this a sacrament exclusively performed by women.[635]

This aside was made to expose the arbitrary nature of canon law. For Bugenhagen, the sacrament of extreme unction introduced a false confidence in human action instead of trusting Christ's work and promises. As an example of this misplaced trust in rituals, he wrote that his opponents would gladly apply unction to kidneys, limbs, ears, noses, lips, hands and feet as signs of God's mercy; but when Lutherans preach the good news of forgiveness through faith in Christ, they get persecuted as heretics.[636] The problem was in trusting the rite itself more than the God who gives and restores life. Like the laying on of hands, Bugenhagen left anointing as a matter of freedom as long as it did not obscure the correct *usus Christi*.

Because Lutheranism emphasizes a "theology of the cross," Bugenhagen's critique of making the sign of the cross raises interesting questions. Bugenhagen clearly stated that the sign of the cross remained a fine practice as a matter of Christian freedom. Luther had included it as part of daily prayer in his Small Catechism.[637] At the same time, Bugenhagen found suspicious origins for this liturgical action in Tertullian. As a non-apostolic source, he said that the sign of the cross cannot reliably deliver any promise of grace it presumed to make and could easily become a superstitious or magical sign, as innocently or piously as it may have begun.[638]

> Thus you see that they started to receive this suggestion, opinion, and superstition from the Montanists: that through the sign of the cross we thought we protected ourselves in body and soul against the power and skill of Satan and against all danger.
>
> We used to sing publicly, "Through the sign of the cross free us from our enemies, our Lord. O glorious cross, O venerable cross, O precious wood and wonderful sign! You, Christ the most godly King, whose cross is a sign of the time, the moment of moments, when you did not fail to defend us. O cross, behold the one and only hope, this time of passion; see godly righteousness and the gifts of kindness."
>
> I do not doubt that the good people who wrote such a song knew through synecdoche and great instruction about Christ crucified that it pertains to faith in Christ, as much as it might be very inconvenient for teachers of the church, who wrote about the holy cross, the wood of the cross, and the sign of the cross. Augustine had written about all such things in his commentary on John. "The sign of the cross," he says, "casts out the destroyer from us, only if Christ is dwelling in our hearts."[639]

But how few are those who knew this or could understand these clear and inconvenient words! So instead from that point on, people accepted these superstitions, idolatries, false worship, and vain faith against the first commandment and against faith in Christ through the hypocrisy of liars like the Montanists."[640]

Recalling a version of the medieval prayer *O Crux gloriosa* ("O Glorious Cross") that he sang as a young priest, Bugenhagen acknowledged that the adoration of the cross can rightly serve as a poetic way to adore the crucified. When not directed toward salvation through Christ alone, however, the cross and the sign of the cross can become new idols, superstitions, or sources of confusion. There is no guarantee from the Bible that the sign of the cross wards off the devil or protects a person from harm. Rather, as Augustine had written about it, its power rests in the Christ who already dwells in the human heart through faith.

Over time, the sign of the cross also became part of the consecration of the elements in Holy Communion.[641] Denying that the sign of the cross or any other human contribution had anything to do with the "efficient cause" of the bread and wine becoming Christ's body and blood, Bugenhagen wrote that Christ serves as his own efficient cause in the sacrament.

> It is granted that only the arrangement, institution, words and omnipotence of our Lord Jesus Christ are properly efficient causes, as you hear in the Lord's Supper from the mouth of Christ himself, who was made a sacrifice for us by the Father. He says, "Take, eat; this is my body, etc." [Matt. 26:26]. From the mouth and hands of Christ, who was crucified for us, there we receive the Lord's body and blood, the Lord's Supper, as Christ instituted for his church. We are obedient to this and do not create out of it other institutions against Christ.
>
> We ministers of Christ's gospel and sacraments are in fact dispensers of the mystery of God, the body and blood of Christ, but not creators of it. As Paul said of the Lord's Supper, "For I received from the Lord what I pass on to you, etc. [1 Cor. 11:23].[642]

This distinction between dispensers and creators of God's mystery shows how Bugenhagen connected justification by faith with his teaching of the ministry and the sacraments. While Catholics and Lutherans agreed that the Lord's Supper gives believers God's grace and that Christ becomes truly present in the bread and wine, the Lutheran position put the sacrament's efficacy outside of human ritual action and located it in God's promise alone. It is also striking that rather than dropping the Aristotelian language of "causes," Bugenhagen reframed it in order to assert that Christ is his own efficient cause. The sacrament is efficacious because Christ attached his promise to it, not because of ritual actions like the sign of the cross.

The Kingdom of God and the Bondage of the Will

Throughout the entire Jonah Commentary, Bugenhagen stressed that God alone saves and liberates people. Thus it is fitting that the commentary's tracts conclude with an Augustinian argument about the bondage of the will. Once again, Bugenhagen found in Tertullian early hints of a teaching that humans contribute to their salvation through good works of the will. In the book *Against Marcion*, Tertullian had written that people clearly have freedom of will after the fall, because God asked Adam "Where are you?" and asked Cain "Why are you angry, and why has your countenance fallen? If you do well, will you not be accepted?" (Gen. 3:9 and 4:6-7).[643] Bugenhagen rebutted this by saying that rather than inspiring good works from Adam and Cain, these questions emphasized their sinfulness and their inability to do the right thing on their own.[644] That is, rather than supporting the freedom of the human will, those verses show instead that goodness comes only from God, as it is God who promises protection and reconciliation to Adam and Eve (Gen. 3:15) and protection to Cain (Gen. 4:15-16).

Bugenhagen further denounced Tertullian's defense of free will based on Luke 17:21: "the kingdom of God is within you." Tertullian had written, "Now, who will not interpret the words 'within you' to be in your hand, within your power, if you hear and if you do God's commandment? The kingdom of God is in the commandments, as Moses said: 'The commandment is not too high for you, nor is it too far away' [Deut. 30:11]."[645] To this Bugenhagen retorted, "You see the abuse of Holy Scripture and the distortion of Christ's gospel immediately after the apostles for people's free will and our power and against Christ the Son of God, the Lord of glory, who was crucified for us."[646] Against Tertullian's idea that the power to do good "is within you," Bugenhagen offered his own interpretation of Luke 17:21.

> That no one can interpret this in any other way is clearly false, because in Luke 17 Christ was talking to the Jews about the kingdom of God, promised in the law and prophets, which had already come into the world through Christ the King. This would not come from outward practices (as under the law) but would rather be among you through the Holy Spirit in the confession of your mouth, the preaching of faith, and in your hearts: first through faith and invocation, then through obedience to the law, that is, love.
>
> Christ is our kingdom of God and the kingdom of heaven, against the kingdom of Satan, sin and death; as we pray: "hallowed be your name, your kingdom come, your will be done in heaven and on earth." For us the kingdom of God is not the law or God's commandment, as the Montanists blasphemed, nor does it come through works of the law. So much less are we justified and saved by extra works of merit. Instead, justification comes through Christ alone when we believe in him who was crucified for us. With their preaching about the free will and its power, those "righteous" and blasphemous spiritualists deny that Christ is our righteousness before God even to the present day, as the Louvain Theologians clearly say in article nine...
>
> For the Louvain Montanists say this: "Faith by which one firmly believe and states with certainty that one's sins are forgiven for Christ's sake and one will obtain eternal life has no support in Scriptures, indeed is opposed to them." These people defect from faith, because they hate, blaspheme and persecute faith in Christ. And removing Christ, whom they deny to be our righteousness and salvation, they send us back to our works and the natural power of our free will for meriting eternal righteousness and salvation. That is, their blasphemy and ungodly doctrine of Christian repentance take us from that which is in Christ's name (Luke 24[:47]) and send us back to false repentance, which is in our name, through the power, freedom and ability of our free will.[647]

Beginning with a refutation of Tertullian's interpretation of Luke 17, Bugenhagen presented his own view of the kingdom of

God being among or within humans: "Christ is our kingdom of God." God's kingdom does not come through the law. It came once through Christ's incarnation and continues through the Spirit-filled gifts of faith and preaching in the Christian community. Because Christ is present in these ways, believers can experience life in God's kingdom by receiving grace, doing the good works that follow faith, and sharing Christian communion with each other.

According to Bugenhagen, the "Louvain Montanists" followed Tertullian by denying certainty of faith, thereby putting the assurance of salvation someplace other than Christ. Bugenhagen identified rituals and works of the law as two places where people seek holiness rather than justification by faith. Therefore, to teach that the human will is able to perform such works of merit was another point at which Bugenhagen could connect Montanus and Tertullian with his sixteenth-century opponents. As evidence that Bugenhagen's argument was still operating under the original umbrella of Jonah 3, the citation above ended with the identification of the discussion of the difference between true and false repentance, the theme that first launched these tracts.

Looking to bridge the centuries between Tertullian and the Council of Trent even more completely, Bugenhagen examined the "scholastic theology" of the preceding centuries. Up to this point in the *Jonah*, Bugenhagen had occasionally mentioned thinkers like Lombard, Lyra, and Aquinas. Sometimes his discussion of them was positive, as when he identified Lombard as a source for Luther's insights about the righteousness of God. More frequently, though, he mentioned these scholastic authorities in order to refute their teachings on the sacraments or rituals.[648] His argument about the bondage of the will challenged the scholastic belief that native goodness remains in the human will after the fall, so that people have an innate moral power to choose good, reject evil, and cooperate with God's grace for their salvation.

As evidence of this tendency, he cited the scholastic axiom, "Do what is in you and God will not deny grace."[649] In *The Harvest of Medieval Theology*, Heiko Oberman identified this phrase as central to the teaching of Gabriel Biel, a fifteenth-century German theologian.[650] Oberman noted that Biel's teaching had not represented a drastic deviation from the tradition but was in line with the majority of medieval theology, including dominant interpretations of Thomas Aquinas.[651] Although Biel and others consistently pointed out that the free will is assisted by God's grace, the emphasis on the will's ability to cooperate with grace made the theology Pelagian, that is, emphasizing human work rather than divine grace.[652] Luther had written against the will's ability to cooperate in matters of salvation as early as his "Disputation against Scholastic Theology" of 1517: "It is false to state that the will can by nature conform to correct precept. This is said in opposition to [Duns] Scotus and Gabriel [Biel]."[653] In the same disputation Luther also asserted, "And this is false, that doing all that one is able to do can remove the obstacles to grace."[654]

To this Lutheran argument for starker teachings about sin and grace than usually taught in medieval traditions, Bugenhagen added his own insights. He asserted that the freedom of the will is something invented by human reason, which always underestimates its own sin and need for God; it is not taught or revealed in the Bible.[655] Bugenhagen did not make this conclusion to denigrate reason but to emphasize faith and the correct use of Christ. While human reason easily and inevitably gets involved in projects of self-justification, faith in Christ frees one from self-deception and opens up new possibilities for truth and love.

This emphasis on Christ's truth was the point of Bugenhagen's personal motto: "If you know Jesus well, it is enough, even if you know nothing else. But if you do not know Jesus, whatever else you learn is nothing."[656] Although not original to Bugenhagen,[657] this saying summarized his personal faith and his work as a pastor. It entered the commentary here as Bugenhagen supposed that people would criticize his opposition to esteemed authorities like Tertullian and Cyprian. In response to such objections, he wrote, "There is nothing to know, except to know Christ as much as possible" before giving the first half of his personal motto: "*Si Christum bene scis, satis est, si caetera nescis.*"[658] To Bugenhagen, honoring leaders like Tertullian and Cyprian is not an excuse for following them where they taught something other than Christ's righteousness.

Bugenhagen's final extended theme in the tract on Tertullian is a further defense of the goodness of marriage. This fits with his larger pattern of moving from theological reflection to matters of daily life. Tertullian had written several severe works about women, marriage, and celibacy. In these, Bugenhagen found historical roots for the clerical celibacy and vows of chastity that Lutherans continued to reject and fought to change. He also identified misogyny in Tertullian's writing that he worked to undo through biblical interpretation, theological reasoning, and support of healthier practices.

Bugenhagen's first defense of the Lutheran practice of clerical marriage was that Christians had always tolerated difference in local customs; these differences should not disturb more important unity in faith and love.[659] Recognizing that an appeal to tolerance was not likely to be persuasive to opponents, Bugenhagen added biblical and traditional reasons for upholding marriage and the marriage of priests so that his audience would at least know why Lutherans practiced as they did. This final section, therefore, builds on the work of the third tract to present positive Lutherans views of marriage, women, and community.

One of Tertullian's main arguments came from his interpretation of monogamy as faithfulness to Christ. He interpreted New Testament passages saying that bishops, deacons, and elders should be husbands of only one wife (1 Timothy 3:2, 12 and Titus 1:6) to mean that all Christians should be celibate, devoted only to Jesus. Bugenhagen said this was nonsense, because those passages refer specifically to marriage between men and women, not to Jesus (especially Titus 1:6).[660] He attributed this poor exegesis to a false understanding of the spirit and the letter, which had allowed Tertullian to invent fanciful allegories. In contrast to Tertullian's ideas against marriage, Bugenhagen found no reason why the passages from Timothy and Titus should not mean what they say; he also saw no reason why priests should not be included in God's blessing to humanity to "be fruitful and multiply" (Gen. 1:28).[661]

Tertullian's spiritual rigor resulted in a disdain for physical things like sexuality, which he considered impure. Bugenhagen rejected that kind of asceticism on the basis of a strong belief that bodies and relationships created by God were good.

> This is Montanist hypocrisy. He says that Christian holiness is not in the bonds of marriage but in living celibately: "Christ did not take a wife; therefore, Christians should not take wives, or else they are not holy. As Peter's Epistle says from Leviticus 19[:2]: 'You shall be holy, for I am holy' [1 Pet. 1:16]." As if the Holy Spirit had said these words against God's marriage![662]

Rather than advancing a kind of holiness based on asexual notions of sanctity, Bugenhagen offered an entirely different way of thinking about holiness. Holiness begins with God and not with people. It is given freely and received through faith. It is for people of all walks of life and does not depend on marital status. Further, because God created and blessed marriage, marriage and holiness are not mutually exclusive but can belong together. While Bugenhagen often spoke of "chastity within marriage," it was always as an effect rather than a cause of divine blessing.[663]

Having removed celibacy as a condition for holiness or church leadership, Bugenhagen denounced ascetic spirituality as a cover for self-righteousness and clerical privileges. Paraphrasing Galatians 3:28, he wrote, "In Christ, there is neither Barbarian nor Greek, male nor female, but in Christ we are all royal priests and priestly kings." This is a dramatic statement of the Lutheran "priesthood of all the baptized." Tertullian, however, had used the idea that all Christians are priests to promote celibacy and degrade marriage. He figured that if all Christians were equally priests, and if priests should be celibate, then all Christians should be celibate. To combat this idea, Bugenhagen responded, "These erring spirits with their foolish wisdom are insane. They are not only against Holy Scripture, against God, against Christ and his Spirit, and against our justification and salvation, but even against common sense and reason."[664] Tertullian's "foolish wisdom" had been to deny the goodness of the bodies and relationships that God created. These were affirmed not only by the Bible but by "common sense." The denial of marriage was a sign of a novel and unbiblical spirituality that made up its own rules about holiness. In contrast, Bugenhagen hoped to show that the Lutheran witness had firm grounding in scripture, the Christian tradition, and everyday experience.

Conclusion to the Tracts on Jonah 3

Bugenhagen's conclusion to this tract tied it together with the sections that came before, including his study of Jonah. Addressing the reader, he retraced how new traditions crept into the church after the time of the apostles through the great Latin writer of Trinitarian orthodoxy, Tertullian, and his willingness to embrace the spirituality of the Montanists. Over time, such teachings rose to prominence through the institution of new canons, regulations and ceremonies. These obscured the apostolic preaching of the gospel and the right use of the sacraments, including the sacrament of repentance. Bugenhagen's final judgment was this:

> This Antichristian blasphemy gave birth to that false and blasphemous repentance of our works, which is not done in Christ's name and leaves people in perpetual doubt. It also condemns and debases Christian repentance and forgiveness of sins, which is done in Christ's name and which Christ commended to us in Nineveh.
>
> You hear this [blasphemy] in the clear words of the Louvain Theologians. Moreover, they teach that our extra works according to human traditions make satisfaction for sin and merit eternal life. You do not receive forgiveness of sins on account of Christ, him who alone was crucified for us and is our righteousness and our salvation. Here you have the entire Antichristendom, evil teaching in the church of Christ, the spirit of error, and the doctrines of demons through the hypocrisy of liars, etc.[665]

Returning to the repentance of Nineveh commended by Christ, Bugenhagen connected all the various parts of his commentary. Already in his preface, he had emphasized that Nineveh's repentance was a Christian repentance. The commentary on Jonah 1 and 2 further explained that the encounter with God through law and gospel worked faith and repentance in both the gentile sailors and the prophet Jonah himself. Now, at the end of the tracts, Bugenhagen showed that rituals, however pious or supposedly spiritual, are neither substitutes nor conditions for the reconciliation available to all people through faith in Christ.

In the first tract, Bugenhagen studied repentance by interpreting Nineveh's experience in light of the Augsburg Confession's definition of repentance as contrition and faith: Nineveh had been saved by believing God's word, recognizing their sins, and trusting in God's mercy. Their good works and renunciation of violence followed this justification rather than preceded it. The second tract expanded upon this biblical example of God freely forgiving sin to teach justification by faith alone. Here Bugenhagen drew not only on Jonah or Matthew 12, but upon Paul, Augustine, Luther and Melanchthon. He also began to refute more directly the teachings of the Council of Trent, the Louvain theologians, and the Augsburg Interim, who denied certainty of forgiveness. Bugenhagen considered the denial of *sola fide* to be a sign of the Antichrist because it rejected Christ's teaching and Christ's power to work in people's lives in favor of traditions and righteousness that had not come from the Bible. To this end, the third and fourth tracts applied justification by faith to matters of Christian worship and daily life like marriage vows, religious rituals, and the sign of the cross.

In all of this, Bugenhagen presented positive arguments for Christian faith and holiness. Instead of unconditionally demanding that his opponents totally agree with him, he asked that they begin to tolerate Lutheran preaching and practice. He did not aim for absolute unity in doctrine or rituals, but allowed for difference, as long as Christ stayed at the center. His condemnation of individuals, groups and institutions was not absolute but was based on the equal status of all people as sinners in need of forgiveness under Christ. For all of its vitriol, Bugenhagen's description of the "Louvain Montanists" as teaching "the entire Antichristendom" hoped to address the problems of minimizing sin and overestimating personal righteousness.

Through his lectures at the University of Wittenberg, Bugenhagen taught students what he had learned over nearly three decades as a reformer. While his *Jonah* presents a negative view of Roman Catholic contemporaries, Bugenhagen was defending a Pauline, Augustinian and Lutheran stream of Catholic Christianity that was under direct physical and spiritual threat. Confronted with the possible end of his reformation movement and aware that he was near the end of his own life, Bugenhagen shared the faith he had taught, preached, practiced and believed with passion and clarity. He also included an unmistakable appeal to the unity of the one church of Christ across time and place. In these tracts, students in the lecture hall and readers of the published commentary learned about a Lutheran tradition that started with biblical interpretation, engaged the Christian tradition, and addressed contemporary realities. Amazingly wide in their reach, the tracts on Jonah 3 give textbook examples of what it means to live by faith alone.

CHAPTER SEVEN

Final Confessions

After the tracts, the book returns to direct interpretation of Jonah 3 and 4. Unlike the sections on Jonah 1 and 2, these chapters do not make verse-by-verse comments. And unlike the tracts, the comments are brief and stay focused on the biblical text. The stylistic difference between these and other sections suggests that Bugenhagen did not simply insert the tracts into a finished commentary after that fact; instead, he seems to have written these last two chapters as a summary of his entire book to that point, letting the prophet Jonah have the last word.

Bugenhagen's return to the text of Jonah 3 revisits the relationship between Nineveh's faith and its works of repentance. It starts by examining Nineveh's experience with the word of God in light of that city's origins, described in Genesis 10. Then, in six fascinating pages, Bugenhagen concluded his commentary by presenting a historically distinctive interpretation of Jonah 4, applying his emphasis on true repentance to the prophet's anger in that chapter. The book therefore ends with a presentation of Jonah as a humble, repentant and faithful preacher, despite the biblical book's abrupt and ambiguous conclusion. In this way, Bugenhagen's *Jonah* teaches the theology of the cross one last time: no one comes out of life perfect or unstained by sin. Even the prophets and saints "have gone to ruin" and are only restored by God's grace. In view of the commentary's tumultuous context in Saxony under the Augsburg Interim, this conclusion stands as a powerful final confession of Bugenhagen's personal faith near the end of his life.

Law and Gospel in Jonah 3

As its heading suggests, the *repetitio tertii Capitis Ionae Prophetae* (Repetition of the Third Chapter of the Prophet Jonah) summarizes themes that Bugenhagen developed earlier. Introducing this section, Bugenhagen remembered Christ's commendation of Nineveh's repentance in Matthew 12.[666] He then denounced past and present attempts to understand or create righteousness through reason or works of the law, which is the argument that he advanced in his second tract.[667] Finally, he wrote that "we put an end to these falsifications in the tract on human traditions, which Paul calls the teachings of demons, which began after the apostles through Montanus and the Montanists."[668] After the detailed historical work of those pieces, Bugenhagen reconnected them here with Jonah 3. To do this, he identified seven mains points of biblical interpretation.

> First, Nineveh was a city of God. Second, Jonah preached nothing other than "Forty days more and Nineveh will be destroyed." Third, "the people of Nineveh believed in God." Fourth, "they proclaimed a fast and wore sackcloth," etc. Fifth, everyone turned from their evil ways and from the violence that was in their hands. Sixth, "who knows if God will turn and forgive," etc. Seventh, "God saw their works," etc.[669]

This is a good summary of both Jonah 3 and the four tracts. Through preaching, people turn to God, recognize their sin, renounce violence, and start doing good works of love. Because the tracts covered most of those seven points, Bugenhagen dedicated the majority of the *repetitio* to two areas that had received less attention: Nineveh's status as a city of God and the preaching of law and gospel.

The first of these was relatively easy for Bugenhagen to explain, because here he agreed with Jerome, the Latin Vulgate Bible, and Martin Luther that Nineveh was a "city of God." Further support for this interpretation came from the account of Nineveh's founding in Genesis 10. There he reasoned that, having been established by Noah's descendents, the people of Nineveh knew God's promise to deliver them from sin and the devil since their founding. While Bugenhagen followed Luther's interpretation and borrowed many of his arguments from Luther's lectures on Genesis, he came to some different conclusions.

Instead of supposing that Jonah's sermon included more than those few words of wrath as Luther and Jerome had, Bugenhagen insisted that Jonah had only preached the few words of divine wrath that the Bible records. His belief that Nineveh was a city of God was ultimately an argument about the power of the gospel. He believed that Jonah really had preached only God's wrath to city, which caused the people to remember the proto-gospel of Genesis 3:15 that they had heard in ages past. After hearing Jonah's words of condemnation, the people of Nineveh had no earthly hope for survival. They received nothing but the righteous sentence of impending death. Yet this knowledge of wrath and doom led them to despair in themselves and turn to God for life.[670]

This was not a new concept in Bugenhagen's commentary. Jonah's experience in the belly of the great fish had led to the similar observation that Jonah really should have died at sea, justly punished for his disobedience. Jonah expected death when he asked to be thrown overboard. No one was there to preach good news to him or assure him of God's goodness. But, Bugenhagen noted, Jonah's time in the fish was not marked by despair but by his prayer of contrition for sin, confession of faith, and thanksgiving. In the midst of death, Jonah had miraculously experienced God's mercy, life and liberation.

Though Bugenhagen did not explicitly make this connection between Jonah and Nineveh's deliverance, both moments exemplify Paul's words that God's law brings the knowledge of sin (Rom. 3:20, 4:15). Bugenhagen then connected Nineveh's miraculous salvation to the "experience of all the saints," who find grace when they least expect or deserve it.[671] This is the same theology of the cross taught in Bugenhagen's comments on Jonah 2. Although separated by hundreds of pages of text and months of lectures, the same theology was at work: faith sees the truth about God most clearly when all illusion is stripped away to reveal that God alone is the source of life.

Bugenhagen's explanation of Nineveh's salvation also revisited the debates with Roman Catholics about certainty of faith. Jonah 3:9 states, "Who knows? God may relent and change his mind." Bugenhagen had only briefly treated this passage in his first tract. Unexamined, it continued to challenge the Lutheran teaching about certainty of faith. In a unique interpretive twist, Bugenhagen managed to turn the King of Nineveh, who had spoken those words, into another preacher of law and gospel. Employing some textual criticism, Bugenhagen rejected the Latin Vulgate's addition of the word "if" (in Latin, *si*) into that verse.[672] With the word "if," the sentence reads, "Who knows if God will relent and forgive and turn from his wrath so that we will not perish?" With that "if," the entire sentence becomes one of doubt, confirming the view that it is a sin of pride to trust in one's salvation and be certain of God's forgiveness. It would support the Augsburg Interim's denunciation of certainty of faith.

Without that little "if," however, the king was not asking one long speculative question. Instead he asked a question and then made a statement. To Bugenhagen, this was a crucial difference. He believed that the "if" was not part of the meaning in Hebrew. Instead, "Who knows?" becomes the question of people under the law who are aware that they deserve God's just punishment. But then the second half of the sentence reads as a hopeful statement: "God may relent and change his mind; he may turn away from his fierce anger, so that we do not perish."[673] In separating the verse into two main clauses, Bugenhagen followed Luther's German translation rather than the Vulgate.[674] At the end of the verse, however, Bugenhagen cleverly decided to agree with the Vulgate. He noticed that in Latin the verse ends with a future indicative, *et non peribimus*: "and we will not perish." For Bugenhagen, the Vulgate's future indicative expressed Nineveh's sure faith in God's grace. "And we will not perish" is a statement of confidence! As he had done with justification of works in James, Bugenhagen turned a passage seemingly against Lutheran teaching into one supporting it. The people of Nineveh were saved through the preaching of the law and faith in God's mercy.

Reminiscent of his comments on Jonah's initial call to preach, Bugenhagen put himself in the Ninevites' place and explained law and gospel from their perspective.

> And so this "who knows?" is a word of law. It says that no one knows the real terror, wrath and judgment of God, which God displayed against us Ninevites because of our sin by means of the prophet Jonah's death sentence. No one who knows his sin and the wrath of God knows that we preach the gospel to you: "God may turn back," etc. For no one truly knows about God's grace and mercy (even in this terrible and righteous judgment of God), if nothing is seen but God's unbearable wrath.
>
> Therefore we who believe in God announce "no one knows" so that you also may believe in God's mercy, which lies hidden under this wrath. Do not despair of your sin.

God forgives you your sin and turns from that righteous fury of his wrath, which to us now is real fury and wrath; soon he will be to us what he truly is in himself – unspeakable grace, mercy, and fatherly love – when we believe according to the gospel which we preach to you, that God might be converted and repent, etc.[675]

Rather than counseling despair or doubt, Bugenhagen aimed to show that this "Who knows?" was a call to faith and personal conversion. Here again, what a thing is (*quid sit*) leads to what it does (*quid effectus*). In this case, the experience of the law leads to despair in oneself and trust in God alone, who is most truly known as a God of "unspeakable grace, mercy and fatherly love." The positive effects of this law and gospel message are deliverance from destruction and an end to "the violence that is in our hands" (Jonah 3:8).

Bugenhagen's interpretation was guided by his concern for people's everyday lives. Through law and gospel, God's word confronts people with their unbelief and their sins, even as it promises and gives liberation. Bugenhagen again stated that this liberation is made possible through faith, which alone receives God's promises and frees people for good works.

> All Holy Scripture or Word of God is either law or gospel, as you have seen was written in these two sermons: "Who knows? God may turn back." Through this "who knows" all people who do not know God's goodness and grace are condemned because they do not know that God is their father; so they do not believe in God, trust in God's goodness, or have any good hopes about God…
>
> Truly through this gospel, "God may turn back" (which God promised in paradise, that the woman's seed shall crush the head of the serpent [Gen. 3:15]), all who believe in the promised seed according to the gospel of God's glory receive forgiveness of sins and will be saved.[676]

For Bugenhagen, forgiveness of sins and salvation are not abstract or internal spiritual categories. They bring a new freedom and a life rightly directed towards God and neighbor. With this passage, Bugenhagen then offered a broad sweep of his biblical theology and evangelical faith, revisiting his main points about repentance, faith and the justification of the ungodly through Jesus

Christ. The king of Nineveh's "two sermons" turned Jonah's words of destruction into an appeal to faith and mercy. The people of Nineveh had experienced scripture's two modes of speaking, law and gospel, which brought them salvation and peace.

As the *repetitio* comes to its close, readers are reminded that what they have heard is the end of something that started much earlier and which had been developed throughout the four tracts. It ends with the following summary, which stands as Bugenhagen's final statement about the nature and benefits of Nineveh's repentance, as commended by Christ himself.

> With this you have a tract on true and Christian repentance,
> which Christ commended to us through the Ninevites,
> against the false repentance which the doctrines
> of demons introduced into the Church of
> Christ and which obscure and negate the
> benefits and use of our Mediator,
> the Lord Jesus
> Christ.

The Ongoing Chastisement of the Saints: Bugenhagen and Jonah 4

In Bugenhagen's six pages on Jonah 4, the tone of the work changes. There is no further mention of Montanists, Louvain theologians, or the papacy. After chapter 3 closed with its final affirmation of Nineveh's faith and denunciation of extra-biblical traditions, teachings and false works of repentance, chapter 4 stands free of such condemnations. It offers an entirely positive conclusion for those who, like Bugenhagen, faced anxious and confusing times. While such a hopeful note had not often entered the *Jonah*, Bugenhagen's encouraging insights remained within the scope of his opening loci, especially those on sin among the saints, repentance as contrition and faith, and all history being in the image of the passion and resurrection of Christ.

Not only is Bugenhagen's conclusion to the commentary free of condemnations, but it differs dramatically from the dominant Christian interpretation of Jonah 4. In that chapter, Jonah went outside of Nineveh to see what would happen to the city. He was "angry enough to die," because he had known that God would spare Nineveh as soon as God first called him (4:2). God then sent a plant to give the angry prophet shade from the heat; just as suddenly, God caused the plant to die. This again made Jonah "angry enough to die." God responded by asking that if Jonah was so upset about the death of the plant, should not God be even more upset about the potential death of the entire city of Nineveh?

> But God said to Jonah, "Is it right for you to be angry about the bush?" And he said, "Yes, angry enough to die." Then the Lord said, "You are concerned about the bush, for which you did not labor and which you did not grow; it came into being in a night and perished in a night. And should I not be concerned about Nineveh, that great city, in which there are more than a hundred and twenty thousand persons who do not know their right hand from their left, and also many animals?" (Jonah 4:9-11).

The book of Jonah ends with that question. This presents the interpretive problem that the book ends with an angry and unrepentant prophet. By the end of the story, Jonah has said for a third time that it is better for him to die than to live. Rather than resolving the prophet's irritation, God posed a question and seems to have left Jonah in his anger.

Jerome explained this conclusion by continuing to view Jonah as a figure of Christ. He interpreted the prophet's complaints to God in light of New Testament parallels like Jesus' lament for Jerusalem (Luke 13:33-35) and Paul's desire to bear the punishment for the unbelief of his contemporary Jews (Rom. 9:3).[677] In that reading, Jonah remains faithful to God, while piously mourning for those who reject God's salvation. Jerome also explained Jonah's statement that "it is better for me to die than to live" (4:5) by connecting them to Jesus' words from the cross: "Father, into your hands I commend my spirit" (Luke 23:46). As Jerome admitted, however, his allegorical interpretation broke down when it comes to the plant that shaded Jonah: the text has God say that God created the shade plant and not Jonah (4:10). This would invalidate Jerome's identification of Jonah with Jesus because Christ also created all things.[678] On this point, Jerome would rather respect the mysteries of God than make any interpretation against the doctrine of the Trinity. He concluded by returning to the more compliant allegory that Nineveh represents the gentile church, which Christ came to save.[679]

Without Jerome's Christological allegory to retain something of Jonah's integrity as a prophet, Luther concluded outright that the prophet's anger foreshadowed Jewish lack of belief in Jesus as the messiah. While sympathetic earlier in his commentary to Jonah's failings as a "saint and sinner," Luther's comments here totally condemned the prophet's unwillingness as a Jew to rejoice in God's salvation to the gentiles; predictably, Luther extended this condemnation to the papacy of his time.[680] Although silent on this point in the 1525 Latin lectures, Luther brought his German lectures on Jonah to a close with three of his own allegorical readings of the entire book, which he called "spiritual" readings.[681]

In Luther's first allegory, Jonah (which means "dove") represents the coming of the Holy Spirit and the gospel to the gentiles. The stormy sea represents the cross and persecution, while the sea is the sinful world and the whale is the devil. Amid such obstacles, God takes care to preserve the gospel. Luther concluded, "Thus, though pastors may be weak and the world powerful, God's Word, the holy Gospel, is still mightier, and no obstacles can impede its progress."[682] This interpretation of trusting God's word to change the world amid persecution certainly spoke to Luther's context after the Peasants War and offered a positive message to beleaguered preachers then.

Similarly, the second "spiritual" reading is about finding strength amid persecution; but this time the persecution comes from God's law, which condemns a sinful conscience. The ship that experiences the storm is free will. The whale is death and hell. The little ship of free will is lost in the coming of God's wrath through the law: "This is the sequence: first the Law, then sin, and finally death."[683] After discussing the firm grip that death has over body and soul, Luther wrote, "Then comes the living Word of God, the Gospel of grace, and addresses the fish, that is, it commands death not to touch man. That is where faith sets in, and man is freed both of sin and of death and lives in grace and righteousness with Christ."[684] If the first allegory taught the saving value of Christian preaching, this second allegory explains the function of the word of God to overcome the bondage of the will. This interpretation also would also have been immediately relevant to Luther's context in 1525, when he was in a dispute over the freedom of the will with Erasmus of Rotterdam. Luther concluded here by saying that Jonah's personal experience of this law and gospel dynamic is what made him such an effective preacher.[685]

After these two positive interpretations, the third allegory considered the shade plant that grew over Jonah. In Luther's reading, the plant represents Judaism, "which was a real wild plant."[686] Here he followed medieval allegorical rules, which stated (already in Thomas Aquinas) that anything interpreted allegorically in one place had to appear literally somewhere else. In this case, Luther used Romans 11:23 to make the connection. This "wild plant" provided only shade and bore no fruit. God's appointing a worm to smite the plant signifies Christ's bringing the gospel to the gentiles and God's verdict against exclusivist Jewish claims about being the chosen people. "Therefore Judaism withered and decayed in all the world, and thus we see it today."[687] Luther then referred again to Romans 9-11 (and very peculiarly to Caiaphas' prophecy in John 11:50) to conclude, "it is better and fairer that Judaism should die... than that it be preserved and the whole world brought to ruin."[688] While Luther's German lectures end with the possibility that Luther may again be referring to the Jews in order to denounce the "works-righteousness" of papal opponents, this allegorical reading ultimately condemns both Jonah and Judaism. It raises the specter that Luther's low regard for Judaism was not only voiced in his later writings but had long informed his theology and his biblical interpretation.[689]

Throughout the Jonah Commentary, Bugenhagen appears to have followed Luther uncritically on this matter of Christian superiority over Judaism. Both reformers similarly advanced Protestant Christianity's frequent claims to have real gospel teachings, as opposed to the "Pharisaical" Roman Catholic Church. Earlier in the commentary, for instance, Bugenhagen had written, "we see the Jews, who were God's people, rejected by God. The papists have also been rejected through God's wrath."[690] And in his opening loci, Bugenhagen had identified Jonah's preaching and Nineveh's conversion as proof of God's condemnation of the Jews.[691]

It is therefore important to note that Bugenhagen's work does not end where Luther's did. In fact, on this point, Bugenhagen's *Jonah* does not end where it began! Bugenhagen's emphasis on Jonah as a book of confession led him to an entirely different conclusion than what his own opening loci would have suggested. Here he presents a rare Christian reading of Jonah 4 that does not practice the same theological exclusivism or supersessionism that it condemns. It is ironic, after all, that an interpretation of Jonah 4 that attacks Jewish exclusivism against gentiles simply creates a new Christian exclusivism.

In the interpretative tradition represented by Jerome, Jonah's anger symbolized Jesus' righteous lament over the unbelief of the Israelites. In Luther's view, Jonah's anger expressed his sinful and (supposedly Jewish) refusal to see God's grace extended to all peoples. But Bugenhagen's unwavering emphasis on repentance and faith resulted in an interpretation that differs dramatically from Jerome, Luther, and the overwhelming majority of interpreters across the Christian tradition. Bugenhagen began his discussion of Jonah 4 by reminding his audience that Jonah is a book of confession and faith from beginning to end.

> Therefore, Christ's church loves the book of the prophet Jonah, in which there are three clear examples of true repentance and the forgiveness of sins. First, Jonah himself sinned and fled from God's face, after which he was cast into a horrible death but was miraculously saved. Second, [the repentance and forgiveness] of Nineveh. The third is about Jonah again. For you read here that he gravely sinned like he did before.
>
> It is a wonder that such a great prophet could sin so defiantly against God and neighbor – that is, against all of God's commandments – after he had been brought back from the dead. But through this God wanted to show the church that when God does great and wonderful works through us, we are not acting on our own, even when we are in the highest stations. So it was for Jonah, David, Paul, Isaiah, Jeremiah, and others. Recognizing these clearly to be works by God and not works by us who are truly sinners, we say what those saints have said, "All that we have done, O Lord, you have done for us" (Is. 26[:12]).[692]

Recalling that Jonah is a book of confession and forgiveness, Bugenhagen continued to interpret Jonah 4 in that light. Jonah's anger and despair remind readers that even the most effective preachers and believers do not stand on their own merit; they too fall prey to sins of pride and self-righteousness. Therefore, rather than condemn Jonah for his unbelief like Luther did, Bugenhagen included him in a list of God's prophets and saints who had also proved themselves unworthy of the gifts they received from God.

As he had mentioned at the beginning of the commentary, this list was headed by such great biblical leaders as David, Peter and Paul. Indeed, after the citation from Isaiah (above), Bugenhagen continued to quote from the Psalms, Jeremiah, Jonah 2 and Paul, beginning with David's confession in Psalm 51:4, "Against you, you alone, have I sinned, and done what is evil in your sight, so that you are justified in your sentence and blameless when you pass judgment."[693] With this citation of Psalm 51, Bugenhagen returned to a passage he had cited in the fall of 1547, when he turned to Jonah as a book revealing the hidden wisdom of the God who justifies the ungodly.[694]

Despite this similarity with earlier portions of the commentary, Bugenhagen seemed much more willing to identify personally with the fallen prophet personally here than he had been at the beginning. His earlier view of Jonah was that the prophet's anger signified Israel's rejection of Jesus and, conversely, God's rejection of Israel. But now, at the commentary's conclusion, Bugenhagen spoke of an "ongoing chastisement" in faith that always leads back to confession of sin and faith in God's mercy. Rather than condemning others, Bugenhagen ended with a statement about self-examination. In the caption that accompanied his comments on Jonah's anger and despair, Bugenhagen summarized, "Thus the saints are chastised all their lives."[695] He explained,

> They are chastised all their lives, I say, not only by the many great and various afflictions that one observes in the saints, but also by various sins, and by terrors before God's face. As they say, "Do not enter into judgment with your servant, for no one living is righteous before you" [Ps. 143:2] and "If you, O Lord, should mark iniquities, Lord, who would stand?" [Ps. 130:3]. That is, no one will be saved. No one will expect your mercy; no one will expect kindness from you.[696]

Instead of rebuking Jonah for his unworthiness and disbelief, Bugenhagen identified with him! Instead of teaching believers to strive for an ever-increasing enlightenment, sanctification, or perfection, the scriptures speak of an "ongoing chastisement" of even the greatest prophets and saints. In this interpretation, Jonah no longer stands as the sign of an unbelieving and apostate Israel but as an example of God's hidden work of redemption among imperfect people. Therefore, Bugenhagen's interpretation of Jonah

4 does not end with the lament for Jerusalem but with encouragement for all people. He then cited Romans 8:28 and Lamentations 3:26-31, passages that promise finding hope and grace amid sin, despair, and destruction.[697]

In his rehabilitation of Jonah, Bugenhagen recalled the examples of two other biblical figures: Elijah and Paul. Like Jonah, Elijah had asked God to take his life when he was fleeing from Ahab and Jezebel. Elijah "went a day's journey into the wilderness, and came and sat down under a solitary broom tree. He asked that he might die: 'It is enough; now, O Lord, take away my life, for I am no better than my ancestors'" (1 Kings 19:4). In response to Elijah's despair, God sent a ministering angel to feed and care for the despondent prophet. Paul wrote in a similar way about his own humiliating "thorn in the flesh," saying: "I prayed three times to the Lord, but received the response, 'My grace is sufficient for you, for my power is made perfect in your weakness'" (2 Cor. 12:8-9).[698] These struggles with faith connect Jonah with figures whose despair brought new insights about God's comfort, strength, and power in times of weakness and hopelessness. Here Bugenhagen not only presented a theology of *simul iustus et peccator* (simultaneously righteous and sinner) but formulated a theology of *simul confessio peccatorum et confessio fides* (simultaneously confessing sin and confessing faith).

This shift from condemnation of Jonah to identification with him constitutes a major statement in Bugenhagen's *Jonah*. Rather than asserting theological supremacy over his opponents, Bugenhagen sided with those who seem to have been forsaken by God: forlorn prophets like Elijah and Jonah, Lamentations' deep pain over the destroyed city of Jerusalem, and the apostle Paul, who would carry that thorn in his flesh until he died. Bugenhagen's refusal to condemn Jonah and the Jews at this point is a major theological change of emphasis. Did he perhaps notice that traditional Christian interpretations of Jonah 4 condemning the Jews merely imitate the exclusive self-righteousness that Lutherans were protesting against? It is possible that in refusing to interpret Jonah 4 as a statement against the Jews, Bugenhagen made his final stand one of contrition and faith, trusting above all in a merciful God rather than striving for theological supremacy over enemies.

This interpretation of Jonah 4 literally stands as Bugenhagen's last major work of biblical interpretation. It is a profound statement. True Christian doctrine is not a set of ideas or a contest for religious purity. Rather, doctrine is valuable because it points back to Christ and his cross. There one finds the divine truth and wisdom that is so easily hidden or lost amid other ways of judging wisdom and virtue in the world. Bugenhagen had recognized this in his statement that "all history is in the image of the passion and resurrection of Christ." Having just survived the Smalcald War, Bugenhagen might have thought that he was well acquainted with the hardships and humiliations of the cross when he wrote that line in 1547. Apparently, however, he would receive more schooling in the theology of the cross through pressures like the Augsburg Interim and conflicts with people who had been friends, students and coworkers. By the summer of 1549, Bugenhagen had identified his Lutheran opponents with the same diabolical spirit that had militarily and politically threatened his church through the war and the Augsburg Interim. He found this spirit even more insidious than Roman Catholic opposition, as it aimed to undermine Wittenberg's teaching from within.

Ultimately unwilling to use justification by faith alone to assert his religious superiority over others, Bugenhagen's interpretation of Jonah 4 turned even more toward the theology of the cross. Bugenhagen's Jonah was angry because God seemed to have treated him unjustly. He accused and condemned God for punishing him when he fled. Speaking again in the first person, Bugenhagen's Jonah says,

> I was right to flee from your face. You were unjust to judge the gentiles with wrath and to punish me, so that when I emerged I was forced to announce the sentence of death against Nineveh, whom you then received in grace. For this, I have been ridiculed and called a false prophet, because what I preached did not happen.[699]

This great distance between God and the prophet matches the theology of the cross. Jonah had suffered tremendously and apparently unnecessarily after God called first called him to preach to Nineveh. Then, after God forgave them (as he knew would happen anyways!), Jonah was left to look like a false prophet. Both human righteousness and divine justice seem to have failed him: he was left utterly empty before God and humans.

But God did not leave Jonah in that despair. Bugenhagen extended Jonah's story to its implied conclusions. Bugenhagen had opened his explanation of Jonah 4 by saying it marked a third moment of confession and forgiveness in the book. But where is this third confession? The book of Jonah appears to end with a despondent prophet and an unanswered question from God. Bugenhagen explained,

> But you say, "It does not say that Jonah repented of that horrible sin, on account of which God showed him his fault." You are wrong, because this was written! For none other than Jonah himself wrote this history of his disgrace, blasphemy, insolence, jealousy, and so on. Therefore, by writing this before the whole church, he repented.[700]

Jonah's final act of confession and faith was that he eventually told his story, including his shameful anger and despair, and allowed it to be recorded for others. The book's mere existence testifies to a final act of confession! Bugenhagen found one final instance of true repentance in Jonah, which presents a uniquely favorable reading of the prophet.

This conclusion did not come from Bugenhagen's imagination but from the text itself. To support his interpretation that Jonah returned to Jerusalem and shared his story, Bugenhagen referred back to the vow that Jonah had made from inside the belly of the great fish: "But I with the voice of thanksgiving will sacrifice to you; what I have vowed I will pay" (2:9). Based on this passage, Bugenhagen presented an inner-textual basis for extending the story.

> Jonah went back to the temple in Jerusalem, returning the vow that he had promised in the song of chapter 2. And I believe that after his fame had spread through Assyria and Judea, those gentiles who with a heavy conscience had cast Jonah into the sea came to Jonah and they confirmed these miracles and preached the name of the Lord with him. Thanks be to Christ. Amen. The end.[701]

Once back in Israel, Jonah told his story as a confession of his sin and God's mercy. Using the same logic, Bugenhagen believed that the gentile sailors would also have gone to the temple to confirm Jonah's miraculous tale and to preach God's mercy with him. After all, they too had promised to pay vows to the Lord after their deliverance from the storm (1:16). This conclusion that the Jews and gentiles would preach the name of the Lord together has roots in both the Old and New Testaments' vision that salvation would begin with the Jews and then be extended to people of all nations. With the phrase "the name of the Lord," Bugenhagen also suggests the same preaching and experience found in the Acts of the Apostles, especially Acts 10:43. In Bugenhagen's view, the prophet Jonah had preached God's free justification of the ungodly to all people, effectively converting the gentile sailors and the evil city of Nineveh, even as he also relearned his own continual need for repentance.

Bugenhagen's 1551 Assessment of his *Jonah*

Although the *Jonah* does not appear to have elicited strong reactions from either friends or foes in public writings, Bugenhagen believed that it met its goals. His next publication after the Jonah Commentary was a treatise entitled "Von den ungeborn Kinder" ("On Unborn Children"). In it, he offered biblical and pastoral council for women and families who had experienced miscarriages, stillbirths and infant deaths, a topic that Luther had addressed in an appendix to Bugenhagen's 1542 exposition of Psalm 29.[702] Printed in conjunction with Luther's republished appendix, Bugenhagen's 1551 piece includes a defense of the Lutheran understanding of baptism and salvation. Discussing the power of the sacraments, Bugenhagen referred to his Jonah Commentary to re-emphasize the connections between the sacraments, true repentance, and salvation through faith in Christ.

> But they were deceived by the new spirit and Paraclete of Montanus and by the great spirituality of the Montanists – who enacted so much physical sanctity and many antichristian laws in their churches, which they called new spiritual ordinances hurled forth by the Montanists after the apostles for the perfection of the church, which crept in under the apostles' cradle (so they imagined) – and they accepted all of these human traditions. They called themselves *Spirituales*, the spiritual ones, which the priestly folk still use to identify themselves as spiritual today.
>
> But in this way faith in Christ is extinguished, as Christ says, "They worship me in vain, teaching human doctrines and commandments" [Matt. 15:9]. They serve me in vain (that is, all their spirituality and great worship is not worth crap, but is the devil's crap and the doctrines of demons), because they preach human teachings and human

commands. With God's word, I wrote strongly against the spiritualism of the Montanists in my *Jonah*. This heresy was first found in Cain and recently is in the world through the works-spirituality that has now taken the upper hand among the papists, against Christ and his dear gospel.

Also, I especially wrote against the words of St. Cyprian, who confirmed (to be sure dreadfully and with blasphemy) two Montanist additions to baptism, namely, the consecration of the water through a holy priest and the "smearing" after the baptism. And he thus misled all the bishops in Africa who were with him at the Council of Carthage, so that they instituted a re-baptism in all of Africa. And what is more, they grabbed the sheep of the other pious bishops who were against Cyprian, if they, too, accepted the twofold spiritualism about baptism.[703]

Many of these statements will appear familiar to readers. His views had not changed over the year: in 1551 Bugenhagen still identified the papacy and monastic life with Montanism and condemned the consecrations that entered the church through Cyprian. He also identified spiritual rigorism with an increase in division and intolerance among Christians.

Bugenhagen followed this summary of his writings against Cyprian and a "Montanist" conception of baptism by saying that spiritual rigor and ritual purity make things that should be optional into necessities. As he had in the Jonah Commentary, Bugenhagen quoted the Papal *Decretals* and Lombard's *Sentences* to show how these optional practices became new laws.

But we say in this clear truth of the gospel, that it is Christian that one condemns this *bene esse* concerning the true baptism of Christ. For one thing, it is a blasphemous lie from the new lying spirit and Paraclete of Montanus, as is clear from Cyprian's words: from his *Opertet* ("it is right") and *Necesse est* ("it is necessary"). I proved this clearly in my *Jonah*, which I brought into the clear light of day, showing what the papists have added with their consecrations, blessings, and anointings, which are things that a Christian now dreads to hear. May God do it better with his Holy Spirit through Jesus Christ his beloved son, our Lord, Amen. But this is also important especially because error and doubt have come to Christian baptism through this.[704]

Here Bugenhagen connected his historical and theological complaints against the papal tradition with practical realities he faced. These included people's concerns about the death of an infant who had not been baptized or the validity of a baptism performed in an emergency without the traditional blessings and presence of a priest. Despite having addressed matters in the *Jonah* in a historical or theological manner, these were also topics that spoke to pressing pastoral and personal concerns. From his perspective, the Augsburg Interim and Council of Trent threatened not only a body of doctrine but the daily spiritual life of local people. His insistence that he had brought this "into the clear light of day" also reminded readers that he had not wavered in his convictions but continued to practice and publish what he preached.

Bugenhagen's last comments about the Jonah Commentary in this 1551 treatise come in a section counseling people to keep trusting God's revelation through Christ.

> How shameful and, in Christ, no longer sufferable is the papist's teaching – as now also decided in Trent – that a Christian should have doubts about this clear light of the truth of Christ's gospel. Whoever likes can read about this and can sufficiently and strongly prove it from my *Jonah* that they cannot be supported by any prophetic writing however much they would like to claim it with great blasphemy against God and denial of Christ, that Christ alone should not be our righteousness before God and our eternal life. For Peter, full of the Holy Spirit in the house of Cornelius condemned the doubters in favor of the gentiles and said, "'All the prophets testify to Christ (this certainly includes Joel and Jonah) that everyone who believes in him receives forgiveness of sins through his name.' And while Peter was still speaking, the Holy Spirit fell upon all who heard the word" [Acts 10:43-44].
>
> Here the Holy Spirit gives testimony to such sure teaching about Christ against all doubters who do not believe God and who make him to be a liar because they do not believe the testimony that God gave about his Son: the testimony that God has given us eternal life and that this

life is in his Son. Whoever has the Son of God has life. Whoever does not have the Son of God does not have life either.[705]

Bugenhagen could hardly have made a more exact summary of his *Jonah*. At the heart of his commentary had stood the practical concerns that people trust in God and receive God's peace in their individual and communal lives: for "whoever has the Son of God has life."

CHAPTER EIGHT

Conclusions

Over the course of its composition, Bugenhagen's *Jonah* grew ever closer to its axiomatic opening statement that "all history is in the image of the passion and resurrection of Christ." Having survived the siege and surrender of Wittenberg, Bugenhagen began his lectures by interpreting Jonah as a sign of the repentance of Psalm 51, which teaches the hidden wisdom of God. Although the people and students of Wittenberg may not have been able to see God's will in Elector John Frederick's military and political defeat, Bugenhagen encouraged them to look to the repentance and faith seen in the book of Jonah.

Over the coming months, the Wittenbergers also needed to respond to the Augsburg Interim, a new religious policy that aimed at bringing Lutherans back to Roman Catholicism through imperial law. Lutheran theologians in Electoral Saxony attempted to work around the Interim, drafting statements intended to preserve civil peace without ceding their gospel teachings. Bugenhagen gave theological and liturgical responses to the Augsburg Interim in his work with Melanchthon, Georg von Anhalt, and others at Altcella. Even more, his critique of the Interim started to appear in his Jonah lectures, as he began writing against the theological uncertainty taught by the Louvain theologians, the Council of Trent, and implicitly the Augsburg Interim in his comments on Jonah 2. Faced with the real prospect that Lutherans would be militarily forced to adopt rituals and teachings that they had either rejected or reformed, Bugenhagen broke with his verse-by-verse commentary at Jonah 3 in order to explain as clearly as possible the Lutheran doctrines of justification by faith, true repentance, and false works or rituals that detract from God's righteousness in Jesus Christ. Remarkably, he never lost sight of the biblical foundation of his theology, writing those tracts under the umbrella of Jonah 3.

Bugenhagen continued writing the Jonah Commentary into 1549. Evidence for this has been shown from the letter of May

1550 to King Christian III, in which Bugenhagen wrote that he would have like his *Jonah* to have been printed six months earlier. Also, the manner in which Bugenhagen addressed the Johannine Comma in the third tract strongly suggests that he was addressing a 1549 edition of the New Testament that included the disputed passage. By that year, significant controversy with other Lutherans had already appeared: Bugenhagen was having to field criticism from other Lutherans already by February of 1549. Thus, the final publication of the Jonah Commentary took place amid controversies not only with Roman Catholic politicians and theologians but with Lutheran leaders as well.

This makes Bugenhagen's conclusion to Jonah 4 all the more remarkable. Amid the heat of the new adiaphoristic controversy, Bugenhagen responded with the same position he had adopted at the end of the Smalcaldic War: repent and believe, for "all history is in the image of the passion and resurrection of Christ." This did not indicate a quietist or defeatist position with respect to either the Augsburg Interim or Lutheran adversaries. As he repeatedly asserted, the Jonah Commentary takes a strong stand on the doctrine of justification and critiques points of worship mandated by the Augsburg Interim. His insistence that he had not been silent but had actively worked for the good of his community and his students is true. Indeed, Bugenhagen was so far from being silent that the nineteenth-century researcher Otto Vogt read this work primarily as an anti-Catholic and excessively polemical diatribe. Although certainty full of invectives, Bugenhagen's *Jonah* cannot be dismissed as merely polemical, partly because the category appears not to have existed at the time; instead, Bugenhagen's forceful statements against the papacy sought to serve a pastorally useful and publicly responsible end. In his *Jonah*, Bugenhagen hoped to teach his audience core points of Lutheran theology, strengthen his community during its afflictions, and serve the church in Saxony. He never named the Augsburg Interim, which would have earned swift reprisal and he did not advocate open rebellion. Instead, while clearly critical of the Interim's teaching and mandates, he recommended following the biblical example of Jonah to claim both Christian freedom and to remind believers of their calls to preach and to work for the common good, especially in hard times.

Even if it did not greatly succeed in winning over Roman Catholic or Lutheran critics, Bugenhagen's *Jonah* can be deemed a remarkable contribution of the time. It teaches readers today how a first generation Lutheran reformer interpreted the Bible and applied its teachings to matters of faith and daily life. In this commentary, we encounter a man who would "rather give his gray head" than lose the good news of justification by faith alone through Christ alone. As an interpreter, Bugenhagen merged insights from across the Bible, the Christian tradition, Luther and Melanchthon's theology, and from his own lifelong pastoral concerns and convictions. After a lifetime of studying, preaching, and teaching the Bible, we find him masterfully summoning up its stories and insights for the sake of those around him.

As a person close to both Luther and Melanchthon, this study of Bugenhagen also helps further clarify a "Wittenberg School" of Protestant theology. First, Bugenhagen's account of Luther's reformation "breakthrough" described Luther as a theologian steeped in the late medieval Catholic tradition and monastic spirituality. By pointing to the righteousness of God (*iustitia Dei*) found in Augustine and Lombard, Bugenhagen shed light on why Luther may have been so convinced of his theology and so disappointed in the early reactions that he received from the Roman hierarchy. His account presents a very Catholic Luther, whose grasp of the Bible and the tradition ushered in a new era.

One also finds many reasons in the *Jonah* for renewed appreciation of Philip Melanchthon's contributions as a leader in the Reformation. As general superintendent of Wittenberg and a professor at the university, Bugenhagen was among the highest ranking Lutheran church officials in Electoral Saxony. Still, for Bugenhagen, Melanchthon never stopped being the *Praeceptor Germaniae* and his great teacher of both theological and secular wisdom. In the *Jonah*, Bugenhagen referred to Melanchthon's *Loci Communes, Commentary on Romans, On the Church and the Authority of the Word*, and the Apology to the Augsburg Confession as esteemed guides for teaching and practice. With Luther, Melanchthon had given Lutheranism its shape and voice. Because Bugenhagen shared Luther's gruff temperament, Bugenhagen's work with the supposedly more timid and peace-loving Melanchthon invites reappraisal of the Wittenberg theologians under the Augsburg Interim. They stayed in Wittenberg and worked with hostile political and Catholic authorities because they believed it was the best way to serve their oppressed congregations. Bugenhagen's sustained refutation of Roman Catholic theology and practices shows that the Wittenbergers did not engage in those debates with a spirit of either surrender or opportunism. On the contrary, Bugenhagen's arguments remind readers that Melanchthon had already been making similarly bold pronouncements for decades and, at great personal peril, had been the first to write against the Augsburg Interim. Bugenhagen's work with his *Praeceptor* during the time and his unequivocally positive references to him in the *Jonah* portray a Melanchthon entering the 1550s who was courageously dedicated to the maintenance of Lutheran teaching and worship.

Although not known as a theological genius like Luther and Melanchthon, Bugenhagen's contributions to the Reformation cannot be reduced to the practical or organizational realm. For one thing, the emphasis on *quid sit* and *quid effectus* shows that that any separation of theory and practice corrupts the Lutheran project. Rather than adding to Bugenhagen's reputation as an expert organizer or implying that he was a weak thinker on his own, Bugenhagen's insistence that faith and practice always belong together suggests that he understood and applied Lutheran theology like few others.

Thus, Bugenhagen's organizational skills were rooted in his biblical scholarship and theological acumen. Luther and Melanchthon had each written extensively and persuasively about the organic relationship between faith and good works. Bugenhagen's early Letter to Hamburg addressed this topic directly, as did his Jonah Commentary almost 25 years later. Nevertheless, the so-called Majoristic controversy of the 1550s reopened this topic, pitting a "genuine Lutheran" view of good works as sources of self-righteousness against a "Philippist" necessity of goods works for salvation. The study of Bugenhagen's theology, however, shows that the apparent need to choose between faith and good works (or between Luther and Melanchthon) is a false dichotomy.

Throughout his career, Bugenhagen addressed the relationship between faith and good works by insisting that justification is God's effective work, received by faith and made manifest in good works. By trusting that life and goodness come from God alone, a person can do good works and follow both tables of the law for the first time: rightly honoring God and loving the neighbor through service. This relationship between faith and works formed the center of Bugenhagen's career. It grounded his interpretation of Jonah and his opposition to the Council of Trent and the Augsburg Interim. Though not the first to formulate this teaching, the clarity he gave it reveals Bugenhagen to have been an exemplary teacher of faith and good works.

Bugenhagen's good work in the Jonah Commentary was to give a principled defense of the Lutheran principle of justification and its effects. Like Augustine, Luther, and Melanchthon, he believed that the true church remains hidden and persecuted in the world. Yet this belief does not lead to quietism or despair. Bugenhagen's career consistently reveals active engagement with social and political realities, tempered by an awareness of human sin. Where Luther often experienced *Anfechtungen* (afflictions) that made him sometimes resemble the despondent prophet of Jonah 4, Bugenhagen sent the prophet back one more time to God's temple, where he again repented and received forgiveness from the community of faith. To a Lutheran community fighting with itself, the pastoral Bugenhagen publicly commended repentance and absolution as the only certain cure for sin and enmity. In his *Jonah*, biblical interpretation became public theology.

APPENDIX ONE

Bugenhagen's Letter to Duke Albrecht of Prussia[706]

Wittenberg, May 25, 1549
Grace and peace to you.

I received your grace's letter on Tuesday after *Misericordia domini* [May 7, 1549]. It came just at the right time for me to give a good and joyful reply. First, I ask your noble grace to believe this is my handwriting. On account of your grace and the grace of God, I do not want to write lies about any man on earth. I have never done it; to this honorable end Christ has preserved me so far, so that I thank God eternally. But it is not without cause that I humbly ask this of your grace.

For I have found before this time that your noble grace has grown somewhat apart from me. Without a doubt, this does not originate with your grace. I know full well how your grace most graciously takes care to share the same mind as us, which your grace has also proven to me with deeds. Rather, it comes from people who have lied about me to your grace, or at least derided and belittled my teaching, in which we are entirely blameless. What they seek by this, God knows. I do not want to judge them. They have a judge, as well as one in their own conscience. For when your grace graciously received my Jeremiah Commentary, your grace wrote to me most graciously and gave thanks for it, and felt that there was much good in the book, which honored Christ and brought people to blessedness and which your grace read through with the hope – as your grace wrote – that your grace should find much happiness in reading it and not be annoyed or burdened by it.[707] I was happy about this: that your grace could have needed to read such a large book so much. That was a sign that your noble grace still sat content with your land and your people. And, to be sure, if I may say so myself, my Jeremiah Commentary is not only an exposition of the prophet, but also many tracts about necessary subjects from the Holy Scripture, not the least of which is the long tract *On the blasphemy against the Holy Spirit*, as Christ said, or

On the sin unto death, as John said, all most diligently and comfortingly written from the Holy Scriptures and from the foundation of Christ's gospel, written with examples and experiences, as no one in this day had put together since the time of the Apostles. You wrote very well before now about this subject, so that people might be led out of human error on those topics that the tract discussed. If now there were nothing else in my book than the one tract (of which I will not speak anymore), then it would still not be anything to scorn. But, gracious Duke, as mentioned before, after this I noticed that I and my book have become suspect [*verdechtig und verechtig*] to your grace through certain people, who could not have done any better, and of that I am confident by the grace of God. I did not write the book to complain about anyone, rather to confess my faith and doctrine for the whole world. The doctrine is correct, but I find that it loses something in translation. If I could rewrite it, then I could improve it myself by God's grace and permit the know-it-alls no such pleasure.

Because of this I came to realize that I need to worry that all the letters I had written to you might be taken the wrong way through certain people. Therefore, I also did not want to write anything to your grace via our judge Hans Lufft. But I could not help it for your grace's sake. I gave him a memorial and commanded him not to tell your grace anything about us other than what he knew and had seen and heard in this land.

Over and above that blow also came this bad luck that certain acquaintances began to write incredible libels against us without using their own names: that we Wittenberg theologians had denied Christ and turned back the entire gospel. God forgive it of those who gave cause for this at Leipzig, they who worked in the name of the theologians for the territory on certain articles, such as they are. Of this, your grace sent me a letter. Against this, we theologians contested rigorously for three days in the time around St. Martin's Day [November 11, 1548]. Then on that third day I offered this gray head of mine before I would accept the blasphemous priestly unctions, consecrations, benedictions, the canon of the mass, and so on. Still to be endured was extreme unction, which those calling themselves theologians defended with Mark 6 and the Epistle of James. From this your grace and an individual interpreter would have noticed full well that we theologians had not set up such things, but crass and ignorant people, who do not even understand the letter of Holy

Scripture. Mark 6 and the Epistle of James say not one letter about the priestly extreme unction with which they blaspheme, etc. What good could your grace now think of us, if such incredible libels come to you? And our adversaries are claiming themselves for your grace and, fully aware of these libels, use them against us. Gracious Duke, what more should I now write, when one does not believe us and when our writings are scorned and evilly interpreted? The more we write, the more they find to complain about, so that I simply must say to such people: "I have spoken nothing in secret, why do you strike me? Ask the ones who have heard" [John 18:20, 23]. This is what I commanded Hans Lufft to do.

All of this made our case harder with your grace, especially the received letter from Jüterbog, of which your grace sent me a copy, along with this word that you wrote to me in the letter: "This writing, in our opinion, shows things clearly and then some. Because such writings refer to certain theologians, it bewilders us, if you and others in Wittenberg also hold with its contents, etc."[708] Your grace judged this correctly, had we theologians prescribed such things. But it hurts me to think how our adversaries have triumphed against us with respect to your grace through this letter, when your majesty also writes, "It bewilders us, etc." Yes, freely and especially [it hurts me] that your grace sees idol foolishness among the theologians in Wittenberg, etc. This is what the devil wanted to have. If I now answer your grace this or that, that we theologians in Wittenberg knew something about the writing, as your grace asks, then I can really do nothing, for – God be praised – then they would quickly say: "See, Gracious Duke, here your grace has Dr. Pomeranus' own confession that it was idol lies that Dr. Pomeranus wrote to you until now. Your grace should expect this and nothing else from him, if he writes any more to you, etc." So it is, gracious Duke, through and through. We cannot get any lower to you.

From this, your noble grace sees with what great need I ask that your grace should believe this to be my personal writing. Without this trust I do not willingly ask your grace anything, because I know that your grace has been graciously and Christianly disposed to us. From this same need, I did not want to answer your noble grace before Hans Lufft came back home, for he might give me more to write about. But because Dr. Sabinus, my dear lord and friend, travels home to your grace, I cannot miss this chance to write to your grace, because I now have something certain and good to write, which Dr. Sabinus will also tell your grace, so that you may believe me more. As your grace is my patron and wants something other than lies to scoff at, God give grace for this: that neither your grace nor anyone else should ever find anything false in me. Dr. Sabinus will also tell your grace a good word from his imperial majesty, as well as a good word from his kingly majesty. We do not write such things about ourselves, for we could not abandon ourselves to such; and when we really need improvement, then we publicly cry out to God with our children in the churches. If we did not, we would still be in the same pathetic need of the gospel as we were earlier. The devil could not kill us with his murder, because Christ has protected us to this day. Now the devil wants to kill us with his lies and provokes our own brother against us. We must then continue on with patience despite the devil's shit and say with Christ: "You dishonor me. But I do not seek my own glory: there is one who seeks it and who judges" [John 8:49, 50]. He will not remain outside for long. "[For the time has come for the judgment to begin with the house of God.] And if first for us, [what shall be the end of them that do not believe God's gospel?]" [1 Pet. 4:17]. He is a faithful God [Dt. 7:9]; he will not reject our prayer forever [Ps. 66:20]. That is my hope.

    The truthful history of the religious issue with us is this. From the beginning, my most gracious Lord, Duke Moritz, Elector [of Saxony, etc.], first in Leipzig commanded many of us theologians, superintendents and pastors to remain faithful in the pure doctrine of Christ's gospel as held earlier and that we should know for ourselves what would be a mistake in this matter with his noble grace. For his grace wanted no one to be able to argue that his grace ever wanted to reaccept papal abuses.

    A second time in Altcella, after last St. Martin's Day, his noble grace again let us similarly make a declaration and that we could peacefully compose an agenda or church order that could be Christianly kept in all of his grace's own lands. Additionally, we worked busily among ourselves with all faithfulness to try to comply somewhat with his imperial majesty in the things that were not against evangelical truth. We wanted to make this effort among ourselves with all faithfulness. We accepted this and peacefully designed an agenda. But then it came to a disputation about the canon of the mass and of unction, and so on. This made our disagreement wider, as said before; in the process we still remain and wanted even then to remain together, as Christ helps us with his Holy Spirit. From this, your grace had a certain answer from me, that neither we Wittenberg theologians nor the Leipzig theologians put forth the article your grace sent to me; instead, we continue to dispute it, as your majesty shall hear more later.

A third time, the theologians were asked about this in Jüterbog, for just one day. Nothing was commanded to them then; rather, I have read for the first time in the letter you sent me about what the two sides covertly prescribed there. In that I was pleased to read this word: "For our subjects, with their approval, etc." For with this, my gracious Lord the Saxon Elector let the prescription go, because his electoral grace's subjects did not approve, rather prayed and spoke against it to the present day. Then the lords in Jüterbog came to experience what had been said to the theologians: that they should have their leave, and one should be able to remain with how things were concluded in Altcella. So with Prince Georg von Anhalt, my gracious lord, they all came happily to us; and we thanked God, for we knew that we had not accepted anything unchristian at Altcella, rather condemned what was unchristian.

Fourth, much good was concluded at the legislative assembly in Leipzig at Christmas, especially that the region wanted to remain in the pure word of God and in the right use of Christ's sacraments. Although such articles as mentioned above were recited in the name of the theologians (by which people have done us wrong), they were not accepted anyway, as also mentioned earlier, praise and honor be to God eternally. I often gave public thanks for such grace of God in the pulpit during the festival of the Lord's Epiphany [January 6, 1549] and made the whole church glad and everyone thanked God with me. After this, I publicly and very earnestly said that someone had done the theologians wrong, because someone had submitted certain articles in the name of the theologians as being Christian, which we are still arguing against to the death. And this person asked teachers, magistrates, the entire school and the whole city to write down themselves what they heard me say about this, along with whatever else they know, see, and hear about how the religious issue is going throughout these lands. Then we publicly cried out from the pulpit more than once that we theologians were not guilty of those articles. I say this so that your grace does not think I am saying this secretly to you alone. I have written all of this to low and high German lands and cities as far as Denmark, as well as to many counts and lords, and also to your grace. For many pious lords and people have also written such things against the lying gossips. I have seen a copy of a letter that Magister George Cracow from Pomerania wrote in my name to your grace, about what he heard here at the Epiphany service from the pulpit. But our adversaries are poisonous, only writing what is evil, and violently pressing us; they write no word of what is good. Whatever happens, God will make it well.

Fifth, during Lent in Dessau, we completed the agenda with Prince Georg von Anhalt, but did not perfect it or finalize it. Finally, in Grimma on the day of Sts. Philip and James [May 1, 1549], we theologians – among whom is also my most distinguished gracious lord Prince Georg von Anhalt, many superintendents and pastors – finally and in a Christian manner finished the agenda with great peace in the name of our Lord Jesus Christ. Then my gracious lord the Elector came to us in boots and spurs, took the book from us, and most graciously thanked us, and asked if we had not made any oversights. Then his electoral grace began to comfort us theologians, as his grace had also done for us earlier by his words when he spoke of how he had read the blasphemous letters that had gone out against us and that we needed to have Christian patience. His grace said, "God will soon bring your innocence to the daylight with honor. Our part, on account of which burdensome things have been written against us, We will bear, and bear all the more gladly, when We observe that you are content, etc. And now that his imperial majesty is content with the agenda, people will start to press you, but this can serve many other churches. For in this We introduce absolutely nothing that we have not already held: the beloved gospel of our churches."

Gracious lord, that is our true history, the parts necessary for your grace and other lords and pious people, so that you do not believe the shameless liars, etc. I pray every day for your grace, for my grace's wife, for land and people, for your school. Christ be with us all eternally; we need it very much.

Written in the City of Wittenberg 1549

Your noble grace's servant,

Dr. Johannes Bugenhagen Pomeranus

Appendix Two

Bugenhagen's Dedication Letter to King Christian III[709]

To the most favorable prince and lord, King Christian of Denmark and Norway, King of Vandals and Goths, Duke of Schleswig, Holstein, Stormar and Detmar, the assembly in Oldenburg and Delmenhorst; to his most merciful lord from Dr. Johannes Bugenhagen Pomeranus, grace and peace from God through Jesus Christ his Son, our righteousness. Greetings.

Christ speaks, most favorable King, in John 8[:44] concerning the devil: "That one was a murderer from the beginning, and he does not stand in the truth because the truth is not in him. When he speaks as a liar, he speaks according to his own nature, for he is a liar and the father of lies," (that is, the fountain of lies) for he killed the human race from the beginning with his lies. One may see this today in the works of the devil, as he horribly works against us afflicted preachers and teachers of Christ's church.

For when he desired, we surrendered our city on the advice, order, and persuasion of the most illustrious imprisoned Prince Elector (may God set him free by his grace). And the Imperial Majesty made us submit and obey peace with this promise: that he would not introduce anything against our religion which we have served to now according to the Augsburg Confession and from which we have not deviated by as much as a finger. The devil, seeing that he could not destroy us through murder (for Christ with his faithful angels preserved us), now clearly desires to defile and oppress us with his lies through adiaphoristic writers. They write many public works in all the world, that we theologians who are faithful servants of Christ (our many Christian churches which we have served so faithfully are witnesses for us and acknowledge our faithful ministry with thanksgiving) accepted money from our magistrates and became traitors of Christ's gospel and that, despising all good order, we defect from faith to the doctrine of demons and worship of the Antichrist.

And the hypocrites dare in public writings to swear in the name of Christ and his judgment against us, most especially against me. They set themselves in Christ's place of judgment and they judge my conscience and threaten upon me the judgment of Christ with this word – this I swear before Christ my Lord and righteous judge – they say this and many other things: Doctor Pomeranus goes against truth and against his own conscience and will not judge rightly what is brought forth. For they say they heard from a worthy man of faith that Father Luther had supposedly said: "After my death, none of these theologians will remain constant, first, because all people lie. Therefore do not swear on the word of men, who can deceive, nor shall you take the name of the Lord your God in vain, for those who do this will not be unpunished." In this manner, they accuse the blessed man Luther of lies. For if you consider the thing itself, these words – "after Luther's death none of these theologians will remain constant" – are simply wrong, insofar as enemies of the gospel think and tell lies and do not suffer the truth.

Moreover, they write out of mere jealousy (as anyone can see) against this our school, which blossoms in Christ, because of his grace. They write these words, "Even if we would have a thousand Wittenberg schools, then we would be better to let them all perish than permit them to become one great evil. For in them the youth are corrupted with false opinions and distorted teaching against the gospel and when they return to their homeland they will corrupt all the other Christian churches." Thus through their lies and blasphemies, the adiaphoristic writers make this divine school to be a common pest of the church of Christ.

Oh Christ, son of the living God, who desired us to be your ministers, these are horrendous and tragic lies of Satan against us miserably afflicted ones, against your church laboring under the cross, against our holy ministers, and against the holy school. These blasphemies have confused your church and many good people, many of whom suffer from our supposed lapse and certain others who, seduced into ignorance, even speak evil about us. But when they learn the truth of the matter, they will rejoice and give thanks to God and be glad about us, and so all things turn to good among God's chosen and beloved ones [Rom. 8:28].

A certain noble and erudite man told us that the captive prince, a holy man, was persuaded by these lies and says bad things about us Wittenbergers, although with customary modesty and a pained soul. The prince had told the man this in lower Germany. For we know that he suffers more from this scandal due to his own condemnation and captivity, just as is the case with the younger princes during this calamity of theirs, too, through human falsehoods.

There are even other preachers who have cast faith aside, primarily arrogant and ambitious ones, and instead of love they hurl hatred against us to the common people. This is their piety and our reward. Occasionally hypocrites, who have gone out from us but who have not been of us, these and other enemies of the gospel pressure such men, saying, "Why don't you defect from that doctrine, from which your teachers have defected, as you see in the adiaphoristic writings?" But I am greatly amazed that they would themselves want brothers who, when they came from another place to us, rejoiced and gave thanks to God for everything that they saw, heard and knew among us. And then they turned back to those who are wrongly accusing all of us, adding affliction to afflictions. Perhaps this is what Christ our head says in Psalm 41[:6?], "Someone approaches, as one exploring with a perverse heart; he seeks in order to falsely accuse, then jumps back and drags down."

And they were with us, who have chosen this disgrace and our mistreatment, who have been embedded that they might catch us either in sermons or in their writings with these lies to others as if recognizing and seeing truth. Perhaps those whom we offended at some point with righteous rebukes and other legitimate punishment, for which I once had good reason, now write to others in order to stir up heaven and earth against us, so that we cannot be supported anywhere – not even in our church – until we at some time get expelled into exile with our wives and our children on account of the truth of the gospel. And the adiaphoristic writers have written to other universities, admonishing that they themselves should write against us, just as our lords and brothers have written to us from the University of Königsberg. Who does not see this evil? Certain people, among whom are some humanists, whom the devil has not blinded with hatred against us, can well and truly judge about those works that they write against us.

Here they are even our lords and brothers, with whom I shared the highest familiarity and friendship, who often were admonishing me to write against such hardships, so that finally they got to be obnoxious to me in their warnings at an open dinner party. I had left it hoping that for at least a happy hour I might dwell there as among brothers during this storm, but it happened to me as Christ said in the Psalm [69:20b-21]: "I sought one who would grieve together with me and there was none; I looked for someone to console me and found none. In my food they gave me gall, and in my thirst they gave me vinegar to drink."

Therefore I have written to your Majesty about these true things. God knows that I do not lie and that these same letters are written down for the rulers and cities to whom I have preached, lest they be scandalized by us through the lies of others. But to the letters mentioned above, the adiaphoristic writers have repaid us with wagons of accusations, threatening us most arrogantly unless we correct our evil. Of them I have said, "Stop! We do what you demand of us. We have corrected all the evil that you have written against us, and you betray us to all the world. 'We are made a spectacle among angels and men'" [1 Cor. 4:9]. They ask, "In what way have you changed?" "Through this," I reply, "that we say that Satan's lies are all that you have written against us." They say, "You put your trust in being allowed to flee to a corrupt state." We respond, "No, rather we accept the testimony of the whole Christian church, which we have preached most faithfully, as I said before, 'I said nothing in secret, why do you strike me? Ask those who have heard me'" [John 18:20, 23].

Then seeing their stubbornness and that sedition in this world against our magistrate is sought through such writings (to which we do not owe our response and strained cooperation and which are fatal to us at this time, as was spoken in Revelation 14:[12] "This is the endurance of the saints and those who have served the commandments and the faith of Jesus"), I say these things, reflecting on myself, that I am beginning to know something of silence and endurance, that which pious, erudite and prudent men among us have since tested. "I said, 'I will guard my ways that I may not sin with my tongue; I have set a guard on my mouth when the sinner stood against me. I kept silent and still from good things and my sorrow was renewed, etc.'" [Ps. 39]. "'Vengeance is mine, I will repay,' says the Lord" [Rom 12:19]. And from St. Paul to the Galatians [5:10], "he who troubles you shall bear the judgment, whoever he be." Christ says, "he who despises you, despises me; and whoever despises me, despises the one who sent me" [Luke 10:16].

If only these writers finally saw how much evil they do in Christ's church by writing against Christ's faithful ministers! If only they could fear God's judgment! I pray to God every day: forgive our enemies, persecutors, and accusers, and may you be thought worthy to convert them to yourself; we pray you to hear us. "Do not turn me over to those who accuse me... do not let the proud accuse me" [Ps 119:121, 122]. "Father, forgive them, for they know not what they do" [Luke 23:34]. And I console myself with this word of Christ, "Blessed are you when people speak evil of you... for so they did to the prophets who were before you" [Matt. 5:11]. Even so did they do to the Son of God in our flesh. "Take courage, for I have conquered the world!" [John 16:33]. For Christ did not return abuse [1 Pet. 2:23], rather "he was led like a sheep to the slaughter, and like a lamb was silent before his shearer, and did not open his mouth" [Acts 8:32].

Because the world truly does not hear us, but perpetually cries out against us, "'You testify on your own behalf; your testimony is not true'" [John 8:13], I say to the Lord, "O Lord my God, if I have done this... [then let the enemy overtake me] [Ps. 7:3]. "All this evil has come upon us, yet we have not forgotten you or done wickedly against your covenant, etc." [Ps. 44:17]. This is recorded in the history of David, as you read [2 Samuel 16:5-14]: "Shimei cried out against David, 'Out, you man of blood!' But David said, 'Leave him alone to curse me, for the Lord has commanded him to curse David.'"

But I truly tell your Majesty that there is the highest harmony in our churches and schools and in all this land, not only in Christian doctrine, but also among persons and among ministers. We rejoice and give thanks to God whenever we hear that others are in such harmony. But for others we pray to the Father in the name of Jesus Christ. And I remind all our brothers in this public writing, that they apply themselves to observe this holy harmony through the Holy Spirit. "If by the Spirit you have put the body to death, you will live" [Rom. 8:13]. "But if you bite one another, see that you are not consumed by one another" [Gal. 5:15].

Good God! How great a forest of their false accusations must I submit us and ours to? Moreover, they will clamor, "You must respond to the Leipzig Interim!" I do not need to respond, neither for it nor against it. For I am not personally aware of anyone's evil doctrine. Neither did our magistrate ever ask this of me; much less has he purchased it, whatever else is judged against us.

Finally they shout, "Now you are all silent and do not want to console the church's afflictions." For this reason, most favorable king, I dedicate to your majesty and your name these my tracts, which contain useful and necessary material, especially for the Christian Church of this age, so that your majesty may read and judge. For God has given your Majesty an intellect, in order that it might know the great mystery of God in Christ and so that all might see that we have not been silent until now. For we have dealt publicly with this in our school from the beginning, since the city's surrender and the college's reopening. We publicly teach this doctrine for the salvation of all who are in the Roman Empire and for all who belong to the Christian Church, including those who go outside the Empire. And if the Empire or Papal Council do not support this doctrine, just as Daniel predicted, it shall be known in turn that Christ, the Son of God who was made the victim for us and the one whom God set as judge of the living and the dead, will not tolerate any more blasphemous sins against the Holy Spirit in this clear light of the gospel truth. For the Council of Trent already stands in blasphemy before Christ with these words: "If any one says that all sins are remitted to the one who believes with certainty that he has remission of sins, and that this is the faith which God requires of a sinner so that he may be justified, let that one be anathema." For they say that this is not in Holy Scripture, in which this stands written against such pride, audacity, and especially false faith: "Who knows if God will turn and forgive?" [Jonah 3:9, Joel 2:14]. To which Paul responds, "Even if we apostles or an angel from heaven should preach a gospel other than that which we have preached, and which you received from us, let that one be anathema" [Gal. 1:8, 9]. "No one is able to lay another foundation but that which has been laid, which is Jesus Christ" [1 Cor. 3:11].

And Peter, full of the Holy Spirit in Cornelius' house and in front of the Roman soldiers who were first among the far off gentiles to receive Christ's gospel from the apostles, stood against this blasphemy and for Christ's glory through the holy prophets. He said, "all the prophets testify about Christ that all who believe in him receive forgiveness of sins through his name" [Acts 10:43]. In this place, Peter – and the Spirit in any holy prophet of the law – negates this foul and blasphemous doubt, which the Papists teach against faith in Christ. Your Majesty will see in this my commentary, too: that the Holy Spirit did not and would not speak of this doubt, either in the Holy Scriptures or anywhere in Joel or Jonah. Therefore, stop fighting the acknowledged truth of the gospel. Daniel already goes forward, and so does the expositor of Daniel in Revelation. Christ defends his church against all gates of hell [Matt. 16:18] into eternal life, AMEN.

    Written in Wittenberg, 1550
    on the first of October

Abbreviations

Ap — Apology of the Augsburg Confession, *The Book of Concord*. Edited by Robert Kolb and Timothy J. Wengert. Minneapolis: Fortress, 2000.

BC — *The Book of Concord*. Edited by Robert Kolb and Timothy J. Wengert. Minneapolis: Fortress, 2000.

Briefwechsel — *Dr. Johannes Bugenhagens Briefwechsel*. Edited by Otto Vogt. Stettin: Saunier, 1888. Reprint, Hildesheim: Olms, 1966.

BSLK — *Die Bekenntnisschriften der evangelisch-lutherischen Kirche*. 11th ed. Göttingen: Vandenhoeck & Ruprecht, 1992.

CA — The Augsburg Confession, *The Book of Concord*. Edited by Robert Kolb and Timothy J. Wengert. Minneapolis: Fortress, 2000.

CR — Philip Melanchthon. *Corpus Reformatorum. Philippi Melanthonis opera quae supersunt omnia*. Edited by Karl Bretschneider and Heinrich Bindseil. 28 vols. Halle: Schwetschke & Sons, 1834-1860.

Denzinger — Denzinger, Heinrich, ed. *Enchiridion Symbolorum et Definitionum, quae in rebus fidei et morum a Conciliis Oecumenicis et Summis Pontificibus emanarunt*. Würzburg: Stahel, 1854.

Geisenhof — *Bibliotheca Bugenhagiana: Bibliographie der Druckschriften d. D. J. Bugenhagen*. Edited by Georg Geisenhof. Leipzig: Heinsius, 1908.

IONAS — Johannes Bugenhagen, *IONAS PRO | PHETA EXPOSITUS | IN TERTIO CAPITE, TRA | ctatus de uera poenitentia, quam Chri= | stus commendat nobis in Niniuitis, & de falsa poeni | tentia, quam doctrinae daemoniorum post Apo | stolos inuexerunt, tantum per opera | nostra, excluso Christo. | Ibidem, Historia certa, ex probatis Scri=| ptoribus, diligentia & iudicio collecta, quemadmo=| dum post defunctum hac uita Iohannem Euangeli=| stam, coeperint defectiones a fide, doctrinae daemonio=| rum sub specie uerbi Dei, prohibitiones nuptiarum & | ciborum, uota coelibatus, pulchrae ordinationes & spi=| ritualitates, quae vocabantur perfectiones Eccle= | siae, quae adhuc regnant, solae faciunt Spi | rituales sine Spiritu sancto, per Spiri= | tum*

	*nouum & Paracletum	Montanistarum &c.	Idem caput repurgatum ab impiis	& blasphemis dubitationibus.* Wittenberg: Creutzer, 1550.
K.A.T. Vogt	Karl August Traugott Vogt. *Johannes Bugenhagen Pomeranus: Leben und ausgewählte Schriften.* Elberfeld: Friderichs, 1867.
LC	Luther's Large Catechism, *The Book of Concord.* Edited by Robert Kolb and Timothy J. Wengert. Minneapolis: Fortress, 2000.
LW	*Luther's Works.* American ed. 55 vols. Philadelphia: Fortress; St. Louis: Concordia, 1955-1986.
MBW	Philip Melanchthon. *Melanchthons Briefwechsel: Kritische und kommentierte Gesamtausgabe.* Edited by Heinz Scheible. 11 vols. to date. Stuttgart-Bad Cannstatt: Frommann-Holzboog, 1977-.
MBW T	Philip Melanchthon. *Melanchthons Briefwechsel: Kritische und kommentierte Gesamtausgabe. Texte.* Edited by Heinz Scheible. 10 vols. to date. Stuttgart-Bad Cannstatt: Frommann-Holzboog, 1991-.
MSA	Philip Melanchthon. *Melanchthons Werke in Auswahl. [Studienausgabe].* Edited by Robert Stupperich. 7 vols. Gütersloh: Mohn, 1951.
PG	*Patrologiae cursus completus. Series Graeca.* 161 vols. Edited by J.P Migne. Paris & Turnhout, 1859-1866.
PL	*Patrologiae cursus completus. Series Latina.* 221 vols. Edited by J.P Migne. Paris & Turnhout, 1859-1963.
SA	Smalcald Articles, *The Book of Concord.* Edited by Robert Kolb and Timothy J. Wengert. Minneapolis: Fortress, 2000.
SC	Luther's Small Catechism, *The Book of Concord.* Edited by Robert Kolb and Timothy J. Wengert. Minneapolis: Fortress, 2000.
Tr	Treatise on the Power and Primacy of the Pope, *The Book of Concord.* Edited by Robert Kolb and Timothy J. Wengert. Minneapolis: Fortress, 2000.
WA	Martin Luther. *Luthers Werke. Kritische Gesamtausgabe [Schriften].* 65 vols. Weimar: Böhlau, 1883-1993.
WA Br	Martin Luther. *Luthers Werke. Kritische Gesamtausgabe. Briefwechsel.* 18 vols. Weimar: Böhlau, 1930-1985.
WA DB	Martin Luther. *Luthers Werke. Kritische Gesamtausgabe. Deutsche Bibel.* 12 vols. Weimar: Böhlau, 1906-1961.
WA TR	Martin Luther. *Luthers Werke. Kritische Gesamtausgabe. Tischreden.* 6 vols. Weimar: Böhlau, 1912-1921.

Bibliography

Primary Sources

Amsdorf, Nicholas von. *Antwort auf Doct. Pommers scheltwort / so er auff der Cantzel aussegeschött hat / am Sontag nach Vdolrici*. Magdeburg: Lotter, 1548.

Bekenntnisschriften der evangelisch-lutherischen Kirche. 11th ed. Göttingen: Vandenhoeck & Ruprecht, 1992.

Book of Concord. Edited by Robert Kolb and Timothy Wengert. Minneapolis: Fortress, 2000.

Bugenhagen, Johannes. *Epistola de Peccato in spiritum sanctum*. Wittenberg: Lotther, 1523.

Bugenhagen, Johannes. *Von dem Christlichen Glauben und rechten guten Werken wider den falschen Glauben und erdichtete gute Werke, dazu, wie man's soll anrichten mit guten Predigern, daß solch Glaube und Werke gepredigt werden, an die ehrenreiche Stadt Hamburg*. Wittenberg: Rhaw, 1526.

Bugenhagen, Johannes. *Johannes Bugenhagens Katechismuspredigten, gehalten 1525 und 1532*. Edited by Georg Buchwald. Leipzig: Heinsius, 1909.

Bugenhagen, Johannes. *Die Pommersche Kirchenordnung von Johannes Bugenhagen, 1535*. Edited and translated by Norman Buske. Greifswald: Evangelische Landeskirche Greifswald, 1985.

Bugenhagen, Johannes. *A Christian Sermon: Over the Body and at the Funeral of the Venerable Dr. Martin Luther*. Translated by Kurt Hendel, with the original German. Atlanta: Pitts, 1996.

Bugenhagen, Johannes, et al. *Agenda, wie es in des Churfürsten zu Sachsen Landen in den kirchen gehalten wirdt*. Edited by Emil Friedberg. Halle: Buchhandlung des Waisenhauses, 1869.

Bugenhagen, Johannes. *IONAS PRO | PHETA EXPOSITUS | IN TERTIO CAPITE, TRA | ctatusde uera poenitentia, quam Chri= | stus commendat nobis in Niniuitis, & de falsa poeni | tentia, quam doctrinae daemoniorum post Apo | stolos inuexerunt, tantum per opera | nostra, excluso Christo. | Ibidem, Historia certa, ex probatis Scri=| ptoribus, diligentia & iudicio collecta, quemadmo=| dum post defunctum hac uita Iohannem Euangeli=| stam, coeperint defectiones a fide, doctrinae daemonio=| rum sub specie uerbi Dei, prohibitiones nuptiarum & | ciborum, uota coelibatus, pulchrae ordinationes & spi=| ritualitates, quae vocabantur perfectiones Eccle= | siae, quae adhuc regnant, solae faciunt Spi | rituales sine Spiritu sancto, per Spiri= | tum nouum & Paracletum | Montanistarum &c. | Idem caput repurgatum ab impiis | & blasphemis dubitationibus*. Wittenberg: Creutzer, 1550.

Bugenhagen, Johannes. *Von den Vngeborn Kinder*. Wittenberg: Klug, 1551; reprint, Wittenberg: Creutzer, 1557.

Bugenhagen, Johannes. *Dr. Johannes Bugenhagens Briefwechsel.* Edited by Otto Vogt. Stettin: Saunier, 1888; reprint, Hildesheim: Olms, 1966.

Denzinger, Heinrich, ed. *Enchiridion Symbolorum et Definitionum, quae in rebus fidei et morum a Conciliis Oecumenicis et Summis Pontificibus emanarunt.* Würzburg: Stahel, 1854.

Flacius Illyricus, Matthias. *Antwort Matth. Fl. Illyr. Auff etliche Beschüldigung D. Gei. Maiores vnd D. Pommers.* Magdeburg: Rödinger, 1551.

Herrmann, Johannes and Günther Wartenberg, eds. *Politische Korrespondenz des Herzogs und Kurfürsten Moritz von Sachsen,* Vierter Band. Berlin: Akademie Verlag, 1992.

Jonas, Justus. *Der Briefwechsel des Dr. Justus Jonas.* Edited by Gustav Kawerau. Halle: Hendel, 1884.

Kolb, Robert and James Nestingen, eds. *Sources and Contexts of the Book of Concord.* Minneapolis: Fortress, 2001.

Luther, Martin. *Luthers Werke. Kritische Gesamtausgabe [Schriften].* 65 vols. Weimar: Böhlau, 1883-1993.

Luther, Martin. *Luthers Werke. Kritische Gesamtausgabe. Briefwechsel.* 18 vols. Weimar: Böhlau, 1930-1985.

Luther, Martin. *Luthers Werke. Kritische Gesamtausgabe. Deutsche Bibel.* 12 vols. Weimar: Böhlau, 1906-1961.

Luther, Martin. *Luthers Werke. Kritische Gesamtausgabe. Tischreden.* 6 vols. Weimar: Böhlau, 1912-1921.

Luther, Martin. *Luther's Works.* American ed. 55 vols. Philadelphia: Fortress; St. Louis: Concordia, 1955-1986.

Melanchthon, Philip. *Corpus Reformatorum. Philippi Melanthonis opera quae supersunt omnia.* Edited by Karl Bretschneider and Heinrich Bindseil. 28 vols. Halle: Schwetschke & Sons, 1834-1860.

Melanchthon, Philip. *Melanchthons Werke in Auswahl. [Studienausgabe].* Edited by Robert Stupperich. 7 vols. Gütersloh: Mohn, 1951.

Melanchthon, Philip. *Melanchthon: Selected Writings.* Edited by Elmer Ellsworth Flack and Lowell Satre. Translated by Charles Leander Hill. Minneapolis: Augsburg, 1962.

Melanchthon, Philip. *Loci Communes Theologici* [1521]. In *Melanchthon and Bucer,* 18-152. Edited by Wilhelm Pauck. Translated by Lowell Satre. Philadelphia: Westminster, 1969.

Melanchthon, Philip. *Melanchthons Briefwechsel: Kritische und kommentierte Gesamtausgabe.* Edited by Heinz Scheible. 11 vols. to date. Stuttgart-Bad Cannstatt: Frommann-Holzboog, 1977-.

Melanchthon, Philip. *Melanchthons Briefwechsel: Kritische und kommentierte Gesamtausgabe. Texte.* Edited by Heinz Scheible. 10 vols. to date. Stuttgart-Bad Cannstatt: Frommann-Holzboog, 1991-.

Mirbt, Carl, ed. *Quellen zur Geschichte des Papsttums und des römischen Katholizmus,* 3rd ed. Tübingen: Mohr Siebeck, 1911.

Scriptorum Publice Propositorum A Professoribus in Academia VVitebergensi, Ab anno 1540, usqae ad annum 1553, TOMUS PRIMUS. Wittenberg: Rhau, 1560.

Patrologiae cursus completus. Series Graeca. 161 vols. Edited by J.P Migne. Paris & Turnhout, 1859-1866.

Patrologiae cursus completus. Series Latina. 221 vols. Edited by J.P Migne. Paris & Turnhout, 1859-1963.
Volz, Hans, ed. *Urkunden und Aktenstücke zur Geschichte von Martin Luthers Schmalkaldischen Artikeln (1536-1574).* Berlin: de Gruyter, 1957.
Walch, Johann Georg, ed. *Dr. Martin Luthers Sämmtliche Schriften*, vol. 21. Halle: Gebauer, 1749.

Secondary Sources

Arand, Charles P. "Melanchthon's Rhetorical Argument for Sola Fide in the Apology," *Lutheran Quarterly* 14 (2000): 281-308.
Bailey, James and Lyle Vander Broek, *Literary Forms in the New Testament: A Handbook.* Louisville: Westminster/John Knox, 1992.
Bieber, Anneliese. *Johannes Bugenhagen zwischen Reform und Reformation.* Göttingen: Vandenhoeck & Ruprecht, 1993.
Brecht, Martin. *Martin Luther.* 3 vols. Translated by James L. Schaaf. Vol. 1: *His Road to Reformation, 1483-1521.* Vol. 2: *Shaping and Defining the Reformation, 1521-1532.* Vol. 3: *The Preservation of the Church, 1532-1546.* Minneapolis: Fortress, 1985-1993.
Brunk, Yvonne. *Die Tauftheologie Johannes Bugenhagens.* Hannover: Lutherisches Verlagshaus, 2003.
Brandi, Karl. *The Emperor Charles V: The Growth and Destiny of a Man and of a World-Empire.* Translated by C.V. Wedgwood. Oxford: Alden, 1939.
Cooper, Derek. *The Ecumenical Exegete: Thomas Manton's Commentary on James in Relation to its Protestant Predecessors, Contemporaries and Successors.* Dissertation: Lutheran Theology Seminary at Philadelphia, 2008.
Dingel, Irene and Günther Wartenberg, eds. *Georg Major (1502-1574): Ein Theologe der Wittenberger Reformation.* Leipzig: Evangelische Verlagsanstalt, 2005.
Dingel, Irene and Günther Wartenberg, eds. *Politik und Bekenntnis: Die Reaktionen auf das Interim von 1548.* Leipzig: Evangelische Verlagsanstalt, 2006.
Dingel, Irene. "The Culture of Conflict in the Controversies Leading to the Formula of Concord (1548-1580)." In *Lutheran Ecclesiastical Culture, 1550-1675*, 15-64. Edited by Robert Kolb. Leiden: Brill, 2008.
Ebeling, Gerhard. *Word and Faith.* Translated by James Leitch. Philadelphia: Fortress, 1963.
Edwards, Mark U. *Luther's Last Battles: Politics and Polemics, 1531-46.* Ithaca, NY: Cornell, 1983.
Ehmann, Johannes. *Luther, Türken und Islam: Eine Untersuchung zum Türken- und Islambild (1515-1546).* Gütersloh: Gütersloher, 2008.
Estes, James. *Peace, Order and the Glory of God: Secular Authority and the Church in the Thought of Luther and Melanchthon, 1518-1559.* Leiden: Brill, 2005.
Eusebius of Caesaria. *The History of the Church from Christ to Constantine.* Translated by G.A. Williamson. Minneapolis: Augsburg, 1975.
Forde, Gerhard. *Where God Meets Man: Luther's Down-to-Earth Approach to the Gospel.* Minneapolis: Augsburg, 1972.
Fowl, Stephen, ed. *The Theological Interpretation of Scripture: Classic and Contemporary Readings.* Cambridge, MA: Blackwell, 1997.

Fraenkel, Peter. *Testimonia Patrem: The Function of the Patristic Argument in the Theology of Philip Melanchthon*. Geneva: Droz, 1961.
Francisco, Adam. *Martin Luther and Islam: A Study in Sixteenth-century Polemics and Apologetics*. Leiden: Brill, 2007.
Frei, Hans. *The Eclipse of Biblical Narrative: A Study in Eighteenth and Nineteenth Century Hermeneutics*. New Haven: Yale, 1974.
Fretheim, Terrence E. *The Message of Jonah: A Theological Commentary*. Minneapolis: Augsburg, 1977.
Geisenhof, Georg, ed. *Bibliotheca Bugenhagiana: Bibliographie der Druckschriften d. D. J. Bugenhagen*. Leipzig: Heinsius, 1908.
Gonzalez, Justo. *The Story of Christianity*. 2 vols. San Francisco: Harper, 1984.
Gritsch, Eric W. *A History of Lutheranism*. Minneapolis: Fortress, 2002.
Gummelt, Volker. *Lex et Evangelium: Untersuchungen zur Jesajavorlesung von Johannes Bugenhagen*. Berlin: de Gruyter, 1994.
Gummelt, Volker. "'Pomeranus hat mich of getröstet:' Johannes Bugenhagen – Freund und Seelsorger Luthers." In *Luther und Seine Freunde*, 89-104. Wittenberg: Drei Kastanien, 1998.
Headley, John M. *Luther's View of Church History*. New Haven: Yale, 1963.
Hedahl, Susan K. "Melanchthon and the Task of Preaching." In *Philip Melanchthon: Then and Now (1497-1997)*. Edited by Scott Hendrix and Timothy Wengert. Columbia, SC: Lutheran Theological Southern Seminary, 1999.
Heen, Erik M. "The Theological Interpretation of the Bible," *Lutheran Quarterly* 21 (2007): 373-403.
Hendel, Kurt K. "Johannes Bugenhagen, Organizer of the Lutheran Reformation." *Lutheran Quarterly* 18 (2004): 43-75.
Hendrix, Scott. *Luther and the Papacy: Stages in a Reformation Conflict*. Philadelphia: Fortress, 1981.
Hendrix, Scott. *Recultivating the Vineyard: The Reformation Agendas of Christianization*. Louisville: Westminster John Knox, 2004.
Holfelder, Hans Hermann. *Tentatio et Consolatio: Studien zu Bugenhagens Interpretio in librum psalmorum*. Berlin: De Gruyter, 1974.
Holfelder, Hans Hermann. *Solus Christus: Die Ausbildung von Bugenhagens Rechtfertigungslehre in der Paulusauslegung (1524/25) und ihre Bedeutung für die theologische Argumentation im Sendbrief "Von dem christlichem Glauben" (1526)*. Tübingen: Mohr Siebeck, 1981.
Karant-Nunn, Susan. *The Reformation of Ritual: An Interpretation of Early Modern Germany*. New York: Routledge, 1997.
Kaufmann, Thomas. *Das Ende der Reformation: Magdeburgs "Herrgotts Kanzlei" (1548-1551/2)*. Tübingen: Mohr Siebeck, 2003.
Kierkegaard, Soren. *The Sickness unto Death*. Edited and translated by Howard Hong and Edna Hong. Princeton: Princeton, 1980.
Kohler, Alfred. *Karl V. 1500-1558: Eine Biographie*. Munich: Beck, 2000.
Kolb, Robert. *Nikolaus von Amsdorf, Knight of God and Exile of Christ*. Dissertation: University of Wisconsin, 1973; published as *Nikolaus von Amsdorf (1483-1565): Popular Polemics in the Preservation of Luther's Legacy*. Nieuwcoop: De Graaf, 1978.
Kolb, Robert. *Confessing the Faith: Reformers Define the Church, 1530-1580*. St. Louis: Concordia, 1991.

Köstlin, Julius. *Martin Luther: Sein Leben und Seine Schriften.* 5th ed. 2 vols. Berlin: Duncker, 1903.

Kötter, Ralf. *Johannes Bugenhagens Rechtfertigungslehre und der römische Katholizismus: Studien zum Sendbrief an die Hamburger (1525).* Göttingen: Vandenhoeck & Ruprecht, 1994.

Leder, Hans-Günter. "Luthers Beziehungen zu seinen Wittenberger Freunden." In *Leben und Werk Martin Luthers von 1526 bis 1546,* Band I, 419-440. Edited by Helmar Junghans. Göttingen: Vandenhoeck & Ruprecht, 1983

Leder, Hans-Günter, ed. *Johannes Bugenhagen – Gestalt und Wirkung: Beiträge zur Bugenhagenforschung aus Anlaß des 500. Geburtstages des Doctor Pomeranus.* Berlin: Evangelische Verlaganstalt, 1984.

Leder, Hans-Günter and Norbert Buske. *Reform und Ordnung aus dem Wort: Johannes Bugenhagen und die Reformation im Herzogtum Pommern.* Berlin: Evangelische Verlaganstalt, 1985.

Leith, John, ed. *Creeds of the Churches,* 3rd ed. Louisville: John Knox, 1982.

Leppin, Volker. *Martin Luther.* Darmstadt: Wissenschaftliche Buchgesellschaft, 2006.

Leppin, Volker. "Martin Luther, Reconsidered for 2017," translated by Anna Johnson, *Lutheran Quarterly* 22 (2008): 373-386.

Lewis, D.B.W. *Charles of Europe.* New York: Coward-McCann, 1931.

Lindberg, Carter. *Beyond Charity: Reformation Initiatives for the Poor.* Minneapolis: Fortress, 1993.

Lindberg, Carter. *The European Reformations.* Malden, MA: Blackwell, 1996.

Loewenich, Walther von. *Luther's Theology of the Cross.* Translated by Herbert Bouman. Minneapolis: Augsburg, 1976.

Lohfink, Gerhard. "Kommentar als Gattung," *Bibel und Leben,* 15 (1974): 1-16.

Lohrmann, Martin. "A Newly Discovered Report of Luther's Reformation Breakthrough from Johannes Bugenhagen's 1550 Jonah Commentary," *Lutheran Quarterly* 22 (2008): 324-330.

Lohrmann, Martin. "Bugenhagen's Pastoral Care of Martin Luther," *Lutheran Quarterly* 24 (2010): 125-136.

Lohse, Bernhard, ed. *Der Durchbruch der Reformatorischen Erkenntnis bei Luther: Neuere Untersuchungen.* Stuttgart: Steiner Verlag Wiesbaden, 1988.

Lohse, Bernhard. *Martin Luther's Theology: Its Historical and Systematic Development.* Translated by Roy Harrisville. Minneapolis: Fortress, 1999.

Lorentzen, Tim. *Johannes Bugenhagen als Reformator der öffentliche Fürsorge.* Tübingen: Mohr Siebeck, 2008.

Madsen, Anna. *The Theology of the Cross in Historical Perspective.* Eugene, OR: Pickwick, 2007.

Mager, Inge. "Three Women Watch Their Husbands' Backs," *Lutheran Quarterly,* 18 (2004): 28-42.

Marty, Martin. "The Modes of Being, Doing, Teaching and Discovering: The Questions about 'the Modes,'" November 1995 report to the Joint Meeting of the American Academy of Religion and the Association of Theological Schools, http://www.illuminos.com/mem/selectPapers/modes.html. Also published in *Criterion* 35 (1996), 23-36.

Matheson, Peter. *The Rhetoric of the Reformation.* Edinburgh: T & T Clark, 1998.

Maurer, Wilhelm. *Kirche und Synagogue: Motive und Formen der Auseinandersetzung der Kirche mit dem Judentum im Laufe der Geschichte.*

Stuttgart: Kohlhammer, 1953.
Miller, Gregory. "Luther on Islam." In *Harvesting Martin Luther's Reflections on Theology, Ethics, and the Church*, 185-203. Edited by Timothy Wengert. Grand Rapids: Eerdmans, 2004.
Moeller, Bernd and Martin Heckel, Rudolf Vierhaus, Karl Otmar Freiherr von Aretin. *Deutsche Geschichte, Band 2: Frühe Neuzeit*. Göttingen: Vandenhoeck & Ruprecht, 1985.
Muller, Richard and John L. Thompson, eds. *Biblical Interpretation in the Era of the Reformation: Essays Presented to David C. Steinmetz in Honor of His Sixtieth Birthday*. Grand Rapids: Eerdmans, 1996.
Muller, Richard *Post-Reformation Reformed Dogmatics: The Rise and Development of Reformed Orthodoxy, ca. 1520-1725*. 2nd Ed. Grand Rapids: Baker, 2003.
Neue Deutsche Biographie. 23 vols to date. Berlin: Duncker & Humblot, 1953-.
Oberman, Heiko. *The Harvest of Late Medieval Theology: Gabriel Biel and Late Medieval Nominalism*. Cambridge, MA: Harvard, 1963.
Oberman, Heiko. *Masters of the Reformation: The Emergence of a New Intellectual Climate in Europe*. Translated by Dennis Martin. Cambridge: Cambridge, 1981.
Oberman, Heiko. *The Roots of Anti-Semitism in the Age of Renaissance and Reformation*. Translated by James I. Porter. Philadelphia: Fortress, 1984.
Oberman, Heiko. *The Dawn of the Reformation: Essays in Late Medieval and Early Reformation Thought*. Edinburgh: T. & T. Clark, 1986.
Oberman, Heiko. *Luther: Man between God and the Devil*. Translated by Eileen Walliser-Schwarzbart. New Haven: Yale, 1990.
Olson, Oliver K. *Matthias Flacius and the Survival of Luther's Reform*. Wiesbaden: Harrassowitz, 2002.
Ozment, Steven. *When Fathers Ruled: Family Life in Reformation Europe*. Cambridge, MA: Harvard, 1983.
Ozment, Steven. *Protestants: The Birth of a Revolution*. New York: Doubleday, 1992.
Ozment, Steven. *A Mighty Fortress: A New History of the German People*. New York: HarperCollins, 2004
Pasig, Julius Leopold. *Johannes VI. Bischof von Meißen: Ein Beitrag zur Sächsischen Kirchen-und Landesgeschichte, ins besondere zur Geschichte des hochstifts Meißen*. Leipzig: J.C. Hinrichs'che Buchhandlung, 1867.
Pelikan, Jaroslav. *The Christian Tradition: A History of the Development of Doctrine*. 5 Vols. Chicago: University of Chicago, 1971-1989.
Pelikan, Jaroslav. *Whose Bible Is It? A Short History of the Scriptures*. New York: Penguin, 2005.
Peterson, Luther. *The Philippist Theologians and the Interims of 1548: Soteriological, Ecclesiastical, and Liturgical Compromises and Controversies with German Lutheranism*. Dissertation: University of Wisconsin, 1974.
Posset, Franz. "John Bugenhagen and the Comma Johanneum," *Concordia Theological Quarterly* 49 (1985): 245-251.
Prothero, Stephen. *Religious Literacy: What Every American Needs to Know – and Doesn't*. New York: HarperCollins, 2007.
Quasten, Johannes and Angelo Berardino, eds. *Patrology: Vol. 4, The Golden Age of Latin Patristic Literature From the Council of Nicea to the Council of*

Chalcedon. Translated by Placid Solari. Westminster, MD: Christian Classics, 1986.
Rabe, Horst. "Zur Entstehung des Augsburger Interims 1547/48," *Archiv für Reformationsgeschichte* 94 (2003): 6-104.
Rajashekar, Paul. *Luther and Islam: An Asian Perspective*. Göttingen: Vandenhoeck & Ruprecht, 1990.
Reiter, Paul J. *Martin Luthers Umwelt, Charakter und Psychose*, vol. 2. Copenhagen: Munksgaard, 1941.
Ruccius, Walter. *Johannes Bugenhagen Pomeranus: A Biographical Sketch*. Philadelphia: United Lutheran, 1924[?].
Rummel, Erika. *The Confessionalization of Humanism in Reformation Germany*. New York: Oxford, 2000.
Sandys-Wunsch, John. *What Have They Done to the Bible? A History of Modern Biblical Interpretation*. Collegeville, MN: Liturgical Press, 2005.
Scheible, Heinz. *Die Anfänge der reformatorische Geschichtsschreibung: Melanchthon, Sleidan, Flacius und die Magdeburger Zenturien*. Gütersloh: Mohn, 1966.
Scheible, Heinz. *Melanchthon: Eine biographie*. München: Beck, 1997.
Schnell, Uwe. *Die homiletische Theorie Philipp Melanchthons*. Berlin: Lutherisches Verlagshaus, 1968.
Schorn-Schütte, Luise, ed. *Das Interim 1548/50: Herrschaftskrise und Glaubenskonflikt*. Gütersloh: Gütersloher Verlagshaus, 2005.
Schulin, Ernst. *Kaiser Karl V: Geschichte eines übergrossen Wirkungsbereiches*. Stuttgart: Kohlhammer, 1999.
Senn, Frank. *Christian Liturgy: Catholic and Evangelical*. Minneapolis: Augsburg Fortress, 1997.
Steinmetz, David. *Reformers in the Wings*. New York: Oxford, 2001.
Steinwachs, Albrecht. *Ich sehe dich mit Freuden an: Bilder aus der Lucas-Cranach-Werkstatt in der Wittenberger Stadtkirche St. Marien*. Altenburg: Akanthus, 2006.
Steinwachs, Albrecht. "The Common Chest as a Social Achievement of the Reformation," translated by Martin Lohrmann, *Lutheran Quarterly* 22 (2008): 192-194.
Stout, Jeffrey. *Democracy and Tradition*. Princeton: Princeton, 2004.
Tjernagel, Neelak. *Martin Luther and the Jewish People*. Milwaukee: Northwestern, 1985.
Tonkin, John. *The Church and the Secular Order in Reformation Thought*. New York: Columbia, 1971.
Vogt, Karl August Traugott. *Johannes Bugenhagen Pomeranus: Leben und ausgewählte Schriften*. Elberfeld: Friederichs, 1867.
Vogt, Otto. "Melanchthon's und Bugenhagen's Stellung zum Interim und die Rechtfertigung des letzteren in seinem Jonascommentar," *Jahrbücher für Protestantische Theologie* 13 (1887): 1-38.
Volk, Ernst. *Dr. Pommer, Johannes Bugenhagen: Der Reformator im Norden*. Gr. Oesingen: Harms, 1999.
Wartenberg, Günther. *Landesherrschaft und Reformation: Moritz von Sachsen und die albertinische Kirchenpolitik bis 1546*. Gütersloh: Gütersloher Verlagshaus Mohn, 1988.

Wartenberg, Günther. "Der Kampf zwischen Kaiser und protestantischen Fürsten: sächsiche Politik unter Moritz von Sachsen zwischen 1546 und 1552," *Dresdner Hefte* 15, 52 (April 1997): 19-26.
Wartenberg, Günther. "Fürst und Reformator – zum Verhältnis zwischen Philipp Melanchthon und Georg III. von Anhalt." In *Reformation in Anhalt*, 47-57. Dessau: Anhaltische Verlagsgesellschaft, 1997.
Wartenberg, Günther and Matthias Zentner, eds. *Philipp Melanchthon als Politiker zwischen Reich, Reichsständen und Konfessionsparteien.* Wittenberg: Drei Kastanien, 1998.
Wengert, Timothy. *Melanchthon's Annotationes in Johannem in Relation to its Predecessors and Contemporaries.* Geneva: Droz, 1987.
Wengert, Timothy. *Law and Gospel: Philip Melanchthon's Debate with John Agricola of Eisleben over Poenitentia.* Grand Rapids: Baker, 1997.
Wengert, Timothy. *Human Freedom, Christian Righteousness: Melanchthon's Exegetical Dispute with Erasmus of Rotterdam.* New York: Oxford, 1998.
Wengert, Timothy. *A Formula for Parish Practice: Using the Formula of Concord in Congregations.* Eerdmans: Grand Rapids, 2006.
Westhelle, Vitor. *The Scandalous God: The Use and Abuse of the Cross.* Minneapolis: Fortress, 2006.
Wiesner-Hanks, Merry. "Women and Men, Together and Apart." In *A People's History of Christianity: Reformation Christianity*, 143-167. Edited by Peter Matheson. Minneapolis: Fortress, 2007.

Endnotes

[1] Wittenberg's Cranach Altar can be viewed at http://www.stadtkirchengemeinde-wittenberg.de/seiten/altar.html. Copyrighted photo by Jürgen M. Pietsch.
[2] Evangelical means "of the gospel." This study also follows the reformers' original usage (as well as contemporary German usage) in using Lutheran and evangelical as synonyms.
[3] Johannes Bugenhagen, IONAS PRO | PHETA EXPOSITUS | IN TERTIO CAPITE, TRA | ctatus de uera poenitentia, quam Chri= | stus commendat nobis in Niniuitis, & de falsa poeni | tentia, quam doctrinae daemoniorum post Apo | stolos inuexerunt, tantum per opera | nostra, excluso Christo. | Ibidem, Historia certa, ex probatis Scri=| ptoribus, diligentia & iudicio collecta, quemadmo=| dum post defunctum hac uita Iohannem Euangeli=| stam, coeperint defectiones a fide, doctrinae daemonio=| rum sub specie uerbi Dei, prohibitiones nuptiarum & | ciborum, uota coelibatus, pulchrae ordinationes & spi=| ritualitates, quae vocabantur perfectiones Eccle= | siae, quae adhuc regnant, solae faciunt Spi | rituales sine Spiritu sancto, per Spiri= | tum nouum & Paracletum | Montanistarum &c. | Idem caput repurgatum ab impiis | & blasphemis dubitationibus. | Per Iohan. Bugenhagium Pomeranum, D. | Impressum Vuittenberge, Per | Vitum Creutzer. | 1550 [hereafter IONAS].
[4] IONAS, B$_{iiii-v}$.
[5] In English, the only full-length biography of Bugenhagen is Walter Ruccius, *Johannes Bugenhagen Pomeranus: A Biographical Sketch* (Philadelphia: United Lutheran, 1924[?]). A more recent summary of Bugenhagen's life is Kurt K. Hendel, "Johannes Bugenhagen, Organizer of the Lutheran Reformation," *Lutheran Quarterly*, 18 (2004), 43-75 [hereafter, Hendel]. Both writers are indebted to the dated but comprehensive study of Bugenhagen's life and work: Karl AugustTraugott Vogt, *Johannes Bugenhagen Pomeranus: Leben und ausgewählte Schriften* (Elberfeld: Friederichs, 1867) [hereafter, K.A.T. Vogt]. Another influential nineteenth-century work is Hermann Hering, *Doctor Pomeranus, Johannes Bugenhagen: Ein Lebensbild aus der Zeit der Reformation* (Halle: Niemeyer, 1888). Other recent works in German include: Hans-Günter Leder, ed. *Johannes Bugenhagen – Gestalt und Wirkung: Beiträge zur Bugenhagenforschung aus Anlaß des 500. Geburtstages des Doctor Pomeranus* (Berlin: Evangelische Verlaganstalt, 1984); Hans-Günter Leder and Norbert Buske, *Reform und Ordnung aus dem Wort: Johannes Bugenhagen und die Reformation im Herzogtum Pommern* (Berlin: Evangelische Verlaganstalt, 1985); Ernst Volk, *Dr. Pommer, Johannes Bugenhagen: Der Reformator im Norden* (Gr. Oesingen: Harms, 1999).
[6] Hendel, 43.
[7] Otto Vogt, ed., *Johannes Bugenhagens Briefwechsel* (Hildesheim: Olms, 1966) [hereafter, *Briefwechsel*], 1-7 (nos. 1-2; April 23, 1512).
[8] Hendel, 45.
[9] Hendel, 45.
[10] Hendel, 45.
[11] K.A.T. Vogt, 17-27; Hendel, 71 n. 9.
[12] K.A.T. Vogt, 27. Translated in Hendel, 47.
[13] Hendel, 47-48.
[14] *Briefwechsel*, 8 (no. 3, 1520).

[15] Hendel, 49.
[16] Volk, 57.
[17] WA Br. 2:410, 15-18; LW 48:351 (ca. December 5, 1521).
[18] WA 10,3:12a, 7 -13a, 1; LW 51:74.
[19] *Briefwechsel*, 8-9 (no. 4, dated April 4, 1521); cf. MBW 142 (T 1: 292-93), where it is dated around May 1521.
[20] *Briefwechsel*, 8-9.
[21] Johannes Bugenhagen, *Epistola de Peccato in spiritum sanctum* (Wittenberg: Lotther, 1523). On the work's original 1521 composition and later publication, see Geisenhof, ed, *Bibliotheca Bugenhagiana: Bibliographie der Druckschriften d. D. J. Bugenhagen* (Leipzig: Heinsius, 1908) [Hereafter, Geisenhof], 42-47 (nos. 20-25).
[22] Hans Hermann Holfelder, "Evangelica veritas und iudicium dei: Zu Johannes Bugenhagens Epistola de peccato in spiritum sanctum (1521)," Leder, ed., *Johannes Bugenhagen, Gestalt und Wirkung* (Berlin: Evangelische Verlagsanstalt, 1984), 89.
[23] Holfelder, "Evangelica veritas und iudicium dei," 89-90.
[24] Martin Brecht, *Martin Luther: Shaping and Defining the Reformation, 1521-1532*, Schaaf, trans. (Minneapolis: Fortress, 1990), 71.
[25] Brecht, *Martin Luther: Shaping and Defining the Reformation*, 72.
[26] WA Br. 2:605, 18-25 (no. 541, October 4, 1522).
[27] Inge Mager, "Three Women Watch Their Husbands' Backs," *Lutheran Quarterly*, 18 (2004), 29.
[28] Mager, 30.
[29] IONAS, C_{ii}.
[30] Steven Ozment, *When Fathers Ruled: Family Life in Reformation Europe* (Cambridge, MA: Harvard, 1983), 50-72.
[31] Heiko Oberman, *Luther: Man between God and the Devil*, Walliser-Schwarzbart, trans. (New Haven: Yale, 1990), 281.
[32] Mager, 30.
[33] Cited in Mager, 30.
[34] Hendel, 55.
[35] Johannes Bugenhagen, *Van dem Christen louen unde rechten guden wercken wedder den falschen louen unde erdichtete gude wercke. Dar tho / wo me schal anrichten myt guden Praedickeren / dat sülck loue und wercke gepraedicket werden. An de ehrenrike stadt Hamborch* (Wittenberg: Barth, 1526). Cf. Geisenhof, 236-248 (nos. 205-213). An edition of the work appears in K.A.T. Vogt, *Von dem Christlichen Glauben und rechten guten Werken wider den falschen Glauben und erdichtete gute Werke, dazu, wie man's soll anrichten mit guten Predigern, daß solch Glaube und Werke gepredigt werden, an die ehrenreiche Stadt Hamburg* (Wittenberg:Rhaw, 1526), 101-267.
[36] Johannes Bugenhagen, *Der Erbarn Stad Brunswig Christlicke ordeninge / to dienste dem hilgen Evangelio / Christlicker lieue / tucht / frede unde Eynicheit. Ock dar under viele Christlicke lere vor de borgere* (Wittenberg: Kluck, 1528). Cf. Geisenhof, 271-276 (nos. 238-240). Cf. K..A.T Vogt, "Die Braunschweigische Kirchenordnung," 281-307.
[37] Carter Lindberg, *Beyond Charity: Reformation Initiatives for the Poor* (Minneapolis: Fortress, 1993), 144. For more on the development of the common chest, see Albrecht Steinwachs, "The Common Chest as a Social Achievement of the Reformation," *Lutheran Quarterly* 22 (2008), 192-194.
[38] Tim Lorentzen, *Johannes Bugenhagen als Reformator der öffentliche Fürsorge* (Tübingen: Mohr Siebeck, 2008), 211.
[39] WA 7:29, 34- 30, 10; 59, 24-36; LW 31:358.
[40] Philip Melanchthon, *Loci Communes Theologici*, Pauck, ed. (Philadelphia: Westminster, 1969), 109-110.
[41] On this controversy, see Timothy Wengert, *Law and Gospel: Philip Melanchthon's Debate with John Agricola of Eisleben over Poenitentia* (Grand Rapids: Baker, 1997).
[42] "The Torgau Articles," *Sources and Contexts of the Book of Concord*, Kolb and Nestingen, eds. (Minneapolis: Fortress, 2001), 93-104.

⁴³ Hendel, 62; cf. *Die Pommersche Kirchenordnung von Johannes Bugenhagen, 1535: Text mit Übersetzung, Erläuterungen und Einleitung,* Buske, ed. (Greifswald: Evangelische Landeskirche Greifswald, 1985).

⁴⁴ Hans Volz, ed. *Urkunden und Aktenstücke zur Geschichte von Martin Luthers Schmalkaldischen Artikeln (1536-1574)* (Berlin: de Gruyter, 1957), 105: "der sey ein heftiger man vnd ein grober Pommer."

⁴⁵ Martin Schwartz Lausten, "König und Kirche. Über das Verhältnis der weltlichen Obrigkeit zur Kirche bei Johann Bugenhagen und König Christian III. von Dänemark," *Johannes Bugenhagen – Gestalt und Wirkung: Beiträge zur Bugenhagenforschung aus Anlaß des 500. Geburtstages des Doctor Pomeranus,* Leder, ed. (Berlin: Evangelische Verlaganstalt, 1984), 144-167.

⁴⁶ For instance, K.A.T. Vogt, 401-442; Hendel, 67-69, and Volk, 182-194.

⁴⁷ Lindberg, *Beyond Charity,* 140.

⁴⁸ Hans Hermann Holfelder, *Tentatio et Consolatio: Studien zu Bugenhagens Interpretio in librum psalmorum* (Berlin: De Gruyter, 1974), 1.

⁴⁹ Johannes Bugenhagen, *Johannes Bugenhagens Katechismuspredigten, gehalten 1525 und 1532,* Buchwald, ed. (Leipzig: Heinsius, 1909).

⁵⁰ Geisenhof, 6-12 (nos. 3-7).

⁵¹ Hans Hermann Holfelder, *Solus Christus: Die Ausbildung von Bugenhagens Rechtfertigungslehre in der Paulusauslegung (1524/25) und ihre Bedeutung für ide theologische Argumentation im Sendbrief "Von dem christlichem Glauben" (1526)* (Tübingen: Mohr Siebeck, 1981).

⁵² Holfelder, *Solus Christus,* 93. WA 7:49, 22-25; LW 31:344.

⁵³ Holfelder, *Solus Christus,* 66-67.

⁵⁴ Holfelder, *Solus Christus,* 73. "Nachfolge Christi als Nachfolge in guten Werken, im Bekenntnis zu Christus bis zum Risiko leiblichen Todes und in 'den Werken gegen sich selbst' (*mortificatio*) kann nur da platz greifen, wo sie aus der Christi Tod und Auferstehung einschließenden Einheit des Glaubenden mit Christus (facile et hilari corde) erwächst."

⁵⁵ Anneliese Bieber, *Johannes Bugenhagen zwischen Reform und Reformation* (Göttingen: Vandenhoeck & Ruprecht, 1993).

⁵⁶ Bieber, *Johannes Bugenhagen zwischen Reform und Reformation,* 117.

⁵⁷ Ralf Kötter, *Johannes Bugenhagens Rechtfertigungslehre und der römische Katholizismus: Studien zum Sendbrief an die Hamburger (1525)* (Göttingen: Vandenhoeck & Ruprecht, 1994).

⁵⁸ Kötter, 69.

⁵⁹ Volker Gummelt, *Lex et Evangelium: Untersuchungen zur Jesajavorlesung von Johannes Bugenhagen* (Berlin: de Gruyter, 1994), 26. "So er [Bugenhagen] hebt hervor, dass die Verkündigung dieses Propheten als eine Predigt von Gesetz und Evangelium zu verstehen sei. Davon ausgehend gliedert er das gesamte Prophetenbuch in Abschnitte, in denen je von 'lex' oder vom 'evangelium' geredet wird."

⁶⁰ Yvonne Brunk, *Die Tauftheologie Johannes Bugenhagens* (Hannover: Lutherisches Verlagshaus, 2003).

⁶¹ Brunk, 193: "Das Schriftprinzip ist bei Bugenhagen immer auch Christusprinzip."

⁶² Brunk, 240.

⁶³ Brunk, 205.

⁶⁴ IONAS, i$_{vii}$.

⁶⁵ Martin Marty, "The Modes of Being, Doing, Teaching and Discovering: The Questions about 'the Modes,'" November 1995 report to the Joint Meeting of the American Academy of Religion and the Association of Theological Schools, http://www.illuminos.com/mem/selectPapers/modes.html. "We pose a thesis: that an individual, a community of scholars, or an institutional complex such as a department or a school, can with integrity and coherence approach theology and religious studies through any number of modes. They can do this without demonstrating intellectual schizophrenia and while avoiding double-talk, double-mindedness, contradiction, or compartmentalization, and in doing so they can therefore enrich the whole enterprise."

⁶⁶ Jeffrey Stout, *Democracy and Tradition* (Princeton: Princeton, 2004), 6.

[67] Stout, 112.
[68] Stout, 113.
[69] Stout, 113.
[70] For Melanchthon's appropriation of these categories, see Wengert, *Human Freedom: Christian Righteousness*, chapter 7. For the impact of these categories on the relation between evangelical princes and their churches, see James Estes, *Peace, Order and the Glory of God: Secular Authority and the Church in the Thought of Luther and Melanchthon, 1518-1559* (Leiden: Brill, 2005), chapter 4.
[71] WA 11:266, 32-37; LW 45:111.
[72] CA XVI (BSLK 71.7; BC 51.7).
[73] WA 44:530, 33-39; LW 7:312.
[74] For Lutherans, God's kingdom is visible and present in the preaching of God's word and the right use of the sacraments; CA VII and VIII (BSLK 61-62; BC 43).
[75] See Luise Schorn-Schütte, ed., *Das Interim 1548/50: Herrschaftskrise und Glaubenskonflikt* (Gütersloh: Gütersloher Verlagshaus, 2005) and Irene Dingel and Günther Wartenberg, eds., *Politik und Bekenntnis: Die Reaktionen auf das Interim von 1548* (Leipzig: Evangelische Verlagsanstalt, 2006).
[76] For instance, Oliver K. Olson, *Matthias Flacius and the Survival of Luther's Reform* (Wiesbaden: Harrassowitz, 2002), 86.
[77] Lindberg, *The European Reformations*, 244. Robert Kolb, *Confessing the Faith: Reformers Define the Church, 1530-1580* (St. Louis: Concordia, 1991), 73.
[78] Luther Peterson, The *Philippist Theologians and the Interims of 1548: Soteriological, Ecclesiastical, and Liturgical Compromises and Controversies with German Lutheranism* (Dissertation: University of Wisconsin, 1974). In his dissertation on the "Philippist" theologians Georg Major and Johann Pfeffinger, Peterson described the efforts of Melanchthon and his colleagues as constituting "an alternative to the Magdeburg brand of Lutheranism, which for the most part won out in the Evangelical camp" (192). This study concurs with Peterson's description. At the same time, this study's emphasis on Bugenhagen, an already well-established leader of the church, allows it avoid the pejorative label of "Philippist" later imposed on Melanchthon's colleagues and to examine this "alternative" within the context of Bugenhagen's long career and his mature theology.
[79] Although dated, recent Renaissance and Reformation encyclopedias still consider the authoritative English work on Charles V to be the 1939 translation of Karl Brandi's *The Emperor Charles V: The Growth and Destiny of a Man and of a World-Empire*, Wedgwood, trans. (Oxford: Alden, 1939). Another English-language resource from the 1930's is D.B.W. Lewis, *Charles of Europe* (New York: Coward-McCann, 1931). Lewis' work is similar to Brandi's, although more inclined to present Charles romantically. Both books dedicate chapters to Charles' earlier and later dealings with his German Protestant subjects. Recent studies of Charles V in German include Ernst Schulin, *Kaiser Karl V: Geschichte eines übergrossen Wirkungsbereiches* (Stuttgart: Kohlhammer, 1999) and Alfred Kohler, *Karl V. 1500-1558: Eine Biographie* (Munich: Beck, 2000).
[80] Brandi, 242.
[81] Brandi, 222.
[82] Brandi, 240.
[83] Bernd Moeller, Martin Heckel, Rudolf Vierhaus, Karl Otmar Freiherr von Aretin, *Deutsche Geschichte, Band 2: Frühe Neuzeit*, (Göttingen: Vandenhoeck & Ruprecht, 1985), 119. Cf. Brandi, 253.
[84] Brandi, 359.
[85] Moeller, et al., *Deutsche Geschichte*, 113-115.
[86] Brandi (citing a letter of July 8, 1530 from Charles to his wife, Isabella), 306-307.
[87] CA Preface (BSLK 44.1-2; BC 31.1-2).
[88] Eric W. Gritsch, *A History of Lutheranism* (Minneapolis: Fortress, 2002), 49.
[89] Brandi, 529.
[90] Gritsch, 61; Lindberg, *The European Reformations*, 243.
[91] Lindberg, *The European Reformations*, 243.

[92] Brandi, 548.
[93] Günther Wartenberg, *Landesherrschaft und Reformation: Moritz von Sachsen und die albertinische Kirchenpolitik bis 1546* (Gütersloh: Gütersloher Verlagshaus Mohn, 1988), 21.
[94] Lindberg, *The European Reformations*, 65.
[95] Wartenberg, *Landesherrschaft und Reformation*, 94-102; Martin Brecht, *Martin Luther: The Preservation of the Church, 1532-1546*, Schaaf, trans. (Minneapolis: Fortress, 1993), 288.
[96] Brecht, *Martin Luther: The Preservation of the Church, 1532-1546*, 292.
[97] Brecht, Martin *Luther: The Preservation of the Church, 1532-1546*, 292-293.
[98] Günther Wartenberg, "Der Kampf zwischen Kaiser und protestantischen Fürsten: sächsiche Politik unter Moritz von Sachsen zwischen 1546 und 1552," *Dresdner Hefte* 15, 52 (April 1997: "Kurfürst Moritz und die Renaissance"), 19-26.
[99] Brandi, 547.
[100] Günther Wartenberg, "Das Augsburger Interim und die Leipziger Landtagsvorlage zum Interim,"*Politik und Bekenntnis: Die Reaktionen auf das Interim von 1548*, eds. Dingel and Wartenberg (Leipzig: Evangelische Verlagsanstalt, 2006), 15, footnote 1. "Im Regensburger Vertrag verpflichtet sich Herzog Moritz, das Trienter Konzil zu beschicken und die Beschlüsse mit den anderen weltlichen Fürsten Germaniens ("Germaniae") anzuerkennen. Bis zu den Konzilbeschlüssen wird der Status quo in der Religion im albertinishen Herzogtum akzeptiert."
[101] Brandi, 551.
[102] Brandi, 555-556.
[103] Brandi, 563-564.
[104] "What the Elbe had never seen / Once happened at this ford / Charles the Fifth high on horse / With army and wagons came across / April 24, 1547."
[105] Wartenberg, "Der Kampf zwischen Kaiser und protestantischen Fürsten," 20. "Die Wittenberger Kapitulation, am 19. Mai 1547 vom besiegten Kurfürsten unterzeichnet, beendete die Kämpfe mit den Ernestinern. Moritz erhielt die Kurwürde und neben dem Kurkreis auch Gebiete im ernestinischen Thüringen. Den Söhnen Johann Friedrichs verblieb ein Restterritorium mit Weimar als Hauptort. Damit behielt der Kaiser ein Druckmittel gegen den neuen Kurfürsten, der sich getäuscht fühlen mußte wie auch bei der unerwarteten Festsetzung Philipps von Hessen am 19. Juni 1547 auf der Moritzburg zu Halle. Die Inhaftierung erfolgte nach dem Fußfall des Landgrafen vor dem Kaiser und traf die um Vermittlung bemühten Kurfürsten Moritz und Joachim II. von Brandenburg (1505-1571) tief."
[106] Wartenberg, "Der Kampf zwischen Kaiser und protestantischen Fürsten," 22. "Wie kein anderer erkannte er [Moritz], daß nur mit Frankreich der Kaiser zum Einlenken gezwungen werden konnte und daß die Albertiner bei einem möglichen Krieg Heinrichs II. mit den antikaiserlichen Kräften im Reich gegen Habsburg nur verlieren konnten. "
[107] Johannes Herrmann and Günther Wartenberg, eds., *Politische Korrespondenz des Herzogs und Kurfürsten Moritz von Sachsen*, Vierter Band, (Berlin: Akademie Verlag, 1992), (*editors' introduction*), 31. "Für dieses Kriegsvolk, das Moritz zur Durchführung der Acht übernommen hatte, bemühte man sich in Augsburg intensiv um die Bezahlung eines großen Teils der Kosten aus dem Reichsvorrat, über den der Ks. [Kaiser] verfügen konnte. Christoph von Karlowitz, dem es immer um Machterweiterung Sachsens ging, ist der Unterhändler, der die Zustimmung des Ks. und der Reichsstände erreichte. Die Reichsstände mußten sich damit verpflichten, den Vorrat wieder aufzufüllen, wofür eine Tagung im April 1551 in Aussicht genommen wurde. Für seine bisherigen Aufwendungen erhielt Moritz 100 000 fl., und für jeden weiteren Monat wurden ihm 60 000 fl. zum Unterhalt der Truppen zugesagt." Cf. Brandi, 602-603.
[108] Heinrich Denzinger, ed. *Enchiridion Symbolorum et Declarationum in Conciliis Oecumenicis et Summis Pontificibus* (Würzburg: Stahel, 1854), 181; for an English translation, see "Canons and Decrees of the Council of Trent," *Creeds of the Churches*, 3rd ed., Leith, ed. (Louisville: John Knox, 1982), 421.
[109] Peterson, 36.

110 For a detailed study of the Augsburg Interim, see Horst Rabe, "Zur Entshehung des Augsburger Interims 1547/48," *Archiv für Reformationsgeschichte* 94 (2003), 6-104.
111 Peterson, 40.
112 See Wengert, *Law and Gospel.*
113 "The Augsburg Interim," Sources and Contexts of the Book of Concord, 147.
114 "The Augsburg Interim," 182.
115 Timothy Wengert, "Not by Nature *Philoneikos*: Philip Melanchthon's Initial Reactions to the Augsburg Interim," *Politik und Bekenntnis*, 35. Melanchthon's first responses appear in MBW 5105 [CR VI, 839-842] and MBW 5130 [CR VI, 853-855].
116 Wengert, "Not by Nature *Philoneikos*," 35.
117 MBW 5130 [CR VI, 865-874].
118 Melanchthon first used that phrase in letters of July 13, 1548; MBW 5221 and 5222 [CR VII, 69-70 (nos. 4293 and 4294)].
119 Peterson, 113-114.
120 Christian Peters, "Der Macht des Kaisers widerstehen: Die süddeutschen Theologen und das Augsburger Interim" in *Politik und Bekenntnis*, 65-81.
121 Kolb, *Confessing the Faith*, 71, 75.
122 Günther Wartenberg, "Fürst und Reformator – zum Verhältnis zwischen Philipp Melanchthon und Georg III. von Anhalt," *Reformation in Anhalt* (Dessau: Anhaltische Verlagsgesellschaft, 1997), 54
123 Wartenberg, "Das Augsburger Interim und die Leipziger Landtagsvorlage zum Interim," 19. "Die Meißner Versammlung vom 2. bis 8. Juli 1548 stellt die Weichen für das weitere Vorgehen in der Interimsproblematik. Zunächst folgen die Verterter von Ritterschaft und Städten den Theologen. Sie lehnen das Augsburger Interim ebenfalls ab."
124 Wartenberg, "Das Augsburger Interim und die Leipziger Landtagsvorlage zum Interim," 20. "Ohne über Einzelheiten des Interims zu disputieren, solle nach einer kuzen Beschreibung von Lehre und Zeremonien in Kursachsen die Bitte an den Kaiser gerichtet werden, den gegenwärtigen Zustand nicht zu verändern, verbunden mit der Zusage, Abweichungen in der Lehre, Ungehorsam gegen die Obrigkeit und Schmähschriften nicht zu dulden."
125 Wartenberg, "Das Augsburger Interim und die Leipziger Landtagsvorlage zum Interim," 21-25. Meetings were held in Meißen (June), Pegau (August), Torgau (October), Altzella (November), and Jüterbog (December) before the Leipzig *Landtag* with the Saxon estates around Christmas of 1548.
126 *Agenda, wie es in des Churfürsten zu Sachsen Landen in den kirchen gehalten wirdt*, Friedberg, ed. (Halle: Buchhandlung des Waisenhauses, 1869). This text differs some from other Altcella documents included in CR VII 198-221 (nos. 4404-4409); cf. MBW 5350-5359.
127 Christian Winter, "Philipp Melanchthon und die albertinischen Räte," *Philipp Melanchthon als Politiker zwischen Reich, Reichsständen und Konfessionsparteien*, Wartenberg and Zentner, eds. (Wittenberg: Drei Kastanien, 1998), 224. "Auf diesen Gebieten war die Zusammenarbeit mit den kurfürstlichen Räten fruchtbar, und es gelang, die kursächsische Politik positiv zu beeinflussen. Auch in den religionspolitischen Fragen des Interims und des Konzils erhielt Melanchthon in seinen Verhandlungen mit den Räten Einfluß auf die albertinische Politik, auch wenn es besonders in der Interimsfrage ein hartes Ringen um das Verhalten zur kaiserlichen Forderung gab."
128 Herrmann and Wartenberg, 11. "Moritz zog deshalb seine bedingte Zustimmung in einer am 18. Mai schriftlich dem Ks. übergebenen Erklärung zurück. Er fühlte sich an die Religionszusage gegenüber seinen Landständen gebunden und wollte mit ihnen erwägen, was sie mit gutem Gewissen tun Könnten, um dem Ks. zu zeigen, daß ihnen an der christlichen Einheit liege."
129 Herrmann and Wartenberg, 33. "Die Interimsverhandlungen hatten ihn in den Überlegungen bestärkt, bei sichtbarer Loyalität gegenüber dem Reichsoberhaupt doch eine möglichst unabhängige Innen- und Außenpolitik anzustreben."
130 Wartenberg, "Der Kampf zwischen Kaiser und protestantischen Fürsten," 22.

[131] Herrmann and Wartenberg, 34. "Hz. Johann Albrecht von Mecklenburg, Mgf. Johann und Hz. Albrecht von Preußen schlossen am 26. Februar das Königsbergers Bündnis, von dem Moritz vermutlich über seinen Bruder erfuhr."

[132] Herrmann and Wartenberg, 34. "Während einerseits die endlosen Verhandlungen zwischen Mortiz, Joachim II. und Hessen über die möglichen Schritte zur Freilassung des Lg. weitergingen, erwog der Albertiner in Geheimgesprächen mit den hessischen Räten Wilhelm von Schachten und Simon Bing ein Bündnis mit Kg. Heinrich II."

[133] Brandi, 604.

[134] Brandi, 605.

[135] Brandi, 610-611.

[136] Brandi, 612; see also Wartenberg, "Der Kampf zwischen Kaiser und protestantischen Fürsten," 24.

[137] Lindberg, *The European Reformations*, 246-247.

[138] *Briefwechsel*, 532 (no. 264, July7, 1552).

[139] Brandi, 613. "Maurice [Moritz] had taken the precaution of asking Ferdinand to ask the Emperor not to liberate the deposed Elector of Saxony. It was a useless request for the old man had been freed some time before. He now followed in the imperial train of his own will."

[140] Robert Kolb, "Controversia perpetua: Die Fortsetzung des adiaphoristischen Streits nach dem Augsburger Religionsfrieden," *Politik und Bekenntnis*, 191.

[141] Robert Kolb, *Nikolaus von Amsdorf, Knight of God and Exile of Christ* (Dissertation: University of Wisconsin, 1973), 189. "Moritz's supporters had joined themselves to the Antichrist of Rome, and Amsdorf cited the angel's command to the people of God to come away from Babylon (from the Roman church, according to Amsdorf), lest they take part in her sins and share her plagues (Rev. 18,4)."

[142] Herrmann and Wartenberg, 19. "Im Kampf gegen das Interim entstand die große Flut der Flugschriften in Magdeburg... Gegen diese Flugschriften werden Druckverbote von Kr. Moritz und noch erheblich schärfere vom Ks. erlassen."

[143] Thomas Kaufmann, *Das Ende der Reformation: Magdeburgs "Herrgotts Kanzlei" (1548-1551/2)*, (Tübingen: Mohr Siebeck, 2003), 53-56.

[144] *Briefwechsel* (no. 196, May 29, 1547), 395-397.

[145] *Briefwechsel*, 396.

[146] Heinz Scheible, "Melanchthon rettet die Universität Wittenberg," *Melanchthon als Politiker zwischen Reich, Reichsständen und Konfessionsparteien*, 70. "Am 17. [1547] Juli traf Melanchthon in Merseburg ein. Am 18. fuhr er mit Georg von Anhalt zum Landtag nach Leipzig, wo er auch die Wittenberger Kollegen Georg Major, Johannes Bugenhagen, Caspar Cruciger, Melchior Fend und Paul Eber traf. Moritz erklärte schon bei der Begrüßung, er werde keine papistischen Mißbräuche einführen, sondern Gottes Wort fördern, für Frieden und Einigkeit wirken, Studien und Recht schützen. Dazu brauche er den Rat der Professoren."

[147] Scheible, 70-71, 73.

[148] Scheible, 68-70.

[149] Scheible, 73.

[150] Scheible, 74-75. "Melanchthons Entscheidung für seine bisherige Wirkungsstätte Wittenberg und gegen die Neugründung in Jena hatte nicht nur die finanzielle Sicherung dieser Institution zur Folge, sondern erwies sich auch pädagogisch als ein voller Erfolg. In den letzten zwölf Jahren der Wirksamkeit Melanchthons war die Frequenz der Universität Wittenberg deutlich höher als zu Luthers Lebzeiten. Die Immatrikulationen stiegen von 1199 in den Jahren 1533 bis 1537 und 2016 von 1538 bis 1542 auf 2520 von 1543 bis 1547, auf 2494 von 1548 bis 1552, auf 3041 von 1553 bis 1557 und auf 3271 von 1558 bis 1562."

[151] "The Augsburg Interim," 180.

[152] *Agenda, wie es in des Churfürsten zu Sachsen Landen in den kirchen gehalten wirdt*, 68.

[153] Wartenberg, "Das Augsburger Interim und die Leipziger Landtagsvorlage zum Interim," 26.

[154] "The Augsburg Interim," 180.
[155] "The Leipzig Interim," *Sources and Contexts of the Book of Concord*, 195.
[156] CR VII, 279 (no. 4444).
[157] WA 10.3:4a, 3-12; LW 51:71.
[158] WA 2:476 n. 4.
[159] Ap XV (BSLK 307.14; BC 230.52).
[160] CA VII (BSLK 62.1; BC 43.2).
[161] CA XV (BSLK 69.1-2; BC 49.1-2).
[162] Herrmann and Wartenberg, 15. "Im Herbst und Winter 1548/49 bemühte sich Moritz, die Probleme zu klären, die ihn als Folgen des Schmalkaldischen Krieges bedrängten. An erster Stelle ging es dabei um die Antwort an den Ks. wegen des Interims. Gleichzeitig mit dem Leipziger Landtag, der am 21. Dezember 1548 begann, wurde zur Exekution gegen die Alte Stadt Magdeburg vom 19. Dezember an in Halle verhandelt."
[163] Herrmann and Wartenberg, 15. "Moritz sucht nach einem eigenstandigen Weg, ohne den Ks. zu reizen."
[164] MBW 5377 [CR VII, 238 (no. 4424, December 11, 1548)].
[165] MBW 5377 [CR VII, 238 (no. 4424, December 11, 1548)]. "Quales autem fremitas erunt, si nos cum Islebio [Agricola] videbimur? Haec iudicio non contemno, deinde revera etiam abhorreo ab his fucosis actionibus, quia manefestum est, quaeri ut priores abusus restituantur et confirmentur."
[166] Herrmann and Wartenberg, 16. "Bald danach, am 17. Dezember, suchten Moritz und seine Räte dise Zellaer Artickel in Jüterbog als Einigungsformel mit Kf. Joachim zu nutzen, den dieser war dem Interim true ergeben. Kontakte zwischen Christoph von Karlowitz und Kf. Joachim hatten das Treffen vorbereitet. Karlowitz hielt die Zustimmung zum Kanon der Messe für möglich, wiel er das evangelische Abendmahl auf die Kommunion in beiderlei Gestalt beschränkte. Doch Melanchthon nahm schon vorher in einer Schrift heftig gegen den Meßkanon Stellung. Georg von Anhalt verhinderte gemeinsam mit ihm einen faulen Kompromiß, den Kf. Joachim erstrebte."
[167] MBW 5398 [CR VII, 293-294 (no. 4455, January 7, 1549)]. Georg Buchholzer wrote to Bugenhagen and Melanchthon, reporting Agricola's words and asking for clarification. According to Buchholzer, Agricola had said, "Damit ihr aber sehet und höret, daß man uns ganz unrecht gethan hat, so haben die Theologen zu Wittenberg auf das Interim eine Beklärung und Ordination gestellet, die den beiden Churfürsten, Sachsen und Brandenburg, überantwortet, die auch bewilligt woren in beiden Churfürstenthumen und Landen zu halten, wie solches beide Ihrer Chf. Gnad. mit eigenen Handen untersiegelt und unterschrieben, und lautet also etc."
[168] MBW 5401 [CR VII, 300 (no. 4460, January 11, 1549)].
[169] MBW 5401 [CR VII, 301 (no. 4460, January 11, 1549)].
[170] MBW 5357 [CR VII, 214 (no. 4408, November 19, 1548)].
[171] Herrmann and Wartenberg, 15-16. "Die Form der [Leipzig] Artikel zeigt, daß sie politisch und nicht theologisch motiviert sind. Sie Stellen alle Verhandlungsergebnisse zusammen, für die eine gewisse Zustimmung auf ksl. Seite bestand. Die Initiative lag bei den Räten, seitdem sich in Meißen erwiesen hatte, daß von den Theologen keine beim Ks. vertretbare Lösung zu erreichen war. Dadurch sind die Artikel nicht aus einem Guß. So ist beispielsweise ein inhaltlicher und stilistischer Bruch zwischen den ersten drei ausführlichen Artikeln zur Rechtfertigungslehre, die Melanchthon in Meißen verfaßt und für die Pegauer Verhandlungen mit den Bf. Gemildert hatte, und den restlichen erkennbar. Der Räte ergänzten auch die Theologischen Artikel für die Verhandlungen in Torgau und Zella durch kurze Abschnitte, um alle Themen des Ausburger Interims zu berücksichtigen. Die Abschnitte bringen keine theologische Definition, sondern stellen Ordnungen und Handlungen für die religiöse Praxis dar."
[172] Peterson, 181.
[173] Wartenberg, "Das Augsburger Interim und die Leipziger Landtagsvorlage zum Interim," 26.
[174] CR VII, 267-268 (no. 4436). "Erstlich berichten wir, daß die übergebenen Artikel nicht von

uns allein bedacht und gestellt sind, sondern von andern mehr Pastoren und Predigern, darum wir sie nicht zu ändern bedächten. So sind sie auch also gestellt, daß sie annehmlich und nicht allein nicht ärgerlich, sondern auch zu guter Unterweisung und zu gutem Exempel dienlich seyn werden. Daß aber etliche Sorgfältigkeit fürfället [vorfallen] in Artikeln Ordinatione, Confirmatione, Unctione, Missa, thun wir diesen Bericht." And CR VII, 270 (no. 4437).

[175] CR VII, 269 (no. 4436, December 28, 1548). "Daß man aber das Chrisma ansicht, dieses Stück ist aufgeschoben, und gehört in den Beschluß: 'in andern Artiklen wolle man sich mit den Bischoffen weiter unterreden.'"

[176] CR VII, 264 (no. 4433, December 23, 1548). Cf. "The Leipzig Interim," 196.

[177] Wartenberg, "Das Augsburger Interim und die Leipziger Landtagsvorlage zum Interim," 27. "Weder Landstände noch die Landestheologen haben der Leipziger Landtagsvorlage jemals zugestimmt."

[178] Peterson, 190.

[179] MBW 5396 [CR VII, 292 (no. 4454, January 6, 1549)]. "Lipsica actio non facit in Ecclesia mutationem, quia controversia de Missa et Canone reiicitur ad alias deliberationes."

[180] Herrmann and Wartenberg, 17-18. "Für Moritz war dieser Brief das wichtigste Ergebnis des Landtages in der Interimsfrage, den dem Ks. hatten Veteter seiner eigenen Partei berichtet, wie Moritz sich für das Augsburger Interim einsetze. Damit hatten die Artikel ihren beabsichtigten politischen Zweck zum Teil erfüllt."

[181] Nicholas Gallus and Matthias Flacius, eds., Beschluss des Landtages zu Leipzig, so im December des 48. Jars von wegen des Auspurgischen Interims gehalten ist, welchs bedencken odder beschluss wir, so da wider geschrieben, das Leiptzigsche Interim genennet haben: mit einer Vorrede und Scholien, was und warumb jedes stuck bisher fur unchristlich darin gestraffet ist; der Theologen bedencken oder (wie es durch die ihren inn offentlichen Drück genennet wirdt) (Magdeburg: [Lotter], 1550).

[182] Irene Dingel, "The Culture of Conflict in the Controversies Leading to the Formula of Concord (1548-1580)," *Lutheran Ecclesiastical Culture, 1550-1675*, Kolb, ed. (Leiden: Brill, 2008), 24.

[183] *Briefwechsel*, (no. 239, June 18, 1550), 476-477.

[184] *Briefwechsel*, 484 (No. 242, Oct. 13, 1550).

[185] Johannes Bugenhagen, *Wie es uns zu Wittenberg in der Stadt gegangen ist in diesem vergangenen Krieg bis wir durch Gottes Gnade erlöset sind und unsere hohe Schule durch den durchlauchtigsten Fürsten und Herrn, Herrn Moritzen, Herzogen zu Sachsen u.s.w. wiederum aufgerichtet ist. Wahrhaftige Historie, beschrieben durch Joh. Bugenhagen, Pommern, Doctor und Pfarrherr zu Wittenberg* (Wittenberg: Creutzer, 1547).

[186] Geisenhof, 421-423 (nos. 378-380).

[187] K.A.T. Vogt, 426. "Der Churfürst [John Frederick] rieth den Bürgern, die Stadt dem Kaiser zu übergeben, derselbe werde seine Zusage halten, auch versprach der Kaiser, es sollten nicht Spanier und andere Nationen, sondern nur Deutsche als Besatzung in dieselbe gelegt werden , und wenn andere wollten eindringen, so möchten die Wittenberger, die wohl stark genug dazu seien, sie mit Scheißen und Stechen zurücktreiben."

[188] K.A.T. Vogt, 426. "So wurde den die Stadt dem Kaiser übergeben; die bisherige Besatzung zog ab, kaiserliche Truppen, doch nur Deutsche, zogen ein. Der König Ferdinand und danach der Kaiser selbst besuchte die Stadt und besah sich auch die Kirchen. Da er hörte, daß, seit die Kaiserlichen im Schlosse lägen, in der Schloßkirche nicht gepredigt und gesungen worden sei, sagte er: wer richtet uns das an? so das geschieht in unserm Namen, so thut man uns keinen Gefallen, haben wir doch nichts gewandelt in der Religion in den hochdeutschen Landen, warum sollten wir es hier thun? Und der Gottesdienst begann wieder. In der Pfarrkirche war derselbe nie ausgefetzt worden. Der Kaiser ließ fleißig die Kirchen und Ceremonien darin besehen und die Predigten hören."

[189] Brecht, *Martin Luther: The Preservation of the Church, 1532-1546*, 380.

[190] K.A.T. Vogt, 426f.

[191] K.A.T. Vogt, 427.

[192] *Briefwechsel*, 445 (no. 230, May 25, 1549).

193 *Briefwechsel*, 434-435 (no. 222, Dec. 18-19, 1548); cf. MBW 5385.
194 CR VII, 249 (no. 4427, December 17, 1548). MBW 5336 dates this letter October 19, 1549 based on similarities with another letter of the same day (MBW 5337). If this were the case, it would refer to deliberations at Torgau rather than Jüterbog. For this argument, it is enough that the citation expresses Melanchthon's attitude toward Brandenburg's style of negotiation.
195 *Briefwechsel*, 435-437 (no. 224, Feb. 1, 1549).
196 *Briefwechsel*, 436.
197 *Briefwechsel*, 439. The unnamed man is likely Matthias Flacius, who published several early attacks against both "Interims" under pseudonymns: *Ein gemein protestation und Klagschrift aller frommen Christen wieder das Interim durch Joannem Warnemundum* (Magdeburg: 1549); *Wider den Schnöden Teuffel, der sich jtzt abermals in einen Engel des liechtes verkleidet hat, das ist wider das newe Interim, durch Carolum Azariam Gotsburgensem* ([Magdeburg: Rödinger], 1549); *Wider das Interim, Papistische Mess, Canonem vnnd Meister Eissleuben ... zu dieser zeit nützlich zu lesen durch Christianum Lauterwar* ([Magdeburg: Lotter], 1549).
198 See, respectively, MBW 5398 [CR VII (no. 4455, January 7, 1549)]; MBW 5495 [CR VII, 366-382 (no. 4516A)]; *Briefwechsel*, 437 (no. 225, February 20, 1549); *Briefwechsel*, 443 (no. 229, April 16, 1549).
199 *Briefwechsel* (no. 229, April 16, 1549), 443.
200 A translation of the letter into English is included in the appendix.
201 *Briefwechsel*, 509 (no. 256, January 11, 1552).
202 *Briefwechsel*, 449.
203 *Neue Deutsche Biographie*, Bd. 15 (Berlin: Duncker & Humblot, 1987), 494.
204 *Biblia / das ist / die gantze heilige Schrifft Deudsch* (Wittenberg: Lufft, 1534); *Tomvs Primvs Omnivm Opervm Reverendi Domini Martini Lutheri, Doctoris Theologiae* (Wittenberg: Lufft, 1545).
205 *Neue Deutsche Biographie*, Bd. 15, 494.
206 *Briefwechsel*, 445.
207 *Neue Deutsche Biographie*, Bd. 22 (Berlin: Duncker & Humblot, 2005), 320. Sabinus was married to Melanchthon's daughter Anna.
208 *Briefwechsel*, 447.
209 *Briefwechsel*, 446.
210 *Briefwechsel*, 462 (no. 232, July 17, 1549). Otto Vogt, the editor of Bugenhagen's correspondence, noted that this letter appeared in other places. The letter was addressed and sent, for instance, to Count Franz of Lüneburg; it was also cited in works by Amsdorf and Westphal.
211 *Briefwechsel*, 454 (no. 232, July17, 1549).
212 *Briefwechsel*, 454.
213 *Briefwechsel*, 455-456.
214 *Briefwechsel*, 458. Cf., Scheible, "Melanchthon rettet die Universität Wittenberg," 70.
215 *Briefwechsel*, 458.
216 *Briefwechsel*, 459.
217 Briefwechsel, 459.
218 IONAS, A$_{ii}$.
219 This use of the term is evident in the titles of several of Flacius and Amsdorf's publications, for instance: Matthias Flacius Illyricus, *Eine schrifft widder ein recht Heidnisch ja Epicurisch Buch der Adiaphoristen, darin das Leiptzische Interim verteidiget wird, sich zu hüten für den jtzigen Verfelschern der waren Religion, sehr nützlich zu Lesen* (Magdeburg: Rödinger, 1549) and Nicholas von Amsdorf, *Das nie nöter gewest ist wider den Römischen Antichrist zu schreiben, unnd predigen denn jtzundt zu dieser zeit do die Adiaphoristen mit gewalt in jhrenn schifften dringen, das man sich unter den Bapst begeben unnd ihn für ein Bisschoff und hirten der seelen widderumb erkennen unnd annemen sol* (Magdeburg: Lotter, 1551).
220 IONAS, A$_{iii}$.
221 Cited in Friedrich Bente, "Historical Introductions to the Symbolical Books of the Evangelical

Lutheran Church," *Concordia Triglotta* (St. Louis: Concordia, 1921), 111-112.

²²² IONAS, A$_{iii}$.

²²³ Nicholas von Amsdorf, *Antwort auf Doct. Pommers scheltwort / so er auff der Cantzel aussegeschött hat / am Sontag nach Vdolrici* (Magdeburg: Lotter, 1548). "Doctor Martinus Luther heiliger gedechtnis hat oft vor vielen andern glaubwirdigen vnd auch vor Doctor Augustin Schurff gesagt diese wort. Nach meinem todt wirdt keiner von diesen Theologen bestendig bleiben. Solchs hat D. Augustinus Schurff D. Pommern erinnert da Wittenberg auffgeben / Vnd ihn vermanet / das ehr bestendig bleiben vnd gedencken wolt / was D. Luther gesagt hett. Aber D. Pomer ist in vnwillen vnd zornig von ihm weggelauffen."

²²⁴ IONAS, A$_{iii}$.

²²⁵ WA TR 4:282, 8-283,23 (no. 4382b): "Wolt ir das thun, weil ich lebe, was werdet ir dann nach meinem todt thun? Wolan, ich will euch vormant haben vnd gebeten, darzu das irs gar eben wisset. Jst euch jo zu wol mit der esels furtzerei, frest sie anders wo vnd macht vns kein gestanck in vnser kirchen!"

²²⁶ WA 48:631, 11-21. "Jm selben Jar (d. i. 1544) hab ich von D. Martinus Luther dise wort gehört: Wann der Bapst oder seine gewalthaber / dz Euangelium wirt verfolgen / wie dann solches nach meinem todt nicht wirt außbleiben / So wirt der Keyser erstlich nachverwandte Fürsten zu hauff hetzen / Nicht der meynung / das er / die seiner lehre anhängig / verschonen werde / sondern dz er beyde teil nit einander auf fresse vnd verderbe. Zu solcher vneynigkeit wirt fürnämlich der Adel helffen / vnd nicht rüwen / biß er endtlich den einen theyl verrathe / das sy gunst bey dem Keyser erlangend / und bey iren güttern bleyben mögen: aber der Keyser wirt jrer nicht verschonen / vnd sy auch vnderstehen außzurotten. / Was darnach vom Adel vberbliben ist / wirdt auch vndergehen: Dann ein yegkliche Statt wirt jren Hauptmann / vnd ein yegkliches Dorf seinen Edelmann / auß dem Landt treyben / Vnd so ich alßdann lebe / wolt ichs nicht woehren."

²²⁷ IONAS, A$_{vii}$.

²²⁸ IONAS, A$_{vii}$.

²²⁹ IONAS, A$_{vi}$.

²³⁰ IONAS, A$_{vii}$.

²³¹ Bugenhagen paraphrased canons 12-14 of the Council of Trent's sixth session (January 13, 1547); Denzinger, 181-182; "Canons and Decrees of the Council of Trent," 421-422.

²³² Bugenhagen referred to chapter 9 of the Council of Trent's sixth session. Denzinger, 173-174; cf. "Canons and Decrees of the Council of Trent," 414: "...no one can know with the certainty of faith, which cannot be subject to error, that he has obtained the grace of God."

²³³ IONAS, A$_{viii}$-B$_{i}$.

²³⁴ K.A.T. Vogt, 431. In his recent examination of this period in Melanchthon's life, Heinz Scheible makes many of the same points; see Heinz Scheible, *Melanchthon: Eine biographie* (München: Beck, 1997), 193-200.

²³⁵ CR VII, 257-258 (no. 4432, December 22, 1548); cf. MBW 5386.

²³⁶ *Scriptorum Publice Propositorum A Professoribus in Academia VVitebergensi, Ab anno 1540, usqae ad annum 1553, TOMUS PRIMUS* (Wittenberg: Rhau, 1560), c (194). "IOHANNES BVGENHAGEN. POM. DOCTOR/ Hodie hora tertia incipiam praelegere Ionam Prophetam, in quo discemus illud Psal. 51. Ecce enim veritatem diligis, quae est in occult, & occultam sapientam tuam manifestas mihi. Christus suo spiritu adsit nobis." This entry is not itself dated but falls between entries of October 24 and November 4, 1547.

²³⁷ *Briefwechsel*, 412 (no. 205, Nov. 13, 1547). "24. October ist unser hohe Schule wider angangen und wir lesen Lectiones offentlich."

²³⁸ *Briefwechsel*, 414 (no. 206, Nov. 29, 1547).

²³⁹ The third volume of Luther's works was published in Wittenberg in 1549 as TOMVS || TERTIVS OMNI=||VM OPERVM, REVE=||rendi uiri, Domini Martini Lutheri, Do=||ctoris Theologiae, Continens enarrationes || Deuteronomij, ultimorum uerborum || Dauidis, multorum Psalmorum || pias luculentas,& ual=||de utiles.|| ... || [Hrsg.v.(Georgio Rorario ... ||)] (Wittenberg: Hans Luft, 1549).

²⁴⁰ A likely reference to Philip Melanchthon, *Die Heubtartikel Christlicher Lere, zusamen gezogen, durch Philippum Melanthon. Im latin genant, Loci communes theologici. Verdeudscht durch Justum Jonam, Doctor. Und im 1549. Jar. Durch Philip Melanth. widerumb durchsehen und gebessert* (Wittenberg: Creutzer, 1549).

²⁴¹ A likely reference to Philip Melanchthon, *Commentarii in Epistola Pauli ad Romanos* (Strasbourg: K. Müller, 1550). It was published in March 1550.

²⁴² "Five books" probably refers to the Jonah Commentary, including its four theological tracts.

²⁴³ *Briefwechsel*, 467-468 (no. 236, March 9, 1550).

²⁴⁴ Philip Melanchthon, *Corpvs Doctrinae Christianae. Das ist, Gantze Summa der rechten waren Christlichen Lehre des heyligen Euangelij: nach jnnhalt Göttlicher, Prophetischen vnd Apostolischen Schrifften, in etliche Bücher gantz richtig, Gottselig vnd Christlich verfasset* (Leipzig: Vögelin, 1560). Melancthon's *Corpus Doctrinae Christianae* included the Augsburg Confession (variata) and its Apology, the Saxon Confession of 1552, the latest edition of the Loci Communes, an examination for prospective ordinands, and a late work against the Bavarian inquisition.

²⁴⁵ IONAS, A$_{vii}$.

²⁴⁶ Among others works about the history of biblical interpretation, see, Fowl, ed., *The Theological Interpretation of Scripture: Classic and Contemporary Readings* (Cambridge, MA: Blackwell, 1997); Jaroslav Pelikan, *Whose Bible Is It? A Short History of the Scriptures* (New York: Penguin, 2005), 205-221; Stephen Prothero, *Religious Literacy: What Every American Needs to Know – and Doesn't* (New York: HarperCollins, 2007); John Sandys-Wunsch, *What Have They Done to the Bible? A History of Modern Biblical Interpretation* (Collegeville, MN: Liturgical Press, 2005), 1-25, 333-339.

²⁴⁷ *Scriptorum Publice Propositorum A Professoribus in Academia VVitebergensi, Ab anno 1540, usqae ad annum 1553, TOMUS PRIMUS* (Wittenberg: Rhau, 1560), c (194). "IOHANNES BVGENHAGEN. POM. DOCTOR/ Hodie hora tertia incipiam praelegere Ionam Prophetam, in quo discemus illud Psal. 51. Ecce enim veritatem diligis, quae est in occult, & occultam sapientam tuam manifestas mihi. Christus suo spiritu adsit nobis." This entry is not itself dated but falls between entries of October 24 and November 4, 1547.

²⁴⁸ Martin Luther, *Explanations of the Ninety-Five Theses*, WA 1:613, 23-28; LW 31:225. For more on the theology of the cross, see Gerhard Forde, *Where God Meets Man: Luther's Down-to-Earth Approach to the Gospel* (Minneapolis: Augsburg, 1972); Walther von Loewenich, *Luther's Theology of the Cross*, Bouman, trans. (Minneapolis: Augsburg, 1976); Vitor Westhelle, *The Scandalous God: The Use and Abuse of the Cross* (Minneapolis: Fortress, 2006); and Anna Madsen, *The Theology of the Cross in Historical Perspective* (Eugene, OR: Pickwick, 2007).

²⁴⁹ IONAS, Biiii-v.

²⁵⁰ Matthew 12:38-41; see also Matthew 16:1-4.

²⁵¹ Luke 11:29-30.

²⁵² In the sixteenth century, many books used letters of the alphabet and roman numerals to mark the pages. Each letter went from one to eight, so that A_i to A_{viii} make up the commentary's first eight pages. Aviii is followed by Bi, and so on. In this particular book, one page includes both the left and right sides of a fully opened book. This commentary begins with A_i and ends with Ggviii, for a total of 424 pages.

²⁵³ IONAS PRO | PHETA EXPOSITUS | IN TERTIO CAPITE, TRA | ctatus de uera poenitentia, quam Chri=| stus commendat nobis in Niniuitis, & de falsa poeni | tentia, quam doctrinae daemoniorum post Apo | stolos inuexerunt, tantum per opera | nostra, excluso Christo. | Ibidem, Historia certa, ex probatis Scri=| ptoribus, diligentia & iudicio collecta, quemadmo=| dum post defunctum hac uita Iohannem Euangeli=| stam, coeperint defectiones a fide, doctrinae daemonio=| rum sub specie uerbi Dei, prohibitiones nuptiarum & | ciborum, uota coelibatus, pulchrae ordinationes & spi=| ritualitates, quae vocabantur perfectiones Eccle= | siae, quae adhuc regnant, solae faciunt Spi | rituales sine Spiritu sancto, per Spiri=| tum nouum & Paracletum | Montanistarum &c. | Idem caput repurgatum ab impiis | & blasphemis dubitationibus. | Per Iohan. Bugenhagium Pomeranum, D. |

Impressum Vuittenberge, Per | Vitum Creutzer. | 1550.
[254] Matthew 12:40.
[255] James L. Bailey and Lyle D. Vander Broek, *Literary Forms in the New Testament: A Handbook* (Louisville: Westminster/John Knox, 1992), 159.
[256] Wengert, *Law and Gospel*, 15, n. 1. Although Wengert elected to leave *poenitentia* untranslated, this study will usually translate *poenitentia* as repentance.
[257] Ap XII: "Absolution can properly be called the sacrament of penance," (BSLK 259.41; BC 193.41). In 1545, Luther asserted, "We gladly confess penance to be a sacrament with the power of the keys," (*Against the Thirty-Two Articles of the Louvain Theologists*) WA 54:427, 26-28; LW 34:357.
[258] WA 1: 540, 42- 541, 7; LW 31:100.
[259] Martin Luther, *The Proceedings at Augsburg*, WA 2:13, 6-16, 11; LW 31:270-275.
[260] Carl Mirbt, ed., *Quellen zur Geschichte des Papsttums und des römischen Katholizmus*, 3rd ed. (Tübingen: Mohr Siebeck, 1911), 192. "Certainty of faith" was condemned in the bull's eleventh point against Luther.
[261] CA XXV (BSLK 98.4; BC 72.4). "It is also taught how God requires us to believe this absolution as much as if it were God's voice resounding from heaven and that we should joyfully obtain forgiveness of sin."
[262] Denzinger, 181; "The Canons and Decrees of the Council of Trent," 421.
[263] Denzinger, 173-174; "The Canons and Decrees of the Council of Trent," 413-414.
[264] Ecclesiastes 9:1: "All this I laid to heart, examining it all, how the righteous and the wise and their deeds are in the hand of God: whether it is love or hate one does not know." Joel 2:14: "Who knows whether he will turn and relent…?" Jonah 3:9: "Who knows? God may relent and change his mind; he may turn from his fierce anger, so that we do not perish."
[265] IONAS, B$_1$.
[266] Heiko Oberman, *The Harvest of Late Medieval Theology: Gabriel Biel and Late Medieval Nominalism* (Cambridge, MA: Harvard, 1963), 217-235. Oberman concluded his examination of Biel's view of hope and faith by stating, "We may conclude that between this kind of *fiducia* and the certitude of salvation stands the categorical imperative of the law of the Old and the New Testament. It is the same movement from mercy to justice that we observed in the doctrine of predestination and justification which stimulates the *viator* to earn his salvation in fear and trembling in a constant oscillation between despair and presumption," 235.
[267] WA 54:412; LW 34:339.
[268] Article 8 of the Louvain Theologians' Thirty-Two Articles condemned justification by faith alone; WA 54:418; LW 34:348. "In adults faith is necessary above all things for justification, by which we firmly believe that Christ Jesus, God's Son, has been given us by the Father as a propitiator for our sins in his blood, without which justification can be obtained by none of our works and by no penance, even as not by faith alone without penance and the intent to live according to God's commands."
[269] WA 54:418; LW 34:348.
[270] "The Augsburg Interim," 154.
[271] Vogt, "Jonascommentar," 27.
[272] Gerhard Ebeling, *Word and Faith*, Leitch, trans. (Philadelphia: Fortress, 1963), 79-81.
[273] Hans W. Frei, *The Eclipse of Biblical Narrative: A Study in Eighteenth and Nineteenth Century Hermeneutics* (New Haven, CT: Yale, 1974), 10. "To state the thesis: a realistic or history-like (though not necessarily historical) element is a feature, as obvious as it is important, of many of the biblical narratives that went into the making of Christian belief. It is a feature that can be highlighted by the appropriate analytical procedure and by no other, even if it may be difficult to describe the procedure – in contrast to the element itself. It is fascinating that the realistic character of the crucial biblical stories was actually acknowledged and agreed upon by most of the significant eighteenth-century commentators. But since the precritical analytical or interpretive procedure for isolating it had irretrievably broken down in the opinion of most commentators, this specifically realistic characteristic, though acknowledged by all hands to be there, finally came to be

ignored, or – even more fascinating – its presence or distinctiveness came to be denied for lack of a 'method' to isolate it. And this despite the common agreement that the specific feature was there!"

[274] Erik M. Heen, "The Theological Interpretation of the Bible," *Lutheran Quarterly* 21 (2007), 375-376.

[275] Frei,1.

[276] Richard Muller, *Post-Reformation Reformed Dogmatics: The Rise and Development of Reformed Orthodoxy, ca. 1520 to ca. 1725* (Grand Rapids, MI: Baker, 2003), 30.

[277] Muller, 51-52. "The theologians of the late Middle Ages did not pose Scripture and tradition against each other neatly as competing norms in theology. Instead, together with the exegetes of the age, they asked questions about pattern and meaning in interpretation that had direct implications for their view of the relationship of Scripture to tradition and their conception of the doctrinal authority of Scripture. On these points there is a clear continuity of discussion between the fifteenth and the sixteenth centuries."

[278] IONAS, B_{i-v}.

[279] IONAS, B_i.

[280] IONAS, B_{i-ii}. "Non potuit Ionas apud Iudaeos, quod potuit apud Gentes, licet miranda per uerbum faceret apud impium Regem Ieroboam, ut scribitur iiii. Regem. xiiii." II Kings 14:25-26: "He [Jeroboam] restored the border of Israel from Lebo-hamath as far as the Sea of the Arabah, according to the word of the Lord, the God of Israel, which he spoke by his servant Jonah son of Amittai, the prophet, who was from Gath-hepher. For the Lord saw that the distress of Israel was very bitter; there was no one left, bond or free, and no one to help Israel."

[281] IONAS, B_{ii}.

[282] For instance, Bugenhagen's commentary ends with a citation of Luther's hymn, "Lord, Keep Us Steadfast in Your Word," WA 35:467-468; LW 53:304-305. IONAS, CC_{vi}: "Erhalt vns HERR bey deinem Wort / Und stewr des Bapts vnd Türken mord etc."

[283] Steven Ozment, *A Mighty Fortress: A New History of the German People* (New York: HarperCollins, 2004), 99-100. See also Wilhelm Maurer, *Kirche und Synagogue: Motive und Formen der Auseinandersetzung der Kirche mit dem Judentum im Laufe der Geschichte* (Stuttgart: Kohlhammer, 1953); Mark U. Edwards, *Luther's Last Battles: Politics and Polemics, 1531-46* (Ithaca, NY: Cornell, 1983), 115-142; and Oberman, *The Roots of Anti-Semitism in the Age of Renaissance and Reformation*.

[284] IONAS, B_{ii}.

[285] Wengert, *Human Freedom, Christian Righteousness*, 52. "Chief among them [dialectical categories] was what Melanchthon called at various times in Colossians the *oeconomia, summa, sententia scriptorum, argumentum, status, scopus,* or hypokeimenon __Without the argumentum, an exegete could easily mutilate a text. With it, one could know the 'organization (*series*) of the entire speech' and could thereby attain the 'certain and sure understanding' (*certa sententia*) of the author, 'which can defend and teach the conscience.'"

[286] IONAS, B_{ii}.

[287] IONAS, B_{iii}.

[288] Muller, 79. Melanchthon's *loci* method "included a movement from textual study to doctrinal statement in the construction of theological *loci* as a final step in the work of exegesis. These *loci* pointed directly from an exegetically grounded theological formulation to the gathering of doctrinal topics into theological compendia and systems."

[289] Melanchthon, *Loci Communes Theologici*, Pauck, ed., 18-19. Cf. MSA II.1, 4.

[290] Wengert, *Human Freedom, Christian Righteousness*, 44. "Melanchthon's exegetical method revolved around his use of commonplaces [*loci*]. Melanchthon viewed each text as a specific example of a more general theological category. By identifying such categories and discussing them, sometimes at length, the exegete was more faithful to the text itself than a simple grammatical explanation allowed. By focusing on a biblical author's *argumentum* either in an entire book or an individual chapter, exegetes obtained a useful lens through which the main topics of theology could be illumined. This allowed exegetes like Melanchthon to skip verses or to subsume them under a more general discussion.

Occasionally, the biblical writer inserted an excursus on another topic, to which exegetes could also turn their attention. In this context the patristic heritage provided for Melanchthon not only interpretations of specific texts – already an important contribution – but also insights into theological topics. Moreover, the theological issues and battles fought by Paul as revealed by the text became simply special cases of the same issues and battles being fought at other times and places. Thus it was perfectly natural, exegetically speaking, for Melanchthon to move from patristic debates to modern ones."

[291] Vogt, "Jonascommentar," 26. "War nun systematische Strenge in Anordung des Stoffes überhaupt nicht sehr Bugenhagen's Sache, da er sich oft allzu sorglos von der Erörterung eines Punktes zu einem andern ablenken last, um danach zum ersten zurückzukehren, so wurde dismal die Planmässigkeit der Anordnung noch erschwert durch die Neuheit und Schwierigkeit der umfassenden Quellenstudien, welche er ersichtlich während des Verlaufs der Vorlesungen noch fortsetzte."

[292] IONAS, Biiii-v.

[293] Vogt, "Jonascommentar," 26. Cited above.

[294] Ap IV, XII, XX (BSLK 177.83, 214.152, 264.65f.; BC 134.83; 198.65, 235.2). Melanchthon's 1543 *Loci Communes* also uses this verse in this way, CR 21:760, 783, 889, 915, & 959.

[295] IONAS, Hii.

[296] "The Confutation of the Augsburg Confession," *Sources and Contexts of the Book of Concord*, 109-110.

[297] Luther had lectured and published on Jonah in 1525 and 1526. For his comments on Jonah 3:10 in the 1526 German Text, see WA 19:239, 6-18; LW 19:90. Melanchthon had included this verse in the Apology's discussion of repentance; Ap XII (BSLK 288.166; BC 216.166): "The example of the Ninevites [Jonah 3:10] is a case in point. By their repentance – we mean the entire scope of repentance [contrition, faith, good fruits] – they were reconciled to God and prevented the destruction of the city."

[298] See Martin Luther, *The Babylonian Captivity of the Church*, WA 6:539, 5-9; LW 36:75: "You will find those who argue and decree that a work done in fulfillment of a vow ranks higher than one done without a vow, and in heaven is to be rewarded above others with I know not what great rewards. Blind and godless Pharisees, who measure righteousness and holiness by the greatness, number, or other quality of the works! But God measures them by faith alone, and with him there is no difference among works, except insofar as there is a difference in faith." And Martin Luther, *The Misuse of the Mass*, WA 8:504, 11-13; LW 36:159-160: "Let this suffice for the present concerning their ungodly priesthood, sacrifice, and service. It will serve to instruct every pious person sufficiently, so that when he recognizes and sees that he is a priest of the devil and of his apostle, the pope, he will soon desist from it and make every effort to become a priest of Christ and his holy church, or else become a layman again and pay no heed whatever to the fictitious character, the anointed and oiled fingers, the tonsured head and the pharisaical dress of these miserable priests." And Ap IV, BSLK 216.282; BC 163.282, "When this entire passage [James 2:24] is examined, it will show that faith also is required. For Christ rebukes the Pharisees for thinking that they are cleansed in God's sight, that is, that they are justified, by frequent washings. Along these lines some pope – I am not sure which one – said that sprinkling of water mixed with salt 'sanctifies and cleanses the people,' and the gloss says that it cleanses from venial sins. Such were also the opinions of the Pharisees whom Christ reprimanded." See also, Scott Hendrix, *Luther and the Papacy: Stages in a Reformation Conflict* (Philadelphia: Fortress, 1981), 95-120.

[299] *Oxford English Dictionary*, 2nd ed. vol. 12, (Oxford: Clarendon, 1989), 21.

[300] "Polemik" in *Deutsches Wörterbuch*, vol. 13, Jacob and Wilhelm Grimm, eds. (Leipzig: Hirzel, 1854-1960), 1977.

[301] "Streitschrift" in *Deutsches Wörterbuch*, vol. 19, 1395.

[302] The uncritical and anachronistic use of "polemic" is a short-coming in the otherwise strong exploration of Reformation language in Peter Matheson, *The Rhetoric of the Reformation* (Edinburgh: T & T Clark, 1998), 1-13.

[303] IONAS, A_{vii}, cited at the beginning of the chapter.

304 IONAS, Cc$_v$, "Sit Christo gratia. | AMEN. | FINIS."
305 IONAS, Cc$_v$-Cc$_{vi}$.
306 IONAS, Cc$_{vi}$.
307 IONAS, Cc$_{vii}$, Ee$_{viii}$, and Ff$_{vii}$, respectively.
308 *Benedictionale siue agenda secundum ritum et consuetudinem Jngenue ecclesie Misnensis* (impressus est in officina libraria Melchiaris Lotter Anno Millesimo quingentesimo duodecimo) (Leipzig: Lotter, 1512). This church order was reprinted in the nineteenth century in Julius Leopold Pasig, *Johannes VI. Bischof von Meißen: Ein Beitrag zur Sächsischen Kirchen- und Landesgeschichte, ins besondere zur Geschichte des hochstifts Meißen* (Leipzig: J.C. Hinrichs'che Buchhandlung, 1867), 233-285.
309 IONAS, Ffiiii. "Hic tangat aquam consecrator in modum crucis (Quis consecrauit aquam Christo in Iordane? Sanctus Cyprianus factis Montaniter dixit Epist. xii. Oportet Mundari & sanctificari aquam prius a Sacerdote qui sanctus sit & Spiritum sanctum habeat, ut posit baptism suo peccata hominis, qui baptizatur abluere, ungi quoque necesse est eum qui baptizatus est, ut accepto Chrismate, id est, unctione, esse unctus Dei & habere in se gratiam Christi posit &c. quae sententiae ab Acclesia damnatae sunt, in primis ab Augustino, ut alias dictum est, & tamen maserunt istae spirituosae aquae consecrationes usque ad nos)."
310 PL 25:1117-1152. Jerome's work also informed the medieval *Glossa Ordinaria*, cf. Muller, 32.
311 PL 25:1118. "Igitur tanto post tempore, quasi quodam postliminio a Jona interpretandi sumens principium, obsecro ut qui typus est Salvatoris, et tribus diebus ac noctibus in ventre ceti moratus, praefiguravit Domini resurrectionem, nobis quoque fervorem pristinum tribuat, ut sancti ad nos Spiritus mereamur adventum. Si enim *Jonas* interpretatur *columba*, columba autem refertur ad Spiritum sanctum: nos quoque columbam, ex adventu [Al. et adventum] ad nos interpretemur columbae."
312 PL 25:1120. "Condemnatur generatio Judaeorum, credente mundo: et Ninive agente poenitentiam, Israel incredulus perit. Illi habent libros, nos librorum Dominum (II Cor. III): illi tenent prophetas, nos intelligentiam prophetarum: illos occidit littera, nos vivificat spiritus (Joan. XVIII): apud illos Barabbas latro dimittitur, nobis Christus Dei Filius solvitur."
313 SCRiptorum / Publice / ProposiTORUM / A PROFESSORIBUS IN / Academia VVitebergensi, Ab anno 1540, usquae ad an/num 1553 | TOMUS PRIMUS | WITTEBERGAE | EXUSUS AB HAE | redibus Georgis Rhaw | Anno 1560, Nn 6$_r$. For more on Bugenhagen's use of Augustine in the Jonah Commentary, see chapter 5.
314 IONAS, B$_{vi-vii}$.
315 See Muller, 33-39, 57. The *quadriga*, the dominant interpretive guide of the Middle Ages, offered four interpretations for any given biblical text: historical, allegorical, tropological, and anagogical. Of these, the historical interpretation offered literal interpretation by providing the basic grammatical and contextual help necessary to understand a passage; the other three were spiritual ways to read a given text for its doctrinal, moral or eschatological insights, respectively. Because those figurative modes of interpretation could lead to erratic readings of scripture, occasional calls for a return to the plain meaning provided by the literal sense also arose in the Middle Ages from scholars like Thomas Aquinas and Nicholas von Lyra.
316 PL 44:203; *On the Spirit and the Letter*, Burnaby, trans. (Philadelphia: Westminster, 1955), 193. "The meaning of 'the letter' in this text [2 Cor. 3:6] is not to be limited to Scripture as understood literally, as against its allegorical interpretation. The 'letter' may also stand for the moral precepts of the law, which must necessarily be taken literally; and so the 'the Spirit that giveth life' may mean, not 'spiritual' or allegorical interpretation of Scripture, but the Spirit's gift of the desire for what is good."
317 IONAS, B$_{vii}$.
318 WA 40.1:657b, 13-19; LW 26:435-436.
319 On Luther as "father," see chapter 4.
320 WA 40.1:664b, 27-33; LW 26:441.

³²¹ Melanchthon, *Loci Communes Theologici* (1521), 77; cf. MSA II.1, 73.
³²² Timothy Wengert, *Melanchthon's* Annotationes in Johannem *in Relation to its Predecessors and Contemporaries* (Geneva: Droz, 1987), 194-198.
³²³ Wengert, *Melanchthon's* Annotiones in Johannem, 196.
³²⁴ For a comparison with Luther's allegorical interpretations of Jonah in the 1526 lectures, see chapter 7.
³²⁵ IONAS, B$_{v\text{-}vi}$.
³²⁶ WA 19:219, 26-27; LW 19:68. "Who would believe this story and not regard it a lie and a fairy tale if it were not recorded in Scripture?"
³²⁷ IONAS, E$_{iiii\text{-}vi}$.
³²⁸ Soren Kierkegaard, *The Sickness unto Death*, Hong and Hong, trans. (Princeton: Princeton, 1980), 18. Kierkegaard wrote this work under the pseudonym "Anti-Climacus."
³²⁹ Wengert, *Human Righteousness, Christian Freedom*, 53. Wengert identified a consistent logical connection between *quid sit* (what a thing is) and *quid effectus* (what is the effect) in Melanchthon's theological and exegetical works. "Here [in the Colossians commentary] Melanchthon moved immediately from one dialectical question, *quid sit*, which provided the conscience a *certa sententia*, to another, *quid effectus* (what is the effect), by adding that this Pauline gospel was 'the greatest consolation' for those same consciences."
³³⁰ WA 7:49, 22-25; LW 31:344.
³³¹ BSLK 515.5, 520.5; BC 359.5-6, 362.5-6.
³³² Melanchthon, *Loci Communes Theologici* (1521), 21; cf. MSA II.1, 7.
³³³ Melanchthon, *Loci Communes Theologici* (1521), 22; cf. MSA II.1, 7. See also Luther's Small Catechism where, in explaining the sacraments he moved from their definition to their benefits (effects), BSLK 515.5, 520.5; BC 359.5-6, 362.5-6.
³³⁴ Martin Brecht, *Martin Luther: His Road to Reformation, 1483-1521*, Schaaf, trans. (Philadelphia: Fortress, 1985), 118. "It was not easy for Frederick to abandon collecting and exhibiting his relics. They were still displayed until 1522, although the indulgence was emphasized less and less."
³³⁵ A picture of Jonas' *Wappen* is viewable at http://de.wikipedia.org/w/index.php?title=Datei:Jonas-und-der-Wal.jpg&filetimestamp=20060325205106. Image belongs to Public Domain.
³³⁶ IONAS, E$_{vi}$.
³³⁷ IONAS, C$_{vi}$.
³³⁸ A hymn by Luther, "Erhalt uns Herr bey deinem Wort," WA 35:467-468; LW 53:304.
³³⁹ A Latin antiphon, "Da pacem Domine in diebus nostris," which Luther translated into German as "Verley uns frieden gnediglich," WA 35:458; LW 53:286.
³⁴⁰ IONAS, E$_{vii}$.
³⁴¹ IONAS, E$_{vii\text{-}viii}$.
³⁴² IONAS, E$_{viii}$.
³⁴³ IONAS, E$_{viii}$.
³⁴⁴ IONAS, D$_{ii}$.
³⁴⁵ Volker Leppin, "Martin Luther, Reconsidered for 2017," *Lutheran Quarterly* 22, (2008), 384. "When one depicts Luther's relationship to the Middle Ages with the historical nuance that is necessary today, one does not lose anything theologically but instead gains something. Instead of creating a rigid border, this model allows Lutheran identity to be depicted as a form of Christianity that, like Roman Catholicism, has preserved the legacy of the Middle Ages but has at the same time understood church and faith in new ways through the radical emphasis on the freedom of a Christian and the resultant priesthood of all believers."
³⁴⁶ There are some studies of the relationship between Luther and Bugenhagen in English and German. For instance, Kurt Hendel, 43-75; David Steinmetz, *Reformers in the Wings* (New York: Oxford, 2001); Volker Gummelt, "Johannes Bugenhagen – Freund und Seelsorger," *Luther und Seine Freunde* (Wittenberg: Drei Kastanien, 1998); and Hans-Günter Leder, "Luthers Beziehungen zu seinen Wittenberger Freunden," *Leben und Werk Martin Luthers von 1526 bis 1546*, Band I, Junghans, ed. (Göttingen: Vandenhoeck &

Ruprecht, 1983).
347 WA Br 2:598, 7-11 (no. 536, September 20 [?], 1522), 598.7-11.
348 Martin Brecht, *Martin Luther: Shaping and Defining the Reformation, 1521-1532*, 71-72.
349 WA 15:8, 10: "Episcopus Ecclesiae Wittembergensis."
350 K.A.T. Vogt, 364; cf. WA TR 5:634, 32-36 (no. 6384).
351 In naming himself as the German pope, Luther made a joke of a serious accusation leveled against him over ten years earlier by Thomas Müntzer. Müntzer had called him, "Father Pussyfoot," "Dr. Liar," and "the Wittenberg pope," among other names; Lindberg, *Beyond Charity*, 153.
352 Schwarz Lausten, "König und Kirche," 152. "Eine Zeitgenössische Quelle berichtet, Luther sei, 'böse vnnd unnmudig' gegen Bugenhagen gewesen, 'dat he sick des Amtes understand hedde, den Koning vnnd Försten tho donde, vnnd gaff em ien groth Ruchte schwar und schalt groß und schwer auf ihn.'"
353 Schwarz Lausten, 152.
354 WA TR 1:140, 10-15 (no. 347); LW 54:49.
355 Volz, 105. See chapter 1.
356 See an interpretation of Melanchthon's principled moderation in Wengert, "Not by Nature *Philoneikos*."
357 WA TR 1:47, 25-48, 2 (no. 122); LW 54:15-16.
358 Hendel, 51, citing K.A.T. Vogt, 71; cf. WA TR 2:390.31-35 (no. 2268b).
359 WA TR 2:390.35 (no. 2268b). "Da verstehet man, was das sei, dein Wort hat mich wieder lebendig gemacht &c."
360 For more on this subject, see Martin Lohrmann, "Bugenhagen's Pastoral Care of Martin Luther," *Lutheran Quarterly* 24, 2 (2010), 125-136.
361 Brecht, *Martin Luther: The Preservation of the Church, 1532-1546*, 378.
362 Johannes Bugenhagen, *A Christian Sermon over the Body and at the Funeral of the Venerable Dr. Martin Luther*, Hendel, trans. (Atlanta: Pitts Theology Library, 1996). This text includes both a copy of the original German text (*Eine Christliche Predigt uber der Leich und begrebnis des Ehrwirdigen D. Martini Luthers* [Wittenberg: Rhau, 1546]) as well as the English translation. The text is available online at: http://beck.library.emory.edu/luther/luther_site/luther_text.html.
363 For instance, Martin Brecht, *Martin Luther: The Preservation of the Church 1532-1546*, 380; Gummelt, "Johannes Bugenhagen – Freund und Seelsorger," 101; and Susan K. Hedahl, "Melanchthon and the Talk of Preaching," *Philip Melanchthon: Then and Now*, Hendrix and Wengert, eds. (Columbia, SC: Lutheran Theological Southern Seminary, 1999).
364 Hedahl, 115. "Bugenhagen's sermon is intensely personal, in several instances referring only to private conversations he had with Luther. He is both anecdotal and rambling. Bugenhagen uses biblical texts, primarily apocalyptic or eschatological in nature, as the foundation of his discourse. Luther's death is portrayed as an exemplar of what it means to die the good death. The focus is generally individualistic in nature. The overall form is loose."
365 Bugenhagen, *A Christian Sermon...*, A_{iv}.
366 Brecht, *Martin Luther: The Preservation of the Church 1532-1546*, 379.
367 Bugenhagen, *A Christian Sermon...*, B_{ii} and D_i.
368 Brecht, *Martin Luther: The Preservation of the Church 1532-1546*, 238. Berndt had married Luther's niece, Lene Kaufmann, in 1538.
369 Bugenhagen, *A Christian Sermon...*, C_i.
370 Bugenhagen, *A Christian Sermon...*, C_{ii}.
371 Bugenhagen, *A Christian Sermon...*, B_i.
372 Bugenhagen, *A Christian Sermon...*, B_i.
373 Oberman, *Luther*, 12. "Luther's measure of time was calibrated with yardsticks other than those of modernity and enlightenment, progress and tolerance. Knowing that the renewal of the Church could be expected to come only from God and only at the end of time, he would have had no trouble enduring curbs on the Evangelical movement. According to Luther's prediction, the Devil would not 'tolerate' the rediscovery of the Gospel; he would rebel with all his might, and must all his forces against it. God's Reformation would

be preceded by a counterreformation, and the Devil's progress would mark the Last Days. For where God is at work – in man and in human history – the Devil, the spirit of negation, is never far away."

[374] Bugenhagen, *A Christian Sermon...*, D_i.
[375] Bugenhagen, *A Christian Sermon...*, A_{iii} and D_{ii}.
[376] *Briefwechsel*, 63. "d. Martini patris nostri." Also in Kawerau, *Der Briefwechsel des Justus Jonas*, 107; Cf. WA TR 3:81 n. 13.
[377] For instance, *Briefwechsel*, 84 (no. 29, March 8, 1529); 126 (no. 49, March 10, 1533); 179, (no. 76, April 28, 1539); 217 (no. 92, December 19, 1540); 234 (no. 106, July 1542); 269 (no. 122, June 17, 1543); 349 (no. 165, January 13, 1546); 356, (no. 169, April 30, 1546); 467 (no. 236, March 9, 1550).
[378] WA 8:576, 1-4; LW 48:335.
[379] WA 8:576, 16-18; LW 48:336.
[380] See Oberman, *Luther*, 139-146.
[381] For instance, WA Br 2:567, 2 (no. 512, June 27, 1522); LW 49:10. "Reverende et optime Pater." And WA Br 3:155, 1-2 (no. 659, Sept. 17, 1523); LW 49:48. "Reverendo in Christo Patri, D. Iohanni, Abbati S. Ord. Benedictini Salisburgae, suo in Domino maiori, patri et praeceptori."
[382] WA Br 3:155,5-156,1 ; LW 49:48.
[383] WA TR 1:80, 6-7 (no. 173). "Jch hab all mein ding von Doctor Staupiz."
[384] LC, 4th Commandment (BSLK 601.158; BC 408.158).
[385] *Briefwechsel*, 306 (no.148, end of 1544): "venerandi Patres et Praeceptores..."
[386] Brecht, *Martin Luther: Shaping and Defining the Reformation, 1521-1532*, 245. Luther's Latin lectures on Jonah appeared in two versions in 1525, WA 13:224-240 and 241-258; LW 19:3-3. An expanded German edition was published in 1526, WA 19:185-251; LW 19:35-104.
[387] WA 19:185-186; LW 19:35-36.
[388] For more on Luther and Bugenhagen's interpretations of Nineveh's founding, see chapter 7.
[389] IONAS, C_{vi-vii}.
[390] See chapter 7.
[391] IONAS, C_{viii}.
[392] See chapter 4.
[393] WA 19:169 (*editor's introduction*).
[394] WA 19:185, 20-25. LW 19:35.
[395] WA 19:169-170 (*editor's introduction*).
[396] WA 13:241, 24-25; LW 19:4.
[397] WA 13:241, 15-17; LW 19:4.
[398] WA 13:243, 20-23; LW 19:6.
[399] WA 13:243, 30-33; LW 19:6.
[400] To describe Calvin's strong position on predestination (or election), Melanchthon privately used the name of the founder of Stoicism, Zeno, to talk about Calvin. Timothy Wengert, *A Formula for Parish Practice* (Eerdmans: Grand Rapids, 2006), 181.
[401] WA TR 3: 550, 20-551, 19 (no. 3705, Jan. 17, 1539[?]).
[402] WA 13:247, 20; LW 19:15. "In this way it came about that, although he [Jonah] was in the midst of death, still he was alive." For the text of *Mitten wir im Leben sind*, see WA 35:453-454; LW 53:274-276.
[403] For more on Luther's exposition of Jonah 4, see chapter 7.
[404] WA 13:257, 20-258, 14; LW 19:31.
[405] WA 19:240, 20-35; LW 19:92.
[406] WA 19:250; LW 19:103.
[407] IONAS, B_{iiii-v}.
[408] WA 19:193. 9-21; LW 19:40.
[409] IONAS, B_{iiii}. See chapter 3.
[410] IONAS, C_{ii-v}.
[411] "The Augsburg Interim," 165. "The sacrament of Order, therefore, was instituted with the

sign of laying on of hands and other appropriate rites, by which those who are consecrated to the offices of the church receive the grace by which they become fit, suitable, and capable of administering the same functions.... Therefore, on whomever in the perpetual succession of the church the bishops place their hands, consecrating them to their order, to them they give the power of discharging their office... The orders recognized by the catholic church are seven: priests, evangelists [German: deacons], epistolers [German: subdeacons], acolytes, readers, exorcists, and thurifers... It is clear that whoever despises or abolishes these offices brings evil on the Christian church."

[412] Tertullian, *De Resurrectione Carnis*, PL 2:806.
[413] IONAS, o$_{vi\text{-}viii}$.
[414] CR VI, 934 (MBW 5182). "Item, daß sie in allen Landen mit großem Fleiß gehalten würde, daß es nicht allein ein Ceremonia und Spectakel wäre, sondern daß die Ordinanden wohl verhöret und unterwiesen würden, und daß bei der Ceremonia ernstliche Gebeth geschehen. Item, daß auch hernach ein fleißig Aufsehen auf die Lehr und Sitten der Priester geschehe."
[415] *Agenda, wie es In des Churfürsten zu Sachsen Landen In den kirchen gehalten wirdt*, 26 and 56.
[416] Justo Gonzalez, *The Story of Christianity*, vol. 1 (San Francisco: Harper, 1984), 76-77.
[417] WA 20:764c,20-765c, 24; LW 30:306-307.
[418] SA III, 8 (BSLK 453.3-454.4; BC 322.3-4).
[419] Wengert, "Not by Nature *Philoneikos*," 35-36.
[420] WA 54:425, 2-426, 2; LW 34:354.
[421] Louvain's article on baptism is cited in WA 54:418; LW 34:347. "Baptism is necessary to salvation for all, also for infants. Through it sins are fully taken away and they become the sons of God and heirs of eternal life. Nor must it ever be repeated."
[422] Brecht, *Martin Luther: The Preservation of the Church, 1532-1546*, 36. "Next to the devil, he regarded as enemies of baptism the Catholic 'Arch-Anabaptists,' who with their works baptized anew, and the 'Epicureans' – meaning the Münster Anabaptists – who with their practice failed to recognize it as a divine work."
[423] WA 54:430, 6-12; LW 34:360.
[424] Gerhard Lohfink, "Kommentar als Gattung," *Bibel und Leben* 15 (1974), 1.
[425] Brecht, *Martin Luther: The Preservation of the Church, 1532-1546*, 136.
[426] WA 44:717, 17-26; LW 8:189.
[427] For the 1545 Preface to the Latin Works, see WA 54:185, 12-186, 24; LW 34:335-37. Accounts of the "tower experience" are found in WA TR 4:72 (no. 4007); LW 54:308-09 and WA TR 3:228 (no 3232c); LW 54:193-194.
[428] Numerous studies on this subject exist. Two works by Bernhard Lohse offer good summaries of recent research: *Der Durchbruch der Reformatorischen Erkenntnis bei Luther: Neuere Untersuchungen*, Lohse, ed. (Stuttgart: Steiner Verlag Wiesbaden, 1988) and Bernhard Lohse, *Martin Luther's Theology: Its Historical and Systematic Development*, Harrisville, trans. (Minneapolis: Fortress, 1999).
[429] See also Martin Lohrmann, "A Newly Discovered Report of Luther's Reformation Breakthrough from Johannes Bugenhagen's 1550 Jonah Commentary," *Lutheran Quarterly* 22 (2008), 324-330.
[430] IONAS, T$_{viii}$-V$_{ii}$. See also, Lohrmann, "A Newly Discovered Report of Luther's Reformation Breakthrough from Johannes Bugenhagen's 1550 Jonah Commentary," *Lutheran Quarterly* 22, 3 (2008), 324-334.
[431] Volker Leppin, *Martin Luther* (Darmstadt: Wissenschaftliche Buchgesellschaft, 2006), 116-117.
[432] WA TR 3:228 (no. 3232c); LW 54:193-194.
[433] WA 1:525, 4-14; LW 48:65-66. "Reverend Father: I remember that during your most delightful and helpful talks, through which the Lord Jesus wonderfully consoled me, you sometimes mentioned the term *"poenitentia."* I was then distressed by my conscience and by the tortures of those who through endless and insupportable precepts teach the so-called method of confession. Therefore I accepted you as a messenger from heaven when you said that *poenitentia* is genuine only if it begins with love for justice and for God and

that what they consider to be the final stage and completion [satisfaction] is in reality rather the very beginning of *poenitentia.*"

434 PL 42:1048. "Sed quemadmodum dicitur etiam justitia Dei, non solum illa qua ipse justus est, sed quam dat homini cum justificat impium..."

435 PL 42:890. "Resuscitatur ergo anima per poenitentiam, et in corpore adhuc mortali renovatio vitae inchoatur a fide, qua creditur in eum qui justificat impium (Rom. IV, 5)..."

436 WA 9:2 (*editor's introduction*): "Unmittelbar unter dem Titel lesen wir die von Luther geschriebenen Worte: 'Moritur b. Augustinus Anno domini .433. Et nunc scilicet 1509. fuit mortuus ad .1076. annos'. Hiernach hat Luther diesen Band im Jahre 1509 benutzt. Derselbe war Eigenthum des Erfurter Augustinerklosters: so besagt die allerdings zehn Jahre jüngere, unter Luthers Worten stehende Bemerkung von anderer unbekannter Hand: 'Conventus ordinis fratrum eremitarum sancti Augustini in Erphordia: 1519:'. In sein Erfurter Kloster aber war Luther 1509, und zwar wohl im Herbst zurückberufen worden, nachdem er im März dieses Jahres zu Wittenberg den Grad eines baccalaureus biblicus erlangt hatte und während er eben im Begriffe war, zum zweiten theologischen Grade, dem eines sententiarius, fortzuschreiten. Als sententiarus war er bis 1511 bei der theologischen Fakultät Erfurts thätig."

437 Where Augustine was discussing how the Father and Son relate to each other in the biblical passage, Luther asked how the life of God becomes part of the life of the believer. In this context, Luther's notes include a discussion of the raising of Lazarus and Christ's words "I am the resurrection and the life" (John 11:25). WA 9:17.

438 Heiko Oberman, "Facientibus Quod in se est et Deus non Denegat Gratiam: Robert Holcot O.P. and the Beginnings of Luther's Theology," *The Dawn of the Reformation: Essays in Late Medieval and Early Reformation Thought* (Edinburgh: T. & T. Clark, 1986), 103. "Not merely the 'young Luther,' but the 'youngest Luther,' even *before* beginning his career as a professor, as a biblical exegete, and eventually as a Reformer, has on points which later prove to be cornerstones in the structure of his thought become independent of the nominalist theological tradition in which he was reared."

439 WA 3:453, 4-5; LW 10:395.

440 WA 3:456, 33-457, 10; LW 10:400. "Therefore a metaphor, not the reality itself, is assumed here in this mode of speaking, when the Law is said to be a reed, but the Gospel a tongue. In this way, that as the reed produces a dead writing on dead parchment, so the Law, or the words of the Law, carnally understood, produces spiritually dead writing, meaning, and understanding in carnal and dead hearts. And as a living tongue naturally produces meaning or living letters, characters, and impressions in a living soul or in a living hearer, so the Gospel spiritually produces spiritual impressions, a spiritually alive and eternal understanding in hearts spiritually alive. For that reason the law of Moses, whether spoken or written, as long as it is spiritually treated, is a living tongue and no longer a dead reed. On the contrary, even the Gospel, when carnally treated, is a dead reed and all that is said about the law of Moses. To this the apostle bears witness in 2 Cor. 4:3: "If our Gospel is veiled, it is veiled for those who perish.""

441 WA 3:457, 38-458, 11; LW 10:402. "*And Thy righteousness, O God, even to the highest.* In this verse at last the correct distinction between divine and human righteousness is depicted. For the righteousness of God reaches up to the heavens of heavens and causes us to reach. It is righteousness even to the highest, namely, of reaching the highest. Not so the human righteousness, but rather it reaches down to the lowest. This is so because he who exalts himself will be humbled, and he who humbles himself will be exalted. But now the whole righteousness of God is this: To humble oneself into the depth. Such a one comes to the highest, because he first went down to the lowest depth. Here he properly refers to Christ, who is the power of God and the righteousness of God through the greatest and deepest humility. Therefore He is now in the highest through supreme glory. Therefore, whoever wants to relish the apostle and other Scriptures must understand everything tropologically: Truth, wisdom, strength, salvation, righteousness, namely, that by which He makes us strong, safe, righteous, wise, etc. So it is with the works of God and the ways of God. All of them are Christ literally, and all of them are faith in Him morally."

442 WA 56:171, 27-172, 5; LW 25:151.
443 WA TR 5:210, 6. "Qui locus primum moverit Doctorem."
444 WA TR 5:210, 24-40 (no. 5518, winter of 1542-1543), author's translation; cf. LW 54:442-443.
445 Vogt, "Jonascommentar," 26, 27.
446 Vogt, "Jonascommentar," 27.
447 Vogt, "Jonascommentar," 32.
448 Vogt, "Jonascommentar," 33. 1 John 5:7-8 reads as follows, with the disputed passage in brackets: "There are three that testify [in heaven, the Father, the Word and the Holy Spirit, and these three are one. And there are three that testify on earth]: the Spirit and the water and the blood, and these three agree."
449 Franz Posset, "John Bugenhagen and the *Comma Johanneum*," *Concordia Theological Quarterly* 49 (1985), 249. "Why did Bugenhagen feel compelled at all to write about this problem? He did so chiefly because in 1549 a volume of gospels and epistles was printed in Wittenberg in which the debated 1 John 5:7 was included quite in contrast to Luther's teaching." Posset's source for this "volume of gospels and epistles" is August Bludau, "Das Comma Ioanneum (I Io 5,7) im 16. Jahrhundert," *Biblische Zeitschrift* 1 (1903), 379. "Die Driezeugenstelle findet sich bereits in einem im Jahre 1549 in Wittenberg gedruckten deutschen Evangelien- und Epistelbuch und forderte den Protest Bugenhagens heraus."
450 Posset, 249.
451 This edition of the New Testament may be *Das newe Testament auffs new zugericht / D. Mart. Luth.* (Wittenberg: Lufft, 1549).
452 Vogt, "Jonascommentar," 37. "Soviel glaubte ich aus jenen Vorlesungen mittheilen zu sollen, welche bisher fast völlig unbeachtet geblieben sind. Der – selbst orthodoxe – Jäncke behauptet (im ‚Gelehrten Pommerland', Stettin 1734), das Buch sei schon zu seiner Zeit ziemlich selten geworden, weil die so nachdrückliche Verwahrung gegen die Textfälschung I. Joh. 5,7 dasselbe bei den späteren Lutheranern missliebig gemacht habe."
453 Vogt, "Jonascommentar," 37. "Es kam aber wohl hinzu, dass Bugenhagen wegen seiner Stellung zu Melanchthon, speciell auch im Streit über die Adiaphora, ohnehin sich geringer Gunst bei ihnen erfreute."
454 This view is shared by the editors of Luther's lectures on 1 John, LW 30:316, n. 13.
455 Posset, 289.
456 Muller, *Post-Reformation Reformed Dogmatics*, 422, n. 225. "Note that the second commentary on 1 John attributed to Luther in the Walch edition (in which the 'comma' is cited as authentic) is now recognized to be by Agricola."
457 Vogt, "Jonascommentar," 25.
458 Vogt, "Jonascommentar," 37-38.
459 IONAS, $E_{vii-viii}$. See chapter 2.
460 IONAS, G_{viii}.
461 IONAS, G_{iiii}. "Expositio primi praecepti."
462 For instance, LC, 1st Commandment (BSLK 560.2-3; BC 386.2-3). "A 'god' is the term for that to which we are to look for all good and in which we are to find refuge in all need. Therefore, to have a god is nothing else than to trust and believe in that one with your whole heart. As I have often said, it is the trust and faith of the heart alone that make both God and an idol. If your faith and trust are right, then your God is the true one. Conversely, where your trust is false and wrong, there you do not have the true God. For thse two belong together, faith and God. Anything on which your heart relies and depends, I say, that is really your God."
463 IONAS, G_{iiii}.
464 "The Augsburg Interim," 154.
465 IONAS, G_{vi-vii}.
466 IONAS, H_i.
467 IONAS, z_i.
468 IONAS, H_{ii}.
469 IONAS, H_{ii-iii}.

470 WA 13:253, 13-21; LW 19:23. *"They proclaimed a fast, etc.* The enemies of faith regularly throw this passage up to us because they think they have found something worthy of the palm against us. Blindly they read the words "God respected the works of the people of Nineveh" and from their own judgment bring forth a witness against justification by faith. Since our eyes have been opened, let us not be blind like these men, but let us look at the words of the Holy Spirit and more thoroughly understand that it is no accident that the first thing that is stated is that *the people of Nineveh believed God.* This is the standard and rule with which all things that are added concerning works must be harmonized. For if faith in the heart is sincere, it does not have need for any teacher of good works; it knows in itself what must be done."

471 IONAS, Aa$_{iii}$.

472 IONAS, D$_v$, D$_{vi}$, F$_i$, G$_{viii}$.

473 IONAS, I$_{iiii}$.

474 WA 26:219, 24-30; LW 40:295-296. "So, the first part of penance is contrition and sorrow. The second part is faith that the sins will be forgiven on Christ's account. This faith effects good resolution. So with faith we receive the forgiveness of sins, as Paul has said in Rom. 3[:35]. But, as we have often said, this faith cannot be there until there has been contrition and sorrow. For contrition without faith is the contrition of Judas and of Saul; it is despair. So faith without contrition, as we shall show, is presumption and carnal security."

475 CA XII (BSLK 66-67.1-6; BC 45.1-6).

476 CA VI (BSLK 60.1-3; BC 41.1-3). CA XX also revisits the theme of faith and good works in a longer discussion (BSLK 75-83a; BC 53-57).

477 IONAS, I$_{ii}$. Cf. CA VI (BSLK 60.2; BC 41.2).

478 Johannes Bugenhagen, *Von dem christlichen Glauben vnd rechten guten Wercken wider den falschen Glauben und erdichtete gute Werke, dazu, wie man's soll anrichten mit guten Predigern, dass solch Glaube und Werke gepredigt werden* (Wittenberg: Rhaw, 1526), included in K.A.T. Vogt, 101-267. On the so-called "Majoristic controversy" see the recent collection on Georg Major: Irene Dingel and Günther Wartenberg, eds., *Georg Major (1502-1574): Ein Theologe der Wittenberger Reformation* (Leipzig: Evangelische Verlagsanstalt, 2005).

479 K.A.T. Vogt, 161-162.

480 IONAS, K$_v$.

481 WA 13:253, 22-25; LW 19:23. "But since the people of Nineveh believed the Word of God, of their own free will and with their faith as the leader and originator they did these works by which they gave external proof of the internal faith. In plain words, faith alone justifies a person, Rom. 3-5."

482 Johannes Bugenhagen, *Die pommersche Kirchenordnung von Johannes Bugenhagen, 1535*, Buske, ed. (Greifswald: Evangelische Landeskirche Greifswald, 1985), 215-216.

483 IONAS, L$_i$.

484 IONAS, L$_i$.

485 PL 25:1139. "*Dominus autem noster post resurrectionem secundo mittitur ad Nineven.*"

486 WA 13:253, 8-12; LW 19:23.

487 WA 19:234, 16-26; LW 19:85. "Undoubtedly he did not confine himself to these words, but he must have enlarged on the themes why such wrath of God would overtake them, what sorts of wickedness were rampant in the city, how one should be a godly person, and all that is involved in this. We are still in the habit of summarizing a sermon today, saying, for example: 'He preached on sin,' or, 'He preached on the Mass.'"

488 PL 25:1139. "*Et Ninive erat civitas magna Dei.*" WA 13:252, 34-37. "Deinde magno errore etiam in latinis bibliis omissum est nomen dei, ut sic legatur: erat civitas magna dei (vel deo), quod nomen magno consensu habent exemplaria hebraea omnia et Hieronymus in translatione sua latina non omisit."

489 PL 25:1139.

490 WA 13:252, 38-39; LW 19:22. Some modern translations, including the New Revised Standard Version and the New International Version, attribute Nineveh's founding to Nimrod. The New Jerusalem Publication Society, among others, concurs with the Vulgate's

reading that Nineveh was founded by Asshur.

[491] WA 42:404, 25-33; LW 2:201-202.
[492] WA 42:405, 9-16; LW 2:202.
[493] IONAS, I$_i$. "Ab Adam a Noe et patribus habuerunt Niniuitae Euangelium."
[494] IONAS, K$_i$.
[495] IONAS, I$_i$.
[496] IONAS, K$_{ii}$.
[497] IONAS, K$_{vi-vii}$.
[498] IONAS, Bb$_{ii-vi}$. See also chapter 7.
[499] IONAS, L$_{ii}$.
[500] IONAS, L$_{ii}$.
[501] IONAS, L$_{iii}$.
[502] IONAS, L$_{iii}$.
[503] Charles P. Arand, "Melanchthon's Rhetorical Argument for Sola Fide in the Apology," *Lutheran Quarterly* 14 (2000), 299.
[504] IONAS, L$_{iii-iiii}$.
[505] WA DB 8:30, 19-28; LW 35:248-249. "Whoever reads this Bible should also know that I have been careful to write the name of God which the Jews call 'Tetragrammaton' in capital letters thus, LORD [*HERR*], and the other name which they call *Adonai* only half in capital letters thus, LOrd [*HErr*]. For among all the names of God, these two alone are applied in the Scriptures to the real, true God; while the others are often ascribed to angels and saints. I have done this in order that readers can thereby draw the strong conclusion that Christ is true God. For Jeremiah 23[:6] calls him LORD, saying, 'He will be called: 'The LORD, our righteousness.'"
[506] IONAS, O$_i$.
[507] IONAS, P$_v$.
[508] IONAS, M$_{vi}$.
[509] IONAS, M$_{vi}$.
[510] On the Lutheran reformers' understanding of James, see Derek Cooper, *The Ecumenical Exegete: Thomas Manton's Commentary on James in Relation to its Protestant Predecessors, Contemporaries and Successors* (Dissertation: Lutheran Theology Seminary at Philadelphia, 2008), chapter 2.
[511] WA DB 7:384, 3-5; LW 35:395.
[512] James 2:13 is cited in WA 19:200, 13-14 (LW 19:47); James 5:17 is cited in WA 13:243, 17; 248, 10-11; 255, 20-22 (LW 19:6, 14, 27).
[513] Ap IV (BSLK 79.23; BC 56.23).
[514] Ap IV (BSLK 209.251; BC 159.252).
[515] IONAS, M$_{vii-viii}$.
[516] Andreas Althamer, *Annotationes in Epistolam beati Iacobi iamprimum editae: Cum Indice* (Strasbourg: Schott, 1527). Althamer was a humanist and reformer active in Franconia until his death in 1539, *Neue Deutsche Biographie*, Bd. 1 (Berlin: Duncker & Humblot, 1953), 219.
[517] IONAS, N$_{ii}$.
[518] See Edwards, *Luther's Last Battles*, 16-17; Hendrix, *Luther and the Papacy*, 62-63.
[519] IONAS, N$_{ii-iii}$. "Si Iacobus potuit instituere nouum Sacramentum extremae unctionis, quod non erat institutum a Christo, possumus & nos Episcopi facere & sanctificare untiones, quas Christus non instituit, & dicere siue docere, quod damus Spiritum sanctum, & sanctificamus alias creaturas nostro oleo a nobis sanctificato, Possumus etiam instituere alia. Sacramenta, quae Christus non instituit, Possumus condere nouos canones, id est, Leges, & imponere hominibus, & uexare atque grauare conscientias, quas Christus suo sanguine liberauit &c."
[520] "The Augsburg Interim," 158.
[521] Luther had come to a similar conclusion in *On the Councils and the Church*, WA 50:560, 4-8; LW 41:68.
[522] IONAS, N$_{iii}$.

523 SA II, 4 (BSLK 430.9; BC 308.9). "Therefore the church cannot be better ruled and preserved than if we all live under one head, Christ, and all the bishops – equal according to the office (although they may be unequal in their gifts) – keep diligently together in unity of teaching, faith, sacraments, prayers, and works of love, etc."

524 Tr 31 (BSLK 480-481.31; BC 335.31).

525 WA 6:567, 32-571, 23; LW 36:117-123.

526 WA 6:569, 37-570, 10; LW 36:121.

527 WA 6:568, 30-37; LW 36:119.

528 IONAS, N$_{iiii}$.

529 IONAS, N$_{iiii}$. Romans 8:9: "Who does not have the spirit of Christ does not belong to him." 2 Corinthians 1:21-22: "But it is God who establishes us with you in Christ and has anointed us." Psalm 45:7: (concerning Christ) "You love righteousness and hate wickedness. Therefore God, your God, has anointed you with the oil of gladness beyond your companions." Isaiah 61:1-2 (which Jesus read in Luke 4:18-19): "The spirit of the Lord God is upon me, because the Lord has anointed me to preach, etc." Acts 4:27: [Peter and John prayed], "they gathered against your holy child Jesus, whom you anointed."

530 IONAS, N$_{iiii-v}$. The citation about Christ's anointing with the Holy Spirit to which Bugenhagen referred is actually in Eusebius' book 1, chapter 3.

531 PG 20:73, 74. "Quibus verbis sermo divinus in primo quidem versu Deum illum nominat; in altero vero sceptrum regale eidem attribuit; ac paulatim descendens, post divinam ac regiam potestatem, tertio demum loco Christum illum, non materiali quidem sed divino laetiae oleo delibutum esse declaret;" Eusebius, *The History of the Church from Christ to Constantine*, Williamson, trans. (Minneapolis: Augsburg, 1975), 44.

532 IONAS, N$_{iiii}$.

533 IONAS, N$_{v-vi}$.

534 For its appearance in the Pseudo-Augustinian *Sermo contra Judaeos, Paganos et Arianos*, see PL 42:1124. John Duns Scotus quoted Pseudo-Augustine as part of his citation of Daniel 9:24, in *Ordinatio*, Prologue, pt. 2 ("De sufficiencia Sacrae Scripturae"), par. 109: "similiter illud Danielis: *Cum venerit Sanctus sanctorum, cessabit unctio vestra*."

535 WA 50:323, 9-19; LW 47:78.

536 John 11:49-52.

537 Johannes Quasten and Angelo Berardino, eds. *Patrology: Vol. 4, The Golden Age of Latin Patristic Literature From the Council of Nicea to the Council of Chalcedon*. Solari, trans. (Westminster, MD: Christian Classics, 1986), 180-190. This study will refer to the work as Ambrosiaster but retain the reformers' own use of Ambrose.

538 CA VI (BSLK 60.1-3; BC 41.1-3) and CA XX BSLK 77.12-13; BC 54.12-13.

539 WA DB 7:39, 28. "So halten wyrs nu, das der mensch gerechtfertiget werde, on zu thun der werck des gesetzs, alleyn durch den glawben..."

540 WA 30.2:642, 26-27; LW 35:197.

541 IONAS, O$_{iiii}$.

542 PL 17:83. "(Vers. [3:]24). 'Justificati gratis per gratiam ipsius.' Justificati sunt gratis, quia nihil operantes, neque vicem reddentes, sola fide justificati sunt dono Dei."

543 PL 17:86-87. "(Vers. [4:]5) 'Ei vero qui non operatur,' id est, ei qui obnoxius est peccatis, qui non operatur, quod mandat lex. 'Credenti autem in eum, qui justificat impium, reputatur fides ejus ad justitiam.' Hoc dicit, quia sine operibus legis credendi impio, id est gentili, in Christum, reputatur fides ejus ad justiam, sicut et Abrahae. Quomodo ergo Judaei peropera legis justificari se putant justificatione Abrahae, cum videant Abraham non per opera legis, sed sola fide justificatum? Non ergo opus est lex, quando impius per solam fidem justificatur apud Deum. 'Secundum propositum gratiae Dei.' Sic decretum dicit a Deo, ut cessante lege, solam fidem gratia Dei posceret ad salutem.

"(Vers. [4:]6) 'Sicut et David dicit.' Hic ipsum munit exemplo prophetae, 'Beatitutidem hominis, cui Deus accepto fert justitiam sine operibus.' Beatos dicit de quibus hoc sanxit Deus, ut sine labore et aliaqua observatione, sola fide justificentur apud Deum. Temporis ergo beatitudinem praedicat, quo natus est Christus, sicut ipse Dominus ait: 'Multi justi et prophetae cupierunt videre, quae videtis, et audire, quae auditis, et non audierunt (Matth.

544 "The Confutation of the Augsburg Confession," 110.
545 "The Confutation of the Augsburg Confession," 110.
546 Brunk, *Die Tauftheologie Johannes Bugenhagens*, 122. "1558 hat Melanchthon in seiner Gedächtnisrede davon gesprochen, daß Bugenhagen aufgrund seiner Augustinstudien zum reformatorishen Durchbruch gelangt ist, der allerdings nicht ohne die Begegnung mit Schriften Luthers stattgefunden haben würde." Although Brunk then cited Hans-Günther Leder to cast doubt on Melanchthon's statement, Bugenhagen's expansive knowledge of Augustine in these tracts suggests a long and influential engagement with Augustine's work.
547 Hendel, 68-69.
548 IONAS, $O_{vii\text{-}viii}$.
549 PL 44:214. "His igitur consideratis pertractatisque pro viribus quas Dominus donare dignatur, colligimus non justificari hominem praeceptis bonae vitae nisi per fidem Jesu Christi, hoc est, non lege operum, sed fidei; non littera, sed spiritu; non factorum meritis, sed gratuita gratia." Translation from *St. Augustine: Anti-Pelagian Writings*, Schaff, ed. (Edinburgh: T & T Clark), 88. "Now, having duly considered and weighed all these circumstances and testimonies, we conclude that a man is not justified by the precepts of a holy life, but by faith in Jesus Christ,—in a word, not by the law of works, but by the law of faith; not by the letter, but by the spirit; not by the merits of deeds, but by free grace."
550 IONAS, O_{viii}, citing Augustine's *De baptismo, contra Donatistas*, book II, chapter 3 in PL 43:128. Translation available in *St. Augustine: The Writings Against the Manicheans and Against the Donatists*, Schaff, ed. (Edinburgh: T & T Clark), 427.
551 IONAS, O_{viii}, "cum sancta humilitate, cum pace catholic, cum charitate Christiana." Cf. PL 43:129.
552 IONAS, P_i. Cf. PL 40: 204.
553 IONAS, P_i. "De tertia quaestione: quod fides ad salutem non sufficit sine operibus." Cf. PL 40:211.
554 IONAS, P_i. Cf. PL 40:211.
555 IONAS, P_{ii}.
556 IONAS, $P_{ii\text{-}iii}$. Cf. PL 40:217.
557 IONAS, P_{iii}. "Philippus Melanthon [sic] etiam in locis communibus & alias, solet uerba Iacobi commode interpraetari."
558 IONAS, P_{iii}, citing BSLK 207.244 [BC 157.244]: "From James [2.24] they quote, 'You see that a person is justified by works and not by faith alone.' No other single passage is supposed to contradict our position more, but the response is easy and clear. James's words do not pose a problem if the opponents would not read into it their own opinions about the merits of works. But wherever works are mentioned, the opponents attach their own ungodly opinions: that we merit the forgiveness of sins through good works; that good works are the atoning sacrifice and payment on account of which God is reconciled to us; that good works conquer the terrors of sin and death; that good works are acceptable in God's sight on account of their own intrinsic goodness; and that they neither need mercy nor Christ as the propitiator. None of these things ever entered into James's mind, yet the opponents now defend all these things under the pretext that this is James's meaning."
559 IONAS, P_{iv}. Ap IV, CR 27:491-492. Bugenhagen's citations of the Apology are exact, matching the April/May 1531 "quarto" edition rather than the September 1531 "octavo" edition (hence this footnote's reference to CR 27). He also rearraged quotations from the Apology throughout, suggesting that he was either citing the Apology from memory or intentionally rearranging it to fit his argument better. Translation from *The Book of Concord*, Tappert, ed. (Philadelphia: Fortress, 1959), 143.252-253; cf. BSLK 209.252; BC 159.252.
560 Ap IV, CR 27:490 (BSLK 208.247; BC 158.247). IONAS, P_{iv}.
561 LC, Lord's Prayer (BSLK 690; BC 456.121-124).
562 IONAS, P_v. "Iudicium Patris Lutheri de Epistola Iacobi, uides in translatione Germanica Noui testamenti."

563 WA DB 7:385, 3-8; LW 35:395.
564 WA DB 7:387, 13-15; LW 35:397.
565 WA DB 6:11, 33-35; LW 35:362, with n. 11. See also, Cooper, *The Ecumenical Exegete*, 271.
566 WA 7:387, 15-18; LW 35:395.
567 IONAS, P$_{iiii}$.
568 IONAS, P$_{vii}$. "Negabant Sola fide nos iustificari... Quia uero negabant Christum esse Deum, consequens erat, ut etiam negarent trinitatem in diuina uintate, quam Deus in suo uerbo nobis reuelauit."
569 IONAS, P$_{viii}$.
570 Wengert, *Melanchthon's* Annotationes in Johannem, 149. Melanchthon had identified his papal opponents with Ebionites in his 1522/23 *Annotationes in Johannem*. "Ebionites are those who deny Christ's divinity. Those are twice Ebionites who, although they attribute divinity to Christ, nevertheless do not put it to use [in remitting sins]."
571 For Luther's understanding of Islam, see Johannes Ehmann, *Luther, Türken und Islam: Eine Untersuchung zum Türken- und Islambild (1515-1546)* (Gütersloh: Gütersloher, 2008); Adam Francisco, *Martin Luther and Islam: A Study in Sixteenth-century Polemics and Apologetics* (Leiden: Brill, 2007); Gregory Miller, "Luther on Islam," in *Harvesting Martin Luther's Reflections on Theology, Ethics, and the Church*, Wengert, ed. (Grand Rapids: Eerdmans, 2004), 185-203; Paul Rajashekar, *Luther and Islam: An Asian Perspective* (Göttingen: Vandenhoeck & Ruprecht, 1990).
572 IONAS, Q$_{iiii}$.
573 WA 50:605, 15-606, 2; LW 41:121.
574 Philip Melanchthon, *De ecclesia et autoritate verbi Dei*, in MSA 1:335; *Melanchthon: Selected Writings*, Flack and Satre, eds., Hill, trans. (Minneapolis: Augsburg, 1962), 141. On the Lutheran reformers' relationships to early church writers, see John M. Headley, *Luther's View of Church History* (New Haven: Yale, 1963); Peter Fraenkel, *Testimonia Patrem: The Function of the Patristic Argument in the Theology of Philip Melanchthon* (Geneva: Droz, 1961); Heinz Scheible, *Die Anfänge der reformatorische Geschichtsschreibung: Melanchthon, Sleidan, Flacius und die Magdeburger Zenturien* (Gütersloh: Mohn, 1966).
575 Melanchthon, *Melanchthon: Selected Writings*, 142; MSA 1:336.
576 The reference to Melanchthon's *De Ecclesia et autoritate verbi Dei* appears on IONAS, a$_v$.
577 IONAS, Q$_v$.
578 Gonzalez, 76.
579 IONAS, Q$_{vi}$.
580 IONAS, R$_{iv-v}$.
581 IONAS, R$_{vii}$.
582 IONAS, S$_{iiii}$.
583 IONAS, S$_{viii}$.
584 IONAS, T$_{i-iii}$.
585 IONAS, T$_{iii}$.
586 See chapter 4.
587 IONAS, V$_{vi}$.
588 WA TR 3:543, 1-4 (no. 3698); LW 54:260.
589 IONAS, V$_{viii}$, citing PL 33:277. The English translation of Augustine above comes from *The Confessions and Letters of St. Augustine*, Schaff, ed. (Edinburgh: T & T Clark), 350.
590 WA 7:838a, 2-8; LW 32:112.
591 PG 20:475-478; Eusebius, *The History of the Church*, 223.
592 IONAS, X$_{vii}$.
593 IONAS, X$_{vii-viii}$.
594 IONAS, Y$_{vii}$.
595 IONAS, X$_{ii}$.
596 LW 39:211, n. 108. "Bishop Ulrich of Augsburg (d. 973), a saint since 993, is associated with a letter criticizing the prohibition against clerical marriage by the pope. Pope Gregory VII

condemned the contents of the letter during a synod in 1074." See also, *Religion in Geschichte und Gegenwart: Handwörterbuch für Theologie und Religionswissenshaft*, 4th ed., vol. 8 (Tübingen: Mohr Siebeck, 1998), 704.

[597] *EPISTOLA DIVI HVLDERICHI AVGVSTENSIS EPISCOPI, ADVERSVS CONSTITVTIONEM DE CLERI COELIBATV, PLANE REFERENS APOSTOLICVM SPIRITVM* (Wittenberg: Lotter, 1520). Interestingly, the same publisher, Michael Lotter, republished the tract in 1550 from Magdeburg, this time edited by Flacius; *EPISTOLA S. HVLRICI EPISCOPI AVGVSTANI, CIRCITER ante sexcentos & 50. annos, ad Pontificem Nicolaum primum, pro defensione coniugii Sacerdotum, scripta, ex qua apparet, quam impudenter Papistae S. Patres iactent, cum & uita & doctrina cum S. Patribus plane ex Diametro pugnent* (Magdeburg: Lotter, 1550). This 1550 publication most likely appeared after Bugenhagen had composed this tract.

[598] Martin Luther, *Answer to the Hyperchristian, Hyperspiritual, and Hyperlearned Book by Goat Emser in Leipzig*, WA 7:677, 13, n. 1; LW 39:211. Luther, *Lectures on Genesis*, WA 42:178, 1-19; LW 1:239 and n. 2, in which readers are directed to a version of the original, in Edmund Martene and Ursinus Durand, eds., *Veterum scriptorum et monumentorum historicorum, dogmaticorum, moralium amplissima collectio*, 1 (Paris: 1724), col. 449–454.

[599] IONAS, Z_{vi}.
[600] IONAS, a_{iii}.
[601] IONAS, $a_{iii\text{-}iiii}$.
[602] IONAS, a_{iiii}.
[603] IONAS, a_{vi}. "Sacramentum baptismi, Sacramentum corporis & sanguinis Domini, Sacramentum poenitentiae siue absolutionis."
[604] PL 41:282, "Sacrificium ergo uisibile inuisibilis sacrificii sacramentum id est sacrum signum est."
[605] IONAS, a_{vi}.
[606] IONAS, e_i.
[607] IONAS, $e_{ii\text{-}iii}$.
[608] IONAS, e_{iii}.
[609] IONAS, c_{vi}.
[610] IONAS, d_{vi}.
[611] IONAS, g_{iiii}.
[612] IONAS, g_v.
[613] On women's roles during the European Reformation, see Susan Karant-Nunn, *The Reformation of Ritual*; Ozment, *When Fathers Ruled*; and Merry Wiesner-Hanks, "Women and Men, Together and Apart," *A People's History of Christianity: Reformation Christianity*, Matheson, ed. (Minneapolis: Fortess, 2007), 143-167.
[614] IONAS, $l_{ii\text{-}iii}$.
[615] IONAS, l_{iii}.
[616] Steinwachs, 193.
[617] IONAS, i_{ii}.
[618] IONAS, l_v.
[619] IONAS, l_v.
[620] IONAS, l_{vi}.
[621] Luther used this interpretation of Matthew 19:6 to make a similar point in his Genesis lectures, WA 43:20, 37-21,3; LW 3:204.
[622] IONAS, l_{vii}.
[623] IONAS, m_i.
[624] Gonzalez, 76.
[625] IONAS, n_v.
[626] IONAS, n_{vii}.
[627] IONAS, o_{ii}. "O Deus, quant mala conscientiae Christianorum per has blasphemias passae sunt?"

628 IONAS, o_{iii}.
629 See chapter 4.
630 IONAS, o_{vi}.
631 IONAS, p_i.
632 "The Augsburg Interim," 154.
633 IONAS, p_{i-ii}.
634 IONAS, p_{ii}.
635 IONAS, p_{iii}.
636 IONAS, p_{iv-v}.
637 SC, Morning and Evening Blessing (BSLK 521.1, 522, 4; BC 363.1, 4).
638 IONAS, p_{vii}.
639 PL 35:1759.
640 IONAS, $p_{vii-viii}$.
641 Frank Senn, *Christian Liturgy: Catholic and Evangelical* (Minneapolis: Augsburg Fortress, 1997), 246-247. "In Franco-German territory the sign of the cross was increasingly regarded as a general form of blessing from the tenth century on, replacing the imposition of hands that had been the customary form of blessing in the first ten centuries. The sign of the cross was made especially at words like 'benedictam' and 'benedices,' leaving no doubt that the signing was a gesture of blessing. Within this general usage, the sign of the cross as certain points in the canon underscored the importance of those words. In particular, the sign of the cross was made almost every time the gifts were mentioned in the canon. The sign of the cross was also made at the words 'gave thanks' in the institution narrative as a way of imitating Jesus' blessing of the bread and the cup."
642 IONAS, q_{ii}.
643 IONAS, q_{viii}-r_i.
644 Luther discussed Genesis 4:7 similarly in *De servo arbitrio*, WA 18:676, 4-27; LW 33:125-126.
645 IONAS, r_i.
646 IONAS, r_i.
647 IONAS, r_{i-ii}.
648 On one page, for instance, Bugenhagen cited Lyra, Lombard and Aquinas as having wrongly supported the sacrament of extreme unction (IONAS, p_{iiii}). In the tract "Montanus Blasphemus," he mentioned Aquinas and Pope Innocent III to contrast the doctrine of transsubstantion and the Corpus Christi festival with his view of the right teaching and use of the sacraments (IONAS, e_v, e_{viii}-f_i).
649 IONAS, r_{vi}. "Quando homo facit quod in se est, tunc certo dat ei Deus suam gratiam."
650 Oberman, *The Harvest of Medieval Theology*, 133. "The baptized *viator* who moves from one point in history another, not knowing whether he is damned or elect, knows by way of the *fides acquisita* that God punishes sin and assists those who call on him for help. To desire God's help is doing one's very best, and those fallen Christians who in this way detest sin and adhere to God their creator may be certain that God will grant them grace, thus freeing them from the bonds of sin." In the "Nominalistic Glossary" that Oberman appended to this work, he presented the following definition, as well as a citation from Lombard's *Sentences*, "*Facere quod in se est*, To do one's very best: To do all that is within one's natural power unaided by grace. In this way man is able to love God above everything else and to earn the infusion of first grace" (p 468).
651 Oberman, *The Harvest of Medieval Theology*, 144-145. "To conclude now this excursus on the late medieval discussion of Thomas' teaching in regard to the preparation for grace, we want to emphasize that the difference between the positions of the mature Thomas and Biel should not be glossed over. But before Biel is accused of ignorance in this matter, it must be pointed out that along with Biel, a significant group of late medieval theologians not only regarded Gregory [of Rimini]'s position as too extreme, but also felt that they had Thomas on their side."
652 Oberman, 177. "It is therefore evident that Biel's doctrine of justification is essentially Pelagian."

653 WA 1:224, 17-18; LW 31:9.
654 WA 1:225, 35-36; LW 31:11. "Falsum et illud est, quod facere quod est in se sit removere obstacula gratiae."
655 IONAS, r_{vi}.
656 K.A.T. Vogt, 442. "Si Jesum bene scis, satis est, si cetera nescis/Si Jesum nescis, nil est, quod cetera discis."
657 This saying had appeared already in the fifteenth century. Luther cited it in a *Tischreden*, WA 48:145, 7-8, and n. 1. Erasmus of Rotterdam also quoted the first half of this phrase in *Antibarbarorum Liber* (Basel: Frobenius, 1520); Desiderius Erasmus, *Opera omnia, recognita et adnotatione critica instructa notisque illustrata*, vol. 1, 1 (Amsterdam: North-Holland, 1969), 84.
658 IONAS, t_{iiii}. "Ais, Sunt ibi multa alia scitu dignissima, Ego autem dico. Hoc est nescire, sine Christo plurima scire. Si Christum bene scies, satis est, si caetera nescis."
659 IONAS, a_{viii}.
660 IONAS, u_{ii}.
661 IONAS, u_{ii}.
662 IONAS, u_{iiii}.
663 IONAS, x_{viii}.
664 IONAS, u_{viii}.
665 IONAS, y_{iiii}.
666 IONAS, z_i.
667 IONAS, z_i.
668 IONAS, z_i.
669 IONAS, z_{ii}.
670 IONAS, Aa_{iii}.
671 IONAS, Aa_{iii}.
672 IONAS, Aa_{viii}. "Latini interpretes qui trastulerunt ex hebreo, similiter & graeci, audaciter satis addiderunt his uerbis Ionae, Si particulam dubitandi, quemadmodum & fecerunt Ioelis ii."
673 IONAS, Bb_{ii}.
674 Luther had divided the verse this way in his translation of Jonah. WA DB 11.2:266, 9. "Wer weis? Gott moecht sich bekeren vnd rewen, vnd sich wenden von seinem grimmigen zorn, das wir nicht verderben."
675 IONAS, Bb_{iii-iv}.
676 IONAS, Bb_{vi}.
677 PL 25:1145.
678 PL 25:1150. Cf. John 1:3.
679 PL 25:1152.
680 WA 19:240, 20-23 and 241, 6-24; LW 19:92-93.
681 WA 19:244, 34-35; LW 19:97.
682 WA 19:246, 4-6; LW 19:98.
683 WA 19:248, 13-14; LW 19:101.
684 WA 19:249, 2-6; LW 19:101.
685 WA 19:249, 6-14; LW 19:101-102.
686 WA 19:250, 1-2; LW 19:102.
687 WA 19:250, 25-26; LW 19:103.
688 WA 19:251, 22-24; LW 19:104.
689 On Luther's writings about Judaism, see Edwards, *Luther's Last Battles*, 115-142; Maurer, *Kirche und Synagogue*; Oberman, *The Roots of Anti-Semitism in the Age of Renaissance and Reformation*; and Ozment, *A Mighty Fortress*, 99-100.
690 IONAS, F_i.
691 IONAS, B_{iiii}. See chapter 3.
692 IONAS, Bb_{viii}.
693 After Isaiah 26:12 and Psalm 51:4, the other citations are Ps. 143:2; Ps. 130:3-4; Ps. 32:6; Jer. 9:23; Jer. 10:23-24; Jonah 2:6; Romans 7:18, 24; and 2 Cor. 12:7.

694 See chapter 3.
695 IONAS, Bb$_{viii}$. "Sic exercentur Sancti per omnem uitam."
696 IONAS, Cc$_{i-ii}$.
697 IONAS, Cc$_{ii}$. Romans 8:28: "We know that all things work together for good for those who love God, who are called according to his purpose." Lamentations 3:26-31: "It is good that one should wait quietly for the salvation of the Lord. It is good to bear the yoke in youth, to site alone in silence when the Lord has imposed it, to put one's mouth to the dust (there may yet be hope), to give one's cheek to the smiter, and be filled with insults. For the Lord will not reject forever."
698 IONAS, Cc$_{ii}$.
699 IONAS, Cc$_{iii}$.
700 IONAS, Cc$_{iii-iv}$.
701 IONAS, Cc$_{v}$.
702 WA 53:202-208; LW 43: 247-250.
703 Johannes Bugenhagen, *Von den Vngeborn Kinder* (Wittenberg: Klug, 1551). This citation is translated from the 1557 edition published in Wittenberg by Veit Creutzer, I$_{vii-viii}$; cf. Geisenhof, 435-436 (no. 392).
704 Bugenhagen, *Von den Vngeborn Kinder*, K$_{i}$.
705 Bugenhagen, *Von den Vngeborn Kinder*, K$_{vi-vii}$.
706 *Briefwechsel*, 443-452 (no. 230, May 25, 1549).
707 Bugenhagen had dedicated his Jeremiah Commentary to Duke Albrecht: Johannes Bugenhagen, *In Ieremiam Prophetam Commetarium* (Wittenberg: Seitz, 1546).
708 *Briefwechsel*, 443 (no. 229, April 16, 1549). Here Bugenhagen cited the letter from Duke Albrecht that had prompted him to write.
709 IONAS, A$_{ii}$B$_{1}$. The dedication letter was also published in 1709 by one Christopher Laemmelius of Hamburg, likely in response to Hamburg's *Theaterstreit*. *D. Johannis Bugenhagii, Pomerani, Epistola Apologetica ad Daniae et Norvegiae Regem, Gloriosissimae memoriae, Christianum III &c., &c., &c. Contra Scriptores adiaphoristicos, aliosque Obtrectatores* (Hamburg: Heylius & Liebezeitius, 1709).